As Light Before Dawn

Stanford Studies in Jewish History and Culture

edited by *Aron Rodrigue and Steven J. Zipperstein*

As Light Before Dawn

The Inner World of a Medieval Kabbalist

Eitan P. Fishbane

STANFORD UNIVERSITY PRESS
STANFORD, CALIFORNIA

Stanford University Press
Stanford, California

Published with the generous support of the Lucius N. Littauer Foundation.

Printed in the United States of America on acid-free, archival-quality paper

Library of Congress Cataloging-in-Publication Data

Fishbane, Eitan P., 1975-
As light before dawn : the inner world of a medieval kabbalist / Eitan P. Fishbane.
p. cm.–(Stanford studies in Jewish history and culture)
Includes bibliographical references and index.
ISBN 978-0-8047-5913-7 (cloth : alk. paper)
1. Isaac ben Samuel, of Acre. 2. Cabala–History–To 1500. 3. Mysticism–Judaism–History–To 1500. I. Title. II. Series: Stanford studies in Jewish history and culture.
BM526.F57 2009
296.1'6–dc22 2009010151

Typeset by Bruce Lundquist in 10.5/14 Galliard

This book is dedicated with love
to the memory of
Leah Levitz Fishbane
1974–2007
כי עזה כמות אהבה

Contents

Acknowledgments

To paraphrase *Sefer Yeẓirah* and its kabbalistic offspring: the end is bound to the beginning like the flame is bound to the coal—and so too the beginning is rooted in the end, the circle turning and returning unto itself. As I prepare to transfer this book to press—this project that has lived with me through several stages of growth and development—I speak from the vantage point of endings, even as the reader takes up these words at the beginning of the way. The last words that are written are the first to be read, the place where preface and postscript meet and merge.

Over the course of this last year I have come to think a great deal about the meaning of endings, about the place of memory in the shadows of tragedy and absence. And now, as I write these lines, the face of my wife Leah stands before me—her voice present as it once was. For it was Leah, *zikhronah livrakhah*, who saw me through the long road of this work. From its very inception in my graduate studies to the shape it bears now, this book was nurtured and loved by my partner in life, the space in which it was born made possible only because of the strength and time that she gave to me. For this, and for so much more, I dedicate this work to Leah's memory—may the blessing she carried always fill the world with light and beauty.

The years spent writing this book were also enveloped with the wonder of fatherhood, and I feel blessed daily for the presence of my daughter, Aderet Shoshanah. The time she had with her mother cut so excruciatingly short, she nevertheless is led by the power of that formative nurturance, and it is from the wellspring of her mysterious young energy that I am drawn back to life, back to these words that were the markers of my path into the world of learning and ideas.

For the twin gifts of life and love, my gratitude to my parents is beyond measure. Their generosity in both the personal and professional spheres continues to sustain me, each of them offering their unique blessings to guide me along the path. At every stage of my intellectual formation, and in countless moments of research and writing, the wise and sensitive voice of my father, Professor Michael Fishbane, has been foundational. That we can share the nuances of our respective writing and teaching lives is a rare beauty, one that I continue to treasure, even as I am just as grateful for his caring love as a father—steadfast and deep. And I am equally blessed to receive the insight and love of my mother, Dr. Mona Fishbane. A person of great intellectual acuity and profound understanding of human relationships, she has guided me along the array of intersecting paths that have led me to this moment. The unwavering interest of both of my parents in my work and development as a human being, their support and sensitivity in every way—these stand among the most resplendent gifts of my life.

I also extend my heartfelt gratitude to other members of my family, all of whom have shown great love and support during the writing of this book: Janet DeKoven, Elisha and Tzippy Russ-Fishbane, Jack and Barbara Levitz, Stephanie Englander, Mitchell Levitz, and Leonore Gibbs. Herman DeKoven (my maternal grandfather) and Bernice Fishbane (my paternal grandmother), of blessed memory, gave of themselves in countless ways, and they both were always supportive of my work and growth as a person. Their presence in this world is deeply missed.

Parts of this work had their origin in my PhD dissertation at Brandeis University, completed under the direction of Professor Arthur Green. Art has been a caring and devoted mentor, seeing me through my growth as an interpreter of texts, advising me as I made my way into the forest of mystical sources. His belief in my work and future has made a great difference on this road, and I stand indebted to him as my teacher. Many other individuals gave of their time and energy in ways that had a decisive impact upon this work. I extend my thanks to: members of the Department of Religion at Carleton College; faculty of the Los Angeles School of Hebrew Union College–Jewish Institute of Religion, as well as the administration of the College–Institute; my current colleagues on the faculty of the Jewish Theological Seminary, and the administration of JTS; members of the Shtibl Minyan community in Los Angeles; members of Congregation Beth Sholom and caring neighbors in Teaneck, New Jersey; Professor Lawrence Fine; Professor Moshe Idel; Professor Reuven Kimelman; Professor Daniel Matt; Professor Bernard McGinn; Dr. Meir Sendor; and Professor Elliot Wolfson. Deep thanks to Rabbi Julia Andelman for her help and support during the proofs stage of this work. Thanks are also due to Professor Aron Rodrigue and Professor Steven Zipperstein for their interest in this work, and to Norris Pope, Emily-Jane Cohen, Mariana Raykov, Peter Dreyer, and David Stein for their diligent care in bringing this work to press. I am delighted that my work appears under the superb imprint of the Stanford Studies in Jewish History and Culture.

At decisive points in the writing of this book, I was the grateful recipient of grants from the Memorial Foundation for Jewish Culture, the National Endowment for the Humanities, and the Lucius N. Littauer Foundation. I thank these organizations for helping to nurture my research. It is likewise my privilege to acknowledge the previous publication of significant portions of Chapters 3 and 4 in the *Journal of the American Academy of Religion* under the title: "Authority, Tradition, and the Creation of Meaning in Medieval Kabbalah: Isaac of Acre's *Illumination of the Eyes*," *JAAR* 72, 1 (2004): 59–95. My sincere thanks go to the editor and publisher of that prestigious journal. Finally, I extend my gratitude and acknowledgment to the UMI division of ProQuest Information and Learning Company for granting me the right to publish earlier work in a new, much expanded form.

As Light Before Dawn

Part I *Context*

One Perspectives and New Directions

Reflections on the State of Scholarship

On the Anticipation of Audience

In its ideal state, scholarship should aim to converse with multiple audiences at once, accomplishing this most challenging goal through concentric circles of dialogue and learning. For if the innermost of these circles is a highly specialized audience (and this rigorous engagement is crucial to the advancement of knowledge), the outermost circle seeks to reach a much broader intellectual discourse, one in which scholars of diverse specialties and tradition-centers may discover lines of connection in their common quest for an understanding of the human phenomenon—the composition of a collective culture, insight into the intersecting threads of the imagination, the ritual of behavior, and the forms of creativity. With this in mind, I have set out to present my research in this book in a manner that will be of some productive interest to diverse scholars of religion and generally educated readers; such interest will be based on where in the spectrum of concentric intellectual concerns each reader stands. And so, while specialists in the literature of Jewish mysticism may find greater value in an array of textual and field-specific analyses, I hope that my attempts to locate specialized research matters within the larger landscapes of the history and phenomenology of religion will keep the doors of invitation opened wide to colleagues in a much larger panorama of disciplinary homes. Likewise, it is my intention that a general readership will find access here to a cluster of ideas and sources that have much to offer all students of religious culture, devotional practice, and spiritual creativity.

As the reader may discern from a perusal of the table of contents, this book centers on a series of issues that have much in common with other mystical traditions, on the one hand, and that share in categories central to the broader study of religious culture, on the other. In addition, the scholar of other subfields in the history of Judaism might appreciate the degree to which the topics and text-studies set forth here bear correlation to other (nonmystical) phenomena in the development of Jewish ideas and textuality. This shared intellectual concern is most evident in three recurrent threads of analysis discussed in the present monograph: (1) The representation and contours of contemplative devotional consciousness, and its situation within a typology of ritual practice. A major dimension of the present work, this category has much to contribute to far broader inquiries in the manifold regions of religious studies. (2) Perceptions of interpretive authority and legitimate meaning in the transmission of religious ideas—the interplay between the processes of spontaneous creativity and the articulation of received wisdom. (3) The dynamics of interiority and exteriority with respect to ritual intention, and the manner in which this polarity serves as the groundwork for greater understanding of the intersecting problematics of body, spirit, and religious experience more broadly. In addressing these and other threads of discourse, this work seeks to locate the thought of a prominent medieval Jewish mystic within several matrices of the study of religion and the transmission of knowledge. In offering a close reading of one kabbalist's creativity, my aim is to contribute to a broad interdisciplinary edifice: through the particular, we seek to clarify the more general nature of religious thought and practice.

The Subject

The late thirteenth century was one of the greatest periods of creativity in the history of Judaism. In the Jewish communities of Aragon, the Kabbalah of Naḥmanides (the giant of medieval Jewish commentary) continued to flourish through his students and their disciples, while Castilian Kabbalah had reached the summit of its intellectual power and literary craft in the *Zohar* and related works. While the kabbalists of these respective schools were most certainly shaped by a concern with the mystical contemplation of God, the dominant character of their writings reflects an emphasis on symbolic meaning and an attempt to depict the inner reality and dynamics of Divinity. To be sure, as recent scholarship has demonstrated,[1] the very process of symbol-construction and knowledge of God through the sacred text was conceived to be an event of illumination and (often) ecstatic-contemplative experience. That fact acknowledged, however, the contemplative orientation of these "western" kabbalists did not reach the same pitch of intensity as that of their "eastern" brothers from the other side of the Mediterranean. Indeed, the Jewish spiritual thinkers and practitioners of the East cultivated a distinctively meditative approach to spiritual practice and mystical thought. They were more heavily influenced by the piety and ideas of their Sufi neighbors in North Africa and the Mediterranean basin—a mode of religious life that was marked by an emphasis on meditative practice and a contemplative orientation. Yet perhaps the greatest difference between eastern and western Kabbalah was its relationship to the act of prescription and instruction. To be sure, we do find numerous examples of prescriptive mysticism among the kabbalistic writings of Aragon and Castile, but these pale in comparison (in this respect, that is) to the writings of the eastern thinkers. Best represented by Abraham Abulafia (a kabbalist who spent considerable time in the Land of Israel, as well as in the Greek islands and the Italian peninsula),[2] the eastern kabbalists sought to present the reader (or disciple) with detailed guidance as to the nature and practice of the Jewish contemplative life. It is this overtly prescriptive element—combined with a vigorous focus on meditative matters—that most concisely embodies the distinction between the two kabbalistic approaches.

It is when this divide in medieval Kabbalah (particularly with respect to geography) is clarified that the significance of our topic emerges into sharper relief. For the figure I propose to study in this work—Isaac ben Samuel of Akko—is first and foremost remarkable as an example of a *bridge* between these two relatively distinct modes of Kabbalah. His work reflects the dominant influences of both the Naḥmanidean

1. Wolfson, *Through a Speculum that Shines*, pp. 270–397.

2. See Idel, *The Mystical Experience in Abraham Abulafia*, pp. 2–3.

Kabbalah of *sefirot* and the Jewish-Sufi/Abulafian-inspired Kabbalah of the East. This unique blend—which also reflects Isaac's geographical migration from the northern Land of Israel to the Iberian peninsula in the 1290s—is most evident in *Me'irat 'Einayim*, a putative metacommentary to Naḥmanides' *Commentary on the Torah*. In Isaac's later work—most notably in *'Oẓar Ḥayyim*[3]—the eastern kabbalistic element is far more dominant, and the Kabbalah of Naḥmanides has been set on the periphery. Yet in general, and especially in *Me'irat 'Einayim*, Isaac emerges as one situated on the borderline of two distinct religious trends and creative mentalities. *Me'irat 'Einayim* is dominated to be sure by the genre of ביאור סודות הרמב"ן ("clarification of the secrets of Naḥmanides"), but is nevertheless permeated with passages that transmit kabbalistic teachings on contemplation in prayer and meditative focus. It is a profoundly *prescriptive* work with respect to the contemplative life, and seeks to function as a reliable conduit for prior teachings pertaining *both* to a sefirotic interpretation of Scripture and to received traditions on the methods for contemplation of Divinity. *'Oẓar Ḥayyim*, on the other hand, is marked by a first-person testimonial discourse of creative process and hermeneutical discovery—a rhetoric that may be contrasted with the prescriptive mode dominant in *Me'irat 'Einayim*, and one that reveals the dynamics of self-perception. As we shall observe in some detail, Isaac's later work presents a model of autobiographical Jewish mysticism and spiritual life-writing—a modality that is rare in kabbalistic literature, and one that provides insight into an alternate dimension of this mystic's inner world. This testimonial discourse also documents Isaac of Akko's deeply contemplative orientation, lending further texture to our understanding of his devotional practice and concerns, to the manner in which a posture of meditative consciousness is cultivated. Given the pivotal position of this kabbalist in the history of medieval Jewish intellectual culture, it is clear that a comprehensive examination of his work is necessary for a full understanding of Jewish mystical trends in the Middle Ages—a fact that stands in marked contrast to what has been conducted hitherto in the way of research.

---

3. As yet this work is only extant in manuscript, the sole complete version of which is to be found in MS Moscow-Ginzburg 775. Portions and fragments of this text are also preserved in MS Oxford 1911, MS Adler 1589, and MS Sasoon 919.

A note to the comparative scholar and the general reader:
In order to do justice to the important research upon which my own work seeks to build, I shall now enter into a detailed (and somewhat technical) assessment of the scholarship completed to date as it relates to our topic. It is through this narrative that the reader may come to appreciate what is new about my own research. That said, however, the nonspecialist may wish to skip this survey of scholarship, which is chiefly intended for the innermost circle of concentric audiences and centers on matters of relatively narrow concern. The broader discussion resumes with the last section of this chapter, devoted to the directional aims and methodological considerations of the present study.

The State of Research

Relative to the considerable attention given to other important kabbalists of the thirteenth and fourteenth centuries, Isaac of Akko has not been a major subject of scholarly study. While two short texts and one voluminous (as well as influential) treatise have been published in critical editions by modern scholars, a large portion of this kabbalist's writing still remains in manuscript. The content of his writings has only begun to be explored, and the significance of his unique cultural position still requires sustained and comprehensive treatment. Despite this fact, valuable advances have been made in several subareas of scholarship, and this chapter will be devoted to a critical examination of them. This discussion will aid in the contextualization of my own research into the subject matter, and will aim to clarify the topics that remain undeveloped and in need of elucidation. The scholarship that has been completed to date may be divided into the following general categories: (1) critical editions and textual/philological analysis; (2) Jewish-Sufism and Abulafian Kabbalah as sources of influence on Isaac; and (3) preliminary analysis of Isaac's contemplative and hermeneutical approach. Additional categories will be treated in subsequent chapters in accordance with specific themes as they arise.

Research into the writings of Isaac of Akko, with an emphasis on the editing of manuscript materials with critical annotation and some analysis, was inaugurated by Gershom Scholem in 1956.[4] In that year, Scholem published a very short section of text (fewer than twenty pages) by Isaac of Akko in which the latter commented on the first section of *Sefer Yeẓirah*.[5] It does in fact seem that this text was originally part of a longer commentary by Isaac on *Sefer Yeẓirah*, and that this complete text was known to the Spanish exile Abraham ben Solomon Adrutiel.[6] Regardless, however, Isaac's exegesis on part 1 of *Sefer Yeẓirah* is all we have. As Scholem states in his brief introduction to the text, Isaac of Akko's work was clearly based on and influenced by the earlier such commentary by Isaac the Blind, one of the very earliest kabbalists in Provence.[7] Nevertheless, Scholem asserts, there are significant differences in approach and ideas between these two commentaries.[8] The very fact that a commentary was composed with such visible influence from Isaac the Blind's laconic and enigmatic text, however, reveals the prominence that the latter's text enjoyed among kabbalists several generations subsequent to its writing. Like Isaac the Blind's *Commentary on Sefer Yeẓirah*, Isaac of Akko's text is deeply contemplative and demonstrates the broad scope of his intellectual activity. At this juncture it is most important to take note of Scholem's own exhortation regarding the importance of Isaac of Akko for a thorough understanding of the history of Kabbalah. He indicated the need (as he did with many other kabbalistic topics) for the pursuit of research on this topic by future scholars—a prescient remark that has been fulfilled by the work of numerous contemporary scholars, and it is a guiding motivation for my own research.

---

4. Isaac of Akko, "Perusho shel R. Yiẓḥaq de-min-'Akko le-Pereq Ri'shon shel Sefer Yeẓirah," ed. Scholem, pp. 379–396.

5. The basis for Scholem's critical edition of this passage is MS JNUL Heb. 8° 404, fols. 15b–33a.

6. Isaac of Akko, "Perusho . . . ," ed. Scholem, p. 379.

7. The most recent study of Isaac the Blind's commentary is Sendor, "The Emergence of Provençal Kabbalah: Rabbi Isaac the Blind's Commentary on *Sefer Yeẓirah*."

8. Isaac of Akko, "Perusho . . . ," ed. Scholem, p. 380. As Scholem states: "R. Isaac of Akko sought to interpret [*Sefer Yeẓirah*] according to his own method, and in a very independent manner. And if the complete version of the commentary [to *Sefer Yeẓirah*] by the '*Ḥasid*'—as R. Isaac the Blind is called here—is published, it will become clear just how far apart most of [Isaac of Akko's] interpretations are from the abstruse intentions of the Provençal kabbalist [i.e., Isaac the Blind]."

A second contribution to textual study bearing on our topic was undertaken by Georges Vajda in an article published at the very end of that same year.[9] The most important element of this work for our purposes is the appendix of fragments authored by Isaac of Akko, published from manuscripts by Vajda. These fragments are mystical comments by Isaac of Akko on the writings of Judah ben Nissim Ibn Malka, particularly Ibn Malka's *Commentary on Pirkei de-Rabbi Eliezer*. It is noteworthy that Ibn Malka's commentary was composed in Arabic, showing Isaac's competence in that language. Vajda has performed an important service to scholarship on Isaac of Akko, insofar as significant mystical passages composed by Isaac are now more accessible. There is not a great deal of commentary or analysis in this article, and its primary value is located in the publication of the Hebrew text along with an annotated French translation. In this regard, let me also acknowledge Vajda's French translation of an important passage from *Me'irat 'Einayim* on the harmonization of conflicting ideas (a theme that I deal with at some length in Chapter 3) in an appendix to one of his major works of scholarship.[10]

As this study will give considerable attention to evidence garnered from Isaac's *Me'irat 'Einayim*, it is fitting to devote greater attention to the extensive research on this text performed by Amos Goldreich some twenty years ago as a doctoral dissertation at the Hebrew University of Jerusalem.[11] It is no exaggeration to state that the critical edition of *Me'irat 'Einayim* prepared by Goldreich transformed the scholarly study of Isaac of Akko, and presented an exemplary model for the systematic and scientific study of medieval Jewish manuscripts in general. As Daniel Abrams noted in an article surveying and analyzing the development of critical text research on Jewish sources,[12] Goldreich's doctoral work was a pioneering effort in a crucial area of scholarly research. Establishing a reliable text that closely represents the original

9. Vajda, "Les observations critiques d'Isaac d'Acco sur les ouvrages de Juda ben Nissim Ibn Malka."

10. Vajda, *Recherches sur la philosophie et la kabbale*, pp. 393–395.

11. Isaac of Akko, "*Sefer Me'irat 'Einayim le-R. Yiẓḥaq de-min-'Akko*," ed. Goldreich (hereafter cited as Isaac of Akko, *Me'irat 'Einayim*).

12. Abrams, "Critical and Post-Critical Textual Scholarship of Jewish Mystical Literature: Notes on the History and Development of Modern Editing Techniques."

work of the author is of paramount importance for the study of medieval Jewish sources. Without this foundational work, technical as it may be, all inquiries into interesting thematic religious issues rest on dubious ground. In completing his work, Goldreich collected an enormous amount of bibliographical information with respect to the many manuscripts of *Me'irat 'Einayim* that are found scattered among the great libraries of the world, consolidated in the microfilm collections of the Jewish National and University Library in Jerusalem. With an eye for minute detail, Goldreich demonstrated that *Me'irat 'Einayim* was copied in a wide variety of scripts and corresponding geographical locations. Dominant among these scripts were the 'Ashkenazic, Sefardic, Byzantine, and Italian methods—a strong indicator of the widespread dissemination of this work. Although Goldreich himself does not reflect in a sustained way upon the fascinating cultural implications of these scribal and paleographical facts, it may be observed that the text's *Rezeptionsgeschichte* (reception history) is ultimately illuminated by the diversity of handwritings and manuscript copies identified. What is revealed through the range of manuscript sources that Goldreich analyzes is an intriguing picture of a text that exercised powerful influence and enjoyed a prominent cultural life in the hands of the Jewish educated elite in the Middle Ages and beyond. Indeed, in the scholarly world prior to the invention of the printing press, the very quantity of surviving manuscripts indicates the degree to which a certain text was distributed and read by members of the scholarly community. Not least among the reasons for this extensive reception was the purported and self-proclaimed goal of *Me'irat 'Einayim*, that of metacommentary to and mystical clarification of Naḥmanides' immensely popular and virtually canonical *Commentary on the Torah*. I shall have much more to say about this aspect of Isaac's work later on.

For a host of reasons spelled out in his work, Goldreich selected MS Gaster (Manchester) 200 for the majority of his edition, a manuscript that Goldreich describes as "not only the source of a majority of manuscripts, but also the most faithful representative of the original work."[13] The part of the text missing from MS Gaster 200 is represented by MS

13. See *Me'irat 'Einayim,* ed. Goldreich, English section, p. 9.

Parma 67, a manuscript that Goldreich deems most reliable.[14] In addition to a thorough and elaborate consideration of the manuscripts involved, Goldreich has also provided scholars with a very rich series of historical annotations to parts of the text. The arguments and conclusions in these notes have contributed significantly to the construction of a historical picture of the times, and of the likely influences exercised on Isaac of Akko in the course of his travels. I have made use of these notes in Chapter 2 (on historical profile and context), and my debts to Goldreich's work on this score are documented there. Several historical observations are also put forward by Goldreich in the Introductory Study in the form of excursuses on matters of influence that are detectable from the content of the text and its manuscript foundations. Perhaps one of the most important conclusions reached by Goldreich in these sections of his work is the identification of a specific manuscript source for an important ubiquitous reference in *Me'irat 'Einayim* to a text unnamed other than by the phrase *maẓ'ati be-yad ḥakham maskil* (I found [written] at the hand of a wise sage). Goldreich argues that this specific formula consistently refers to a manuscript anthology of kabbalistic traditions from the Geronese school of mystics as edited by a mysterious and anonymous Castilian scribe from the latter part of the thirteenth century or early in the fourteenth.[15] The pervasive presence of these traditions in *Me'irat 'Einayim* are a window into Isaac's process of receiving traditions from others—an issue that will be dealt with more extensively later on. Goldreich notes that this manuscript is found in its entirety in MS Oxford Christ Church College 198, and that Isaac of Akko's frequent citations from this source are almost always precisely copied. Goldreich further argues that Isaac must have come into contact with this manuscript on his sojourn in the cities and towns of Castile in the course of his famous search for the *Zohar*. Thus Goldreich links the integration of this manuscript material into *Me'irat*

14. See the discussion of this selection, along with a panoramic analysis of the entire spectrum of manuscript witnesses, in Chapters 1 and 2 of Goldreich's introductory study to *Me'irat 'Einayim*. Also see a full listing of the many manuscripts consulted on pp. 436–441, and see the English section, pp. 3–4.

15. For evidence regarding this claim, see Goldreich's Introduction to his critical edition of *Me'irat 'Einayim*, p. 91.

'Einayim to the year 1305, when Isaac (by his own admission, preserved in a passage from Abraham Zacuto's *Sefer Yuḥasin*, cited and discussed in the next chapter) was in Castile.

Most of the *maẓ'ati be-yad ḥakham maskil* citations, which Isaac supposedly only encountered on his visit to Castile in 1305, are well integrated into *Me'irat 'Einayim*, thus suggesting that much of the treatise was composed later.[16] As Goldreich himself notes, some of these citations were appended to the text of *Me'irat 'Einayim* after Isaac had completed a fair amount of his text (thus indicating that at least some of Isaac's writing was completed *prior* to 1305), but the overwhelming majority were integrated into the flow of writing in such a way as to suggest that they were available to Isaac before he began to write those sections (thus *after* 1305). Goldreich observes that while numerous citations from the *ḥakham maskil* manuscript were appended to Isaac's commentary on the book of Genesis (included right at the end), this does not occur at all with respect to the other books of the Pentateuch. For the subsequent four biblical books, Isaac was able to integrate the citations into the flow of the text itself. The logical conclusion that Goldreich draws is that Isaac encountered the *ḥakham maskil* manuscript *after* he had already completed writing most of his commentary on Genesis—a time frame directly linked to the year 1305. Of course, this entire hypothesis rests on the reliability of the testimony preserved in *Sefer Yuḥasin*, that Isaac first traveled to Castile in 1305, and that it was there that he came into contact with the texts of the *ḥakham maskil* (this second deductive point is asserted by extension in Goldreich's analysis—it is not itself discernable from the *Sefer Yuḥasin* passage). As Goldreich also notes, however, we have no reason to doubt the historical legitimacy of this evidence.

While the above-mentioned advances in text-critical scholarship are indispensable in the construction of a solid portrait of Isaac of Akko and his mystical thought, the most substantial treatment of Isaac's larger cultural position has come in the form of discussion of his role in the impact of Jewish-Sufi piety on medieval Kabbalah. Isaac was one of a select few Jewish mystics who bridged the distinct cultural worlds

---

16. See *Me'irat 'Einayim*, ed. Goldreich, Introduction, pp. 98–99.

of eastern and western Jewish mystical circles, two arenas that exhibited markedly separate spiritual concerns. We encounter in him a fascinating cross-cultural combination of ideas and approaches to the mystical life as they were practiced in these two geographical zones. This domain of scholarship has been pursued by Moshe Idel[17] and Paul Fenton,[18] with special attention to a practice known as *hitbodedut* (literally, "seclusion") in kabbalistic and other pietistic documents. These scholars have shown the practice of *hitbodedut* to be a meditative technique of special concentration, intimately related to a discipline of ascetic detachment and emotional equanimity. Both Idel and Fenton focus on the place of Isaac of Akko in the history of this practice in Jewish mystical piety, and their research has revealed the likely influence of Sufi-inspired Jewish mystics upon Isaac.

Let us now briefly consider three studies that deal directly with Isaac of Akko. The first treats aspects of Isaac's conception of mystical experience, and the other two deal with the subject of kabbalistic interpretation in Isaac's work. The last of these studies, in accord with a new awareness among scholars of Kabbalah,[19] seeks to clarify the interconnected nature of contemplative experience and interpretive modalities in parts of Isaac's writing. The first article was composed by Ephraim Gottlieb,[20] and for many years was the only scholarly discussion of Isaac's contemplative orientation. Though only a preliminary foray into the field, Gottlieb's study offers a valuable selection of textual fragments from Isaac's *'Oẓar Ḥayyim*, as well as pioneering insights into their typologization, and it is the point of departure for my analysis of numerous issues and themes. The early seeds of thematic work undertaken by Idel and Fenton (particularly with respect to *hitbodedut* and its textual evidence in Isaac's writings) may also be found in this seminal

17. Idel, *Studies in Ecstatic Kabbalah*, pp. 73–169.

18. Fenton, "Solitary Meditation in Jewish and Islamic Mysticism in the Light of a Recent Archeological Discovery." Cf. id., "La 'Hitbodedut' chez les premiers Qabbalistes en Orient et chez les Soufis."

19. See M. Fishbane, *The Exegetical Imagination*, pp. 105–122; Idel, *Kabbalah: New Perspectives*, pp. 234–249; Wolfson, *Through a Speculum That Shines*, pp. 326–333.

20. Gottlieb, "Illumination, *Devequt*, and Prophecy in R. Isaac of Akko's *Sefer 'Oẓar Ḥayyim*."

article by Gottlieb. Furthermore, it should be noted that Amos Goldreich was originally Gottlieb's student at the Hebrew University (after Gottlieb's death in 1973, Goldreich's doctoral supervision was assumed by Gershom Scholem). Gottlieb must thus be regarded as a pioneer in modern scholarship on Isaac of Akko.[21]

Gottlieb's article concentrates exclusively on Isaac's *'Oẓar Ḥayyim*—though he does give some tangential attention to *Me'irat 'Einayim*. As Gottlieb notes (and as Scholem mentioned in the introduction to his critical edition of Isaac's *Commentary on Sefer Yeẓirah*), the best manuscript of this important text is MS Moscow-Ginzburg 775, which contains the most complete copy available, but pieces of the text are also found in several other manuscripts, including MS Oxford 1911, MS Adler 1589, and MS Sasoon 919.[22] Gottlieb himself notes that *'Oẓar Ḥayyim* is not a diary in the traditional sense, inasmuch as there is no presumption of privacy in the text.[23] Indeed, throughout *'Oẓar Ḥayyim*, Isaac addresses his readers directly and offers numerous bits of prescriptive advice on the mystical life (though the testimonial-confessional genre is certainly dominant). While Gottlieb makes mention of this important distinction between the presumptions of the diary mode and the operating assumptions of *'Oẓar Ḥayyim*, he singles out its markedly spontaneous approach to mystical experience and the written report thereof. Gottlieb observes that in this treatise Isaac of Akko explicitly asserts that he has not received these traditions from anyone else, but arrived at his mystical insights through spontaneous spiritual illumination. This fact is significant in my own analysis of Isaac's approach to cultural reception and transmission, insofar as it presents a radically different model from *Me'irat 'Einayim*, which is more conventional in its construction of authoritative reception and new transmission, whereas *'Oẓar Ḥayyim* clearly privileges spontaneous moments of spiritual insight and illumination over the usual chain of tradition.

The three issues to which Gottlieb gives the greater part of his attention are: (1) visualization practices oriented toward the divine name;

21. See the preface to *Me'irat 'Einayim*, ed. Goldreich.

22. Gottlieb, "Illumination, *Devequt*, and Prophecy in R. Isaac of Akko's *Sefer 'Oẓar Ḥayyim*," p. 231.

23. Ibid., p. 232.

(2) negation of all worldly thought and experience (which he, too, correlates to Sufic doctrine); and (3) the subject of *devequt* as an event of *unio mystica*. This last topic was one of the early divergences from Scholem's categorical rejection of the possible place of *unio mystica* in Jewish thought[24]—a position that was first articulated by Isaiah Tishby in 1961,[25] and later elaborated on by Moshe Idel.[26] Gottlieb adduces two primary examples of this phenomenon in *'Oẓar Ḥayyim*: (a) *devequt* as a state of being swallowed by the divine[27]—and thus incorporated into that divine Being; and (b) the metaphor of a pitcher of water poured into a flowing stream as an analogy for the completely unitive character of mystical experience.[28] From these cases, Gottlieb contributed to a growing awareness of the prevalence of this significant religious feature in medieval Kabbalah. Building upon this foundational work, a broader analysis of contemplative issues (and its relationship to the concept of *devequt*) will show that there are many different aspects to Isaac's contemplative orientation, each of which needs to be examined on its own terms as a type of mystical consciousness and practice.

A more recent study by Boaz Huss has set out to illuminate the intersection of such experiential mysticism with elaborate hermeneutical strategies in Isaac of Akko's writings.[29] In this respect, the work of Huss directly impacts the analysis undertaken in this book. The focus of Huss's article is an exegetical system developed by Isaac in his later works (i.e., *'Oẓar Ḥayyim* and his paraphrastic notes to Judah ben Nissim Ibn Malkah's *Commentary to Pirkei de-Rabbi 'Eliezer*) called "NiSAN." Huss argues that Isaac presents NiSAN as a hermeneutical system that transcends the PaRDeS method—the other standard fourfold system of exegesis employed in the Middle Ages.[30] NiSAN—an acronym for *Nistar* (N), *Sod* (S), *'Emet* ('A), and *'Emet Nekhonah* (N)—is

24. See Scholem, "*Devekut*, or Communion with God."

25. See Tishby, *Mishnat ha-Zohar*, 2: 289.

26. Idel, *Kabbalah: New Perspectives*, pp. 35–73.

27. Gottlieb, "Illumination, *Devequt*, and Prophecy," p. 237.

28. Ibid.

29. Huss, "NiSAN—The Wife of the Infinite: The Mystical Hermeneutics of Rabbi Isaac of Acre," pp. 155–181.

30. Idel, "PaRDeS: Some Reflections on Kabbalistic Hermeneutics," pp. 249–268.

explained by Huss as an exegetical process of ever-deeper kabbalistic meanings. Whereas the PaRDeS system is only kabbalistic with respect to its fourth mode (i.e., *Sod*), the NiSAN system is entirely kabbalistic, the distinctions between the four modes only corresponding to the different ontological gradations. Thus, as Huss demonstrates, *Nistar* (N) reads the sacred text in light of human psychological meaning, *Sod* (S) corresponds to the angelic world (particularly the domain of Meṭaṭron, for whom Isaac has a particular affinity), *'Emet* ('A) correlates to the lower levels of sefirotic Being, and *'Emet Nekhonah* (N) to the higher rungs of the *sefirot*. The primary conclusion that Huss draws from this complex exegetical model is that like the interpretive system of Abraham Abulafia, the levels of interpretation correspond directly to hierarchized levels of human experience as it ascends through the dimensions of divine reality. Huss further argues (and this point is especially relevant for our purposes) that climactic hermeneutical experience is correlated by Isaac to the moment of prophecy, an assertion that finds an immediate parallel in the writings and methods of Abulafia.

The most recent piece of scholarship to be written on Isaac of Akko, and therefore the concluding subject of this review of scholarship, is a short section at the end of Moshe Idel's monograph *Absorbing Perfections*.[31] The primary issue addressed by Idel in that context pertains to the kabbalistic use of a symbolic code (i.e., the sefirotic system) to resolve all apparent hermeneutical difficulties in the encounter with the sacred text of Torah and with all paradigmatic rabbinic interpretations thereof. Through a close reading of a long passage from *'Oẓar Ḥayyim*, Idel demonstrates the manner in which Isaac of Akko manipulates the sefirotic code to rebuff the derision of certain contemporary philosophers regarding the seeming contradictions in an ancient rabbinic passage. The network of sefirotic associations that arise from a classical or biblical text serves as the master key for all perceptions of problematic meaning and interpretive quandaries. Kabbalistic symbolism emerges as the meta-meaning that clarifies all exegetical dilemmas.

Idel argues that Isaac of Akko (and in this respect Isaac represents a larger kabbalistic mentality, which Idel documents throughout *Absorb-*

31. Idel, *Absorbing Perfections: Kabbalah and Interpretation*, pp. 449–460. See also E. Fishbane, "Jewish Mystical Hermeneutics: On the Work of Moshe Idel," pp. 94–103.

ing Perfections) treats the sefirotic system *not* as a symbolic structure that points beyond itself to the Unknowable,[32] but rather as a self-evident code that functions to unlock the complexities and perplexities of the canonical texts of the tradition. In contrast to other scholars, who have persuasively claimed that medieval kabbalists used the hermeneutical event vis-à-vis the Torah as a means for contemplative experience of the Divine,[33] Idel argues that the symbolic associations of the sefirotic system were *taken for granted* by the kabbalists, and that the real mystery and enigma was the sacred text. The symbolic system of the *sefirot* was therefore considered to be the great key to the locked meaning of the text, as opposed to the view that considers the text to function as the prism for understanding the mysteries of Divinity. In Idel's estimation, the truth about Divinity (reflected in the sefirotic system) served as a priori knowledge that the kabbalist brought with him to the exegetical act vis-à-vis the sacred canon. As such, the primary task (and ultimate goal) of the kabbalist was the interpretation of the text, and not the elusive search for theological knowledge.

Aims and Approach

In the chapters that follow, I argue that neither of these two models is entirely sufficient (though both lend deep insight into the kabbalistic view of interpretation and contemplation). Indeed, we must ask to what degree the exegetical construction of meaning predicated on knowledge of the divine, on the one hand, and the search for mental experience of Divinity through contemplation of the text's symbolic meaning, on the other, are truly distinct modalities. Can these two priorities be *separated* in attempting to understand the mystical approach in Isaac of Akko's works? As we have now seen in some detail, several important advances have been made in contemporary scholarship toward a full understanding of this remarkable medieval

32. This view of sefirotic symbolism, which was adapted from Goethean aesthetics, was most famously advanced by Gershom Scholem (e.g., Scholem, "Kabbalah and Myth," pp. 87–100), and was further developed in the writings of Isaiah Tishby (e.g., Tishby, "Symbol and Religion in the Kabbalah," pp. 11–22).

33. See esp. Wolfson, *Through a Speculum that Shines*, pp. 383–392.

kabbalist. Moreover, the subject of contemplative mysticism in the history of Jewish thought has been substantially developed in recent years. Nevertheless, despite these crucial beginnings—upon which subsequent scholars must inevitably stand—a comprehensive consideration of the modes of thought and features of creativity in Isaac of Akko's writings is a clear desideratum of contemporary scholarship. What are the forms of thought and practice in *Me'irat 'Einayim* and *'Oẓar Ḥayyim* (along, of course, with the other surviving fragments of his writing)? How does the author relate to prior authorities, and how does he seek to communicate with his readers as a pedagogue? In what ways does Isaac reveal his self-perception and inner creative process through the genre of testimonial mysticism? What are the specific ways in which Isaac of Akko may be understood to be a crucial bridge between centers of Jewish religious creativity in the High Middle Ages? Why should Isaac be characterized as a *contemplative* mystic, and what are the contours of his rhetoric of prescription?

These are some of the guiding questions of the present work. In seeking answers and explanations, I employ a methodology that aims to combine the history of ideas (as manifested in the uncovering of diachronic textual layers and a clarification of the reception history of ideas and practices) with the construction of a *typological* picture—one related in spirit to the morphology of religion.[34] Thus, while attempting to situate Isaac's thought historically (within the development of medieval Jewish mysticism and the larger history of Jewish thought), probing ideas and words in *Me'irat 'Einayim* and *'Oẓar Ḥayyim* for earlier reverberations and innovative uses, I am primarily concerned here with the discernment and analysis of *types* of contemplative consciousness and mystical practice, on the one hand, and models of the reception and transmission of kabbalistic wisdom, on the other. This latter process seeks to understand religious expression as the disclosure of forms and structures in the mind as they are shaped by a very particular cultural context. To only seek a picture of diachronic history, without always searching (synchronically) for deeper understanding of the nature and motives of human thought

34. On the study of forms and types as a discrete methodology (and framed as religious morphology), see Jones, *The Hermeneutics of Sacred Architecture: Experience, Interpretation, Comparison*, 2: 6.

and action, is to succumb to a flat reductionism in which *meaning* is relegated to the periphery in favor of establishing a linear progresion.[35] My aim is rather to uncover a particular life of contemplation and the modalities of kabbalistic ritual intention. Though history, context, and the configurations of influence must never be far from this work, they must likewise never eclipse the centrality of the *forms* of religious expression as they emerge through a particular thinker. It is in this respect that I seek a dynamic interplay between three methodological avenues: (1) the historical-contextual; (2) the phenomenological-typological; and (3) the textual-hermeneutical. These multiple lenses offer a view of the mystical life of one notable kabbalist, which I approach through the dense prism and historical gateway of textual hermeneutics.[36] In centering on a discrete set of texts, I aim to construct a taxonomy of the contemplative imagination, a morphology of ritual engagement and the transmission of wisdom.

---

35. On the delicate balance between reception-history and phenomenology in the study of religion, see Crouter, "Schleiermacher's *On Religion*," pp. 1–3, 11–12.

36. A felicitous description of the phenomenological method as viewed from within a particular historical-textual matrix is put forth by Capps, *Religious Studies: The Making of a Discipline*, p. 107: "The shift from unambiguous simples to organically interrelated plurals also represents a historical and theoretical turn taken by scholars of other approaches, many of whom choose to refer to themselves as 'phenomenologists of religion.' The word *phenomenology* is important and appropriate, for it denotes an intention to concentrate on phenomena—that is, on the perceptible, manifest, empirical, and sometimes visible features or characteristics of religion. Again, instead of trying to identify the single and definitive core element . . . phenomenologists have worked to describe the manner and form in which religious phenomena appear in human experience." In the course of his survey of various theorists, Capps highlights the degree to which the work of Geo Widengren reflects a deep integration of the historical-textual with the phenomenological. Ibid., pp. 136–139. This methodological bridge is also proposed by Elliot Wolfson as a guiding principle in his monograph on mystical vision and prophetic imagination. See Wolfson, *Through a Speculum that Shines*, pp. 5–9, 52–58.

Two The Wandering Kabbalist

Historical Profile and Context

As a mystic who lived a life of travel, journeying from the Land of Israel westward through Aragon and Castile, absorbing new ideas and practices along the way, Isaac of Akko was a man of context who learned from his many environments. He seems to have begun his education in the Jewish community of Akko (Acre), a port at the northern end of Haifa Bay (shaped by the teachings of Naḥmanides), escaped during the Muslim reconquest of that city in 1291, and renewed his adherence to Naḥmanidean Kabbalah under the influence of Solomon Ibn Adret in Catalonia.

Crusader Akko in the Thirteenth Century

Thirteenth-century Akko was a cosmopolitan port city, bustling with international commerce and the arrival of large trading ships from European harbors. Under Christian Crusader rule since 1104 (and continuing unabated until 1291), Akko was the maritime center of the Latin Kingdom of Jerusalem, and functioned as the major commercial and immigrational bridge between the European lands and the Mediterranean Levant.[1] In this role, Akko was the meeting ground of individuals from a wide array of geographical origins—an environment that cultivated a heterogeneous ethos, and a palpable air of ethnic diversity, in which Christians, Muslims, and Jews interacted on the street on a daily basis. Indeed, according to the Muslim chronicler Ibn Jubair, Akko was

1. See Graboïs, "Akko as a Gate for Immigration to the Land of Israel in the Crusader Period," pp. 93–94.

a labyrinth of streets teeming with people to the point that there was barely space to walk, and people of different faiths were everywhere present. Ibn Jubair goes so far as to liken it to Constantinople (Istanbul) in terms of its sheer size.[2]

In addition to its commercial function, the city also served as the main gateway for immigration and pilgrimage from Christian Europe to the Holy Land. The overwhelming majority of Christian pilgrims disembarked in the port of Akko, and proceeded from there to their final destinations elsewhere in the Land. Despite the fact that Akko itself was not technically deemed part of the *terra sancta* that was the object of the Christian pilgrim's journey, a great many immigrants stayed in the city of Akko over the years, and it quickly became a busy urban center dominated by the influx of goods, merchants, and travelers from the West. As a commercial crossroads, the port of Akko—in which goods were rigorously taxed—also generated a significant and steady flow of revenue for the royal coffers of the Crusader kingdom.[3]

The role of Akko as the unofficial capital of the Crusader Levant was due to the consolidation of Crusader enclaves on the coast of the Holy Land—the fortification of which constituted a movement away from the inland cities and establishments that were characteristic of Muslim rule. The inland areas were still under Muslim control during the thirteenth century, and the Christians focused instead on the strengthening of more easily defensible positions on the coast. In this respect, Akko grew in importance throughout the thirteenth century as Muslim forces continued Saladin's tactic of systematically destroying coastal fortifications as a way of fending off a further European Crusade.[4] Moreover, by the early 1240s, Jerusalem had been conquered by the Muslims, and the fortified walls of that city (built by the Crusaders) were demolished. It was against this background that the center of the Crusader establishment—in the realms of politics, society, and economy—shifted to the coastal cities of Akko and Tyre, and primarily to the former.

After the Christians took over Akko from their Muslim predecessors,

2. Ibid., p. 98.

3. Ibid., p. 93.

4. Prawer, *History of the Jews in the Latin Kingdom of Jerusalem*, p. 264.

mosques were transformed into churches, minarets into bell towers, and the city was progressively divided up between the various interests of European states. Over the years, through official territorial grants of authority from successive kings of England, residents of Pisa, Genoa, Venice, Provence, and Marseille assumed residence in self-sustained quarters in the city.[5] These quarters existed (often in violent conflict with one another) in addition to the presence of the two main military orders of the Crusader kingdom—the Hospitallers and the Templars—each of whom also established separate quarters. This division in Akko led to a highly decentralized form of government and urban fragmentation along ethnic lines. This type of homogenized division among the satellite European communities was actually far more characteristic of urban life in Arab cities of the time, as opposed to the state of urban affairs in contemporaneous European cities.[6]

When Akko was conquered by the Crusaders in the first decade of the twelfth century, the European victors settled in the older part of the city, the section of Akko whose southern end met the port area. This was certainly the more desired area of the city, given its already established character, as well as its easy access to the harbor. At this point in time there was some infighting over property between the Franks who had lived in the city prior to Saladin's conquest some five years earlier and the other European Crusaders. As a result, all persons who were not European Christians (which included Jews, Muslims, and Eastern Christians) were required to live in the less prestigious section of the city, known as Montmusard.[7] At this time, Montmusard was the unfortified suburb of Akko, situated just to the north of the Hospitallers' quarter. It appears that some progressive fortification of Montmusard was undertaken by the Crusaders in the course of the century after the reconquest of Akko, and that major fortification of this zone was accomplished under the auspices of the French king Louis IX during his visit to the Holy Land from 1250 to 1254.[8] This requirement of all the so-called minority inhabitants of Akko (that they live in Montmusard) had the added result of situating

5. Jacoby, "Crusader Akko in the Thirteenth Century," p. 1.

6. See ibid., p. 43.

7. See Prawer, *History of the Jews*, p. 260.

8. See Jacoby, "Montmusard, Suburb of Crusader Akko," pp. 211–214.

these people on the hill up above the royal market of the city, which was clearly meant to serve the economic interests of the Crown by forcing those inhabitants to shop exclusively at the royal market, which lay between Montmusard and the center of Akko, and prevented them from making use of other independent markets, such as the one located in the old part of Akko.[9]

Jewish Social, Religious, and Intellectual Life in Akko

The factors noted above also seem to have shaped the growth of a substantial Jewish community within Crusader Akko. The commercial and political vitality of Akko, combined with its cosmopolitan ethos, proved to be a hospitable and attractive environment for the Jews, particularly after their expulsion from Jerusalem in 1229 and the city's virtual destruction by the Muslims just prior to 1244.[10] Beginning in the earlier part of the thirteenth century, Akko was also the destination and place of settlement of successive waves of immigration from Jewish communities in France. These first émigrés, who arrived in Akko between 1209 and 1211, consisted of some of the most eminent Jewish scholars from Ashkenaz at the time—*tosafists* (rabbis who wrote glossses on the Talmud) among whom were the well-known Rabbi Samson of Sens and his disciples. In addition to Samson of Sens, the group also included such scholars as R. Yonatan ha-Kohen of Lunel, R. Joseph of Clisson, R. Barukh ben Isaac of Worms, and R. Samson of Coucy, along with many of their disciples and colleagues.[11] Unlike other tosafist émigrés who made the trip during these years, Samson of Sens's group did not travel to the Holy Land via Egypt (a route that others had taken in order to visit the illustrious Abraham Maimonides), but traveled directly to Akko. While earlier scholarship suggested that various socioeconomic factors were the likely impetus for this move from France to the Land of Israel,[12] more recent work

9. Prawer, *History of the Jews*, pp. 261–262.

10. See Graboïs, "L'école Talmudique d'Akko," p. 52.

11. Kanarfogel, "The *'Aliyah* of 'Three Hundred Rabbis,'" pp. 193, 195.

12. Urbach, *The Tosafists*, pp. 125–126; Chazan, *Medieval Jewry in Northern France*, pp. 86–87.

has convincingly argued that intrareligious and pietistic concerns were at the forefront of the decision. Of the latter, Ephraim Kanarfogel has put forward the thesis that a desire to expand the range of halakhic observance through performance of Holy Land–bound commandments (*mizṿot ha-teluyot ba-'areẓ*) formed the core of tosafist reasoning on this issue.[13]

Once settled in Akko, Samson of Sens and his colleagues transplanted the main approach of the Franco-German school of tosafist pietism and talmudic study to the Land of Israel. This method, which continued and expanded the project begun by RaShI (Rabbi Solomon ben Isaac) several generations prior, was primarily focused on the clarification and explanation of the *peshat* meaning of the talmudic text, and reflected the dialectical manner of talmudic analysis for which the tosafists were famed.[14] Through this influence of Ashkenazi scholarship, the nascent talmudic academy in Akko focused on the characteristic tosafist method of elucidating the particular talmudic *sugya* under analysis, as opposed to the dominant Sefardi method of reading the talmudic text with the primary goal of ascertaining the final halakhic decision to be used in ritual practice. The latter method was most prominently employed in the scholarship of Moses Maimonides and is in evidence in his classic multivolume work the *Mishneh Torah*.[15] The vitality and strength of the Akko Ashkenazic school seems to have been sustained financially by the numerous Jewish merchants and affluent businessmen who attended the talmudic academy upon their visits to the Holy Land for commercial purposes, some of whom abandoned business altogether for the pursuit of scholarly study in the yeshivah of Akko.[16] One of the most famous of these cases was that of the merchant Shem Ṭov ben Isaac of Tortosa, who originally came to Akko on business in 1226 and stayed to study for many years.

---

13. Kanarfogel, "*'Aliyah* of 'Three Hundred Rabbis,'" p. 197.

14. Graboïs, "L'école Talmudique d'Akko," pp. 50–52.

15. It should be noted of course, that despite the highly dialectical character of tosafist analysis of talmudic *sugyot* (which reflects the dialogue between master and disciple in the *yeshivah*), the practical questions of applicable halakhah were almost always present. See Urbach, *Tosafists*, pp. 676–680.

16. See Graboïs, "L'école Talmudique d'Akko," p. 51.

Under the leadership of Samson of Sens, the talmudic academy of Akko continued to grow in numbers and reputation, and by the 1230s, the city had become a highly significant center of Jewish learning,[17] particularly devoted to the tosafist approach to talmudic study and recognized for its scholarly stature by the eminent rabbis of European cities.[18] Yet for all the prestige of this early group of tosafist immigrants to Akko, the talmudic academy underwent a dramatic expansion and veritable renaissance several decades later with the arrival of a large contingent of tosafist scholars who were the disciples of the Ashkenazi luminary Rabbi Yeḥiel of Paris.[19] Yeḥiel and his followers appear to have departed from Paris in the spring of 1259, sailing to Akko via Marseille.[20] Yeḥiel's presence in Paris can be dated to the end of 1258 by a divorce document that he signed there, and the next ship leaving for the Levant would not have been until April or May of the following year.[21] Aryeh Graboïs has argued that the move to Akko by Yeḥiel of Paris was likely precipitated by the public disputation between R. Yeḥiel and a Jewish convert to Christianity, and the subsequent burning of the Talmud in Paris during the years 1242–44.[22] We may, however, recall the argument of Kanarfogel that pietistic views of ritual observance associated with the Land of Israel among the French tosafists were also decisive factors in such immigrations during the thirteenth century, and the causal effects of external events should not be given too much weight. Yeḥiel himself died during the voyage to Akko, but his students built upon the existing academy of Akko and the legacy of Samson of Sens (as well as the model and inspiration of their teacher), and developed what soon became known as the "Academy of Paris in Akko." It can therefore be stated with some certitude that talmudic study in the tosafist mold flourished in Akko throughout the thirteenth century.

---

17. See Prawer, *History of the Jews*, p. 266.

18. See comments to this effect, as well as further references, in Schein, "Between East and West: The Latin Kingdom of Jerusalem," p. 158.

19. Prawer, *History of the Jews*, p. 150.

20. See ibid., p. 274, n. 65.

21. Ibid., p. 274.

22. Graboïs, "L'école Talmudique d'Akko," pp. 49, 51.

Less than ten years after the arrival of the disciples of Yeḥiel of Paris in Akko, another towering figure of medieval Jewish scholarship arrived in that city, having met a similar fate to that of Rabbi Yeḥiel on the European continent. Moses Naḥmanides, the great jurist and mystic of Barcelona, had left Spain for the Land of Israel approximately four years after his famous disputation with the convert Paulus Christiani (in July of 1263)—an event sponsored by King James of Aragon to test the efficacy of Paulus Christiani's new method of proselytizing, which sought to use the Talmud itself to demonstrate the truth of Christianity to Jews.[23] Irrespective of these circumstances, however, it is clear from Naḥmanides' own writings that the Land of Israel held a special place in his thought and religious imagination,[24] and it is therefore not surprising that he chose to emigrate to the Holy Land when he became advanced in years. In 1267, Naḥmanides disembarked in the Holy Land and first traveled to Jerusalem. It was there that he delivered one of his famous sermons, the text of which records the degree of destruction that Naḥmanides witnessed in the sacred city.[25] It was likely this experience that contributed to his decision to move on to Akko. The master gave his well-known sermon for Rosh ha-Shanah in Akko in 1269, just a year before his death.[26] In Akko, Naḥmanides completed work on his monumental *Commentary on the Torah*[27] and established a school of his own, where he taught until his death in 1270. He was buried in the community cemetery at the base of Mount Carmel.

Among the scholars of Akko to be influenced by Naḥmanides during his years there was Solomon ben Samuel Petit—a man who became notorious ten years later for his active role in the Maimonidean controversy of Akko.[28] The personality of Solomon Petit and his role in

23. See Chazan, *Barcelona and Beyond*, p. 1.

24. On this subject, see Pedayah, "The Spiritual vs. the Concrete Land of Israel in the Geronese School of Kabbalah," pp. 264–289.

25. See the text cited and discussed in Prawer, *History of the Jews*, p. 160.

26. Naḥmanides' "דרשה לראש השנה" has been published in *Kitvei RaMBaN*, 1: 214–252.

27. In addition to the scholarship of Prawer on this point (as well as the bitter and prejudicial writing of Graetz [*History of the Jews* 3: 605–606]), note the autobiographical comment of Naḥmanides at the very end of his *Commentary*: ... ברכני השם עד כה שזכיתי ובאתי לעכה (God has blessed me to this point that I have merited to come to Akko . . .).

28. See Graboïs, "L'école Talmudique d'Akko," p. 56.

the intellectual-religious culture of Akko in the 1280s are particularly important for this study, owing to testimony provided by Isaac of Akko regarding the time he spent studying with other students under the tutelage of Solomon Petit:

ואני יה"ב שנ"ר דעת"ו מעיד עלי שמים וארץ ואת בוראם כי בעכו ת"ו היינו יום אחד אנחנו התלמידים יושבים ושונים לפני מורי הרב ר' שלמה צרפתי הקטן ז"ל . . .

> I, Isaac . . . of Akko . . .[29] call heaven and earth and their Creator as witnesses to my testimony that one day in Akko, may it be rebuilt, we the students were sitting and studying before my teacher, the Rabbi R. Solomon the Frenchman Petit, of blessed memory . . .[30]

Isaac then goes on to relate an antiphilosophical tirade that was delivered by Solomon Petit to the students who were gathered there, mocking the philosophy of Aristotle and his medieval followers among Jewish intellectuals. Although Maimonides is not mentioned by name in this particular context, it is clear from the fact of the Maimonidean controversy of the late 1280s that the philosopher's controversial writings constituted the background to Solomon Petit's virulence. It should also be noted that (in the aforementioned passage) Isaac quotes Solomon Petit as encouraging his students to study the Talmud, as opposed to the corrupting influence of philosophy.

Solomon Petit was a scholar educated on the tosafist model of talmudic learning, and seems to have been a kabbalistic and talmudic student of Naḥmanides in the few years before the master's death.[31] It therefore appears likely that it was Solomon Petit (presumably among others) who was responsible for the continued cultivation of a school of Naḥmanidean Kabbalah (which also devoted considerable attention to talmudic study on the tosafist model)[32] in Akko from the death of Naḥmanides until the fall of the city in 1291. We may indeed

29. The acronym יה"ב שנ"ר דעת"ו corresponds to the following words: יצחק הצעיר בן שמואל נטוריה רחמנא דמן עכו תבנה ותכונן (Isaac, the young one, son of Samuel—may the Compassionate One protect him—from Akko, may it be rebuilt and restored).

30. See Isaac of Akko, *Me'irat 'Einayim*, p. 56.

31. Prawer, *History of the Jews*, p. 278.

32. On Naḥmanides' use of the tosafist method of study and analysis, see Assis, *The Golden Age of Aragonese Jewry*, p. 308.

hypothesize that Isaac of Akko's formative influence in Naḥmanidean Kabbalah (which would ultimately function as the impetus for his great work of commentary on Naḥmanides' kabbalistic allusions, *Me'irat 'Einayim*) was initiated under the guidance of Solomon Petit. It thus also makes perfect sense why Isaac of Akko sought out the Naḥmanidean kabbalistic school of Solomon Ibn Adret in Barcelona upon his escape from Akko in 1291 during its conquest by the Muslims (more on this below). As Joshua Prawer has noted, it is clear that Solomon Petit was the leader and instigator of the anti-Maimonidean contingent in Akko,[33] thus departing in a significant way from Naḥmanides' more respectful manner of disagreement with the writings of Maimonides.[34]

The foundations for this anti-Maimonidean posture had been laid earlier in the century by Samson of Sens, who transplanted the negative reactivity of French tosafist scholars toward Maimonides' philosophical work, just as he had transplanted Ashkenazic exegetical and pietistic trends to Akko. Indeed, even before his immigration to Akko, Samson of Sens joined other rabbinic scholars in the excommunication of Maimonides' *Guide of the Perplexed*, and Akko became host to a great deal of anti-Maimonidean sentiments in the wake of the arrival of Samson and his disciples.[35] Generally speaking, the divide over Maimonides' writings, which had already begun to germinate at this early point in the Ashkenazi immigration to Akko, was structured by an East-West polarity—between Jews of Oriental descent, for whom Maimonides was the paragon of intellectual and religious perfection, and the French tosafists, whose authority structures were more deeply rooted in the great talmudic academies of Europe. While far less vicious than the Maimonidean controversy in Montpellier two generations earlier, the controversy at Akko reached a high pitch of ferocity

33. Prawer, *History of the Jews*, p. 283, and see my comments above on *Me'irat 'Einayim*, p. 56.

34. The most extraordinary and eloquent example of Naḥ- manides' attempt to balance a critique of philosophy with high esteem for Maimonides as a halakhist and speculative thinker is Naḥmanides' epistle that begins with the biblical words of humility טרם אענה אני שוגג (Ps. 119:67). An annotated version of this text has been published in *Kitvei RaMBaN*, 1: 336–351. In addition to an articulation of disagreement on certain issues, this classic of medieval polemical literature is filled with praise of Maimonides.

35. Prawer, *History of the Jews*, p. 268.

toward the end of the 1280s with the arrival of David Maimonides in the city in 1285.[36] The grandson of the illustrious philosopher had been temporarily removed from his position as *nagid* of Egyptian Jewry,[37] and he settled in Akko until his return to Egypt in September of 1290. As has been noted in the historiographical research of Prawer and Graboïs,[38] the focal points of the Maimonidean controversy of Akko were David Maimonides and Solomon Petit, and the debate raged primarily from 1286 to 1289, radiating from there outward to other parts of the Jewish world.

Like his brother 'Obadyah (the author of *The Treatise of the Pool*),[39] David Maimonides combined Jewish-Sufi pietism with the transmission of his grandfather's Neoaristotelian philosophy. Thus, David's stay in Akko during the 1280s seems (at least in part) to account for the presence of Jewish-Sufi themes and motifs in Isaac of Akko's written work (whether Isaac received direct transmission on these matters from David Maimonides, or whether he learned them from other members of David's pietistic circle, is still unclear). If not for this explanation, the convergence of these two facts would be highly coincidental.

Nevertheless, it is also quite plausible that the so-called Jewish-Sufi themes in Isaac of Akko's writing were not restricted in origin to David Maimonides and his circle, and may in fact have also been influenced by pietistic trends stemming from tosafist spirituality in Ashkenaz as they were imported to Akko through the immigration of tosafist scholars. Let us recall that the primary content of the Jewish-Sufi ideals found in Isaac's writing was a fundamentally ascetic form of pietism. The devotee was instructed to transcend all concern for physicality and mundane emotion in favor of a state of complete equanimity in which all corporeal matters were deemed equal in their inability to disquiet the mystical concentration of the pietist. This state of equanimity was directly correlated to an extreme form of humility, in which the pietist would be indifferent to the rebuke or praise

---

36. Ibid., p. 286.

37. Ibid., p. 282.

38. Ibid., p. 286; Graboïs, "Akko as a Gate for Immigration to the Land of Israel in the Crusader Period," pp. 102–103.

39. See Fenton, *The Treatise of the Pool by 'Obadyah Maimonides.*

bestowed upon him by others. In Isaac of Akko's *'Oẓar Ḥayyim*, this mentality was also associated with a social group known as the *perushim ha-mitbodedim,* which might be loosely translated as "the ascetics who meditate in seclusion" (for more on this, see Chapter 8). As Ephraim Kanarfogel has demonstrated recently,[40] the extensive use of the term *perushim*, as well as the content of this form of asceticism and extreme humility, was a dominant feature of Ashkenazi pietism as it was expressed and practiced among tosafist scholars in the twelfth and thirteenth centuries. For despite the fact that such ascetic ideals were known to have been employed among the *Ḥasidei 'Ashkenaz*, the presence of this mentality among the tosafists has only recently come to light through Kanarfogel's pioneering work. Given the strength of the tosafist religious establishment in Akko, I would suggest that the formative influence upon Isaac may have been a convergence of Near Eastern Jewish-Sufism (as transmitted primarily through the Maimonides family) and Ashkenazi pietism as it was derived from the Franco-German schools of tosafist religious culture. Such a convergence would indeed reflect the essential character of Akko in this period—a place that served as a crossroads for politics, commerce, ideas, and practice from different parts of the world.

With respect to the personalities associated with Jewish-Sufism in Akko and the transmission of these ideas to Isaac, we would do well to add mention of another individual who remains something of an enigma to modern scholarship. Indeed, it is hard to determine the identity of the ABNeR (אבנ"ר) figure mentioned several times by Isaac of Akko in *Me'irat 'Einayim* (see further in Chapter 8), but we may speculate that this person was associated with colleagues or students of David Maimonides during his five-year stay in Akko, or with advocates of an equanimic pietism as derived from Ashkenazi thought and practice. Yet the likelihood is that such ideas only rose to prominence in Akko with the *convergence* of Maimonidean Sufism and Ashkenazi asceticism. From what we know of David Maimonides' time in Akko, it is only logical to assume that Isaac of Akko encountered the Jewish-Sufi teacher ABNeR in Akko some time during the second half of the

40. Kanarfogel, *Peering Through the Lattices*, pp. 33–92.

1280s (i.e., after David Maimonides' arrival in Akko, and before the fall of the city to the Muslims in 1291, which prompted Isaac's escape to the European continent). The other possibility is that Isaac encountered this ABNeR figure in North Africa some time between the years 1305 and 1310 (on the relevance of these years see below).

While we are still unable to precisely identify the actual name of this person, I would like to offer a few notes toward a partial resolution of the enigma. The second half of this acronym—נ"ר—may likely be the ubiquitous honorific נטוריה רחמנא (May God protect him), which Isaac frequently appends to the names of people he reveres, a common epithet in Jewish scholarship appended to the names of the living who were esteemed by the author of a text. Such, for example, is the case with Isaac's respectful references to Solomon Ibn Adret, as well as his attributions to Yom Ṭov Ashvili, another highly significant halakhist who participated in the circle of Adret in Barcelona (to be discussed in more detail below). The presence of this honorifical suffix with respect to Ibn Adret lends important insight into the chronology of Isaac's writing of *Me'irat 'Einayim*, clueing us in to the fact that Adret was still living at the time of Isaac's writing and/or editing of his treatise (more on this below as well). By the same token, we learn of Isaac's living relationship with Yom Ṭov Ashvili, and under our present hypothesis, ABNeR as well. If this estimation is plausible, then we need only solve the enigma of the first two letters of the acronym, א"ב, and the so-called name ABNeR becomes misleading. What the letters א"ב may in fact signify remains a matter of speculation, but we may assume that they indicate a person who was intimately involved with Jewish-Sufi pietists, and with whom Isaac of Akko had direct oral contact. Perhaps focusing on the first half of the אבנ"ר acronym will aid us in identifying this mysterious figure, who clearly had a formative impact on Isaac's thinking. In Chapter 3, I shall have occasion to further discuss the range of figures to whom Isaac attributes the status of teacher (or transmitter) with respect to himself (and the complex rhetoric involved in these attributions)—a discussion that will aim to contextualize the few personalities just mentioned.

As can now be ascertained, the city of Akko in the thirteenth century (and for present purposes, primarily the last quarter of that century) was a place of meeting for Jews of diverse geographical origins, as well as of diverse intellectual-religious orientations. Tosafists, mystics, and philosophers (not to mention the many merchants and pilgrims who passed through Akko during these years) met and debated their highly varied perspectives on religious thought and practice. Talmudic learning thrived alongside Naḥmanidean Kabbalah, and advocates of philosophy and Jewish-Sufi piety also cultivated deep roots in the Jewish community of Akko. It was against this background and in this milieu that Isaac of Akko lived the first part of his life, and his subsequent eclectic method of tradition collection was no doubt shaped by the significantly heterogeneous character of his city of origin. He was very likely educated in the talmudic (tosafist) academy of Akko, was clearly schooled in the thought and exegetical ways of Naḥmanidean Kabbalah, had received oral instruction from masters of Jewish-Sufi piety, and was evidently very close to the front lines in the battle over Maimonidean philosophy (through his close connection to Solomon Petit). Owing to its centrality as a political and commercial crossroads for the Crusaders, Akko functioned as an intellectual crossroads for Jewish scholars and pietists of the time.

The Fall of Akko: Trauma and Memory

This period of flourishing in Jewish intellectual and spiritual life in Crusader Akko came to a dramatic and tragic end with the famous battle of 1291 between the Christian rulers of the city and the Mameluk Muslim invaders—a bloody fight in which many Jewish residents of Akko were caught in the middle and killed. Due to the inescapable impact that this event had upon Isaac of Akko[41]—a trauma that directly caused his move westward to the Jewish communities of Aragon and Castile—it is worthwhile to depict the details of that momentous and terrifying occasion. As mentioned earlier, Akko was one of the very last strongholds of the Crusader kingdom in the Holy Land, and the defeat at Akko meant the ultimate fall of Christian power in the Mediterranean Levant.

41. See the document discussed below on pp. 34–35.

Indeed, this collapse has been viewed by historians of the period[42] to be one of the single most transformative events in the respective histories of the Muslims and the Christians in medieval times. The battle of Akko dramatically shifted the balance of power in the Holy Land, and represented the ultimate demise of the Latin Kingdom of Jerusalem. Much to the benefit of the modern historian, both Christian and Muslim eyewitnesses chronicled the battle and its aftermath extensively and carefully, thereby leaving us a remarkably clear window onto those fateful events of 1291.

According to two of the reports discussed by Andreas D'Souza,[43] the conquering Muslim army reached the fortified walls of Akko on the fourth or the fifth day of April 1291. At this point in time, according to the Christian chronicler Gerard de Montreal, the number of people living in the city of Akko was somewhere between thirty and forty thousand individuals—a number that included 600–700 cavalry soldiers and 13,000 infantry.[44] The siege of the city continued for more than a month, and on the eighteenth day of May 1291, Akko fell to the Muslims. All the eyewitness chroniclers of the event report that the final charge by the Muslim fighters was presaged by a frightening sound of beating drums.[45] Once the walls of the city were breached, a bloody rampage of killing and destruction ensued, and the Christians were defeated and overrun in less than three hours of the Friday morning attack.[46] The castle tower of the city center was set on fire with 10,000 people holed up inside, collapsing and further killing 2,000 people on horseback in the street below.[47] One of the main synagogues of the city was also burned with Jews inside—a horrible massacre that was recorded by Isaac of Akko himself.[48] After the Muslim conquest, the city of Akko was utterly destroyed by the invaders so as to forestall any future Christian Crusade from European lands.

42. See D'Souza, "The Conquest of 'Akkā," p. 234.

43. Ibid., p. 241.

44. Ibid., p. 240.

45. Ibid., pp. 244–245.

46. Ibid., p. 245.

47. Ibid., p. 246.

48. Isaac of Akko, *'Oẓar Ḥayyim*, fol. 111b.

The Wandering Scholar: Travels and Intellectual Influences in Aragon and Castile

The fall of Akko, and the collapse of the vibrant Jewish community therein, was a pivotal event in the life of Isaac ben Samuel, just as it was for the larger history of religion and society in the Middle Ages. With the intellectual and spiritual Jewish center of the Levant in ruins, the surviving Jews from the battle of 1291 sought out new associations in other parts of the Jewish world. For Isaac of Akko, that shift led to the European continent, and particularly to the Iberian regions of Aragon and Castile, in which Jewish religious life was still flourishing in numerous and diverse settings. We learn some of the details of this geographical move on Isaac's part from a well-known document preserved in Abraham Zacuto's *Sefer Yuḥasin*—a passage most familiar to scholars of medieval Kabbalah for its relevance to the question of the authorship of the *Zohar* and Isaac's famous encounter with the illustrious Moses de Leon. The majority of this remarkable text records Isaac of Akko's personal testimony regarding his journeys throughout the Castilian region in the year 1305 (a year to which we shall return in due course), but the text begins with several details that shed light on the effect of 1291 on Isaac's life:

> In the month of Adar, Rabbi Isaac of Akko wrote that Akko had been destroyed in the year fifty-one [i.e., 1291], and that the pious of Israel had been slaughtered there with the four statutory kinds of death.[49] In 1305, this Rabbi Isaac of Akko was in Navarre, in Estella, having escaped from Akko, and in the same 1305, he came to Toledo. And I found the diary of Rabbi Isaac of Akko,[50] the man who wrote a kabbalistic work in 1331 and in whose time Akko was destroyed and all its inhabitants captured.[51]

---

49. These were stoning, burning, beheading, and strangling. This list likely means, in-effect, "in all kinds of terrible ways." See *Mishnah Sanhedrin*, 7: 1.

50. Isaac of Akko refers to this lost work (called *Divrei ha-Yamim*) in *'Oẓar Ḥayyim*, fol. 8b.

51. Here I have provided the translation of David Goldstein in his rendition of Isaiah Tishby's General Introduction to *The Wisdom of the Zohar*, p. 13. Also see the critical discussion of this text in B. Z. Kedar, "Judeans and Samarians in Crusader Kingdom of Jerusalem," pp. 405–407. Kedar further notes (p. 406, n. 78) the testimony provided by Isaac to the burning of a synagogue during the battle of Akko in 1291.

Thus Isaac's escape from the massacre of Akko resulted in a westward journey away from the Land of Israel and the Mediterranean Levant toward Jewish centers of distant lands embedded within the kingdoms of Christian Europe. Although the foregoing text does not reveal any biographical information between the time of Isaac's escape from Akko (1291) and his pursuit of the *Zohar* in 1305, we can certainly assume on the basis of internal evidence from *Me'irat 'Einayim* that Isaac spent considerable time in the intellectual circle and religious environment of Rabbi Solomon Ibn Adret (RaShBA), the great successor to Naḥmanides in the coastal city of Barcelona.[52] As will be documented through sources cited in Chapter 3, Isaac of Akko refers on several occasions to specific kabbalistic teachings that he heard directly from the mouth of the RaShBA, as well as from other notable Barcelonese scholars, including Yom Ṭov Ashvili (of Seville). R. Yom Ṭov was himself a disciple of Adret who grew to great fame of his own accord in the area of legal reasoning and decision making. Both of these scholars were major halakhic figures of the end of the thirteenth / beginning of the fourteenth centuries, each of whom composed voluminous *responsa* to legal queries from throughout the Jewish world. In addition to this massive halakhic literature, for which they are both famed in Jewish history, the RaShBA and the RIṬBA (Rabbi Yom Ṭov) were clearly notable kabbalistic thinkers and teachers as well. Due to the fact that the dominant mode of textual creativity undertaken by both men was that of halakhic responsa, neither of them is particularly well known to students of history as kabbalistic figures. Nevertheless, the attribution of kabbalistic teachings to them both by Isaac of Akko attests well to this fact. In this respect, the Naḥmanidean school of Kabbalah was characterized by leaders who embodied the complete fusion of esotericism (Kabbalah) and applicable exotericism (law and responsa) in their intellectual life. Like others in the history of the Jewish religion, Naḥmanides, Adret, and Yom Ṭov Ashvili all sought to attain an ongoing balance of these two different realms of thought and practice.[53]

---

52. On the features of this circle around the RaShBA, with particular attention to their struggle with the ongoing conservatism of Naḥmanidean Kabbalah, see Schwartz, "Between Conservatism and Intellectualism: The Analytical Thought of the Circle of the Rashba."

53. For a study of this phenomenon in the life of a later kabbalist, see Werblowsky, *Joseph*

Adret in particular continued the esoteric traditions of Naḥmanides, and like his illustrious predecessor, he limited his teaching of Kabbalah to a highly restricted circle of close disciples. Adret's yeshivah in Barcelona was famed for its holdings in talmudic manuscripts, and was a meeting place for scholars from throughout the Jewish world.[54] This latter fact can be attributed to Adret's scholarly renown—a reputation that brought many promising young Jewish intellectuals to his school.[55] Just as Akko served as an intellectual crossroads for diverse trends in medieval Judaism, so too did Barcelona under the leadership of the RaShBA. Another prominent teacher in the yeshivah of Barcelona was Rabbi Aharon ha-Levi de Na Clara—a master who taught many students in common with Adret, and who served alongside Adret as a judge in Jewish legal proceedings.[56] It is therefore reasonable to assume that Isaac of Akko would have encountered this teacher as well during the time that he may have spent in Barcelona.

In the fourteen years between his escape from Akko and his arrival in Toledo in 1305, Isaac appears to have entrenched himself in the study and exposition of Naḥmanides' terse kabbalistic allusions to Scripture, collecting the diverse teachings and viewpoints through oral discussions with many different people and the perusal of a wide range of written sources. The composite result of his travel and study was *Me'irat 'Einayim*—a work that reflects the unique blend of eastern and western intellectual influences received by Isaac as he made his way from one part of the world to another. As noted in Chapter 1, Amos Goldreich has convincingly argued that Isaac had written the majority of his

---

Karo: Lawyer and Mystic. A further parallel may certainly be drawn to Moses Maimonides' extraordinary combination of law and philosophy in his intellectual life and creativity. See Twersky, *Introduction to the Code of Maimonides*, pp. 356–514.

54. On the broader phenomenon of great rabbinic masters and *yeshivot* who attracted advanced disciples from all across the Jewish world in medieval Ashkenaz and Sefarad, see Goldin, "Communication in Jewish Intellectual Circles," p. 130. Goldin discusses the existence of a type of intellectual fellowship that surrounded a revered and charismatic teacher, which frequently led to the establishment of major centers of higher Jewish education. Speaking about the master, Goldin observes: "At the center stood the charismatic personality of the teacher. Rather significantly, the *yeshiva* was known by his name, not by the town or the community where it was located."

55. Assis, *Golden Age of Aragonese Jewry*, p. 309.

56. Ibid., pp. 310–311.

metacommentary pertaining to the book of Genesis by 1305, and that the addenda to the Genesis commentary were added after this time.[57] Building upon this conclusion reached by Goldreich, it may be argued that most of *Me'irat 'Einayim* was written, or at least edited together, between the years 1305 and 1310. This hypothesis is predicated on the fact that we find scattered references throughout *Me'irat 'Einayim* to teachings that Isaac of Akko heard orally from R. Solomon Ibn Adret in which Adret's name is consistently postscripted with the honorifics given to a person who is still living.[58] Given the fact that we know Ibn Adret died in the year 1310,[59] it seems quite probable that most of the treatise was composed prior to 1310.

According to the secondhand evidence preserved in Zacuto's *Sefer Yuḥasin* (cited above), Isaac of Akko arrived in Toledo after first passing an unspecified length of time in Estella (in the kingdom of Navarre). If Isaac's sojourn did in fact take him from Barcelona to Estella to Toledo, then we can imagine a southwesterly path of travel into Castile—a route that probably would have had to overcome the Iberian Mountains and the imposing Central Sierras. Toledo could be reached just south of those Central Sierras—a mountain range that posed a formidable challenge and barrier to many medieval travelers.[60] Further, it is clear from the evidence in *Sefer Yuḥasin*[61] that Isaac's southwesterly course took him through Valladolid in north-central Castile, and then south to Avila in his pursuit of Moses de Leon and the truth about the *Zohar*. It remains unclear whether Isaac went to Toledo *before* seeking out Moses de Leon in Valladolid, but this seems highly unlikely given Isaac's northern point of origin in Estella, and the aforementioned obstacle of the Central Sierras to the north of Toledo.[62] It therefore seems probable that Isaac followed a route that led from Estella to Valladolid to Avila—eventually

57. See Goldreich, "Notes to *Me'irat 'Einayim*," p. 354.

58. I.e., נטוריה רחמנא (may God protect him). Numerous examples of Isaac's rhetoric of oral reception from Adret are discussed in Chapter 3.

59. See the discussion in the *Encyclopedia Judaica*, s.v. "Solomon Ibn Adret." Also see Werblowsky and Wigoder, eds., *The Oxford Dictionary of the Jewish Religion*, p. 20.

60. See Ruiz, *Crisis and Continuity: Land and Town in Late Medieval Castile*, pp. 15–17.

61. See the text as cited in Tishby, *Wisdom of the Zohar*, 1: 14.

62. See the relevant maps in Assis, *The Jews of Spain: From Settlement to Expulsion*, unnumbered pages appended at the end of the volume (map titled: "The Iberian Peninsula—From

arriving for a protracted stay in the city of Toledo. Irrespective of this somewhat speculative reconstruction, however, it does appear that Isaac was greatly influenced by several scholars from the Jewish community of Toledo, and that these points of contact were anchored in the year 1305 (if not beyond that as well). In this regard, Amos Goldreich cites and discusses very significant testimony from *Me'irat 'Einayim* indicating that Isaac first received traditions concerning the "Kabbalah of the Left Side" (i.e., the Kabbalah focused on intradivine manifestations of evil cultivated in Castile and exemplified in the writings of Isaac and Jacob ha-Kohen, Todros Abulafia, and the *Zohar,* along with its related Hebrew literature) from David ha-Kohen (referred to in *Me'irat 'Einayim* primarily through the acronym מרדכ"י), who had in turn received these traditions from Todros Abulafia himself.[63] By 1305, R. David ha-Kohen was a prominent rabbinic figure in Toledo (R. Todros had been the major rabbinic leader in that city until his death in the early 1280s) and, together with R. Solomon ben Ami'el (referred to in *Me'irat 'Einayim* as, רשנ"ר)[64] influenced the thought and religious development of Isaac of Akko when he migrated from Aragon to Castile (via Navarre).

The extent to which Isaac integrated this particular brand of Kabbalah after his apparently sustained stay in Toledo is substantially reflected in his later work, *'Oẓar Ḥayyim* (on the dating of this work by Goldreich, see below). What is evinced relatively marginally in his earlier writing of *Me'irat 'Einayim* is amplified and developed significantly in *'Oẓar Ḥayyim*—indeed, the two books are markedly different in this regard. In numerous passages scattered all throughout the voluminous text of *'Oẓar Ḥayyim* (more than 450 pages of manuscript), Isaac makes repeated references to the doctrine of the demonic/evil dimensions that directly parallel (and oppose) the "holy and pure" *sefirot*.[65] Isaac's term

---

the Middle of the 13th Century Until 1492"); Baer, *A History of the Jews in Christian Spain* (Hebrew version), p. 614 (map appended to the very end of the book).

63. See Goldreich, "Notes to *Me'irat 'Einayim*," p. 361. Goldreich also notes (p. 362) that Isaac of Akko surprisingly refers to David ha-Kohen as גדול דורו—a designation usually reserved in *Me'irat 'Einayim* for the RaShBA. Uses of this phrase with respect to the RaShBA are documented and discussed in the next chapter.

64. See the extensive discussion of this enigmatic figure by Goldreich in "Notes to *Me'irat 'Einayim*," pp. 389–390.

65. See, e.g., Isaac of Akko, *'Oẓar Ḥayyim*, fols. 100b, 123a. As noted above, this is a well-

of choice when referring to these demonic forces is "the external rungs" (*ha-madregot ha-ḥiẓoniyot*),[66] and this specific usage is nothing short of widespread in *'Oẓar Ḥayyim*.[67] What is more, distinctions in orientation (based on this exact terminology) between the kabbalists of Castile and Aragon are observed and noted by Isaac of Akko in several different passages[68]—a phenomenon that attests well to Isaac's unusual ability to discern the panorama of kabbalistic approaches in his own time. Let us consider a particularly striking example of this comparative awareness on Isaac's part. After offering a symbolic interpretation that makes explicit allusion to the '*madregot ha-ḥiẓoniyot*,' Isaac states that this exegesis is according to

> **זהו על דרך מקובלי ספרד אשר זכו לקבל קבלת המדרגות החיצוניות. אמנם על דרך מקובלי כתלוניא, אשר קבלתם נכונה בעס"ב [=עשר ספירות בלימה], אלא שלא קבלו דבר במדרגות החיצוניות . . . ירמזו . . .**

> the way of the kabbalists of Sefarad [*mequbbalei Sefarad*], who have merited receiving the Kabbalah of the *madregot ha-ḥiẓoniyot*. However, according to the way of the kabbalists of Catalonia—whose Kabbalah is correct with respect to the ten *sefirot*, but who have not received a tradition pertaining to the *madregot ha-ḥiẓoniyot*—[the words in question] allude to [a different meaning] . . . [69]

As is also the case elsewhere in *'Oẓar Ḥayyim*,[70] the phrase *mequbbalei Sefarad* is used in overt contrast to the phrase *mequbbalei Catalonia*,[71]

---

known and characteristic feature of Castilian Kabbalah, a schema that is developed in many zoharic passages. See the seminal essay on the matter by Scholem, "*Siṭra Aḥra*: Good and Evil in the Kabbalah," in id., *On the Mystical Shape of the Godhead*, pp. 56–87. Also see the broad and detailed work of Isaiah Tishby on this subject in his *Wisdom of the Zohar*, 2: 447–546. Tishby addresses our subject with attention to both historical and thematic concerns.

66. This is an established usage in kabbalistic literature to refer to the demonic forces of impurity. See Klatzkin, *Thesaurus Philosophicus*, 1: 289; Ben-Yehudah, *Complete Dictionary and Thesaurus of the Hebrew Language*, 2: 1537.

67. Examples of this phrase include, but are not limited to, *'Oẓar Ḥayyim*, fols. 12a, 13b, 28b, 53a, 67b, 85b, 96b, 100b, 123a, 164b.

68. See Isaac of Akko, *'Oẓar Ḥayyim*, fols. 12a, 13b, 85b.

69. Ibid., fol. 12a. Also see the discussion in Huss, "NiSAN—The Wife of the Infinite," pp. 160–161.

70. Isaac of Akko, *'Oẓar Ḥayyim*, 13b and 85b.

71. In Isaac's day, Catalonia was already subsumed under the Crown of Aragon. Isaac was almost certainly referring to the well-known kabbalists from Gerona and Barcelona.

and the context clearly indicates that Sefarad was understood by Isaac (in most cases) to connote the Castilian region in particular. In this passage, Isaac displays an acute awareness of the divide between Castilian and Catalonian Kabbalah on the issue of the "impure evil" dimensions that exist alongside the "holy and pure" *sefirot*. This awareness of fundamental differences in geographically defined kabbalistic schools reflects a relatively broad sense of the intellectual climate and concerns of his day, and is, I believe, in large part a function of his itinerant profile. Familiarity with the diversity of traditions and practices among his contemporaries is also reflected in Isaac of Akko's stated awareness of differences in liturgical ritual practice between the Ashkenazic (what he calls *ḥakhmei ẓorfat ve-'ashkenaz* [the sages of France and Germany])[72] and Sefardic communities (which he lists as *sefarad, yavan, ve-yishm'a'el* [Sefarad, Greece, and Muslim lands]).[73] In this instance (unlike in the passage previously considered), the word "Sefarad" would appear to connote *both* the regions of Castile and Aragon, though we cannot say for certain.

Let us now turn to the historical puzzle (repeatedly pondered by historians of medieval Kabbalah, and alluded to above) involving Isaac of Akko, Moses de Leon, and the emergence of the *Zohar*. This well-known connection involved Isaac's persistent search for the truth about the *Zohar*'s authorship, his purported encounter with Moses de Leon just before the latter's death (at which time de Leon reportedly affirmed the antiquity of the *Zohar* to the curious traveler), and Isaac's subsequent conversation with another scholar who himself heard a very different story, if only thirdhand: both de Leon's widow and de Leon's daughter had claimed that their husband and father had composed the work himself and did *not* copy it from an ancient manuscript. All of these elements are preserved in Abraham Zacuto's *Sefer Yuḥasin*, and all have been turned and considered over and again by generations of *Zohar* critics.[74] Yet in addition to the rather tenuous character of this

72. Compare this with a parallel line on fol. 45a: "A *qabbalah* [a tradition] is in my hands from the righteous ones of France and the *ḥasidei 'ashkenaz* . . ."

73. Isaac of Akko, *'Oẓar Ḥayyim*, fol. 54a.

74. For the most recent summary and consideration of this evidence, see Green, *A Guide to the Zohar*, pp. 164–165. Full citation of the evidence, as well as a detailed discussion of its

document as historical evidence regarding Moses de Leon's authorship of the *Zohar*, historians have also been left somewhat in the dark as to Isaac of Akko's ultimate conclusions regarding the *Zohar* mystery. In the first-hand testimony that Isaac offers regarding his quest (albeit a "first-hand" account that is only preserved by Zacuto's later anthology, owing to the fact that Isaac's original diary is now lost to us), he reports that those with whom he discussed the matter were quite divided in opinion over de Leon's claim that the *Zohar* was ancient. Assuming that the document preserved in *Sefer Yuḥasin* represents some shred of historical truth, we must also resolve the question of Isaac's own opinion after investigating the enigma. Was Isaac convinced by Moshe de Leon or by the story of de Leon's widow and daughter? Did he accept the claim that the *Zohar* was composed in tannaitic times by R. Shimon bar Yoḥai (as was accepted by subsequent kabbalists and bearers of religious memory)? On the basis of the evidence that I have seen in *'Oẓar Ḥayyim*, it is clear that this question is to be answered in the affirmative. Indeed, overt attributions of the *Zohar* to R. Shimon bar Yoḥai are found in at least six different cases in *'Oẓar Ḥayyim*, and none of these instances appear artificial or interruptive to the flow and context of Isaac's writing.[75] That is to say, unlike several lengthy citations from the *Zohar* in *'Oẓar Ḥayyim*[76] (which appear to be an insertion of the sixteenth-century scholar and copyist Avraham Saba),[77] the attributions of the *Zohar* to Shimon bar Yoḥai are seamlessly integrated into the text, and are of a piece with the stylistics generally characteristic of Isaac of Akko's composition. There is therefore no justifiable reason to assume that these are the additions of a later copyist. It is a significant fact that such evidence does not exist in Isaac's *Me'irat 'Einayim*—a further support for the hypothesis that the marked influence of Castilian Kabbalah on Isaac's thought took place toward the end of his writing of *Me'irat 'Einayim* and the beginning of work on *'Oẓar Ḥayyim*.

---

reliability and implications, can be found in the classic analysis of Tishby, *Wisdom of the Zohar*, 1: 13–18.

75. Isaac of Akko, *'Oẓar Ḥayyim*, fols. 60a, 65a, 65b, 95a, 102a, 120a.

76. See, e.g., ibid., fols. 62b, 68a.

77. I thank Prof. Boaz Huss of Ben-Gurion University for calling this intriguing fact to my attention.

An additional feature of religious life in Toledo at this time was the rising power and influence of R. 'Asher ben Yeḥiel (the R'oSh)[78] and his institution of intellectual conservatism and repression—a fact that likely affected Isaac of Akko during his stay in that city. In fact, Goldreich argues that Isaac of Akko's perception of the narrow-mindedness of 'Asher ben Yeḥiel and his followers, and the repressive intellectual environment that resulted, may have contributed to Isaac's decision to leave Toledo (one of the great Jewish communities and intellectual environments of the High Middle Ages)[79] for the notably less fecund intellectual atmosphere of North Africa, in which he seems to have written his later (and more Sufi-inspired) work.[80]

'Oẓar Ḥayyim appears to have been written in this North African environment (quite probably Morocco) sometime in the early 1330s. Goldreich determines this dating primarily on the basis of the fact that almost all of the extant manuscripts of Isaac's later work were composed and/or copied in North Africa.[81] This general geographic and temporal provenance would also seem to apply to Isaac's kabbalistic comments on Judah Ibn Malkah's work that were published with critical annotation by G. Vajda (as mentioned in Chapter 1). Indeed, *'Oẓar Ḥayyim* in particular is marked by a persistent focus, consistent throughout that voluminous work, on Jewish-Sufi piety and mysticism (with great attention to asceticism and the concept of *hitbodedut*). It is further notable that even the relatively sparse pieces in Isaac's kabbalistic commentary to Ibn Malkah's work contain clear elements of this ascetic strain of

78. See Baer, *History of the Jews in Christian Spain*, 1: 316–325.

79. The hypothesis that Isaac of Akko was negatively impacted by the influence of R. 'Asher in Toledo might also be bolstered by the fact that R. 'Asher all but ignored the halakhic legacy of the great Sefardic jurists (including that of Adret, whose support had paved the way for R. 'Asher's successful move from 'Ashkenaz to Toledo). Indeed, it even appears that R. 'Asher was dismissive of Adret's halakhic reasoning in at least one instance. On this peculiarity, which may very well have troubled Isaac of Akko (owing to his great reverence for Adret and the Naḥmanidean tradition), see Ta-Shma, "Between East and West: Rabbi 'Asher b. Yehi'el and His Son Rabbi Ya'akov," pp. 181–183. On the dramatic transformation of Jewish culture in Toledo under the sway of the *R'oSh*, see Ilan, "The Jewish Community in Toledo at the Turn of the Thirteenth Century and the Beginning of the Fourteenth," p. 68, who also notes the decidedly pluralistic ethos of Toledan society, nurtured by "cultural interfacing between the Muslims, Christians, and Jews" (p. 75).

80. Goldreich, "Notes to *Me'irat 'Einayim*," p. 412.

81. See ibid., pp. 364, 368.

thought and practice.[82] By contrast, *Me'irat 'Einayim* gives far less attention to these modalities, and the overwhelming majority of this material is found in the last sixth of the treatise. The kabbalistic concerns of the earlier sections of *Me'irat 'Einayim* (while still powerfully contemplative) are molded according to the forms of Naḥmanidean Kabbalah, and less along the lines of Sufic ascetic ideals.

This fact leads me to suppose that although Isaac was certainly influenced by the ascetic-meditative modalities advocated by some teachers in his native Akko, his interest in this type of thought and practice only fully matured toward the end of the first decade of the fourteenth century (i.e., *after* he may have left Toledo for North Africa, but *before* the death of the RaShBA in 1310). For if we assume that Isaac wrote *Me'irat 'Einayim* in a reasonably linear fashion with respect to time, then it may be concluded that the sections that most pertain to Sufic pietism were composed at the end of the writing process when he may have been drawn to, if not already settled in, the more Sufi-inspired Jewish community of North Africa.

Isaac of Akko's historical profile as an itinerant mystic who journeyed through both Christian and Muslim-dominated lands put him in the relatively unique position of being able to reflect upon his interactions and relations with the religious "Other" in different sociopolitical environments. From the heterogeneous, though Christian-governed society of Akko, through the Christian kingdoms of Aragon, Navarre, and Castile, and finally southward to Muslim Granada[83] and North Africa, Isaac ben Samuel traveled a road that would almost ineluctably lead to a comparative awareness in his relation to people of other religious cultures. What then were his perceptions of the Muslims and the Christians that he met along the way, and what light might this shed (however limited in scope) on the texture of these societies? How did he construe and construct their *otherness* as one whose religious tradition inevitably placed him on the margins? Put differently: how did Isaac of Akko experience the reality of living as part of a minority religious faith within the social contexts of distinct religious majorities, and how was

82. Vajda, "Les observations critiques d'Isaac d'Acco," p. 66 (text #11).

83. This is a logical presumption given the fact that a traveler would have had to cross through Andalusia on the way from Castile to Morocco.

this experience shaped by his wandering lifestyle? There is not a great deal of such evidence to be found in Isaac's writings, but I have located one remarkably revealing piece of testimony on his part. At the very least, this comment gives us insight into Isaac of Akko's unique experience of the religious Other:

שלום סודו עשו שכן בני ישמעאל עם שונא שלום אמנם בני עשו אוהבי שלום כי בארץ ישמעאל אם יאמר יהודי לישמעאלי סלאם עליכום שר"ל שלום עליכם מתחייב בנפשו כי יפול עמהם בצער ובסכנה גדולה ואם יתן יהודי שלום לבני עשו ישמחו בו ויכבדהו.

> The secret [meaning of the word] *shalom* [peace] is Esau.[84] For indeed the children of Ishmael[85] are a people who hate peace, while the children of Esau[86] are lovers of peace. In a Muslim land [*be-'erez̤ yishm'a'el*], if a Jew says "*salam aleikum*"—which means *shalom 'aleikhem* [peace unto you]—to an Ishmaelite [a Muslim], he risks his life, and will fall into sorrow and grave danger. [By contrast,] if a Jew offers a greeting of peace to the children of Esau [to Christians], they will rejoice in him and respect him.[87]

So what are we to make of this testimony? We can certainly speculate that Isaac's formative experience during the massacre of 1291 in Akko left an indelible impression upon him, and that he associated the greater part of violence with Muslims rather than Christians. And yet, beyond this probable bias—based as it was in a traumatic experience—we learn something of the texture of this scholar's everyday social experience, and of the societies in which he lived. One can certainly hypothesize, on the basis of this evidence, that Isaac enjoyed extremely positive social interactions with his Christian neighbors. By the same token, it is fair to assume that he had mostly negative and belligerent contact with his Muslim counterparts—relations in which he was clearly afraid even to extend a greeting.[88] In both instances, the historian would have to

84. This correlation is made through the exegetical technique of *gematria* (numerology). The numerological identification is observed between the words שלום and עשו (both = 376).

85. A medieval Hebrew term used to refer to Muslims.

86. A common term used to refer to Christians.

87. Isaac of Akko, *'Oẓar Ḥayyim*, fol. 154b.

88. This is particularly surprising given the fact that Isaac was so clearly influenced by Sufi piety and spiritual thought.

assume that these assertions were based either on firsthand experiences of the Other (whether in the positive or the negative), or predicated on the secondhand report of someone else. Certainly no broad generalizations can be made about interreligious life on the foundation of this one piece of testimony. Isaac's contrasting perceptions of Muslims and Christians are all the more surprising when we recall that the preponderance of historical evidence does not support such a dichotomy at any level of generalization.[89] In light of this fact, we must assume that these remarks primarily represent the idiosyncratic experience of Isaac of Akko, and are not applicable on the larger scale of social history. Yet in constructing a profile and image of this kabbalist, we can certainly envision an individual who was far more comfortable conversing with Christians than with Muslims—a characteristic that is further reflected in Isaac's stated willingness to hear and appreciate the wisdom of a Christian contemporary.[90]

In an article on the role of elites in kabbalistic society,[91] as well as in a further study on the sociological category of mobility in the history of Jewish mysticism,[92] Moshe Idel has made the argument that one may discern a distinction between types of kabbalists in direct relationship to their social position—a typology that Idel labels "first and second order elites." Scholars such as Naḥmanides, Todros Abulafia, Solomon Ibn Adret, and Yom Ṭov Ashvili were first and foremost halakhic figures. Their high status within the Jewish community was primarily linked to their erudition in legal matters and their mastery of talmudic sources and discourse. Nevertheless, all of these men were also masters of kabbalistic tradition, and they each cultivated disciples for the transmission of Jewish mystical doctrine and practice. What is particularly notable as a unifying characteristic of such leaders is that their public roles as adjudicators of Jewish law caused them to adopt a highly guarded and conservative approach to kabbalistic teaching and

89. See the discussion of sociability between Jews, Muslims, and Christians in M. R. Cohen, *Under Crescent and Cross*, pp. 129–136.

90. Isaac reports this encounter in *'Oẓar Ḥayyim* (fol. 85a).

91. Idel, "Kabbalah and Elites in Thirteenth-Century Spain."

92. Idel, "On Mobility, Individuals and Groups."

writing.[93] Moreover, their halakhic roles within specific communities necessitated a rather rigid geographical stasis. Naḥmanides was best known as the great rabbi of Barcelona (hence his role in the famous disputation of 1263), Adret as his successor in that same city, and Yom Ṭov Ashvili after him. Todros Abulafia was the pillar of the rabbinic aristocracy in Toledo until his death in the first part of the 1280s. Thus, major kabbalistic figures who were best known for their halakhic erudition and their position as leaders of specific communities generally stayed in one place and did not wander about. By contrast, according to Idel, kabbalists who were markedly less interested in halakhic creativity and leadership were very often prone to frequent wanderings throughout the Jewish world, moving from center to center and from town to town.

Such was the life of Isaac of Akko—a fate that paralleled the journeys of Abraham Abulafia, Shem Ṭov Ibn Ga'on, and numerous others. This mobility and incessant movement came to define Isaac of Akko's intellectual-religious life. Each new place brought with it an encounter with new ideas and new people, and Isaac's writings reflect the frequency and diversity of these encounters. From the Near East to the coast of Catalonia, from the towns of Castile to the communities of North Africa, Isaac sought out new lands and new intellectual environments. His own developing thought appears to have changed subtly and then dramatically through the course of his journey, and mobility also provided the context for an impulse to collect numerous and variegated kabbalistic traditions. It is to this process of collection—which can be characterized as a form of eclectic authority construction—that I now turn.

93. This statement should, perhaps, be qualified with regard to Todros Abulafia, who did compose substantial kabbalistic treatises (i.e., *'Oẓar ha-Kavod* and *Sha'ar ha-Razim*). Nevertheless, his approach to greater kabbalistic secrecy and reticence is notable when contrasted with subsequent Castilian kabbalists (i.e., Moses de Leon, Joseph Gikatilla, Joseph of Hamadan, Joseph ben Shalom 'Ashkenazi). If we provisionally accept Y. Liebes's suggestion (Liebes, *Studies in the Zohar*, pp. 135–138) that R. Shimon bar Yohai of the *Zohar* was partly modeled on the historical persona of R. Todros (and therefore on the teacher of the early circle of the *Zohar*), then the repeated assertion that earlier sages had argued for a more stringent level of esotericism and nondisclosure of mystical teachings (see my "Tears of Disclosure") may be understood as a possible allusion to the position taken by R. Todros on esotericism with his disciples. On the contours of Todros Abulafia's kabbalistic thought and historical context, see Kushnir-Oron, Introduction to Todros Abulafia, *Sha'ar ha-Razim*, pp. 13–22.

Part II *Reception and Transmission*

Three Receiving Tradition, Constructing Authority

How does the transmitter of an interpretive religious culture navigate between the weight of historical tradition and the impulse to innovate and to create? Why is the past so often endowed with legitimacy and regarded with reverence from the vantage point of the present? Through what exegetical means are received ideas deemed authoritative, and how is accepted meaning consequently established? In partial contrast to the later work of *'Oẓar Ḥayyim*, Isaac of Akko's *Me'irat 'Einayim* reflects an eclectic and anthological approach. In it, he seeks to act as a reliable conduit for the vast array of opinions and views espoused by predecessors and contemporaries in the kabbalistic arts of interpretation. Interspersing his own innovation with this eclecticism, Isaac aims to communicate the full panorama of past authoritative wisdom, on the one hand, and to establish new meaning through creative interpretation, on the other.

The idea of eclecticism has mainly been viewed by intellectual historians in one of two ways. The first, which originated in the study of ancient Greek philosophy, considered eclectics to be individuals who were more prone to the collection and combination of earlier divergent traditions than they were inclined to innovative thinking in their own right.[1] According to this argument, the patterns of intellectual history point to a recurring alternation between periods of high and low creativity—a model that was based on the dialectical nature of Hegelian historiosophy. Writers who follow an era of great innovative creativity inevitably function only as eclectic custodians of their predecessor's genius and

1. See discussion of this in Donini, "The History of the Concept of Eclecticism."

do not produce masterworks of significant originality. A rather different view of eclecticism, one that was most famously expressed by Diderot in the *Encyclopédie* (1755), argues that the eclectic thinker is defined by the courage to defy the conformity of rigidly articulated schools of thought and to receive insight from a wide variety of influences, considering each on its own merits and based on one's own independent judgment.[2]

To be sure, both of these are generalizations, but they nevertheless offer helpful heuristic models with which to understand Isaac of Akko's specific cultural role as an eclectic thinker. Indeed, Isaac's highly eclectic method of tradition collection did follow in the wake of a period of immense literary creativity in the medieval schools of Jewish mysticism. The most obvious of these great predecessors is the Naḥmanidean opus that Isaac sets out to clarify through metacommentary (the basic premise of *Me'irat 'Einayim*), but the outpouring of creativity in the years just prior to Isaac's writing hardly ended there. As Moshe Idel has noted in a different context, the last quarter of the thirteenth century (Naḥmanides' *Commentary on the Torah* was written prior to this—it was completed in the Land of Israel in 1270) witnessed enormously creative endeavors by kabbalists such as Abraham Abulafia, Moses de Leon, Joseph Gikatilla, and Joseph of Hamadan, among many others. Idel goes so far as to suggest that this explosion in creativity (post-1270), in which kabbalistic matters were articulated with greater openness than before, was primarily caused by the death of Naḥmanides, the figure most responsible for the highly conservative and esoterically guarded approach to Kabbalah.[3] Even if this is not a conclusive characterization, Isaac's eclecticism in the light of this fact is quite suggestive. That is not to say, however, that Isaac of Akko's work should be viewed as part of an era of "low creativity" but, rather, as part of a genre of eclecticism that reacted directly to the masterworks and great personalities that immediately preceded that eclectic thinker.

With regard to Diderot's idealization of the eclectic as a person who thinks for himself and shuns all manner of intellectual conformity, we once again cannot directly graft this notion onto Isaac of Akko. Kab-

---

2. Ibid., p. 19. See also Hatcher, *Eclecticism and Modern Hindu Discourse*, pp. 3–46.

3. See Idel, "Kabbalah and Elites in Thirteenth-Century Spain"; and id., "Nahmanides: Kabbalah, Halakhah, and Spiritual Leadership."

balah in general walks the fine line between the conservatism of tradition and the assertion of individual creativity and innovation. However, *Me'irat 'Einayim* and *'Oẓar Ḥayyim* are filled with representative examples of Isaac's ability simultaneously to collect traditions as an eclectic and to assert his own individual voice as an authoritative transmitter of the esoteric tradition. Isaac of Akko, like the many eclectics who preceded him, sought delicately to balance the desire to be a faithful transmitter of the various interpretations on a given matter with which he was familiar with the effort to present himself as a legitimate and innovative master in his own right. The genre of eclecticism to which *Me'irat 'Einayim* in particular belongs is indeed highly characteristic of the fourteenth and fifteenth centuries and may be an important piece in the general periodization of Jewish mystical history. These two centuries, which have been relatively underresearched by scholars, were marked by numerous kabbalists who composed works with a distinctive method of anthologization or eclecticism. Alternatively called "mosaic" compilations, these treatises formed a new genre in Jewish mysticism, one that sought to break down the boundaries among different kabbalistic schools and to offer a more pluralistic approach to kabbalistic meaning than we find in earlier sources.[4] Among the kabbalists whose writings made up this genre were Baḥya ben 'Asher, Menaḥem Recanati,[5] Shem Ṭov Ibn Ga'on, and Menaḥem Ẓiyyoni.

It is precisely this eclecticism of tradition reception on Isaac of Akko's part that makes him a remarkable case study for the very essence of Kabbalah: the process of receiving and transmitting Jewish esoteric traditions from master to disciple and from one informed peer to another.[6] Indeed,

4. See the discussion of this matter, along with a specific analysis of the kabbalist Menaḥem Ẓiyyoni and a more general call for a comprehensive scholarly corrective, in Laura, "Collected Traditions and Scattered Secrets: Eclecticism and Esotericism in the Works of the 14th Century Ashkenazi Kabbalist Menahem Ziyyoni of Cologne," pp. 19–44.

5. On this phenomenon in the writings of Recanati, see Idel, *R. Menahem Recanati the Kabbalist*, pp. 13–32, 81–121.

6. The rhetoric of transmission as one of the defining features of Kabbalah has also been studied recently by Moshe Idel, who has adapted categories from the sociology of scientific knowledge for the understanding of the religious culture of Kabbalah. He has focused on the interplay between four components in the event and rhetoric of transmission: the "learned Informant, the Content of the information, the process of Transmission itself, and last but not least, the Recipient." See Idel, "Transmission in Thirteenth Century Kabbalah," p. 140.

the very meaning of the word *Kabbalah* connotes this phenomenon.[7] Before it can be characterized as anything else, Kabbalah must be understood as a specific cultural process that involves secretive and highly exclusive relationships between carriers of ideas considered to be the deepest core of the Jewish tradition. For, as has been recently observed, despite the fact that Kabbalah has come to be defined under the all-inclusive term "mysticism," a far more accurate characterization, and one with which the kabbalists themselves might identify, is esotericism. Elliot Wolfson has noted[8] that the kabbalists themselves refer to their lore as *torat ha-sod* (the secret teaching) or *ḥokhmat ha-nistar* (concealed wisdom) precisely because the essential nature of Kabbalah is that of extreme esotericism, which sought to preserve certain religious teachings under the control and purview of elite individuals and abhorred the idea that such sensitive teachings might become exposed to the public at large.

Thus, in medieval culture Kabbalah was the furthest thing possible from popular religion or spirituality—a fact that has been almost inverted in modern times by popular appropriators of Judaism's esoteric side.[9] Although it would be unwise to fully separate content from form, it may be argued that Kabbalah is more a transmittive and educative process than it is purely a phenomenon of distinctive doctrine. Indeed, throughout the ages, many different doctrines have come under the name Kabbalah, but in all of these manifestations, the word represented a similar phenomenon of interpersonal relationships between masters and disciples oriented around "secrets of the Torah" and the hidden inward meaning of the Jewish canon. Whether one takes as an example Abulafia's prophetic Kabbalah of divine names, the Kabbalah of *sefirot* cultivated in the circles of Catalonia and Castile, or the esotericism of the Rhineland Pietists (*Ḥasidei 'Ashkenaz*), the essential unifying feature

---

7. In the *Zohar*, the term *qabbalah* is replaced frequently with Aramaic variations on the word *mesirah* (transmission). See *Zohar* 1: 23a, 225a; 2: 9b, 11a, and many other passages.

8. See Wolfson, "Occultation of the Feminine and the Body of Secrecy in Medieval Kabbalah" and *Abraham Abulafia—Kabbalist and Prophet*, pp. 9–38.

9. My argument here does not aim to exclude the fact that many folk motifs—particularly those that concern demonology—are to be found in kabbalistic literature, most especially in the *Zohar*. In that sense, Kabbalah contains elements of popular religion. This caveat aside, however, kabbalistic religious society was highly elitist and by its very nature (esotericism) excluded the larger sectors of society.

is less mysticism abstractly conceived (a term that was originally adapted from the lexicon of Christian piety and that has come to connote a wide range of phenomena in the modern study of religion) than it is a common sociological conception of the authoritative transmission of secretive and purportedly deeper insights into theological and cosmic reality.

In the view of the kabbalists themselves, what makes something "Kabbalah" has everything to do with the reliability and authority of the transmissional source. The term alludes to a *specific method of transmission*—one that is entirely predicated on the authority of the real or purported transmitter. The ability on the part of the kabbalist to invoke a reliable reception functions as an empowering cultural commodity whose value is determined by its particular societal context. Every social situation that involves hierarchical communication between two sides—the authoritative speaker/actor and the receiving audience—involves specific objects, times, and places of legitimation. As Bruce Lincoln has observed,[10] such particulars as the policeman's uniform, the physician's stethoscope, the professor's podium, and the clergy's pulpit (to name only a representative few) serve powerful functions in the bestowal of legitimacy and authority on the speaker/actor in question. The receiver or audience more often than not accepts the authority of such persons in connection with (if not solely on the basis of) these objects and situations. Such is the case, I contend, with respect to kabbalistic social constructions of legitimacy, in which the item of authentication is the ability to posit a reliable source in the unbroken chain of masters and disciples. Put more broadly, it may be argued that attitudes to legitimacy within a given social setting, and constructions of authority vis-à-vis one's fellows, are of the essence to understanding human nature and its social situation.

Models of Authoritative Transmission in Kabbalistic Literature

Before proceeding to analyze the terms and modes of authoritative transmission in Isaac of Akko's writings, I shall first examine several intriguing antecedents and earlier models in the writings of medieval kabbalists. These examples will contextualize the concerns found in *Me'irat 'Einayim*

10. Lincoln, *Authority: Construction and Corrosion*, pp. 7–13.

and *'Oẓar Ḥayyim*, and will shed light on the larger conceptions of reception and transmittive authority in medieval Kabbalah. As *Me'irat 'Einayim* is a supercommentary to Naḥmanides' *Commentary on the Torah,* it is fitting to open this discussion with Naḥmanides' well-known cautionary remark at the close of his introduction to that commentary:

> With a solid oath I hereby give sound advice to every person who looks into this book [ואני הנני מביא בברית נאמנה והיא הנותנת עצה הוגנת לכל מסתכל בספר זה]: He must not try to reason or think thoughts about any of the allusions which I write with regard to the secrets of the Torah [לבל יסבור סברה ואל יחשוב מחשבות בדבר מכל הרמזים אשר אני כותב בסתרי התורה]. For I inform him reliably that none of these matters may be comprehended or known by way of the intellect and mental understanding [כי אני מודיעו נאמנה שלא יושגו דבר ולא יודעו כלל בשום שכל ובינה], unless they are received from the mouth of a wise kabbalist into the ear of an understanding kabbalist [זולתי מפי מקובל חכם לאוזן מקובל מבין]. . . . For only bad things can come from his reasoning [כי לא תבואו בסברותיו רק רעה].[11]

Legitimate meaning thus only arises out of a proper dialogical relationship between an informed transmitter and a receiver who possesses a certain degree of knowledge and understanding of these matters to begin with. Such, of course, is the stated requirement of ancient tradition, that a recipient of esoteric knowledge must first be one whose mind is properly attuned to such subtleties.[12] Naḥmanides here excludes

11. Naḥmanides, *Commentary on the Torah*, 1: 7–8. On this passage, and its implications for understanding the place of orality and esoteric transmission in Naḥmanides' thought, see Idel, "We Have No Kabbalistic Tradition on This," pp. 59–60, and "Transmission in Thirteenth Century Kabbalah," pp. 144–145; Wolfson, "Beyond the Spoken Word," p. 181; Abrams, "Orality in the Kabbalistic School of Nahmanides: Preserving and Interpreting Esoteric Traditions and Texts," p. 88; Pedayah, *Nahmanides: Cyclical Time and Holy Text*, pp. 142–144; Halbertal, *By Way of Truth: Nahmanides and the Creation of Tradition*, pp. 311–312.

12. Consider the following passage in BT *Ḥagigah*, fol. 14b: "Our Rabbis have taught us: Once Rabbi Yoḥanan ben Zak'ai was riding on a donkey. And as he was going down the road, Rabbi 'El'azar ben 'Arakh was riding a donkey after him. [R. 'El'azar] said to him: 'Master, teach me one teaching on the Account of the Chariot.' [R. Yoḥanan] replied: 'Have I not already instructed you that one must not [transmit] the Account of the Chariot to an individual unless that person is a sage who understands through his own mind? [לא כך שניתי לכם: ולא במרכבה ביחיד אלא אם כן היה חכם מבין מדעתו?]." Compare this *beraita* with *Mishnah Ḥagigah* 2: 1: "One must not teach matters of sexual prohibition [in the presence of] three [or more] people. And [one must not teach] about the Account of Creation [in the presence of] two [or more]

human reason as a force capable of constructing meaning in and of itself (at least with respect to kabbalistic truth)—a position that seeks to establish what may be called *a closed and exclusive sense of meaning*, fully circumscribed within the legitimacy of the act of transmission. The fact that an interpretation is transmitted through a reputed kabbalist becomes an a priori condition for establishing its truth. This stands irrespective of whether the exegesis makes any sense from a logical or rational perspective, provided reason has no bearing on the construction of ultimate meaning.

We might compare the invocation of a reliable source of transmission to that other great Jewish method of interpretive justification and validation of meaning: the scriptural proof-text. Indeed, the midrashic or kabbalistic exegete is able to establish automatic validation for an asserted piece of interpretation simply by linking the insight to sometimes playful uses of the sacred canon, often no matter how far-fetched.[13] In the framework of textual exegesis, the words of the original paradigmatic text have the cultural power to validate simply through the act of invocation or creative citation. In this sense, the personality of the reputed kabbalistic master assumes a parallel legitimating stature to the scriptural proof-text. The oral context requires a "proof-person" in much the same way that the literary event requires a "proof-text." Legitimate meaning ultimately *only* requires that the source of transmission be considered authoritative within the specific cultural context. Without the living oral clarification from a reliable master, all symbolic meaning

---

people. And [one must not teach] about the Account of the Chariot [in the presence of] one person, unless that person is a sage who understands through his own mind."

13. To be sure, midrashic exegesis also invokes the oral chain of tradition to generate authoritative meaning. The parallel is therefore better made between oral and textual constructions of authority, and need not juxtapose midrashic and kabbalistic discourse as entirely distinct methods. Regarding the dynamic of transmission in rabbinic literature and society (and with particular attention to the question of orality and discipleship), see Jaffee, "The Oral-Cultural Context of the Talmud Yerushalmi," pp. 27–30, 51–57, and notes. Cf. the more recent article by S. Pachter, "Transmission of the Esoteric Tradition," pp. 5–17, wherein the author deals with the issue in both rabbinic and kabbalistic sources. The biblical roots of these exegetical-cultural dimensions of transmission have been explored and illuminated in great depth in M. Fishbane, *Biblical Interpretation in Ancient Israel*, and the exegetical character of the transmission of mythic motifs is analyzed in id., *Biblical Myth and Rabbinic Mythmaking*, pp. 95–249 (esp. pp. 193–220). For general comments on the process of transmission and its relation to the creation of myth, see ibid., pp. 23–27.

hinted at through kabbalistic language remains locked and inaccessible to the reader of Naḥmanides' text. Whether or not this assertion is actually true is quite another matter, though Naḥmanides' symbolic exegesis is often highly enigmatic, lacking the more open clarity that is characteristic of subsequent kabbalistic writing. As can be gathered from Naḥmanides' own words, this abstrusity was intentional—requiring the living voice of a teacher to unlock the mysteries and terse allusions.[14] Authoritative meaning is the exclusive property of an established transmitter, and it is not open to just any individual who chooses to read the book. Thus the *textuality* of the written commentary presupposes and demands *orality*, just as the orality of authentic transmission is based upon and shaped by the textuality of the exegetical culture (insofar as it always relates to an orienting and foundational text).[15] The written

---

14. The use of a cryptic method of writing as a way to ensure the enduring necessity of orality was continued through the practice of Naḥmanides' disciples, and (at least in principle) in the written transmissions of the disciples of his disciples. Consider the remarks of Shem Ṭov Ibn Ga'on (*Keter Shem Ṭov*, 2a ['*Amudei ha-Kabbalah* edition]) regarding his decision to commit the esoteric traditions of Naḥmanidean Kabbalah to writing. Ibn Ga'on tells his reader of his sojourn in the city of Barcelona to learn from the reputed masters Solomon Ibn Adret and Isaac ben Todros, and reports that these teachers revealed the secrets of Naḥmanides to him until they were firmly fixed in his mind. Having attained this knowledge and understanding, Ibn Ga'on proceeds to ponder whether it would be appropriate for him to record the teachings in a written form: "And I consulted with them [Solomon Ibn Adret and Isaac ben Todros] as to whether I should, for the sake of memory, write down some of the esoteric [lit., hinted] matters of our rabbi of blessed memory [the RaMBaN] through the way of hinting [ונתיעצתי עמהם אם אכתוב לזכירה ברמיזה על מקצת הדברים הנרמזים לרבינו ז"ל]. And they permitted me to do this [והרשוני על כן]. My teacher, Rabbi Isaac ben Todros of blessed memory, even asked me to write down for him that which was accepted by us [in the realm of] hidden matters. Even so, my heart did not allow me to write in an open manner [לא הרשני לבי לכתוב מפורש], but only in permutated hints and with switched letters for each and every hint, and for each and every hidden matter [רק ברמזים מצורפים ואותיות מחולפות על כל רמז ורמז ועל כל סתר וסתר]." Ibn Ga'on thus derives his authority to transmit directly from the permission of his own teachers (והרשוני), but he nevertheless chooses to preserve the element of concealment and esotericism in his written record. Thus, even in the act of elucidating the hidden meanings of Naḥmanides' *Commentary*, the kabbalist feels the imperative to obscure easy understanding of the matters without oral explanation. So great was the anxiety of esotericism that the moment of disclosure and clarification inevitably metamorphoses into one of concealment and enigma. This paradox, which lies at the heart of the kabbalistic mentality and orientation toward transmission, has been analyzed and explained in significant detail by Elliot Wolfson. See his "Beyond the Spoken Word," pp. 176–183 (on the issue of writing as an antidote to forgetfulness, see pp. 183–184), and *Abraham Abulafia*, pp. 9–38.

15. This latter point was made by Wolfson in "Beyond the Spoken Word," pp. 193–206, and his insights have influenced my formulations here.

aspect serves as a mode of concealment for the uninitiated, and the orality of the master-disciple encounter functions as the key that opens the esoteric character of the written commentary. It is in this way that these two modes of creativity and cultural transmission play off one another in dynamic tension.

In addition to Naḥmanides, another major influence on Isaac of Akko was Abraham Abulafia, and therefore Abulafia's rhetoric on these matters is of particular interest to us. The following passage is taken from Abulafia's *Sefer ha-Ḥesheq*,[16] one of his short works on the means required to attain prophetic experience:

> So that you will understand my meaning in the matter of the "voices," I shall transmit to you well-known traditions [קבלות ידועות]—those that I received orally from the wise of this generation [שקבלתים מחכמי הדור פה אל פה]; those that I received from the books called "books of the Kabbalah" [שקבלתים מהספרים הנקראים ספרי הקבלה], which were composed by the wise ones of earlier times, the kabbalists, of blessed memory, which deal with the wondrous topics that I shall discuss with the help of God; and those that were revealed to me by God, may He be blessed, in the image of a *bat qol*. These [divine revelations] are [the most] exalted *qabbalot*.[17]

In this passage Abulafia outlines three distinct sources of authority for the various interpretations he is imparting to his readership: (1) oral (authoritative communication from a reliable master), (2) textual (reading a text that is considered to embody the words of a reliable master), and (3) revelatory (direct from heaven). It is clear that all three of these function as legitimators of meaning and that the kabbalist derives the authority to transmit esoteric lore on the basis of access to any one of these sources. In a striking fashion, Abulafia asserts without the least hesitation or timidity that he himself has received such revelations from Divinity, thus imbuing him with the ultimate authority as a source of kabbalistic wisdom. Transmission based on this third form of reception is explicitly asserted by Abulafia to be superior to reception from either an oral or a textual source. And, indeed, how could it be otherwise?

16. Cf. Idel, "Transmission in Thirteenth-Century Kabbalah," pp. 150–151.

17. Abulafia, *Sefer ha-Ḥesheq*, ed. Safrin, p. 7.

Nevertheless, Abulafia has established a form of authoritative reception that is entirely based on the testimony of the individual to whom such matters were revealed from heaven. There is no personality or written work known to a third party who can corroborate the authenticity of the transmission. In this sense, the third form of reception establishes a line of transmission whose *human* point of origin (insofar as it has been transferred directly from the divine to the human without any additional intervening human transmitter) is the present transmitter himself! It is a transmittive act that seeks to return to the Source of all sources and at the very same time to inaugurate a radically new transmission.

In other cases the authority of transmission is established through recourse to the larger chain of tradition. A specific piece of kabbalistic interpretation is considered to be authoritative if it can be traced to a reliable transmitter, who in turn ultimately traces his own lineage back to an original divine revelation at the dawn of time. Thus, transmittive authority in the present is predicated on the reconstruction of an entire history of the transmittive process, which follows the history of the Jewish people. Consider the following representative example from Moses de Leon's *Sefer Sheqel ha-Qodesh*:

> This is what is called "Kabbalah" (reception), owing to the fact that it is a reception [traceable back] to Moses from Mount Sinai. Moses transmitted it to Joshua, and Joshua transmitted it to the elders, and the elders transmitted it to the prophets, and the prophets transmitted it to the men of the Great Assembly, according to the same process as the reception of the Torah. They transmitted this wisdom one to the next. In fact, this path of wisdom was given to the first man at the moment of his entrance into the garden of Eden. The secret of this wisdom was given to him [ונתן לו סוד החכמה הזאת], and it was with him until he sinned, and was expelled from the garden of Eden. After that, when the first man died, his son Seth inherited this wisdom. After that, this wisdom made its way to Noah the righteous, and he transmitted it to his son Shem, [and this continued] until Abraham our father inherited it, and with this wisdom he worshipped his Creator [ובחכמה הזאת עבד לבוראו]. He transmitted it to Isaac, and Isaac to Jacob, and Jacob to his sons, [and this continued all the way] to the moment when the later generations stood at Mount Sinai and it was transmitted to Moses our master. From there it was transmitted and received

orally, person to person, through all the subsequent generations [ומשם קבלו איש מפי איש כל הדורות הבאים אחריהם]. But in the exile this wisdom was forgotten, except for among the very few, and they reawakened this wisdom in each and every generation [והם התעוררו את החכמה הזאת בכל דור ודור]. For this reason, this wisdom is called "Kabbalah" (reception), transmitted orally from person to person. The entire Torah, the written Torah and the oral Torah, is grounded in this wisdom [וכל התורה, תורה שבכתב ותורה שבעל פה, מיוסדת בחכמה הזאת].[18]

Moses de Leon opens this excursus by restating the ancient formulation of oral Torah as it appears in *Mishnah 'Avot* 1: 1. In his rendition, however, the essence of oral Torah as it reaches back into the deepest origins of human existence is itself kabbalistic in content. Indeed, he extends the historical reach of kabbalistic origins all the way back to Adam in Eden. Significantly, despite the fact that a line of reception is posited from Adam to Jacob's sons, de Leon then inserts the paradigmatic moment of Mosaic revelation at Sinai, thus implying that the esoteric tradition was retransmitted and reinitiated to Moses from the divine Source after having been transmitted by human beings for the prior length of history. Yet what is particularly interesting here for our present purposes is the kabbalist's *rhetoric of authority construction*, which is rooted in a proper and complete line of transmission. The ultimate source of authority for the human process of transmission is an original *divine* revelation—in the first instance as given to Adam, and in the second, as revealed to Moses during the ascent to Sinai. The direct claim of the text is that, following Sinai, awareness and cultivation of kabbalistic wisdom passed into a state of forgetting, and only a few sages in each generation prevented the tradition from being lost altogether. The implication of this statement is that knowledge of Kabbalah was (in this particular kabbalist's conception of sacred history) much more widespread prior to the great cultural amnesia of Israel's exile.[19] Despite this statement,

18. Moses ben Shem Tov de Leon, *Sefer Sheqel ha-Qodesh le-R. Moshe de Leon*, ed. Mopsik, pp. 17–18.

19. Isaac of Akko makes a remarkably similar statement in his *'Oẓar Ḥayyim* (fol. 183a). There he asserts that the forgotten wisdom of Kabbalah was reawakened by several great masters in different geographical locations, thereby resurrecting an authentic tradition that had become submerged beneath the surface. Isaac links this end of forgetting, this awakening of memory, to the emergence of "the devout master in Egypt" (הרב המאמין במצרים—a reference

however, de Leon does assert that the exclusive and secretive character of Kabbalah is fundamental to its present nature and context—a depiction that accords well with my general remarks earlier in this chapter. For this kabbalist—who may indeed be viewed as paradigmatic—the very definition of Kabbalah is tied to a historical and cultural process. The matters that he sets out to discuss are "Kabbalah" precisely because of the line of *unbroken* historical transmission that he, as a reliable master, is able to posit and assert. His legitimacy and authority to transmit esoteric ideas and practices are entirely dependent on his ability to establish such a firm foundation for reception. To put the matter another way: reliable reception (whether established by invocation of a specific reputed master or through a reconstruction of the larger historical chain of tradition) makes for legitimate transmission.[20]

The Rhetoric of Reception

Having surveyed several prior models of kabbalistic authority-construction so as to gain an appreciation for context, let us now consider the particular manner of tradition-reception and legitimation-building in

---

to Abraham Maimonides?); the masters of Provence (though only the names of Ya'akov ha-Nazir and the RABaD are mentioned here); "the devout master [הרב המאמין] in Catalonia" (a reference to Naḥmanides?); "R. Ya'akov ha-Kohen and R. Yosef Gikatilla of Segovia"; and by [the emergence of] "R. Shimon bar Yoḥai's *Zohar*" in Sefarad (Isaac's term of choice for Castile). The last item on this list particularly fits the model of recovering lost wisdom, inasmuch as the kabbalists believed that Moses de Leon had "found" the heretofore "lost" and ancient work of R. Shimon bar Yoḥai. It is in this reawakening of forgotten wisdom that the medieval kabbalists collapse the abyss between the supposed antiquity of kabbalistic wisdom and the seeming originality of the ideas they expound. In this way, authentic *creativity* becomes a mode of *rediscovery* and remembering of truths already known to the paradigmatic sages of antiquity. Nevertheless, there is an implicit awareness on the part of the kabbalist that something (at least *apparently*) new has taken place in the literary emergence of medieval Kabbalah. This type of rhetoric might be compared to the association of "revelations from Elijah" (גילוי אליהו) with the teachings of the Provençal kabbalists. Both formulations mark a subsurface awareness that something new has emerged in Jewish medieval culture while still preserving the belief in an ancient, and ultimately unbroken, chain of tradition.

20. This conception of the history of oral transmission, culminating in the social configuration of the elite in the Middle Ages, was also a centerpiece of Maimonides' Introduction to his *Mishneh Torah*. See discussion of this phenomenon in Maimonides' work in Twersky, *Introduction to the Code of Maimonides*, pp. 28–29.

Isaac of Akko's writing. Through an examination of the forms of rhetoric employed by Isaac, we will be in a position to further appreciate the interrelated roles of orality and textuality in the making of authoritative meaning.

We begin with a case that reflects a similar conception of history and authenticity to the one already observed in de Leon's *Sheqel ha-Qodesh*:

> Happy is the person who contemplates these words of mine, and who uses them in his enactment of blessings, prayers, supplications, and praises. He who [acts in this manner] is certainly [considered] among the disciples of the father of all sages, the master of all prophets, Moses our master, peace be unto him [הרי הוא ודאי מתלמידיו של אב החכמים אדון הנביאים הוא מרע"ה].[21]

Like his predecessors, Isaac seeks to root the legitimacy of his kabbalistic interpretation in the esoteric lineage of biblical Moses, anchoring present authenticity in the master figures of Israel's sacred history. The kabbalists are perceived to be the true bearers of the Mosaic revelation; they are the disciples and inheritors of the hidden truth transmitted to Moses.[22] Indeed, the wisdom of the Kabbalah is conceived to be the ultimate core of the revelation at Sinai—*the deeper word* that Moses received on behalf of Israel.

This theme of historical authentication is further borne out in Isaac of Akko's attempt (in two representative cases) to reconstruct an unbroken path of oral transmission extending back to Isaac the Blind, the father of Kabbalah in Provence—and thus to align his own interpretive legitimacy with the remembrance and reawakening of this wisdom in the Provençal circle. In the first instance in particular (and by implication in the second case), it is precisely the belief that Isaac the Blind's teachers received instruction directly from Elijah the prophet that legitimates the chain of tradition and present meaning, insofar as it constitutes an otherworldly insertion of wisdom into the human historical stream. As

---

21. Isaac of Akko, *'Oẓar Ḥayyim*, fol. 70b.

22. The kabbalists who authored the *Zohar* extended this lineage even further: they asserted that R. Shimon bar Yoḥai directly correlated with (and was perhaps a reincarnation of?) the biblical Moses, based on R. Shimon's unique function as revealer of mystical secrets. For discussion of this issue, see Boaz Huss, "A Sage Is Preferable to a Prophet: Rabbi Shim'on Bar Yoḥai and Moses in the Zohar," pp. 103–139.

such, this construction discloses a remarkably self-conscious realization of the innovative character of kabbalistic thought as it emerged under Isaac the Blind and his teachers.[23] Nevertheless, it is highly revealing of Isaac of Akko's attempt to speak authoritatively for the esoteric tradition and to legitimize his own transmission through its connection to historical authenticity and paradigmatic authority structures. The key feature here from a rhetorical point of view is the use of the phrases *mi-pi* and *'ish mi-pi 'ish* ("from the mouth of" and "orally from person to person"): (1) "for the interpretation of this verse has been transmitted orally from person to person [איש מפי איש] back to R. Isaac son of the Rabbi [R. Abraham ben David of Posquieres, or "the RABaD"], all the way back to Elijah the prophet";[24] (2) "from the mouth of a disciple of the *ḥasid* [pious] R. Isaac, the son of the Rabbi."[25]

Likewise pertinent is the assertion in *Me'irat 'Einayim* that Isaac of Akko received kabbalistic teachings directly from the Barcelona halakhist and kabbalist Adret, whose name also had the power to bestow legitimacy: "From the mouth of [מפי] the RaShBA [Rabbi Solomon ben Abraham Ibn Adret], the great one of the generation, may God protect him [נ"ר = נטוריה רחמנא], who heard from the mouth of [ששמע מפי] the RaMBaN [Naḥmanides]."[26] A direct line of oral communication is thus established from Isaac to Naḥmanides himself via Adret. The terms *mi-pi* (from the mouth of) and *shama' mi-pi* (heard from the mouth of), insofar as they establish an unbroken chain of oral transmission, serve as the ultimate legitimators of meaning. To use this formulation is to as-

---

23. On this question of "revelation from Elijah" (*gilui 'eliyahu*) and its larger implications for understanding the medieval emergence of kabbalistic literature, see Scholem, *Origins of the Kabbalah*, pp. 35–39, 238–243; Abrams, "Orality in the Kabbalistic School of Nahmanides: Preserving and Interpreting Esoteric Traditions and Texts," p. 85; Wolfson, "Beyond the Spoken Word," pp. 191–192.

24. Isaac of Akko, *Me'irat 'Einayim*, p. 62.

25. Ibid., p. 87. Compare the lines of the first quotation with Isaac's use of a tradition he attributes to Shem Ṭov Ibn Ga'on's *Keter Shem Ṭov* in *Me'irat 'Einayim*, p. 84. According to Moshe Idel, this passage does not exist in the text of *Keter Shem Ṭov* that we possess. It does, however, exist in a separate manuscript that also transmits teachings from Isaac the Blind. See Idel, "On Isaac the Blind's Intentions for the Eighteen Benedictions," p. 48. Compare the second quotation with *Me'irat 'Einayim*, p. 155, and see an earlier precedent in Jacob ben Sheshet, *Sefer ha-'Emunah ve-ha-Biṭaḥon*, p. 357. As is well known, Isaac the Blind is frequently referred to as "the *ḥasid*" in the writings of early kabbalists.

26. Isaac of Akko, *Me'irat 'Einayim*, p. 2.

sert that there was no intermediary in the transmission, thereby raising its stature and authority.[27]

Consider another highly instructive example, which may very likely refer to Adret. After citing a continuous piece of text from Naḥmanides' *Commentary,* Isaac of Akko ventures to explain his literary practice of lengthy citation and, in so doing, further reveals the premise behind orally based authority construction:

> I have written all of the Rabbi's language [i.e., words] in this place, because most books are mistaken [with regard to] this language. There [are those] who add [to the words], and there [are those] who subtract [from the words]. *But I have received this* [קבלתיו] *from the mouth of* [one who heard it directly from] *the Rabbi RaMBaN* of blessed memory, and [I received it] from his book, which was copied from the manuscript of the Rabbi of blessed memory [himself]. [I have also written the] clarification of his [RaMBaN's] words as I received them from the mouths of reliable people[28] [כאשר קבלתיו מפי אנשי אמונה].[29]

---

27. Compare the examples from Isaac of Akko's work with the following instance from Shem Ṭov Ibn Ga'on's *Keter Shem Ṭov*: "You must accept [צריך אתה לקבל] the view of the Rabbi, our master of blessed memory, in [both the] revealed and concealed [matters], just as I have received [them] from the mouth of the Rabbi RaShBA [כמו שקבלתי אני מפי הרב הרשב"א], who received from the mouth of the Rabbi [שקבל מפי הרב], our master of blessed memory" (*Keter Shem Ṭov*, p. 35a; also cited in Idel, "On Isaac the Blind's Intentions," p. 46). Also note the relevant line that employs the technical rhetoric of authoritative oral reception and which appears at the very end of Ibn Ga'on's *Keter Shem Ṭov*: "[Thus] conclude the [mystical] allusions of the RaMBaN of blessed memory as we have received them from mouth to mouth [i.e., by oral transmission]" (54a).

28. The phrase, מפי אנשי אמונה, which is clearly used to authenticate Isaac's transmission, may also be translated as: "from the mouths of people of faith." The clear implication of this expression, however, is to refer to *reliable kabbalists*—proponents of a particular form of theological "faith." The use of the technical term אמונה specifically to denote a theology structured according to the *sefirot* is also a recurring feature in the *Zohar*, and variations on the phrase are used to characterize membership in the esoteric society of mystics (those who subscribe to a particular form of theology and practice). This term appears in the *Zohar* through the Aramaic word מהימנותא, and it is used in the above-described fashion more than two hundred times. This usage is also a prominent feature of Moses de Leon's Hebrew writings, and is one of the notable terminological correlations between de Leon's Hebrew writings and the *Zohar*.

29. Isaac of Akko, *Me'irat 'Einayim*, p. 203, emphases added. "One who heard it directly from the Rabbi RaMBaN" is a translation of the phrase מפי שני לרב רמב"ן—a formula not easily translatable word for word into English, but that indicates a person who was an intermediary between the original spoken words of Naḥmanides and Isaac of Akko himself. The literal meaning of this line might be "from the second to the Rabbi RaMBaN."

Here we see an extraordinary use of the rhetoric of legitimation on Isaac's part, an act of transmission that derives its authority from the oral linkage to Naḥmanides himself. Given what we know of Isaac's disciplic relation to Adret, it is highly probable that the "second from the master" (i.e., the one who heard it directly from the master) mentioned in this passage is in fact the Barcelona master (the RaShBA thus serving as an intermediary to Naḥmanides' original speech).[30] The authenticity of the transmission, which is contrasted positively to other mistaken (according to Isaac, that is) and *inauthentic* renditions of Naḥmanides' teaching, is established through both the posited *oral* line of reception and the assertion that the textual rendition that Isaac has followed was based on a direct *written transcription* of Naḥmanides' own self-authored manuscript copy. In both instances of authority derivation, greater legitimacy emerges through the connection and proximity of the present transmitter (Isaac of Akko) to one who was privy to an *unmediated connection* to the spoken or written words of RaMBaN himself.[31]

Isaac's clear intention is to restrict esoteric meaning to that which has been reliably transmitted, and to reject the possibility of understanding such matters without an authenticating reception. In my view, this is the force of the phrase *'al derekh qabbalah* (by way of *qabbalah*), which should not be misunderstood as simply referring to "the mystical approach." Instead, it is my contention that while the mystical approach is certainly implied, the phrase is better read through a hyperliteral lens: "by way of reception from a reliable master." The author thus defines the interpretation as legitimate based on its method of reception and communication. As Isaac states in another passage:

> On the [kabbalistic] secret regarding prohibited sexual relations, I have received a wondrous secret [קבלתי סוד מופלא], and it cannot be under-

30. Compare this with a similar construction of the authoritative line of transmission, this time stemming from Naḥmanides to Isaac by way of R. David ha-Kohen (*'Oẓar Ḥayyim*, fol. 22a): כתבתיו מפי ה"ר דוד כהן ז"ל גדול דורו ששמע מפי המקובל הרמב"ן ז"ל... (I have written [this tradition down as I heard] it from the mouth of R. David ha-Kohen, of blessed memory, the great one of his generation, who heard [it] from the mouth of the kabbalist . . . the RaMBaN, of blessed memory).

31. Isaac also employs this rhetoric (על דרך קבלה / קבלה שקבלתי ממורי) with respect to R. Yom Ṭov Ashvili. See *Me'irat 'Einayim*, pp. 44, 68.

> stood by a person who has not received the secret[32] [ולא יבינהו . . . אדם אשר לא קבל סוד] of the true unity that is known to the modest ones. And this is what I have received from the mouth of [וזהו אשר קבלתי מפי] Rabbi "S"—may God protect him [רשנ"ר].[33]

As we saw in the case of the passage by Naḥmanides cited earlier, coherent meaning for the kabbalist resides primarily in the legitimacy of its source. Establishing that source, here asserted with the now familiar forms *qibbel* (received) and *qibbalti mi-pi* (I have received from the mouth of), unlocks an encrypted meaning and infuses the author with a new sense of authenticity. Indeed, truth *cannot be understood* unless it has been transmitted through the proper authoritative channels.[34]

The preponderance of evidence indicates that these channels of legitimate transmission were limited to reliable *kabbalistic teachers*—figures who embodied and spoke for an *internal* chain of tradition. But just how broad and inclusive was this conception of authenticity? Could kabbalists (or more to the point, could Isaac of Akko) conceive of a legitimate reception that came from outside the usual lines of internal kabbalistic tradition? In what ways would the construction of authority have to be transformed to accommodate such a traversal of social boundaries? The following example from *'Oẓar Ḥayyim* contributes

---

32. Or "one who has not received according to the way of *sod*."

33. *Me'irat 'Einayim*, p. 157. The mysterious רשנ"ר mentioned here has been discussed in a lengthy note by Goldreich ("Notes on *Me'irat 'Einayim*," p. 389), and the status of this not infrequently referenced kabbalist does require brief mention here. As Goldreich notes, Scholem had argued (albeit with some hesitation) that this personality was Adret himself—owing to the significant similarities between Adret's explicitly referenced teachings and those attributed to רשנ"ר as well as the plausibility of reading Adret's name into the acronym itself. Given the fact that Isaac of Akko ubiquitously appends the honorific suffix נ"ר (which stands for the words נטוריה רחמנא [may God protect him]) to Adret's name (see the case cited earlier in which this terminology appears), the possibility is intriguing. If this is the case, then the acronym might be parsed as ר' שלמה נטוריה רחמנא (R. Solomon Ibn Adret, may the Compassionate One protect him). However, I am inclined to agree with Goldreich that this is somewhat unlikely, given the fact that in the numerous other cases in which Isaac explicitly refers to the רשב"א, he adds the praise גדול הדור (the great one of the generation). Moreover, why would he employ an enigmatic acronym to refer to Adret, when he could just as easily write the acronym רשב"א—a method that he does in fact employ in his work. Goldreich's concluding hypothesis is that רשנ"ר was a Castilian kabbalist who was also a prominent disciple of Adret. Goldreich tentatively speculates that the identity may be a certain kabbalist by the name of ר' שלמה בן יוסף בן עמיאל.

34. Parallel uses of this form can also be found in *'Oẓar Ḥayyim*. See fols. 144b, 158a, 202b.

much to our understanding of this phenomenon, and of Isaac's relative exegetical (and social) openness:[35]

> I heard a very strange thing from the mouth of an uncircumcised non-Jew [שמעתי מפי גוי ערל דבר זר מאד]. And despite the fact that *he did not receive it* [ואע"פ שלא קבל אותו], the small amount of intellect that is within me [says that] it is a sound tradition [קבלה נכונה], since he is an Edomite [i.e., Christian], and Edom destroyed the Second Temple.[36] I saw fit to write it down here, for despite the fact that this matter is not true according to its literal sense [שאע"פ שאין דבר זה אמת כפשטו], *it is true and correct according to the way of the hidden secret* [אמת נכון הוא על דרך הסוד הנסתר].

Let us pause here for a moment to unpack the import of this opening rhetoric of transmission. The first (if obvious) element to be noted is that Isaac of Akko was a Jewish scholar who clearly engaged in conversation with his non-Jewish contemporaries about the content of particular religious traditions, and that he was receptive to learning from non-Jewish scholars. This in itself is no small matter, and underscores my observations in Chapter 2 regarding Isaac's highly positive perception of the Christian religious Other. In this case, although Isaac makes it clear that the Christian with whom he spoke stands outside of the chain of authentic tradition (ואע"פ שלא קבל אותו), Isaac nevertheless deems it appropriate to derive a kabbalistic secret from the tale and tradition that the non-Jew reports to him (אמת נכון הוא על דרך הסוד הנסתר)—indeed, to *align* the Christian's words with authentic kabbalistic meaning! This strikes me as immensely significant and revealing of Isaac's core beliefs regarding tradition, social boundaries, and interpretive authenticity: the Christian person in question is considered to be a carrier (if in a veiled way) of a wisdom that can, on occasion, be recognized as in *accord with the deepest esoteric truth of Judaism*. Isaac's resolve to transcribe the tradition is based on the fact that the transmitter is a so-called Edomite—a support that

35. Ibid., fols. 85a–85b. On this passage, see Idel, "Prometheus in Hebrew Garb," pp. 119–122. Cf. Huss, "NiSAN—The Wife of the Infinite," p. 170, who also suggests that the multi-layered exegetical system of NiSAN may reflect the competitive tension between different schools of kabbalistic thought in Isaac's day (ibid., p. 172).

36. That is to say: Edom = Christianity = Rome (the historical confusion of associating Rome with Christianity at this time notwithstanding). On this motif and symbolic association, see G. Cohen, "Esau as Symbol in Early Medieval Thought," pp. 19–48.

initially appears quite puzzling, but that is subsequently resolved by the content of the tradition.[37] This aside, however, what does it mean for the kabbalist to discover (what he believes to be) an authentic tradition (one that has bearing on the inner Divine Truth) from the supposedly impure words of the uncircumcised Other? How does this alter the perception of validity in reception, and of the "recovery" of legitimate meaning?

Let us summarize the rhetorical modalities of authentication that are employed by Isaac of Akko in his project of transmission. First, authoritative *oral reception* is denoted by the following technical phrases: "I have

---

37. Having provided this preface, and having affirmed the esoteric legitimacy of the tradition, Isaac proceeds to relate the very bizarre and enigmatic tale that he heard from his Christian source. It is a tale that we might say belongs to the literary genre of magical realism (and appears to be a direct parallel to the Myth of Prometheus—see Idel, "Prometheus in Hebrew Garb"). According to his retelling, a certain non-Jewish pious ascetic (characterized as *ḥasid ʾeḥad me-ḥasidei ʾumot ha-ʿolam* and as a *parush mitboded*) was traversing roads and deserts with miraculous speed until he came upon King Solomon seated on his royal throne, there in the midst of a remote desert, far from any settlement (a scene that, like other cases of magical realism, presents a wildly alternate and "fantastic" picture of reality, despite the fact that the story is told as though it represented nothing at all out of the ordinary). And Solomon is forced to sit there, unable to move while a multitude of crows descend upon him and eat all the flesh off of his bones. Within one day, all the flesh returns to King Solomon's body, but the crows return and eat him to the bone yet again. This cycle of torturous pain recurs day after day in a seemingly unyielding stream of suffering. Solomon tells the miraculously transported ascetic that it is only when the Messiah will arrive (born of Solomon's seed) that God will forgive Solomon (for what we are not told, but the forgiveness comes only on the account and merit of the Messiah), and only then will his suffering end. After reporting the tradition as he heard it from his Christian contemporary, Isaac tells his reader of the esoteric meaning that he (Isaac) has discerned in this tale (the justification for including this seemingly strange story in *ʾOẓar Ḥayyim*): "And the secret that I saw in this is that this Solomon is the King of Peace, and He is the Assembly of Israel, the *Shekhinah* who dwells in the souls of the children of Israel who are in exile under the yoke of the nations of the world. The crows (who eat the flesh off of Solomon's body) are, according to the hidden way of interpretation (ע"ד הנסתר), the nations of the world who cause suffering for the children of Israel. . . . According to the way of truth [ע"ד האמת] (a still deeper level of interpretation for Isaac of Akko, one that correlates meaning to the *sefirot* within God), this Solomon hints at (the *sefirot*) *Tifʾeret* and *ʿAtarah (Shekhinah)*. And the crows, according to the way of the kabbalistic sages of Sefarad (that is, Castile) hint at the external rungs that ascend and cause trouble for the Divine Attributes (the *sefirot*)." Isaac's initial justification for including the words of a non-Jew (it is a sound tradition since he is an Edomite, and Edom destroyed the Second Temple—leaving aside the anachronistic ascription of Christianity to Rome *before* Constantine) thus become a bit more clear, if still a bit of a stretch: the deeper meaning of the tradition is about the suffering of Israel at the hands of the nations of the world (and the corresponding torment of *Shekhinah* by the demonic forces that surround Her). So (the Jew in exile reasons) who better to be the source of such a tradition than a Christian ("Edomite"), a member of the religion that inflicted much of this very suffering on the Jews?!

received from the mouth of" (קבלתי מפי); "by way of reception from" (על דרך קבלה מ . . .) though this is not exclusively oral; "I heard from the mouth of" (שמעתי מפי); "from the mouth of one person to another" (איש מפי איש); "*X* said that . . ." (אמר ש . . .); and "on this matter I asked the mouth of *X*, and he said . . ." (שאלתי על זה את פי ואמר . . .). In a parallel fashion, written reception also adheres to a specific set of lexical constructions that serve to validate transmission. The majority of these cases revolve around two central terms that imply the act of reading: ראיתי (I have seen) and מצאתי (I have found).[38]

In addition to the rhetoric of orality and textuality in the construction of authority and its transmission, certain phrases exist whose primary function is the validation of meaning based on its association with paradigmatic forebears and revered tradition: "Here are further reliable teachings [דברים נכוחים] and true Kabbalah [קבלת אמת] on the secret of . . ."[39] The particular phrases employed here—"reliable teachings" and "true Kabbalah"—are exceptionally revealing of Isaac's attempt to present his transmission with an aura of authority.[40] He seeks to convey to his readers that what he is about to transmit to them has been received through the proper channels and is part of the authentic corpus of esoteric meaning. To characterize a piece of interpretation as "true Kabbalah" (or true reception) is consciously to contrast that act of transmission with an interpretation that is invalidated purely on the basis of not participating in the unbroken chain of tradition (or as not in accord with authentically received tradition). It is to speak of an *exclusive authenticity*—one whose legitimacy is predicated on reception. However, the stamp of authenticity given here by the word *'emet* (true), which serves to distinguish legitimate Kabbalah from inauthentic speculation, does frequently allow for a diversity of views within that kabbalistic chain of tradition. In that sense, the phrase *qabbalat 'emet*

---

38. See Isaac of Akko, *Me'irat 'Einayim*, pp. 30 ("As we have received from the mouth of scribes, and as we have seen in books"), 39 ("I have seen hints in the books of a few kabbalists, who hint that . . ."), 52; *'Oẓar Ḥayyim*, fol. 70b. For an extended discussion on the cultural role of scribes and copyists in medieval kabbalistic culture, see Beit-Arie, "Publication and Reproduction of Literary Texts in Medieval Jewish Civilization: Jewish Scribality and Its Impact on the Texts Transmitted."

39. Isaac of Akko, *Me'irat 'Einayim*, p. 45.

40. The phrase *devarim nekhoḥim* originates in Proverbs 24:26.

can be used as an *inclusive* characterization, so long as one is referring to disparity among *properly transmitted* interpretations.

Harmonization and Hermeneutical Pluralism

If a major feature of Isaac's early work in *Me'irat 'Einayim* is the attempt to transmit a wide array of traditions, to construct an anthological mosaic of oral and textual reception, the inevitable dilemma emerges: what is the exegete to do with conflicting interpretations and opinions? How does the transmitter resolve the apparent lack of congruence between different receptions? Must they all be in agreement, or does each individual tradition maintain a degree of autonomous truth and validity? These are the core questions that stand behind a discernable type of rhetoric and hermeneutics in *Me'irat 'Einayim*—one that serves as an orienting premise for the project of eclecticism: *the ideal of harmonization and hermeneutical reconciliation*. This issue is essential to an understanding of the motivations behind Isaac's self-perception as a reliable conduit for kabbalistic meaning:

> The *maskil* will make peace between [will reconcile] these [different] receptions [המשכיל ישים שלום בין הקבלות האלו], just as it is proper for a wise individual to make peace between the different teachings of sages, and to reconcile each and every word by the way of truth [ולייׁשב כל דבר ודבר אחרי דרך האמת], and not to completely reject the word of wisdom of one in favor of that of another. If God gave you the intellect to do this, then you will know that all [of these words of wisdom] are true.[41]

Isaac of Akko thus adheres to what we may call a *pluralistic hermeneutic*. The task of the truly enlightened individual is to realize that there is no essential hierarchy in kabbalistic interpretive meaning, so long as the views involved were all transmitted through the proper channels of reception. All received traditions (from reputable sources) may be included under the legitimating shelter of the term *'emet* (true/

---

41. Isaac of Akko, *Me'irat 'Einayim*, p. 55. *Maskil* literally means "the intelligent person." However, the word *maskil* is a standard technical term used to refer to a kabbalist. The term itself, of course, is derived from Daniel 12:3. For further discussion of its use in kabbalistic literature, see Wolfson, *Through a Speculum That Shines*, pp. 276–277, 285.

truth)—a conception of truth that allows for a broad range of diversity, and ultimately seeks to resolve all apparent contradictions. I would argue that we encounter here a nondeterminate and unstable meaning structure, insofar as Isaac seeks to posit a conception of meaning that is not restricted to one fixed line of argument and interpretation.[42] Meaning, under the expansive rubric of kabbalistic reception, may be characterized as a fluid pluralism, owing to the fact that no single interpretation is to be given priority over another, and no single view is to be entirely rejected in favor of another. In this sense, the kabbalistic reader is endowed with a significant degree of freedom. Of course, we must emphasize again that this pluralistic stance does not equate authentically received traditions with individually innovated perspectives into the sacred canon. Yet, once within the boundaries of kabbalistic cultural definition, seemingly disparate meanings are legitimized with ultimate inclusiveness. The imperative of inclusion—phrased as "he should make peace between the different receptions," "it is proper for a kabbalist to make peace between the different teachings of sages," and "to reconcile each and every word by the Way of Truth"—calls on the kabbalist to harmonize or reconcile interpretations that may seem

42. My use of this terminology should not be entirely conflated with the rather different implications of literary indeterminacy as it has been employed in the postmodern discourse of deconstruction and "reader-response criticism." Indeterminacy in that context is bound up with a reading strategy in which meaning is not wholly determined by authorial intent, and often depends considerably on the premises and strategies that the reader brings to the act. The initial assumptions that a reader makes can dramatically affect the interpretive outcome. See Iser, "Indeterminacy and the Reader's Response in Prose Fiction," pp. 3–30; Fish, *Is There a Text in This Class? The Authority of Interpretive Communities*, pp. 1–17, 21–67, 338–355. Despite the fact that I make no claim to the *identity* of the kabbalistic construction of meaning with reader-oriented indeterminacy, the unfixed nature (and thus the limited relativism) of the hermeneutics that I shall presently consider is remarkably parallel to the model of deconstruction. For a prior study of hermeneutical issues related to indeterminacy in kabbalistic literature, see Idel, "Between Authority and Indeterminacy—PaRDeS: Some Reflections on Kabbalistic Hermeneutics," pp. 249–268. In his most recent study to date (*Absorbing Perfections: Kabbalah and Interpretation*, pp. 457–458), Idel has noted that Isaac of Akko was part of a larger tendency toward polysemous interpretation in the exegetical application of sefirotic symbolism for the elucidation of the canonical Torah text. Idel asserts that a *monosemic* approach (one that would posit a single and exclusive meaning with respect to the symbolic interpretation of the text) was not characteristic of Isaac of Akko or many of his contemporaries. Instead, such kabbalists were open to the implementation and coexistence of numerous hermeneutical strategies and meanings, a posture intimately related to the hermeneutical phenomena I discuss in this section.

on the surface to be incompatible. Such is the underlying premise for a project guided by an eclectic and syncretistic methodology.

Although Isaac of Akko does not fully explicate this connection between ideology and method, we may indeed argue that the imperative of interpretive reconciliation and harmonization provides justification for the eclectic method, lending it legitimacy through an implicit theory of unfixed and nondetermined meaning. The attempt to reconcile disparate meanings under a single exegetical roof rests on an assumption of interpretive *flexibility* (i.e., not unequivocal, not stable)—pluralism is possible because a fixed determinate meaning is not. At the level of kabbalistic sociology, it would also seem that Isaac was faced with a crisis of diverse traditions. If kabbalistic meaning was locked into a single determinism, then how was he to explain the fact that multiple views from equally authoritative sources were in existence? Instead, he resolves that conflicting interpretations are all pieces of a single overarching Truth (אמת). Thus true in theory to his eclectic practice, Isaac seeks to harmonize contrasting views and to integrate them into a single whole.

A few lines later on the same page of *Me'irat 'Einayim*, Isaac extends this notion of reconciliation to certain elements within the *philosophical* camp—a move that is quite surprising and highly revealing:

> Not only should the wise individual [the kabbalist] make peace between the words of two different sages by the way of Truth [i.e., Kabbalah], but even with respect to matters of Philosophy, which seem to the masses as if they are opposed to our teachings [Kabbalah], the wise individual should make peace between them, and he should rectify the matter in his mind so that matters [of philosophy] are joined with matters of Kabbalah [ישים המשכיל שלום ביניהם ויתקן הענין בשכלו הנכון שיתחברו דבריהם עם דברי הקבלה].[43]

This is indeed a rather remarkable statement for a medieval kabbalist, and it indicates the very different approach taken by an eclectic thinker of the fourteenth century to that adopted by most of his intellectual predecessors.[44] According to this view, the distinction in

43. Isaac of Akko, *Me'irat 'Einayim*, p. 55.

44. By and large, kabbalists of the classical thirteenth-century period were far less inclined to draw such explicit and pluralistic correlations between kabbalistic and philosophical meaning. Philosophy did indeed have a powerful impact on medieval kabbalistic

meaning between Kabbalah and philosophy is only a superficial and apparent one. Such is the way it appears to the untrained eye of the common individual. But a far more perceptive and unfixed approach is expected of the "intelligent kabbalist" (the *maskil*). He must understand that these two seemingly different systems are ultimately capable not only of mutual toleration but of *mutual integration* as part of a single underlying structure of meaning and theological wisdom.[45] To the eclectic writer, diverse forms of wisdom must be combined, and in some cases synthesized, so as to reveal the ultimate unity of spiritual *'emet*.

One final example of harmonization will be sufficient. Upon referring to a teaching attributed to 'Azriel of Gerona, Isaac states:

> All of these are the words of the sage, Rabbi 'Azriel, of blessed memory. And because I have seen great value and innovation in his words, I have written them down. Even though it is understood from [perusing] his words that his *qabbalah* [i.e., the tradition he has received] is not one and the same as the *qabbalah* of the RaMBaN, of blessed memory, every *maskil* can recognize the differences between them, and nevertheless make peace between their receptions [מכל מקום כל משכיל יוכל להכיר ההפרש שביניהם ולשים שלום בין קבלתם], as I wrote in [my commentary to the *parashah* of] *Beshalaḥ*. For many things that R. 'Azriel

---

thinking, but the overt character of that influence was mainly submerged beneath the surface. On this phenomenon, see E. Fishbane, "Mystical Contemplation and the Limits of the Mind." For a relatively unique example of the conscious identification of kabbalistic and philosophical meaning (an exception to the more general pattern), see Jacob ben Sheshet, *Sefer ha-'Emunah ve-ha-Biṭaḥon*, p. 386. Having just referred to "the language of the philosophers," ben Sheshet asserts: "*'Aleph* in our language [i.e., *Keter*] corresponds to the Divine Will in their language. *Yod* in our language [i.e., *Ḥokhmah*] corresponds to the Active Intellect in their language." The particulars of the second correlation (*Yod* = Active Intellect [שכל הפועל]) are surprising. The more logical correlation to the Active Intellect would be *Malkhut*, the tenth *sefirah*. To be sure, there were numerous other kabbalists in the Middle Ages who sought overtly to bridge the discourses of meaning in Kabbalah and philosophy. This phenomenon is particularly evident in the pages of Joseph ben Shalom Ashkenazi (Pseudo-RABaD)'s *Perush Sefer Yeẓirah*. Also see the discussion of these matters in Wilensky, "The *Guide* and the *Gate*: The Dialectical Influence of Maimonides on Isaac Ibn Latif and Early Spanish Kabbalah," pp. 266–278.

45. As we shall see later in this chapter, Isaac of Akko appears to have changed his position on this issue dramatically between the writing of *Me'irat 'Einayim* and *'Oẓar Ḥayyim*. The later work clearly reflects a hierarchical approach to Kabbalah vis-à-vis philosophy, and seems to contradict the harmonizing tendency found in *Me'irat 'Einayim*.

> associates with [the *sefirot* of] *Ḥesed* and *Paḥad*, the Rabbi, of blessed memory [i.e., Naḥmanides], associates with *Tif'eret* and *'Atarah*. But it is all one, for the essence of *Tif'eret*'s reception[46] is from *Ḥesed*, which is the Right side. Hence you will find in many places that the Rabbi, of blessed memory, calls *Tif'eret* "the Right side."[47]

Alluding to his earlier remarks on reconciliation, Isaac of Akko again emphasizes the importance of harmonizing seemingly different kabbalistic interpretations. In this instance, Isaac seeks to demonstrate the underlying identity of the hermeneutics presented by 'Azriel and Naḥmanides by positing their respective adherence to a common deep structure of sefirotic thought. In Isaac's view, it makes no substantial difference that 'Azriel correlates certain words to *Ḥesed* and Naḥmanides correlates those same words to *Tif'eret*, insofar as these two *sefirot* both represent the Right Side of Divinity.[48] Conversely, the same identity applies to respective uses of *Paḥad* (on 'Azriel's part) and *'Atarah* (on Naḥmanides's part), insofar as these two *sefirot* both represent the Left Side. Though it is fair to argue that the polarity of Right and Left was a deep unifying structure for medieval sefirotic thought, it is Isaac of Akko's own exegetical ideology that is most visible here. Motivated by his eclectic project of constructing a mosaic of kabbalistic opinions that may ultimately be reconciled, Isaac seeks to downplay the differences that exist between 'Azriel and Naḥmanides. The basic premise of this harmonization, therefore, is the ultimate unity of kabbalistic theologies, despite the fact that this common truth is expressed in significantly different ways. This point may be summed up in Isaac of Akko's own words regarding the reconciliation of the interpretations: *ve-ha-kol eḥad* (it is all one).[49] The task of the kabbalist, as outlined by Isaac, is to see beyond superficial differences and to harmonize the work of distinct thinkers into a single whole of meaning.

---

46. The term *qabbalah* (reception) is thus also used to connote the reception of emanational flow from one *sefirah* to another in addition to its technical usage as a form of authoritative communication.

47. Isaac of Akko, *Me'irat 'Einayim*, p. 146.

48. *Tif'eret* is in the Center of the sefirotic structure, but leans to the Right Side.

49. It is clear from the context that this is not the ubiquitous phrase employed by kabbalists to assert the monistic unity of the entire sefirotic system. Instead, the phrase is used to establish the unity, or homogeneity, of the two meanings in question.

This pluralistic hermeneutic of harmonization is significantly qualified by Isaac in a separate passage in *Me'irat 'Einayim*. Here he again affirms the validity of multiple simultaneous meanings, but he cautions against an overly cavalier combination of distinct receptions. No single interpretation may be viewed as determinate meaning, but there are certain guidelines for such an open exegetical posture:

> Even though all the words of the RaMBaN of blessed memory are the words of the living God, and his Kabbalah is strong, reliable and true in the eyes of all the wise kabbalists [וקבלתו מוחזקת נכונה ואמתית בעיני כל המקובלים המשכילים], nevertheless you are permitted to adopt one path from among the [several] paths mentioned [מכל מקום הרשות בידך לאחוז דרך אחת מהדרכים הנזכרים . . .]. However, take caution that you not confuse your mind by adopting from this one and from that one, thereby combining receptions [אמנם הזהר שלא תשבש שכלך לאחוז מזה ומזה ולערבב הקבלות], lest you be called [Eccles. 2:14] "a fool who walks in darkness." For even in matters of prohibition and permission [i.e., matters of law], our Sages of blessed memory said in [tractate] *Ḥulin*:[50] that one who acts according to the strictures of [both] the House of Shammai and the House of Hillel, about him Scripture says [Eccles. 2:14]: "the fool walks in darkness." Rather, he must act either according to the strictures and leniencies of the House of Shammai, or the strictures and leniencies of the House of Hillel. Thus you find many followers of Kabbalah[51] who are confused, for they receive from here and from there, and they want to adopt all of them [ועל כן תמצא הרבה מרודפי הקבלה משובשים שמקבלים מזה ומזה ורוצים לאחז בכלן]. It is therefore prudent for every wise kabbalist who has eyes in his heart [כל מקובל משכיל אשר עינים בלבו],[52] who desires to grasp the truth, to draw himself

50. See BT *Ḥulin*, fols. 43b–44a.

51. The term רודפי קבלה (followers of Kabbalah) is rather unusual and seems to indicate adherence to a specific social group who practiced this form of communication and esoteric exegesis. As I mentioned earlier in this chapter, it would be a gross distortion to consider medieval Kabbalah as a widespread social movement along the lines of popular religion.

52. The term "eyes of the heart" was used in medieval Jewish writing to connote a mode of perception deeper than physical sensation, and the term *lev* was used to refer to both the heart and the mind. Yehudah ha-Levi (ca. 1075–1141)—poet, philosopher, and mystic—made remarkable use of this phrase in his conception of visionary experience. On this phenomenon in ha-Levi, see Wolfson, "Merkavah Traditions in Philosophical Garb: Judah Halevi Reconsidered," pp. 215–235, and *Through a Speculum That Shines*, pp. 163–181. In the text I have cited above from *Me'irat 'Einayim*, the "wise kabbalist who has eyes in his heart" is directly con-

> after the words of the Rabbi Moshe ben Naḥman of blessed memory with all his strength until he comprehends them. Then he will be complete in the Way of Truth without any doubt [ואז יהיה שלם בדרך האמת בלא ספק].[53]

Despite the fact that Isaac indicates a clear preference for the Naḥmanidean perspective and encourages his reader to adopt that path, he explicitly allows for a highly pluralistic and nonexclusivist approach to esoteric meaning. Numerous possible paths lie before the discerning kabbalist, and one is given the *exegetical freedom* to choose whichever among them one prefers. Implicit in Isaac of Akko's statement is that there is no one objective path that must be adopted to the exclusion of all others. *The legitimacy of any one given meaning is entirely predicated on its reception from a reliable master* and not on a commonly accepted stable structure of meaning that exists independently of the human act of transmission. For if meaning were stable and fixed, there would be no need for the requirement that disparate *qabbalot* not be conflated and combined. Why would they be ultimately irreconcilable if they meant essentially the same thing? It is precisely because the contrasting receptions are *equally legitimate but often incompatible* that the unfixed character of kabbalistic meaning emerges. The ways of interpretation open to the kabbalist are multiple—"you are permitted to adopt one path from among the [several] paths mentioned"—but they must all be implemented independently, because they are not reducible to one and the same truth, and such a conflation would only be confusing. As Isaac states: "However, take caution that you not confuse your mind [הזהר שלא תשבש שכלך] by adopting from this one and from that one, thereby combining receptions [קבלות]."

The key issue to be noted here is that the various *qabbalot* are not merely different components of the same foundational truth. If each of

---

trasted with the individual who foolishly seeks to combine different receptions (they may all be considered "Truth," but each reception must nevertheless function as a circumscribed unit unto itself). Thus, Isaac of Akko has implicitly correlated the two types of people adumbrated in Eccles. 2:14 to the two types of kabbalistic receivers. For the verse in Ecclesiastes contrasts the characterization "the fool walks in darkness" (הכסיל בחשך הולך) with the ideal type of piety: "the wise man has eyes in his head" (החכם עיניו בראשו), which is to say, a wise man is able to see matters in a deeper way.

53. Isaac of Akko, *Me'irat 'Einayim*, pp. 91-92.

the traditions conveyed essentially the same meaning, then there would be no logical problem with the free and arbitrary combination of them by the receiver. On the contrary, there is an explicit awareness that different *qabbalot* actually reflect different perspectives on and conceptions of the divine world. Because these traditions are fundamentally different, they cannot be combined at will, insofar as they do not cohere as a system of thought within the larger rubric of sefirotic thinking (a position that is markedly different from that of several of the texts cited earlier). It is precisely this *principle of difference*, however, that is respected by Isaac of Akko. Each of the different teachings, provided that it has been transmitted through a reputable and legitimate source (a master or a text), possesses an autonomous authority and must be respected by the holders of a conflicting tradition (as we saw in an earlier text: "It is proper for a wise individual . . . not to completely reject the word of wisdom of one in favor of that of another").[54] The autonomous but incompatible nature of disparate *qabbalot* underscores the exegetical freedom of the individual in question, insofar as that individual may choose which tradition to follow, so long as it derives from an authentic source. In this respect, we encounter a construction of pluralistic meaning that is even more extreme than the model of harmonization. Here Isaac's implication goes a step further: truth does not adhere to a single predetermined meaning, insofar as two interpretations may both be true and nevertheless be completely contradictory and incompatible.

---

54. Ibid., p. 55.

Four Intentions and the Recovery of Meaning

The Construction of Naḥmanidean Authorial Intent in *Me'irat 'Einayim*

In the discourse of modern critical theory, exegetical indeterminacy and the question of authorial intent lie at opposite ends of the conceptual spectrum. In the hands of their respective advocates, these two approaches to textual meaning are in perpetual struggle, and one must choose between two radically different alternatives: (1) is meaning solely determined by the intention of a text's author, which is timeless, irrespective of its reader,[1] or (2) is the author's intent irrelevant to the meaning of the text, inasmuch as a text is only actualized by the reader, who approaches it with a unique set of assumptions and strategies?[2] For the medieval kabbalist, however, these two positions were not mutually exclusive—in fact, they were two integral pieces of a single hermeneutical phenomenon. Isaac of Akko's *Me'irat 'Einayim* takes meaning to be unfixed or flexible, but he nevertheless does not assert the full autonomy of the individual reader/interpreter. Rather, the legitimacy of

---

1. This position has been most conspicuously argued by Hirsch in his *Validity in Interpretation*. For a recent discussion of the relationship of authorial intent to classical Jewish literature, see Halbertal, *People of the Book: Canon, Meaning, and Authority*, pp. 45–50.

2. In fairness, this position has not consistently been formulated with this degree of hyperbole, and numerous critics have argued that meaning is constructed in the *interplay* between author, text, and reader. For representative studies advocating a more reader-centered approach to the construction of meaning, see the two pieces of work by Iser and Fish referenced earlier, along with the classic formulation of Gadamer, *Truth and Method*, pp. 265–474. A further and particularly nuanced discussion of the reading process may be found in Hartman, *Criticism in the Wilderness*, pp. 161–188.

each reading is predicated on its reception from a reliable source, whose "intention" should be clear to the recipient. Thus, despite the persistent argument for the instability of kabbalistic meaning on Isaac's part, we do encounter a high valuation of "authorial" or "transmissional" intent. Given that *Me'irat 'Einayim* is a metacommentary on Naḥmanides' work, it should come as no surprise that it is considerably taken up with the process of establishing Naḥmanides' authorial intent with respect to a host of esoteric exegetical issues. In this respect, true understanding cannot be based purely on the act of reading the master's *Commentary* at face value. One requires access to the underlying intent of the author (the subtext indicated through allusion) in order to fully appreciate the depth of meaning conveyed by the text. This unveiling of intention is further tied to the tradition of esotericism within which the metacommentator functions—for it is the orality of received explanation that unlocks the closed door of textual secrecy and enigma.[3] As an exegete who stands in direct lineage to the oral transmission of Naḥmanidean doctrine, Isaac of Akko (along with his colleagues in the genre of metacommentary) believes himself able to apply the clarifications and elaborations that he received in oral form,[4] thus empowering him to posit the correct intention of the master.

This phenomenon is markedly parallel to a similar conception in medieval Christian textual culture, in which the reconstruction of an author's *intentio* was a crucial factor in the determination of meaning.[5] Without access to that *intentio*, the reader's interpretation would be fundamentally flawed. This medieval conception has been revived in recent years by the literary critic E. D. Hirsch. I would also add the following observation: Building on the assumption of modern commonsense philosophy that our forms of ordinary speech and rhetoric reflect our deepest assessment of what is true, it may be argued that the prioritization of original intent vis-à-vis the finished product is reflected in commonplace

---

3. See the observations of Wolfson, "Beyond the Spoken Word," p. 197.

4. On metacommentary on Naḥmanides' work—and the manner in which this genre sheds light on the place of orality in the kabbalistic creation and conception of tradition—see Abrams, "Orality in the Kabbalistic School of Nahmanides: Preserving and Interpreting Esoteric Traditions and Texts," pp. 90–98.

5. Minnis, *Medieval Theory of Authorship: Scholastic Literary Attitudes in the Later Middle Ages*, pp. 16–21.

vernacular constructions. How often can a certain action or statement be resolved or mitigated through recourse to original intent? Consider the following common rhetorical constructions: "I did not *mean* to say that . . . but, rather . . ."; "That was not my *intention* . . ."; "I didn't mean it!" Such phraseology reveals very deep human assumptions about the need to defer to the original intention of an actor, speaker, or writer. We believe at a visceral level that what a person *meant* to do or meant to say is to be given more weight than the external action or speech.

In *Me'irat 'Einayim*, Isaac of Akko frequently seeks to establish authentic meaning by alluding to a postulated intention of the author. The assumption of this rhetoric is that the underlying truth of the text's meaning requires *implied* information (the unwritten mental intent of the author) that is not necessarily provided at the text's surface level. As we shall see, this implicit knowledge is at the disposal of the interpreter (in this case, Isaac of Akko) because of an oral reception to that effect or through his unique hermeneutical ability to discern the implied intentions of the master (Naḥmanides). The authenticity of Isaac's role as transmitter rests on his ability to posit the true authorial *intention* of Naḥmanides. Understanding this phenomenon will elucidate a further essential piece of Isaac's method of authority-construction.

Consider a prayer offered by Isaac as a reflection on his own act of writing and on the ideal of discerning the intended meaning of Naḥmanides' text:

> May it be the will of the One who illuminates the eyes of those who see, that He should always illumine our eyes so *that we may understand the entirety of the intention* in all the words of Rabbi Moshe ben Nahman of blessed memory [שתמיד יאיר עינינו להבין כל כונת הרב ר' משה בן נחמן ז"ל בכל דבריו], [that we may] add to those words [ולהוסיף עליהם], and that He [the Holy One] open our eyes so that we may see wonders from [the RaMBaN's] teachings. Amen.[6]

This text is important on a number of levels, not least of which is the light that it casts on Isaac's self-perception of his own divinely inspired creative process.[7] What concerns us here is the emphasis placed on

6. Isaac of Akko, *Me'irat 'Einayim*, p. 106.

7. Isaac's prayer in this passage expresses the desire on the part of the mystic for pneumatic

discerning authorial *intention* in the process of exegesis. For Isaac, the text as it is cannot be separated from the mental intentions of the author at the time of its writing. Understanding what Naḥmanides meant when he wrote the words that he did is of even greater importance than the reader's ability to decipher the semantic signs of the text itself.

Compare this formulation with the following additional cases of this rhetoric in *Me'irat 'Einayim*:

> If you consider the way in which the Rabbi of blessed memory began to interpret the scriptural structure you will understand that what we wrote regarding the verse "let there be a firmament between the waters" is in fact the intent of the Rabbi [שהוא כונת הרב ממש].[8]

Here it is quite clear that Isaac perceives his own interpretive legitimacy to be rooted in his ability to effectively and authentically represent the *implicit intent* of Naḥmanides. Proper exegesis is the correct reconstruction of authorial intent (a reconstruction in which oral tradition is the cipher for textual secrecy); the reader is not free to assert an opinion that is contrary to that original intent: "Indeed I have received that the intention of the Rabbi [קבלתי כי כונת הרב] was to offer proof that the word . . . is the language of. . . ."[9] In this instance, Isaac has combined two modes for establishing transmittive authority—the construction of original intent and the rhetoric of formal reception (קבלתי). The specifics of Naḥmanides' inner mental intentions at the time of his writing are the subject of an authoritative reception/transmission (and thus an *oral* tradition):

> I have received an additional matter on this subject which is an authentic reception [קבלת אמת], and it is certainly the opinion [intended view] of the Rabbi [שהיא בודאי דעת הרב], of blessed memory.[10]

---

illumination in his quest for understanding the canonical text of Naḥmanides. The phrasing clearly evokes the language and imagery of Ps. 119:18, a biblical passage that reflects a concern for revealed exegesis in ancient Israel (see M. Fishbane, *Biblical Interpretation in Ancient Israel*, pp. 539–541). This image was also prominent in religious literature from Qumran (ibid., p. 542), and was used to connote revelatory exegesis throughout the history of Judaism (ibid., p. 541, n. 29). For an extended discussion of pneumatic exegesis in kabbalistic literature, see Idel, *Kabbalah: New Perspectives*, pp. 234–249.

8. Isaac of Akko, *Me'irat 'Einayim*, p. 18.

9. Ibid., p. 37.

10. Ibid., p. 39.

The fact that Isaac must state that "it is certainly the opinion [intended view] of the Rabbi" demonstrates that Naḥmanides' view on the matter is not self-evident from the text itself but, in fact, requires that the *actual* view or *intended* meaning of the master be asserted. Such a formulation would make no sense if the implication were otherwise. Thus, Isaac's task as a reliable transmitter is to assert what he believes to be the properly reconstructed (pre-written) view of Naḥ manides. Such mental intention exists prior to and outside of the text within the original author's mind. It is therefore necessarily *implied* and not explicit.

It should further be observed that the invocation of intent seeks to correlate true meaning with its origin in life, the living mind that exists prior to and beyond the created text. In certain instances, the establishment of original authorial intent has recourse to a transmission to that effect from a reliable disciple of Naḥmanides, who by virtue of that intimate relationship was purportedly privy to the unwritten intentions of the master when he wrote the words that he did. In this regard, consider the following case:

> Despite the fact that these words are sound and proper, and they are words of truth [אע"פ שדברים אלו נכוחים וישרים והם דברי אמת], nevertheless, that which was hinted above [from a different source], that East corresponds to *Tif'eret* and West corresponds to *'Atarah*, is not the way of the Rabbi of blessed memory [לו זו היא דרך הרב ז"ל]. For the RaShBA and the pious one RYBT, students of the Rabbi of blessed memory, said that the *qabbalah* of the Rabbi is . . . [11]

Naḥmanides' authentic meaning is established through reference to a direct chain of oral reception from the master himself, thus overriding other interpretive speculation with insight (through the direct relation of discipleship) into what Naḥmanides *actually meant* in his text (i.e., the "subtext"). Here Isaac invokes the authenticating discipleship of Solomon Ibn Adret (RaShBA) and Isaac ben Todros (RYBT), two of Naḥmanides' main students in Barcelona. The fact that these two figures were able to vouch for the true meaning of Naḥmanides' text through the cultural power of direct reception becomes the ultimate

11. Ibid., p. 171.

"proof text" (or "proof person") for Isaac of Akko in his search for Naḥmanidean authorial intent.

Among the disciples of Adret there was frequent disagreement over Naḥmanides' authentic intention. In *Me'irat 'Einayim*, Isaac of Akko's greatest competition in this regard is Shem Ṭov Ibn Ga'on's *Keter Shem Ṭov*, one of the other major metacommentaries on Naḥmanides' *Commentary on the Torah*. On more than one occasion, Isaac's attempt to reconstruct Naḥmanidean intent is postulated over against Ibn Ga'on's view:

> With respect to what is written in *Keter Shem Ṭov*, that the Rabbi here calls *Tif'eret* "the Right Side," ***know that this is not the Rabbi's intent at all*** [דע כי אין זה כונת הרב כלל]! For he only calls *Ḥesed* "the Right Side," and he calls *Tif'eret* "the Holy One blessed be He." Now also see that with respect to the matter of the Rosh ha-Shanah prayer, which he [Ibn Ga'on] thought was proof for his words—on the contrary, it is the exact opposite, and it is a complete support for *my* words! So give ear and listen to the correct clarification of the Rabbi's words [באור דברי הרב על נכון].[12]

We should first note that Isaac here seems to contradict his earlier remarks on Naḥmanides' conception of the sefirotic "Right Side," in which Isaac postulates the reconciliation between Naḥmanidean and 'Azrielean meaning. This aside, however, we encounter here a salient example of a debate within the extended Naḥmanidean school over the *intended* meaning of Naḥmanides' written text. Isaac forcefully rejects Ibn Ga'on's construction of Naḥmanidean intent, essentially subverting his own repeated assertions regarding the pluralistic character of kabbalistic hermeneutics. In this passage, Isaac seeks to position himself as *the* authentic spokesman for Naḥmanidean textual meaning, framed through his self-perceived ability to discern the subtext (the pre-written, mental intent) of the *Commentary*. Authentic meaning is not simply found in the reader's actualization of the text before him but, rather, in the reconstruction of the author's intent at the time of writing.[13]

12. Ibid., p. 67.

13. And thus kabbalistic theory here accords better with the view espoused in contemporary literary criticism by E. D. Hirsch than with that expressed by Wolfgang Iser and others.

The process of discerning intent, and in some cases distinguishing that intent from the surface meaning of the text, reveals a great deal about the exegetical posture of the interpreter himself. In his role as metacommentator, Isaac of Akko often seeks to posit true meaning as an implicit phenomenon, as a datum that requires his authoritative insight as a transmitter. The final example that I shall consider in this section elucidates this hermeneutical process by exhibiting Isaac's attempt to hyperesotericize the Naḥmanidean text. He posits that a proper understanding of the text requires an esoteric subtext, even in instances where Naḥmanides' esoteric project does not *appear* to be operative:

> Even though he [Naḥmanides] did not state above that this matter alludes to "the Land of the Living," *nevertheless his intention was to do so* [אעפ"כ כוונתו היתה כן]. For just as words of a verse refer explicitly to the lower world, and yet allude to the upper world, so too in the majority of places the words of the Rabbi of blessed memory also [function in this way]. And even though those words may seem to be referring to a simple meaning [ואע"פ שנראים פשט בעלמא], know that what the Rabbi of blessed memory has said is an exalted and hidden secret [סוד נשגב ונעלם הוא]. For we must understand that "the Land" alludes to *ʿAtarah*.[14]

According to this view, the reader of Naḥmanides' text must always search beyond the appearance of a simple literal meaning, and must strive to retrieve the implied and hidden intentions of the author. The reader is instructed to look probingly for an esoteric subtext, even in those countless instances where Naḥmanides expounds on a *nonkabbalistic* interpretation. In effect, Isaac of Akko has sought to subject Naḥmanides' own words to the esoteric rigors that the master himself applies to Scripture! Or at the least, Isaac claims to transmit an orally received esoteric meaning that is not even textually *implicit*—that is, a kabbalistic meaning that Naḥmanides intentionally concealed through a presentation of *peshat*, without any of the usual signifiers of *sod* (i.e., the Naḥmanidean terminology of *ʿal derekh ha-ʾemet*—"by way of truth," the kabbalistic method of interpretation). We may characterize

14. Isaac of Akko, *Meʾirat ʿEinayim*, p. 161.

this exegetical posture as *hyperesotericism*—seeking to find esoteric meaning even in the admittedly *exoteric* lines of the work. Such a hermeneutical approach attempts to go above and beyond the acknowledged esotericism of Naḥmanides' text and to subsume all apparent *peshat* (literal meaning) within the encompassing rubric of kabbalistic *'emet* (truth)—a framework in which all meaning (with very few exceptions) is kabbalistic meaning.[15] Our kabbalist is clearly unable to imagine that the RaMBaN might actually have intended to convey a *peshat* meaning—the *sod* as core truth is understood to be all-pervasive and all-inclusive. As with the other cases considered above, Isaac of Akko asserts access to an *implied* textual meaning, arguing that he as a transmitter can speak for the less-than-obvious features of the text in question and for the inexplicit intentions of its author.

Tradition and Authenticity: Kabbalistic (Re)constructions of Rabbinic Intent

We have seen that the medieval kabbalists considered themselves to be the bearers of a Truth that reached back to Sinai, and indeed back to Adam in Eden. In this understanding of sacred history, the "concealed wisdom" of the Kabbalah is viewed to be the deep structure of knowledge that has been passed down through the generations. A thoroughgoing continuity is constructed—one that subsumes all innovation within the authority of a perennial truth, and the gap in time that divides the medieval kabbalist from the masters of old is decisively bridged. Within this conception of time and tradition, the *new* is refigured as the *old*, and the classic enduring truth is recovered as new once again. If the theology and interpretive schema of the *sefirot* is not immediately apparent in the writings of classical Judaism, it is

---

15. A related argument was made by Wolfson in his "Beautiful Maiden Without Eyes: *Peshat* and *Sod* in Zoharic Hermeneutics," pp. 155–203. Cf. Wolfson, "By Way of Truth: Aspects of Naḥmanides' Kabbalistic Hermeneutic," pp. 110, 131, and elsewhere (though Wolfson also extensively documents Naḥmanides' adherence to a hermeneutic in which two ontological planes are affirmed, one denoted by literal interpretation and the other by symbolic allusion). On this subject, also see the recent analysis of Idel in his *Absorbing Perfections: Kabbalah and Interpretation*, p. 456.

(the mystics assure us) only because that intention has been concealed within the outer garments of perception, and the implied levels of rabbinic meaning must be unearthed from their hiding place by the keen *maskil*. To the kabbalists, it was inconceivable that the great Sages of talmudic and midrashic literature were not kabbalists themselves—a core assumption that was dramatized by the belief that the *Zohar* was the work of Shimon bar Yoḥai and his tannaitic disciples. This method of rereading earlier canonical sources through the lens of a later thought-structure—a recasting of apparent meaning through the conception of subsurface intention—is not dissimilar to the way tannaitic and amoraic masters radically reinvented the modalities of biblical religion in their own image.[16] From the perspective of the medieval mystics, the Sages of old were themselves kabbalists (even if that "fact" is hidden beneath the surface), and therefore all of rabbinic literature is to be read through the lens of kabbalistic symbolism; the hidden intent of the Sages is discerned to be of a piece with the medieval kabbalists' theology and exegetical approach. Among the many instances in medieval kabbalistic literature, this attitude and interpretive method is reflected in Naḥmanides' *Commentary on the Torah*, wherein the master explains perplexing *'aggadot* according to the symbolic associations of kabbalistic thought, and overtly argues that the real intent of the Sages was kabbalistic in nature.[17] So, too, in a manner parallel to the project

---

16. Among the many examples that could be adduced to support this point, note the classical rabbinic assertion that the biblical patriarchs actually fulfilled all the rabbinic precepts of law (even if only at an "internal" level). On this, see Green, *Devotion and Commandment*, pp. 9, 30–33.

17. An indicative passage may be observed in Naḥmanides' commentary on Gen. 1:1 (*Perush ha-RaMBaN 'al ha-Torah*, 1:9). Reflecting on the famous midrashic tradition that the purpose of the creation narrative (given that the Torah was perceived to be a law book, first and foremost) was to justify Israel's claim to the Holy Land (in that, the midrashic logic runs, the Creator of the world surely may decide to whom he will give the land, and from whom he will take it!), Naḥmanides argues that the Rabbis of old had a far more lofty intention in mind. They unquestionably intended to allude to the way in which the world was created via the ten divine *sefirot*, but offered this other interpretation in order to conceal the deep truth from the uninitiated. In his words: שמעשה בראשית סוד עמוק אינו מובן מן המקראות, ולא יוודע על בוריו אלא מפי הקבלה עד משה רבינו מפי הגבורה, ויודעיו חייבין להסתיר אותו, לכך אמר רבי יצחק שאין להתחלת התורה צורך בבראשית ברא (Creation is a deep secret that cannot be understood through the Scriptures alone. It can only be fathomed through the tradition—the *qabbalah*—that extends back to Moses our teacher, who received revelation from the mouth of God, and those who know this secret are obligated to conceal it. For this reason did Rabbi Isaac

of reconstructing the implied intentions (and subsurface meanings) of Naḥmanides' writing, Isaac of Akko approached the classical rabbinic texts with a similar agenda. Like many other kabbalists of his time, Isaac believed that the Sages employed the wisdom of the *sefirot* in their writings, and that one only needs to discover and lift the veils of external meaning to retrieve their true intent.

Consider a particularly striking case of this interpretive phenomenon from Isaac's *'Oẓar Ḥayyim*.[18] Citing the classic rabbinic dictum that a person must not touch an unclothed Torah scroll with bare hands (a position that follows in the Babylonian Talmud from the assertion that bare hands may contaminate a holy object),[19] Isaac of Akko argues that the intention of the Sages is not to be discerned through a literal interpretation of the dictum—the truth of the remark is only to be gathered by way of its hidden sense (וראיתי שכוונת רז"ל בזה אינה ע"ד הפשט אלא ע"ד הנסתר). Isaac goes on to claim that (contrary to the appearances of literalism) the dictum of the Sages was actually directed at those people of "little faith" who read the Torah and assert that it possesses no secrets and hidden matters, none of the concealed mysteries of existence—it is (they claim) only composed of plain meanings, of matters that are readily apparent to the interpretive eye. Such simpletons leave the Torah naked, bereft of any outer clothing and any sense of hidden depths (אומרים שאין בה נסתרות וסתרי המציאות כולו רק הנגלה לבדו פשטי המעשיות ועושין התורה ערומה בלי לבוש . . .). Thus Isaac of Akko radically transforms a rabbinic statement about the tension between the sacred scroll and the profane human hand (a fascinating belief in and of itself, which sheds light on rabbinic conceptions of ritual and taboo) into an altogether different kabbalistic assertion about the layers of

---

[of the *midrash*] say that the Torah did not need to begin with *In the Beginning, God Created* . . .). On this conception of concealment in the act of transmission, see Wolfson, "By Way of Truth: Aspects of Naḥmanides' Kabbalistic Hermeneutic," pp. 153–178. It must be noted that this symbolic approach to the interpretation of rabbinic *'aggadot* is also reflected in the writings of 'Azriel of Gerona (in his *Perush ha-'Aggadot*) and Todros Abulafia (in his *Sefer 'Oẓar ha-Kavod*). For recent reflection on the range and character of 'Azriel's kabbalization of the *'aggadot* (with particular attention to the manner in which these moves lend insight into the exegetical history and reception of Jewish myth), see M. Fishbane, *Biblical Myth and Rabbinic Mythmaking*, pp. 260–266.

18. Isaac of Akko, *'Oẓar Ḥayyim*, fol. 118a.

19. BT *Shabbat*, fol. 14a.

hidden meaning that are to be discerned in the scriptural text. Most critical here, however, is the unequivocal assumption that the Sages had this kabbalistic-esoteric meaning *in mind*, and that the latter-day kabbalist is able to unveil these latent intentions. As we saw earlier with regard to Isaac's attempts to recover Naḥmanides' esoteric intentions, the transmitter here believes that a deeper structure of truth lies hidden in the unwritten intentions and implied meanings (כוונת רז"ל) of the received texts. The following other short examples also reflect this exegetical approach: "I was writing down a passage from the words of our Rabbis of blessed memory, and I was unable to complete [the writing] until I comprehended a great secret that was [contained] in it" (the continuation of the text in *'Oẓar Ḥayyim* clarifies that this "great secret" is indeed sefirotic in content);[20] "according to the way of truth, [the word] 'heavens' [שמים] hints at [symbolizes] *Tif'eret*—and this was the intended [meaning] of our Rabbis of blessed memory";[21] "I was contemplating a passage from our Rabbis of blessed memory, and I saw in it a secret [ראיתי בו סוד] that was correct in my eyes";[22] "I saw the secret of a passage from our Rabbis of blessed memory."[23] In this way, the medieval kabbalist reads his own perceptions of exegesis and esotericism into the canonical words of talmudic discourse—believing that he is legitimately disclosing the original subsurface intention and concealed true meaning of rabbinic prescription.

This conception of truth, tradition, and rabbinic intention is also dramatized by Isaac of Akko through direct contrast with the interpretive approach of the philosophers. In a starkly different manner from the views expressed in *Me'irat 'Einayim*—wherein Isaac sought to harmonize the exegetical methods and meanings of Kabbalah and Philosophy[24]—Isaac's argument in *'Oẓar Ḥayyim* overtly rejects the philosophical outlook, and postulates the kabbalistic *sod* as the deep

20. Isaac of Akko, *'Oẓar Ḥayyim*, fol. 172a.

21. Ibid., fol. 197b.

22. Ibid., fol. 146a.

23. Ibid., fol. 121b.

24. It is important to note, however, that Isaac did not see philosophy and Kabbalah in a mutually affirming light; he ultimately subsumed philosophical hermeneutics under kabbalistic symbolism, notwithstanding the attempts in *Me'irat 'Einayim* to reconcile them.

structure of truth as it extends back through rabbinic literature to the dawn of human time. In this way, the kabbalist seeks to position himself as the authentic inheritor of the rabbinic tradition over against the competing claims of the philosophers. The views articulated in *'Oẓar Ḥayyim* are markedly more polemical toward philosophical exegesis—a characteristic that appears to reflect a significant shift in approach that occurred between Isaac's composition of *Me'irat 'Einayim* (approximately 1308) and that of *'Oẓar Ḥayyim* (approximately 1330). We cannot pinpoint the cause for this change in attitude (though Isaac's journey into new regions and influences would be the most logical explanation), but we may at least observe the evolution of our kabbalist's perception of interpretive authenticity and his unwillingness to reconcile competing modes of hermeneutical construction. Our first case of this phenomenon in *'Oẓar Ḥayyim* pertains to the contrast between the kabbalistic and philosophic readings of the older rabbinic assertion that the Torah existed in a primordial state of black fire upon white fire for two thousand years prior to the creation of the world.[25] Seeking to assert the authenticity of the kabbalistic interpretation (and explicitly polemicizing against the philosophers), Isaac states:

> For even though their argument is sound, they have not merited knowledge of the Rabbis' intention [לא זכו לדעת כוונת רז"ל]. You should know that as the heavens are higher than the earth, so too is the Rabbis' intention in their words many times higher [or greater] than the way in which the philosophers [חכמי המחקר][26] understood them—for their intention [concerned] the secret of the ten *sefirot* [כי כוונתם בסוד עס"ב].[27]

Thus rabbinic meaning is aligned with (or subsumed within) kabbalistic meaning, and Isaac of Akko positions the mystic as the authentic inheritor of the rabbinic mantle. As already noted, this framing of tradition and meaning is accomplished through a self-proclaimed ability to "reconstruct" the implied intentions of the Sages—a move that es-

---

25. This text is also discussed in Idel, *Absorbing Perfections*, pp. 449–460. Idel's core argument—comprehensively argued throughout his book—pertains to the kabbalistic project of constructing and employing an exegetical code for the deciphering and explanation of Scripture.

26. Literally, "the sages of [philosophical] investigation"—a medieval term commonly used to refer to philosophers.

27. Isaac of Akko, *'Oẓar Ḥayyim*, fol. 129a.

tablishes an unbroken chain of interpretive authority and a particular (re)vision of sacred history. Like the broader human tendency to privilege intention over manifestation,[28] the supposedly implied meaning is repeatedly vested with far more legitimacy than what is actually stated at a literal level.

Consider one other remarkable example of this phenomenon.[29] After asserting that the kabbalists effect unifications within the sefirotic realm through their recitation of the daily benedictions with proper intention (a practice claimed to have been transmitted orally all the way back to Moses on Mount Sinai), Isaac demeans the practice of the philosophers as simply empty sounds, devoid of any cosmic import:

> With respect to the philosophers—even though they are Jews who utter [benedictory] unifications with their mouths, it is only comparable to the chirping of a bird [ידמה לצפצוף העוף]. For the goal of their minds with respect to the unity [or unification] of the One and Only Master is nothing other than the negation of corporeality [ושתכליתשכלם בייחוד האדון היחיד אינו אלא שלילת גשמות]. They do not understand and do not comprehend the secret of His name . . . [30] for they do not possess the secret of the ten *sefirot*, correct and received [כי אין בידם סוד עס"ב הנכון המקובל]. . . . The root of the Torah, the correct [conception of] unity and faith is the secret of the ten *sefirot* [ושורש התורה והייחוד והאמונה הנכונה היא סוד עס"ב].[31]

Here the kabbalist makes it clear that proper intention is the element that lends meaning to the interpretation of Scripture and the performance of ritual. For without a conscious awareness of the sefirotic resonances latent in the liturgical benediction (as well as a cultivated ability to effect the unification of the *sefirot* through that ritual action and

28. See more detailed discussion of this phenomenon above.

29. This polemical rhetoric concerning the superiority of *sod* over the limited and flawed views of the philosophers is found in a few other cases in Isaac's *ʾOẓar Ḥayyim*. See, e.g., fol. 49a (where Isaac of Akko directly rejects and criticizes philosophers who don't recognize the "truth" of the ten *sefirot*, instead relying on their analytical skills) and fol. 71a (a strong critique of the philosophical focus on the negation of any divine corporeality to the neglect of kabbalistic *sod*).

30. The divine name (the Tetragrammaton) is a common symbol for the totality of the ten *sefirot*.

31. Isaac of Akko, *ʾOẓar Ḥayyim*, fol. 28a.

intention), the prayer of the devotee will be of no greater cosmic significance, and possess no more meaning, than the chirping of birds. It is the symbolic associations of the ten *sefirot* that make prayer meaningful—and it is just this awareness (Isaac asserts) that the philosophers lack. The cipher of the ten *sefirot* links the kabbalist back to an authenticating revelation—one that Isaac believes was also transmitted through the Sages of old. In the process of asserting this distinction, Isaac sets the kabbalistic conception of theology and cosmic truth against one of the core issues of medieval Jewish philosophy: the attempt to purify theological discourse of any and all anthropomorphic language (שתכלית שכלם בייחוד האדון היחיד אינו אלא שלילת גשמות). Isaac of Akko aggressively maintains that such theological goals completely miss the point of prayer—which for the medieval kabbalist is deeply theurgical and structured around a comprehension of the inner divine dimensions. Thus the kabbalist is engaged in the struggle to assert his inheritance of the rabbinic legacy—an ideological battle that is best reflected on the philosophical side through the literary project of Moses Maimonides and his radical reinterpretation of the rabbinic terms מעשה בראשית (the Work of Creation) and מעשה מרכבה (the Work of the Chariot). Indeed, it has been argued in contemporary scholarship that it was this very issue that prompted the early kabbalists to move from orality to textuality in the formulation of their ideas and teachings. As Moshe Idel has proposed,[32] Maimonides' interpretation of מעשה בראשית and מעשה מרכבה as physics and metaphysics (and the consequent reconceptualization of rabbinic meaning) compelled the kabbalists to construct a literary defense of their own that sought to restore what they believed to be the true esoteric intent of the Sages.

In sum, we may point to several converging issues in the kabbalistic self-perception of authenticity—each of which also stands as a pillar of the exegetical religious culture, broadly conceived. They are: revelation and the endurance of a perennial truth; tradition and the reception of authoritative wisdom; authorial intention and the disclosure of subsurface meaning; the bridging of gaps in time and the unity of meaning in Jewish religious history.

---

32. See Idel, "Maimonides and Kabbalah." This argument contrasts with the earlier position of Gershom Scholem (see, e.g., *Major Trends*, pp. 11–12, 22–32) that medieval Kabbalah arose in direct response to the rationalism of the philosophers.

The Idea of Authorship: A Theoretical Interlude

Beyond the persistent attempt to reconstruct authoritative reception through the establishment of authorial intent, Isaac of Akko also displays a remarkable self-consciousness with regard to his own status as an author. Repeatedly, and often in formulaic terms, Isaac asserts his own position as a legitimate transmitter of kabbalistic traditions. Thus, despite the desire to posit reliable *sources* for the issues he presents (whether they be oral or textual), Isaac simultaneously seeks to establish an independent stature for himself as a person worthy of delivering esoteric truths. In this sense, we encounter an ongoing dialectic in Isaac's writing between the eclectic method of tradition collection (predicated on the reliability of the particular reception) and the construction of individual authority on the part of the author himself.[33] There are several theoretical considerations, however, before we proceed to the textual specifics that represent these ideas in *Me'irat 'Einayim* and *'Ozar Ḥayyim*.

The first question is one that has been the subject of some reflection in the discourse of modern literary theory and philosophy: What is the relationship between the overtly stated name of an author and the text associated with that author? How does the author perceive herself with regard to the book that she is in the process of producing? Does he conceive of himself as one endowed with enough authority and legitimacy to assert original opinions in the form of written discourse? In what way does the name of the author affect the *reader's* perception of that book's authority? As Michel Foucault has pointed out,[34] it was not until the rise of scientific method in the seventeenth and eighteenth centuries that the legitimacy of a text (or discursive argument) could be separated from the personality and authority of the author of that text. Prior to that time the legitimacy of the author to which a specific text was attributed was the primary point of reference for determining the worthiness and authority of the text in question. Scientific method

33. The status of the individual and the dynamics of self-perception were prominent features of religion in the High Middle Ages. See Bynum, "Did the Twelfth Century Discover the Individual?" pp. 82–109.

34. Foucault, "What Is an Author?" p. 453.

changed this perception (at least within its own circles), asserting that the ultimate factor in determining the truth and authority of a textual argument is the plausibility of independent verification and validation. If the reader was able to verify the process and results of a scientific argument (based on certain collectively accepted criteria), then the text automatically could be considered authoritative. The identity of the original author of that text became essentially irrelevant to the process of legitimization. The author was not disregarded, of course, but was also not the determining element in establishing the truth and authority of a specific textual claim.

I would argue that despite the self-avowed connection of the modern study of religion to scientific method (*Religionswissenschaft*), the significance of an author's name in the formation of a reader's prejudgments of a text should not be underestimated. The so-called scientific arguments made in the humanistic disciplines, including the study of religion, are inescapably affected by the name that is attached to the text being read. Can we honestly say that our reading of an article or a book is not shaped and to some extent predetermined (whether favorably or pejoratively) by our preconceived notions of the author? Does not our knowledge of an author's prior work or personal reputation affect the manner in which we read and judge a present work? Indeed, this fact seems to lie at the root of the double-blind system employed for the peer review of articles for contemporary scholarly journals. The identity of the author is concealed precisely because of the fear that knowledge of that identity will inevitably affect the reader's judgments regarding the scholarly value of the written work in question. Furthermore, as Martin Jay has observed, the invocation of an esteemed author's name in modern humanistic discourse functions to bestow legitimacy on the particular idea in question, as well as to bolster the authority of the later writer or scholar who invokes that respected name.[35] I would argue that this phenomenon lies at the heart of the scholarly enterprise and ac-

35. Jay, "Name Dropping or Dropping Names?: Modes of Legitimation in the Humanities," pp. 19–34. Jay considers this phenomenon in several different contexts, with particular emphasis on the manner in which the invocation of Freud's name is still intimately tied to the legitimation of psychoanalysis, and the name of Karl Marx to that of specific socialist perspectives. The same may be said for other fields of study in which allusion to the names of revered scholars has the power to bolster the authenticity of a particular line of argument.

curately captures an essential dimension of human communication and exchange. The writer or speaker in the present constructs his or her own legitimacy as a transmitter and interpreter of ideas through reference to a paradigmatic and charismatic personality from the past.

In the medieval world, the identity and reputation of an author were not only operative factors in the prejudices of readers, but also were the primary criteria for determining the legitimacy and value of a text. As A. J. Minnis has shown,[36] medieval Christian scholasticism placed the identity of the author above all else, and a text was excluded from a status of legitimacy if a worthy *auctor* could not be posited. The actual historical truth of such attributions was not rigorously verified by medieval scholastics, and certain texts were ascribed to personalities of antiquity who were given a special authenticity simply by virtue of their historical distance in the revered times of old. Such was also the case in the scholarly world of medieval Judaism. Indeed, the attribution of the *Zohar* to the ancient sage Rabbi Shimon bar Yoḥai, and the consequent canonization of the *Zohar* on this basis, attests well to the authoritative power involved in positing antique authorship to works that were actually written in the Middle Ages.[37] The question of authorship was therefore deeply central to the medieval construction of textual legitimacy.[38] It is against this background that we must understand Isaac of

---

36. Minnis, *Medieval Theory of Authorship: Scholastic Literary Attitudes in the Later Middle Ages*.

37. In the case of the *Zohar*, this matter is complicated by the phenomenon of pseudepigraphy. One wonders in fact whether the author(s) of the *Zohar* did not themselves identify with the personalities of antiquity who are the subject of the zoharic narratives. Nevertheless, it was precisely the *perception* of antique authorship (along with its great literary and imaginative character, to be sure) that vouchsafed for the *Zohar* such a prominent (indeed canonical) role in the history of Jewish religious literature. I plan to deal with these issues at much greater length in a future study. On the question of the canonization of the *Zohar* as a sacred text, the sociocultural implications of this phenomenon for the reception-history of Jewish sources, see Huss, "*Sefer ha-Zohar* as a Canonical, Sacred and Holy Text: Changing Perspectives on the Book of Splendor Between the Thirteenth and Eighteenth Centuries," pp. 257–307; Giller, *Reading the Zohar: The Sacred Text of the Kabbalah*, pp. 13–33; Abrams, "*Zohar, Sefer, Sefer ha-Zohar*: A History of the Assumptions and Expectations of Kabbalists and Modern Scholars," pp. 201–232.

38. Medieval Jewish scribal culture did not, however, share our modern concept of intellectual property: it saw ownership of a text as collective, and scribes felt free to alter the work they were transmitting. Medieval Jewish texts thus survive in a wide variety of manuscript readings. See M. Beit-Arie, "Publication and Reproduction of Literary Texts in Medieval Jewish Civilization: Jewish Scribality and Its Impact on the Texts Transmitted."

Akko's persistent act of self-referencing in his written work, as well as his self-conscious reflections on the process and significance of his own authorship.

The Self-Perception of Authorship and the Act of Writing in *Me'irat 'Einayim*

Despite Isaac's deeply eclectic method, self-reference recurs in his writings as a rhythmic refrain. This refrain serves to lift the identity of the author from the shadowed background of eclecticism, in which his individual persona functions as a passive cultural conduit, to the foreground of active communication with the reader, and it consistently appears in a predictable acronymic formulation of Isaac's name. The meaning of this acronym and the method of its use are explicitly commented on by Isaac at the beginning of *Me'irat 'Einayim* (p. 2): "I, Isaac, the young one, the son of Samuel—may God protect him—from Akko, may it be rebuilt, alluded to in all places by [the acronym] 'YHB SNR DATV.'[39] I, the author of this book [מחבר ספר זה], say that . . ." True to his statement here, Isaac employs this acronym with tremendous frequency in *Me'irat 'Einayim* (along with similar variations in *'Oẓar Ḥayyim*), often in a manner clearly intended to juxtapose his own individual opinion on a given subject with those he cites and paraphrases. Noteworthy also is Isaac of Akko's self-characterization of authorship, phrased here by the distinctly medieval term *meḥabber*.[40] Variations of this word, Aramaicized in the *Zohar*, served as one of the philological clues for Gershom Scholem in his argument for the medieval provenance of that book.[41]

In his assertion of his own identity as an author, Isaac frequently employs a rhetoric designed to bolster his authority as a transmitter of

39. As mentioned in Chapter 2, the acronym *YHB SNR DATV* (יה"ב שנ"ר דעת"ו) corresponds to the words יצחק הצעיר בן שמואל נטוריה רחמנא דמן עכו תבנה ותכונן.

40. Ben-Yehudah suggests that this term (particularly in the sense of authorship) entered into the Hebrew lexicon (via Arabic influence) through the linguistic projects of Menaḥem ben Jacob ibn Saruq and Dunash ben Labrat in the tenth century. See Ben-Yehudah, *Dictionary and Thesaurus of the Hebrew Language*, p. 2893.

41. See Scholem, *Major Trends in Jewish Mysticism*, p. 390.

Kabbalah. He self-consciously asserts the boldness of his transmissional endeavor, and he positions himself in this regard in direct contrast to the efforts of other kabbalists. In one particular passage, Isaac sets his project against that of his greatest rival, Shem Ṭov Ibn Ga'on: "I, Isaac, the young one . . . say that [the subject on] which this sage did not want to offer any [kabbalistic] hint whatsoever, I now come to clarify according to that which I have received [על פי אשר קבלתי]."[42] Where Ibn Ga'on is reserved and reluctant to expound on a certain kabbalistic matter, Isaac of Akko presents himself as one who dares to engage in the precarious act of transmission and authorship.[43] It is his identity as a legitimate author—one who is willing to be bolder in that endeavor than his peers and colleagues—that Isaac seeks to convey to the reader of *Me'irat 'Einayim*.

The act of authorship for Isaac of Akko is therefore a complex blend of retransmitting reliable receptions ("according to that which I have received") and his own individual ability to clarify matters on his own ("I now come to clarify"). This dialectical conception of authorial creativity is well demonstrated by a further passage: "I, Isaac, the young one . . . will speak about this secret, and I will write down regarding it the discovery I have made[44] [התעוררות אשר התעוררתי בו] from the principle that I received from the kabbalists [אשר קבלתי מהמקובלים]."[45]

The term התעוררות (awakening/arousal) is widely used by medieval kabbalists to connote the process of creativity—a phenomenon that is best demonstrated in the zoharic literature by the Aramaic equivalent אתערותא and the corresponding repeated usage of התעוררות in Moses de Leon's Hebrew writings. Of late, Melila Hellner-Eshed has studied this very important concept in the *Zohar*, using the term as a window into the zoharic conception of mystical experience.[46] For our

42. Isaac of Akko, *Me'irat 'Einayim*, p. 39.

43. On ambivalence and boldness in the drama of kabbalistic disclosure, as well as several other issues involved in the act of transmission in the *Zohar*, see E. Fishbane, "Tears of Disclosure: The Role of Weeping in Zoharic Narrative."

44. Literally, "the awakening that I have awakened."

45. Isaac of Akko, *Me'irat 'Einayim*, p. 33.

46. See Hellner-Eshed, "The Language of Mystical Experience in the *Zohar*," pp. 16–32, and *A River Issues Forth from Eden: On the Language of Mystical Experience in the Zohar*, pp. 237–267.

purposes here, the התעוררות to which Isaac testifies is clearly meant to be distinguished from the content that he received from other kabbalists (i.e., reliable human sources of esoterica). He received the principle for the interpretation from other kabbalists, but his own creative act of התעוררות is the true cause for the self-consciousness of his own authorial/scriptive act.

This balance between reception and innovative transmission is also framed by Isaac as the divide between קבלה (reception or tradition) and סברא (reason and/or innovative thought)—the two models of interpretation that were famously discussed by Naḥmanides.[47] Isaac takes his cue in this sense from Naḥmanides, but develops the dialectic in his own singular fashion:

> I have here mentioned my own opinion [סברתי] for the following reason: In the Way of Truth [דרך האמת], one must not employ reason [סברא], but only reception [קבלה בלבד]. Everyone who employs reason in these matters, who invents things out of his own heart [ובודה דברים מלבו], and writes or says them as if they were a reception [וכותבם או אומרם בלשון קבלה]—his sin is too great to bear. For [in so doing], he gives false testimony, and he profanes the name of Heaven . . . Every individual who has the Spirit of God within him with respect to wit and logic [כל אשר רוח אלהים בו בחדוד ובפלפול], and who understands one thing from another[48] [ומבין דבר מתוך דבר]—that issue which he has understood he is permitted to write down or speak *in his own name* [אותו דבר שהבין מותר לו לכתבו או לאמרו בשם עצמו] . . . Thus every person who, in matters of the Way of Truth, says things in the name of the person who first articulated them, and speaks matters that have been understood in the name of the one who has understood them, he surely sanctifies the name of Heaven [לפיכך כל האומר בדרך האמת דברים בשם אומרם והמובן בשם המבין הרי הוא מקדש שם שמים].[49]

47. For technical usage of the phrase על דרך סברא in Naḥmanides' exegesis, see *Perush ha-RaMBaN ʿal ha-Torah*, 1: 212 (commentary on Gen. 38:2); 2: 261 (commentary on Num. 16:21).

48. The origin of this phrase in the sense of reasoned deduction and innovation is to be found in talmudic sources. See, e.g., BT *Shabbat*, fol. 31a; *Ḥagigah*, fol. 14a; *Sanhedrin*, fol. 93b.

49. Isaac of Akko, *Me'irat ʿEinayim*, p. 90, emphasis added. The formulation "too great to bear" is based on Gen. 4:13. It should be noted that the value of proper attribution was already asserted in classical rabbinic literature, and the reverberations of that precedent are clearly manifest in Issac of Akko's rhetoric. See, e.g., M. *ʾAvot* 6:6; BT *Ḥulin*, fol. 104b.

Note first of all that, in this instance, the terms דרך האמת (the way of truth) and קבלה are not synonymous.[50] דרך האמת connotes the larger rubric of esoteric thought and hermeneutics, whereas קבלה refers to the specific method of transmission—the process of receiving insight through the authoritative chain. As I emphasized earlier, Kabbalah is first and foremost a characterization of a specific form of cultural communication. *Derekh ha-'emet* signifies the system and method of thought involved—it is a technical term that was used most prominently by Naḥmanides and his school. In this sense both the methods of קבלה and סברא (reasoned innovation or deduction) are acceptable approaches to the process of expounding the "Way of Truth," provided that the individual involved in their usage explicitly separates the two methods, indicating clearly to the reader or hearer when each one is being employed. The act of writing about esoteric (kabbalistic) matters requires this open and honest rhetoric directed toward the recipient of the transmission. According to Isaac, if any confusion is left to the reader on this score, then the author has committed a grave sin. The reader must know what has been innovated by the author of the text and what has been reliably transmitted from earlier sources.

These two modes are thus not culturally equivalent. Transmission by way of קבלה is superior to that of סברא—as Naḥmanides himself makes clear. Nevertheless, they are both legitimate forms of expression and are both modes of mystical/kabbalistic interpretation.[51] In this respect we encounter a significant difference between the views of Naḥmanides and Isaac of Akko. For whereas the RaMBaN explicitly rejected the ability of an independent סברא to yield any kabbalistic understanding (stipulating the necessity of received tradition from a reliable master), Isaac does appear to affirm the autonomy of individual

50. This is particularly surprising given the manner in which the phrase דרך האמת functions in Naḥmanidean Kabbalah. See Wolfson, "By Way of Truth: Aspects of Naḥmanides' Kabbalistic Hermeneutic," esp. pp. 129–153; Pedayah, *Nahmanides: Cyclical Time and Holy Text*, p. 127; Halbertal, *By Way of Truth: Nahmanides and the Creation of Tradition*, p. 318.

51. I use the word "kabbalistic" here only to connote a recognized mode of medieval discourse that has become a commonplace in modern scholarship. If we use Isaac of Akko's terminology more strictly, the discourse should be characterized as דרך האמת, and the term קבלה should be reserved for the specific mode of communication and reception. I believe this distinction is essential to understanding the way Jewish esoterics viewed their own endeavor.

interpretive insight as it may arise in certain cases. Furthermore, it would be incorrect to read the juxtaposition here of קבלה and סברא as the polarity between the rationality of philosophy and the so-called antirationalism of mysticism—the manner in which the issue was framed by Scholem in his application of a Hegelian conception of dialectical historiosophy.[52] Instead, *qabbalah* and *sevara'* are two methods of Jewish mystical exegesis—the former being predicated on authoritative *reception* and the latter a mode of *innovative creativity*. This interpretive creativity seems to be a form of pneumatic exegesis—a moment of insight believed to be inspired by the deity (here characterized as "the Spirit of God"—*ruaḥ 'Elohim*). In this respect both modes are considered to be authoritative and function in a parallel fashion to the Abulafian text observed at the beginning of this chapter (wherein I note three modes of authority construction: oral, textual, and revelatory). Even the modality of individual creativity presupposes an inspiration from Elsewhere. The persons capable of innovative deduction are so able precisely because they are *inspired by the Divine* or, more literally, the "spirit of God" dwells within them. Creativity is primarily authoritative because of its origin in a revelation from God. Yet, whether the act of exposition is based on reception or innovative creativity (a polarity that might also be compared to the tradition/charisma distinction articulated by Max Weber),[53] it is the responsibility of the kabbalistic author to reflect accurately the method and source of the esoteric exegesis in question.

This passage is remarkable testimony to the fact that Isaac of Akko did not advocate an unequivocal blind fidelity to received traditions

52. Scholem, *Major Trends in Jewish Mysticism*, pp. 22–32, argues that Kabbalah arose as a negative reaction to the prevailing rationalism of medieval Jewish Philosophy. My point here is not necessarily designed to dispute this (though it is certainly a position in need of modification), but rather to claim that *sevara'* is not meant to represent philosophical rationalism here. Instead, I would argue that the term refers to the construction of an individual's innovative opinion as juxtaposed with the process of authoritative reception. Such is the force of its widespread usage in talmudic discourse. See, e.g., BT *Berakhot*, fol. 35a; *Shabbat*, fol. 96b; *'Eruvin*, fol. 15b.

53. See Weber, *The Protestant Ethic and the Spirit of Capitalism*, pp. 36, 84–85, 178, 281, and "Politics as a Vocation," p. 79. Weber's typologization of authority into "traditional," "charismatic," and "rational," with particular attention to its application to Judaism, is analyzed in Eisen, *Rethinking Modern Judaism*, pp. 57–61, 275–276.

in the construction of authentic meaning. Room is explicitly left for the innovative character of individual creativity. A kabbalist who is blessed with a sharp deductive mind capable of original interpretation (that derives from divine inspiration) is here given cultural legitimacy. The major caveat posited for this legitimation of creativity is that it be honestly stated as such and not falsely attributed to the authority of reception. This emphasis is highly revealing of the dramatic difference between the medieval and modern scholarly worlds. Whereas our contemporary culture of writing and authorship warns against the sin of dissimulating originality when a prior author has already made a certain argument (i.e., plagiarism), the medieval conception as articulated by Isaac asserts the exact inverse perspective! The impulse of the medieval author was to attribute his originality to a prior reception so as to gain greater legitimacy for the idea; authoritative reception was considered superior to individual innovation—thus the need to warn against this in *Me'irat 'Einayim*. Indeed, as discussed earlier, this phenomenon also lies behind the pseudepigraphical impulse in medieval Jewish esoteric authorship, in which an author attempts to ascribe responsibility for the text to a paradigmatic figure in antiquity. We may recall that this cultural-literary dynamic is exemplified by texts such as the *Bahir*, which was attributed by medieval Provençal scholars to the ancient sage R. Neḥuniah ben Haqanah; the *Zohar*, which was attributed by Castilian mystics to the Tanna R. Shimon bar Yoḥai; and several other cases, including works produced by the Rhineland Pietists in the late twelfth century and the writings of the *'iyun* (contemplation) circle.[54] By contrast, in contemporary culture it is considered shameful to claim innovation when the idea was in fact *received* (or copied) from someone else. In this sense, the different hierarchizations of originality and reception in medieval and modern culture shed light on the evolving conception of the individual, the status of authorship, and the value of tradition.

This balance between reception, self-awareness, and transmission

---

54. On the practice of pseudepigraphy among the *Ḥasidei 'Ashkenaz*, see J. Dan, *The "Unique Cherub" Circle: A School of Mystics and Esoterics in Medieval Germany*, pp. 1–15. For a detailed analysis of the *'iyun* texts that sheds much light on the problem of medieval Jewish pseudepigraphy, see Verman, *The Books of Contemplation*.

goes to the heart of Isaac's conception of his own authorial purpose. As he puts the matter:

> Since God, may He be blessed, has caused me in His compassion to merit to receive from the mouths of men of Truth [לקבל מפי אנשי אמת], it is proper and obligatory for me [ראוי ומחויב אני] to bring the matter out of potential and into actuality [להוציא הענין מן הכח אל הפועל], so that the intellective [dimension] will be understood from the sensory [dimension] [למען יובן מן המורגש המושכל]. As it is written [Job 19:26]: "From my flesh I shall see God" [מבשרי אחזה אלוה].[55]

The act of transmission—and, by extension, authorship—is the self-perceived duty of the kabbalistic master; he is bound by the imperative to serve faithfully as a link in the chain of tradition. Having been entrusted with sacred reception from authoritative kabbalists (אנשי אמת) and further viewing that reception as the compassionate gift of God, Isaac considers it to be his responsibility to aid others in their comprehension of esoteric matters. As a process of education, the pupil matures into a teacher, viewing that role as a vocation (or a calling) bestowed on him by divine destiny. The function of the kabbalistic teacher is to enable others to cultivate a mystical mentality—a mode of perceiving reality that constantly seeks to penetrate beyond the surface level of worldly encounter. From the physical flesh and the elements of sensory perception, the mystic seeks to perceive the elusive spiritual inner core of Being. This is certainly one of the ultimate aims of mysticism broadly conceived, and this is the stated purpose of Isaac of Akko's act of writing *Me'irat 'Einayim*. As a kabbalistic author, his goal is to instruct others in the art of perceiving the world with a mystical eye.

---

55. Isaac of Akko, *Me'irat 'Einayim*, p. 118.

Five Seeing the Secret

Creative Process and the Hermeneutics of Insight

Whereas authorial self-awareness and the use of the first-person voice are clear features of *Me'irat 'Einayim*, the testimonial mode assumes an entirely new level of maturity and development in Isaac's *'Oẓar Ḥayyim*. In the latter work, there is a substantial shift away from the reception-focus of *Me'irat 'Einayim*—a transformation from the eclecticism of tradition-collection to the rhetoric of individuality and innovation. This is not to say that Isaac of Akko ceases to collect and report received traditions in *'Oẓar Ḥayyim*. On the contrary, there are a good many examples of this mode to be found in his later work, and his writing reflects a broad array of intellectual influences and debts. Nevertheless, there is a profound difference in the proportion and manner in which Isaac allows his own persona to rise to the surface of the discourse in *'Oẓar Ḥayyim*, and this text reflects a startlingly new use of first-person testimony and autobiography in the communication of kabbalistic wisdom. In notable contrast to the vast majority of Jewish mystical literature (which is far better characterized as exegetical and prescriptive), *'Oẓar Ḥayyim* offers sustained confessional moments and autobiographical vignettes throughout the pages of a voluminous manuscript.[1] In this respect, *'Oẓar Ḥayyim* should be contextualized within a larger and much-neglected substream of Jewish mystical literature: a genre of first-person confessional speech in which the otherwise obscured selfhood of the kabbalist comes to the foreground of the text.[2] The regnant assumption among scholars

1. In *'Oẓar Ḥayyim*, fols. 8b, 22a, 49b, 101b, 111b, Isaac of Akko alludes to an even more autobiographical work of his titled *Sefer Divrei ha-Yamim* (Chronicle of the Days), now lost.

2. See Chajes, "Accounting for the Self: Preliminary Generic-Historical Reflections on Early

of Kabbalah has been that, unlike counterparts in other religious traditions, Jewish mystics deliberately avoided extended first-person rhetoric and autobiographical testimony regarding the personal nature of their spiritual lives.[3] This generalization is certainly justified with regard to the vast majority of kabbalistic literature, where experiential dimensions are most often expressed through the exegesis of paradigmatic moments in Scripture (e.g., divine revelation to the patriarchs, Moses, and other biblical prophets) or through a pedagogical rhetoric aimed at the instruction of novice readers in kabbalistic practice. In the case of the latter, the rhetoric of prescription—while not confessional—proves to be highly revealing of the experiences and personal practices *of the one who prescribes*.[4] Nevertheless, the broader characterization of Jewish mystical literature as decidedly and vigorously nonautobiographical is in need of significant qualification and adjustment, insofar as we must account for the good number of kabbalists who went against the grain and engaged in just such a testimonial discourse.[5] These cases provide rare opportunities for the historian of Jewish mysticism to view the life of mystical experience through the lens of intimate self-awareness on the part of the subjects. A comprehensive inquiry into the contours and features of this autobiographical genre will ultimately be necessary for a broad and balanced assessment of Jewish mystical literature and practice.[6]

Modern Jewish Egodocuments," p. 3. An extended analysis of early modern autobiography is presented in Moseley, *Being for Myself Alone: Origins of Jewish Autobiography*, pp. 82–193.

3. See Scholem, *Major Trends in Jewish Mysticism*, pp. 14–17, 38. On the autobiographical dimensions of Jewish mystical literature, see *Jewish Mystical Testimonies*, ed. Jacobs, pp. 3–19, as well as Idel, "Preface," pp. xv–xx, and Faierstein, "Translator's Introduction," pp. 3–39, in *Jewish Mystical Autobiographies*, trans. Faierstein. See also comments and bibliographic references in Wolfson, *Through a Speculum That Shines*, pp. 331–332 (esp. n. 21). And for an annotated translation and study of Abraham Yagel's *Gei Ḥizayon*, see Yagel, *A Valley of Vision: The Heavenly Journey of Abraham ben Ḥananiah Yagel*, trans. Ruderman. See, in particular, pp. 23–27, for Ruderman's reflections on the topos of early modern Jewish autobiography.

4. On the contemplative techniques discernible in Isaac of Akko's writing, see also Chapter 7 ("Techniques of Mystical Contemplation").

5. Some representative examples of this genre (aside from Isaac of Akko's *'Oẓar Ḥayyim*) include Abraham Abulafia's *'Oẓar 'Eden Ganuz*; Natan ben Sa'adya's *Sha'arei Ẓedeq*; selections from Shem Ṭov Ibn Ga'on's *Keter Shem Ṭov* and *Baddei ha-'Aron*; Ḥayyim Vital's *Sefer ha-Ḥezyonot*; Yosef Karo's *Maggid Mesharim*; Elazar Azikri's *Milei de-Shemaya*; and Moshe Cordovero's *Sefer Gerushin*.

6. I plan to deal with this subject in much greater detail in a future study.

How did Isaac of Akko understand the moment of insight into kabbalistic meaning, and what were the lived frameworks for attaining such insight? What was his self-perception of his own creative process? Here, the kabbalist passes from one state of knowing to another, morphing from eclectic receiver to individual transmitter and teacher. It is in these moments, which form the core of Isaac's autobiographical reflection in *'Oẓar Ḥayyim,* that the mystic "sees the secret" of the scriptural and liturgical texts—that original insight into metaphysical reality is attained.

Waking from Sleep

Historians of religion have long been attuned to the manner in which religious people of diverse cultural backgrounds have understood sleep to be a particularly propitious time for divine revelation and prophetic inspiration. Dreams were believed to be portals of otherworldly perception, windows onto a hidden divine truth, forecasting future events. Those mysteries of the unconscious have long held a deep fascination for the religious mind, and the interpretation of the putatively symbolic content of dream-visions (seen from the reflective vantage point of the waking state) has constituted a cross-cultural and elemental form of religious practice and creativity.[7] The experiential phenomenon that I wish to explore in this section is undoubtedly anchored in a perception of the illuminative power of sleep, but is less concerned with the state of sleep itself (and the dreams that occur therein) than it is oriented around *emergence from sleep*—the hermeneutic discovery that takes place upon traversing the mental threshold from slumber into wakefulness. For while autobiographical reports about sleep and insight abound in *'Oẓar Ḥayyim*, they only center upon the event of dreaming to a minor degree. Instead, the focus of Isaac's discourse of insight concerns the moment of waking from the

7. This phenomenon has stimulated a rather extensive scholarly literature, but the following works are representative: Oppenheim, "The Interpretation of Dreams in the Ancient Near East"; Niehoff, "A Dream Which Is Not Interpreted Is Like a Letter Which Is Not Read"; Kalmin, "Dreams and Dream Interpreters"; Shulman and Stroumsa, eds., *Dream Cultures: Explorations in the Comparative History of Dreaming*.

unconscious state, that liminal condition in which the human mind crosses from one boundary of awareness to another. The preponderance of textual evidence seems to indicate that this kabbalist experienced the passage from sleep to waking as a powerful stimulus for his hermeneutic insight and creative perception.

This causal relationship between waking up and attaining new hermeneutic insight is manifested through two recurring expressions in Isaac's *'Oẓar Ḥayyim*: (1) "I awoke from my sleep and I saw the secret of . . ." (הקיצותי משנתי וראיתי סוד), and (2) "in a state of being asleep and yet not asleep I saw the secret of . . ." (בנים ולא נים ראיתי סוד). Both of these formulations emphasize the stimulating power of the moment of waking, though each with notably different experiential nuance. While the former (הקיצותי משנתי) serves as a standard refrain to indicate a general emergence from sleep, the latter (בנים ולא נים) evokes a state of semiconsciousness, of a liminal mode in which the kabbalist reports himself to be betwixt and between[8] these two baseline conditions of mind and perception—both asleep and not asleep, awake and not awake.[9] There are a great many cases in which the two forms are combined—a characterization of the semiconscious (or half-asleep) state that often occurred precisely at the moment of waking.

It should be noted at the outset that Isaac of Akko's experience of *nim ve-lo nim* (the condition of being asleep but not asleep) as a state of mind conducive to attaining hermeneutic insight appears to have been consciously inspired by the reported practice of the great eleventh-century Muslim philosopher Avicenna.[10] This report clarifies Isaac's foundational assumption that exegetical quandaries are often

8. Here I have borrowed the anthropological terminology employed by Victor Turner in his highly influential studies of the "liminoid phenomenon" in religious practice (see, e.g., V. Turner and E. Turner, *Image and Pilgrimage in Christian Culture: Anthropological Perspectives*, pp. 1–39).

9. The particular phraseology of נים ולא נים is derived from a usage in earlier rabbinic sources, where the characterization is coupled with תיר ולא תיר (awake and yet not awake), both of which convey essentially the same meaning: a state of being half-asleep or half-awake. See its use in BT *Pesaḥim*, fol. 120b; *Ta'anit*, fol. 12b; *Megilah*, fol. 18b; *Yevamot*, fol. 54a; *Niddah*, fol. 63a.

10. For mention of this practice in the larger context of Avicenna's life, see Goodman, *Avicenna*, p. 14. For reference to this phenomenon as it relates to Isaac's hermeneutical system and conception of prophetic experience, see Huss, "NiSAN—The Wife of the Infinite," p. 162.

best solved in a state of sleep (i.e., dreaming) or, more often, in the semi-conscious state that obtains between full sleep and full waking. In Isaac's words:

> ושמעתי שאחד מגדולי הרוחניים מן חכמי המחקר שכאשר יקשה לו דבר שלא יוכל להולמו ולהקיפו בשכלו יעמוד וישתה כוס יין טוב ויישן במחשבת שכלו על הדבר ההוא ובנים ולא נים ישכילהו ויעמוד ויכתבהו.

> I heard [the following about] one of the great spiritual [masters] from among the Sages of Investigation [i.e., philosophy]: whenever he would be challenged by a matter that he could not grasp and wrap his mind around, he would stand and drink a cup of good wine and sleep thinking the matter over in his mind. And in [the state of being] asleep but not asleep [*nim ve-lo nim*] he would comprehend it, and he would then stand up and write it down.[11]

That which is elusive and incomprehensible in the ordinary waking state is therefore opened to the mind through the processes of sleep and semiconsciousness. *Nim ve-lo nim* is construed to be a time of insight and hermeneutic discovery—a state in which the mind becomes capable of heightened understanding by virtue of its position between the ordinary planes of consciousness. The difficult matter is contemplated during the sleeping state—a practice that attributes a higher order of cognitive clarity to the unconscious condition of the mind—and it would appear that final and complete understanding is only achieved once the individual passes into the border zone between sleep and waking, the state of *nim ve-lo nim*. It is precisely this conception of *nim ve-lo nim*—here attributed indirectly to Avicenna[12]—that is operative in Isaac of

---

11. Isaac of Akko, *'Oẓar Ḥayyim*, fol. 36a.

12. Despite the fact that the tradition reported by Isaac of Akko seems to allude to Avicenna, the actual testimonial report recorded in Avicenna's autobiography tells of a somewhat different practice: "At night I would return home, set out a lamp before me, and devote myself to reading and writing. Whenever sleep overcame me or I became conscious of weakening, I would turn aside to drink a cup of wine, so that my strength would return to me. Then I would return to reading. And whenever sleep seized me I would see those very problems in my dream; and many questions became clear to me in my sleep" (Gohlman, *The Life of Ibn Sina*, pp. 29–31). Whereas the rendition offered by Isaac of Akko implies that the wine was imbibed in order to induce a state of sleep that would in turn yield dream insight into the conceptual problem at hand, Avicenna's words depict wine in its stimulating and arousing capacity—giving the philosopher renewed mental energy and seemingly dissociated from the sleep that would come later. Moreover, we do not encounter mention of a semiconscious

Akko's recurrent use of the expression elsewhere in his text. Though he rarely articulates the transition from perplexity to comprehension in as overt a manner as cited above with regard to Avicenna, I contend that the vast majority of Isaac's uses of this phrase in *'Oẓar Ḥayyim* come to evoke just such a mental transformation and the resolution of interpretive difficulty.

So that we may follow the experiential progression from dreaming to the waking state, and that we may properly assess the relation between states of consciousness and new interpretive creativity, let us begin with consideration of Isaac's dream reports in *'Oẓar Ḥayyim*. For despite the aforementioned fact that the number of dream reports in Isaac's writing are markedly disproportionate to the number of cases in which waking from sleep is mentioned as a stimulative phenomenon in and of itself, the correlation of dreams to new insight is best seen as part of the same experiential continuum that characterizes the waking and *nim ve-lo nim* states. The following case combines all three modes—the report of a dream's content, waking to interpretive insight into the dream, and the unique exegetical "seeing" that occurs in the liminal state of *nim ve-lo nim*:

> I, the young one,[13] was still sleeping in my bed, and I dreamed a dream [עוד אני הצעיר ישן במטתי וחלמתי חלום]. And behold [in this dream] Abba Mari of blessed memory[14] gave me a pitcher of clear white glass filled with red wine, and there was a spout extending from it. From the opening of this spout I drank all of the wine, and it pleased me greatly [וערב לי מאד]. . . . After I drank the wine [in the dream], I awoke from my sleep [הקיצותי משנתי] and explained [the dream] as follows: the wine is nothing other than wisdom [אין יין זה אלא חכמה]. For the Holy One

state—a *nim ve-lo nim* condition. Regardless of these discrepancies, however, it is indeed sleep and dream that provide the desired clarity and insight into perplexities that the philosopher seeks. That is the key feature for understanding Isaac of Akko's practice and framing of insight. Fresh understanding and interpretive clarity emerge either in the dream state or in the liminal time threshold between sleep and waking. Comprehension that is apparently impossible in the waking state becomes possible in the shifting planes of the subconscious.

13. As elsewhere, the term צעיר here denotes self-effacement, rather than an actual indication of age.

14. This is most probably a reference to Abba Mari of Lunel, a close associate of Solomon Ibn Adret's (and thus the historical connection to Isaac of Akko) as well as a staunch opponent of the Maimonidean tradition.

> blessed be He gives wisdom to all the children of Israel so that they may worship Him [שיתן הקב"ה חכמה לכל בני ישראל לעבודתו]—and to me, His servant, the son of His maidservant, among them [ולי אני עבדו בן אמתו בכללם]. As it is written [Prov. 9:5]: "Come, eat my bread and drink the wine that I have mixed [לכו לחמו בלחמי ושתו ביין מסכתי]." And I read good verses about wine [וקראתי פסוקים טובים על היין] that are recorded in the books of Proverbs, Psalms, and the Song of Songs.[15]

It is the hypostatized Lady Wisdom of Proverbs 8 and 9 who utters this invitation to eat and drink from the food and wine that she has prepared. And it is on the basis of this contextual association that Isaac interprets his dream. To drink the wine symbolizes the imbibing of divine wisdom (the wine that Wisdom has mixed), of ingesting a God-given ability to engage in worship of that deity. In this manner, the contents of dream consciousness are read as a figurative and allusive text; the details of the subconscious point the way to a deeper meaning that the dreamer can only fully understand and interpret from the vantage point of the waking state. This passage in *'Oẓar Ḥayyim* then continues to narrate, in an autobiographical fashion, the staccato rhythm of Isaac's sleep cycle and its relationship to his attainment of hermeneutic clarity:

> I fell asleep again. Then I awoke from my sleep, and in my mouth was the verse [וישנתי עוד והקיצותי משנתי ובפי פסוק] [Ps. 115:16]: "The heavens [השמים] belong to the Lord [YHVH], but the earth [ארץ] He gave over to humans." And in the state of being asleep but not asleep [*nim ve-lo nim*], I saw that the meaning of this verse is that . . . the "heavens" allude to the *muskalot* [the intelligible/spiritual dimensions] . . . and the "earth" alludes to the corporeal, sensate dimensions [ובנים ולא נים ראיתי שענין פסוק זה . . . השמים ירמוז למושכלות והארץ ירמוז למורגשות העפריות הגופניות].[16]

Isaac repeatedly wakes from his sleep with new interpretive insight—sometimes through direct extrapolation from his dream-content, and at other times in a creative moment that is facilitated by the experience of passing through distinct domains of consciousness. Notably, it is in the climactic and liminal state of *nim ve-lo nim* (climactic because it follows

15. Isaac of Akko, *'Oẓar Ḥayyim*, fol. 158b.

16. Ibid., fols. 158b–159a.

on the heels of a clear sequence: dreaming; then a waking interpretation of the dream; return to sleep; and waking yet again to contemplate a particular verse) that Isaac frames the final exegetical association of שמים and ארץ (heaven and earth) to מושכלות and מורגשות (the intellective and the material/sensate), respectively. Both the remembrance of symbolically rich dreams and the threshold of emergence from the unconscious state proved to be particularly creative times for this kabbalist.

Yet in addition to the processes of hermeneutic insight, we also learn a great deal about autobiographical expression and the dynamics of self-representation. Isaac of Akko considered his experiences (be they in dreams or while awake) to be openings into a symbolic unveiling of an incessantly meaningful reality, and he often embeds such reports in revealing testimonies about his own life story:

> Close to dawn I dreamt a dream, and behold my mother was seated to my left, and my brother Rabbi Menaḥem of blessed memory was seated to my right, and I was seated between them chanting the benediction for the *Haftarah* that the *maftir* recites before beginning the *Haftarah*. And I chanted it with the melody of the Land of Israel. And after I chanted it I saw the secret of it according to the way of proper truth [על דרך האמת הנכונה].[17]

Isaac then proceeds to explain the symbolic sefirotic associations that he has discerned from the *Haftarah* benediction . . . הבוחר בתורה ובמשה עבדו. Having established these, he concludes with the remark: "And with that I awoke from my sleep very happy [ובזה הקיצותי משנתי שמח מאד]." This text is remarkable on many levels, not least of which is the striking fact that in Isaac's dream, he sees himself chanting the *Haftarah* benediction while seated beside a woman—his mother. Given the sociological implausibility of such a ritual practice (unless, of course, it was a recitation removed from the public ritual context), the dream scene appears instead to represent an odd creation of the retrospective and fantastic imagination. What is more, we learn that Isaac had a brother named Menaḥem, and that this brother was already deceased at the time of Isaac's composition of *'Oẓar Ḥayyim*. These historical matters aside, however, the passage further reflects the manner in which this kabbalist arrived at new

17. Ibid., fol. 40b.

insights; how fresh symbolic associations emerge through ritual performance (though it is critical to emphasize that here we are speaking of a ritual performance that is dreamed); and how dream itself serves as a stimulus for the process of kabbalistic insight.

Isaac's discourse on insight and creativity—his testimonial reports regarding his own hermeneutic process—stands in marked contrast to the emphasis on proof texts and proof persons for the assertion of interpretive legitimacy documented above, and aligns well with Isaac's competing desire to posit his own authenticity as a kabbalistic innovator. The drama of sleep, dream, and waking—the prevalent autobiographical refrain regarding the eruption of insight and exegetical understanding in the border zones of consciousness—constitutes a distinct conception of the self and the individuality of the creative process. Extricated (at least to a large extent) from the authenticating discourse of reception, the kabbalist as innovator and transmitter rises to the foreground of the text—indeed, the image and language of the self assumes a prominence otherwise obscured by the culture of tradition (and thus more akin to the aforementioned method of *sevara'* as opposed to *qabbalah*). Yet if an interpretation of the symbolically laden dream "text" still preserves some of the character of reception and authoritative derivation, the refrain of waking as an experiential topos in and of itself reflects a far greater validation of the eruption of originality and the legitimacy of an individually innovated transmission. Given the frequency with which Isaac of Akko reports such experiences of insight upon waking, we may justifiably view these moments as crucial points of orientation in his discernment and construction of meaning—in the structure and unfolding of his hermeneutic creativity. Consider the following representative cases:

1. "And with that I awoke from my sleep very happy. I returned again to my sleep a third time, and after that I awoke and saw the secret of . . . [ובזה הקיצותי עוד מנמנומי שמח מאד מאד ושבתי עוד לשנתי פעם ג' . . . ואח"כ הקיצותי וראיתי סוד]."[18]
2. "I awoke from my sleep, and suddenly I saw a wondrous [meaning] . . . [הקיצותי משנתי ופתאום ראיתי פלא . . .]."[19]

18. Ibid., fol. 80b.

19. Ibid., fol. 84a.

3. "I, the young one, Isaac of Akko, awoke from my sleep [הקיצותי משנתי], and suddenly I saw the secret [ופתאום ראיתי סוד] of the statement of our Rabbis of blessed memory, that while Moses our master was writing down the Torah, he saw it written in the air of the Heavens, black fire upon white fire."[20]
4. "I awoke from my sleep, and I was reading . . . and in the state of being asleep but not asleep I saw . . . [. . . הקיצותי משנתי ואני קורא . . . ובנים ולא נים ראיתי]."[21]
5. "And with that I awoke from my sleep very happy, and I was reading . . . I returned to my sleep, and in the state of being asleep but not asleep [בנים ולא נים] I further saw [the following hint] . . . And with that I awoke from my sleep a second time. I contemplated [the following] two words, and I saw their secret according to the four ways of NiSAN."[22]
6. "Close to dawn, in the state of being asleep but not asleep, I saw a secret pertaining to the human soul [סמוך לשחר בנים ולא נים ראיתי סוד בנפש האדם]."[23]
7. "In the state of being asleep but not asleep, I saw the secret of . . . [. . . בנים ולא נים ראיתי סוד]."[24]

As these and other examples amply demonstrate, Isaac of Akko drew a direct line of correlation—even causation—between the experience of rising from sleep consciousness and the hermeneutic act of "seeing the secret." To be sure, this rhetoric of "seeing" is a standard figure of speech and should not be overemphasized. Nevertheless, the recurrent language reflects the very texture of this experience—the clear connection between an awakening of exegetical in-*sight* and the awakening of consciousness from the state of sleep. The function of the mental condition of נים ולא נים as a frame (even stimulus) for the climax of hermeneutic discovery underscores this phenomenon in *'Ozar Ḥayyim*. For it is at the crossroads of conscious states that the act of "seeing into" symbolic meaning takes place in this work—reflected by a cluster of core terms

20. Ibid., fol. 106b. See *Midrash Tanḥuma', parashat bereishit*, § 1; JT *Sheqalim*, fol. 25b.

21. Ibid., fol. 110b.

22. Ibid., fols. 122b–123a. See Chapter 1 of this book for an explanation of the acronym NiSAN and for reference to the work of Boaz Huss on this exegetical system.

23. Ibid., fol. 123a.

24. Ibid., fol. 100b.

that serve as the rhetorical markers of an experiential process and cyclical pattern.

Consider one final example of this topos—a case in which the נים ולא נים state of mind is linked not only to the hermeneutical process of symbolic insight, but also to a powerful visual experience aroused within the imagination of the kabbalist. In view of the fascinating experiential portrait presented in this passage, I have chosen to translate it here in full:[25]

> (A) During the third watch of the night,[26] asleep but not asleep, I saw the house in which I was sleeping to be filled with a very sweet and pleasing light [עוד במשמרה שלישית בנים ולא נים ראיתי הבית אשר אני ישן בו מלא אור מתוק ערב מאד]. And this light was not like the light that comes from the sun, but it was like the light of day, the light of dawn just before the sun shines [כי לא היה אור זה כאור הבא מהשמש אבל היה אור כאור היום שהוא אור השחר טרם יזרח השמש].
>
> (B) This light stood before me for something like a third of an hour, and I hurried to open my eyes to see if dawn had risen or not, [to see whether it was time] to get up to pray [ועמד לפני אור זה כמו שליש שעה ומהרתי לפתוח את עיני לראות אם עלה השחר אם לא למען אקום להתפלל]. I saw that it was still night, and I returned to my sleep very happy [וראיתי כי עדיין הוא לילה ושבתי לשינתי שמח מאד].
>
> (C) [Subsequently], after I arose from my bed to pray, I suddenly saw a secret pertaining to the letter *alef* that is written in Assyrian script [ואחרי קמתי ממטתי להתפלל ראיתי פתאום סוד באות האלף הנכתב כתב אשורי]. [The form of the *alef* in Assyrian script] is a clear proof for the unity and simplicity and eternity of the Singular Master, blessed be the name of His glorious kingdom for ever and ever, for He has no beginning and He has no end, and He has no place, for He is the Place for everything [שהוא ראייה ברורה על ייחודו ופשיטותו וקדמותו של האדון היחיד בשכמל"ו

25. Ibid., fol. 197a.

26. This temporal demarcation, and its significance for the ritual enactment of prayer and the study of Torah, is discussed in a foundational way in BT *Berakhot*, fols. 3a–3b. Dimensions of this theme of midnight and predawn study and devotion (as used later on in the *Zohar*) have been considered at some length in Wolfson, "Forms of Visionary Ascent as Ecstatic Experience in the Zoharic Literature." For reflection on a zoharic text (*Zohar* 3:166b) that exemplifies the predawn moment of illumination and revelation, see E. Fishbane, "Tears of Disclosure: The Role of Weeping in Zoharic Narrative," pp. 42–46.

> [שאין לו ראשית ואין לו אחרית ואין לו מקום כי הוא מקום לכל]. . . . The *alef* is simple with complete simplicity, without any composite [multiplicity whatsoever] [שהאלף הוא פשוט בתכלית הפשיטות בלי שום הרכבה בעולם].

In an extraordinary confessional form, Isaac here reports a particular event of ocular sensation in consciousness that ultimately leads (following a series of changing states of sleep and waking) to an insight concerning the symbolic relationship between the letter *alef* and the *'Ein-Sof* (possibly also including *Keter*).[27] His reference to the אדון היחיד is a standard term for the *'Ein-Sof* in *'Oẓar Ḥayyim*,[28] and the characterization of *'Ein-Sof* as one, simple, and eternal (ייחודו ופשיטותו וקדמותו) most certainly reflects the influence of Neoplatonic metaphysics.[29] In breaking up the manuscript text into parts *A*, *B*, and *C*, I wish to underscore a discernable experiential progression, one that is tied directly to the rhythms of sleep and waking. In section *A*, we find: (1) testimonial reflection that Isaac was in a state of semi-consciousness (נים ולא נים) when he had the experience; (2) a vision of light that is pleasurable to the mystic's senses; (3) a light that appears to be indirect, mysterious, and dim—certainly not bright ("the light of dawn just before the sun shines"). Section *B* reveals the kabbalist to be in a state of sensory confusion—unsure whether the light he sees is the natural light of daybreak (which would necessitate waking to recite the morning prayers) or if it is (as it indeed turns out to be) a light conjured up within the semiconscious imagination. Isaac does not indicate that he was sleeping and dreaming at the time of this light vision; on the contrary, he tells us that he was in the liminal state of נים ולא נים. The נים ולא נים condition is therefore one that is experienced with the eyes closed (thus his need to say: "I hurried to open my eyes to see if dawn had risen or not"), but nevertheless with enough waking consciousness to feel the impulse to open his eyes in anticipation of the morning prayers. We therefore learn that Isaac experienced an

---

27. In some earlier kabbalistic literature, the letter *alef* is associated with *Keter*—the first *sefirah*. See Isaac's own *Me'irat 'Einayim*, p. 213; Asher ben David's *Sefer ha-Yiḥud* (*R. Asher ben David*, p. 106); *Bahir*, p. 181 (§ 96).

28. Isaac of Akko, *'Oẓar Ḥayyim*, fols. 44b, 29b, 70b, 129a.

29. See Hyman, "From What Is One and Simple."

unusual state of consciousness at this time—one in which the pleasurable light (resembling pre-dawn natural light) was visualized for approximately twenty minutes while the kabbalist remained in the mysterious and ambiguous border zone between sleep and waking. The light that he sees in his semi-conscious state is consequently viewed in the interior eye of meditative and imaginal construction, thereby presenting the reader with the experiential distinction between vision as veridical sensation, on the one hand, and vision as docetic or constructed sensation, on the other.[30] It is a sensory experience of the imagination (that is, the objective reality in which he was situated was actually nocturnal and dark), and it should be underscored that the mystical experience here is marked by the degree to which it gives the mystic great pleasure and delight (אור מתוק ערב מאד . . . וראיתי כי עדיין הוא לילה ושבתי לשינתי שמח מאד). What is more, that sustained moment of sensory pleasure appears ultimately to engender a hermeneutical association and conclusion upon the awakening to full consciousness. Based on the progression of the text (and placed within the larger phenomenology of נים ולא נים states in Isaac's writing), the reader of this autobiographical account can fairly assume that the insight into *'Ein-Sof* that occurs upon Isaac's final waking from sleep (section *C*) is the consequence and culmination of his illuminative experiences during the night—one that is framed within the experience of passing from נים ולא נים into waking (to see that it was still night), into further sleep, and into waking again. Though autobiographical reports of this kind are relatively rare in Jewish literature, it should be noted that similar visions of light are a common feature of mystical experience across the historical spectrum of Judaism, and across the divides of several

30. In making use of the term "imaginal" in this context (as well as my allusion to the veridical/docetic distinction in discussions of sensory mystical experience), I am building on the insights of Elliot R. Wolfson in his explication of the imaginal divine body of contemplative visualization. The reality that is seen in the interior domain of consciousness—distinct from the objects that are seen externally with the physical eyes of sensation—is understood to be held within the frame of human imagination and mind, while simultaneously reaching the kabbalist as a divine revelation of that which cannot be viewed directly with the physical eye. Wolfson has developed these issues in sophisticated detail in his *Through a Speculum That Shines*, and most recently in an article entitled "Iconicity of the Text: Reification of the Idolatrous Impulse of Zoharic Kabbalah." See esp. pp. 218–221.

different religious traditions.[31] Indeed, one contemporary scholar of mysticism has observed the manner in which many different mystics and practitioners of meditation report seeing a white light illumined in the mind's eye just after a period of intense meditative practice.[32]

The Performance of Ritual

As outlined above, self-conscious reflection on the ways and processes of his own hermeneutic creativity forms the core of Isaac's fragmented autobiographical discourse. In assessing the topography of this genre in *'Oẓar Ḥayyim,* we do not encounter a sustained and linear autobiographical narrative about the kabbalist's life. Such is likely what we have lost in the text of *Divrei ha-Yamim* that did not survive the unfortunate vicissitudes of manuscript history. Instead, in the voluminous pages of *'Oẓar Ḥayyim*, we catch brief glimpses of a kabbalist ruminating in the first-person voice about the symbolic meaning that he found to be everywhere present, reporting the modalities by which he attained moments of exegetical clarity. After the dominance of the waking topos, we find abundant reports about the insight achieved through the daily acts of ritual performance, and the manner in which the prescribed patterns of sacred behavior serve as one of the foundations for hermeneutical creativity. In a wide range of cases, Isaac of Akko gives autobiographical testimony to the symbolic meanings and interpretive correlations that were made manifest to him through the enactment of a particular ritual—a direct link thereby established between the performative dimension and the cognitive-creative process. Indeed, it is through such confessional moments that the historian may begin to appreciate the degree to which kabbalistic creativity was rooted in the lived and daily experience of the mystic. These autobiographical reports (however fragmentary they might be) ultimately reveal the manner in which the life of a kabbalist (and here

31. See the observations and references provided by Wolfson, *Through a Speculum That Shines*, pp. 270–288 (a section on the ontology of light and mystical vision). On the presence of this phenomenon in other mystical traditions, see the representative remarks of Hollenback, *Mysticism: Experience, Response, and Empowerment*, pp. 44–48, 56–74, and McGinn, *The Growth of Mysticism*, pp. 101–105.

32. See Forman, *Mysticism, Mind, Consciousness*, pp. 48–49.

we might justly extend this generalization to include a broad array of medieval Jewish mystics) is guided by an enduring search for the patterns of interpretive correlation between the upper and lower worlds—a path of discovery that encompasses multiple realms of his daily routine. What is more, the report of lived experience as the frame for new hermeneutic insight implies a bold validation of the individual kabbalist as authoritative interpreter—a model that is to be contrasted with the legitimacy derived from existing channels of reception and tradition. For while the ascription of symbolic meaning to the life of *mizṿot* may be a commonplace in kabbalistic literature, the use of an autobiographical discourse to record the self-conscious process by which such associations were made (and in which the flashes of interpretive creativity erupted in the vigilant mind of the kabbalist) is far more rare and notable. Consider the following array of pertinent evidence from *'Oẓar Ḥayyim*:

1. "On the evening of Shabbat I was praying [the words], 'You have sanctified the seventh day' [בעודי מתפלל ליל שבת אתה קדשת את יום השביעי], and I saw [וראיתי] that this 'seventh day' is surely *Tzedeq* [i.e., the *sefirah Shekhinah*]."[33]
2. "I was reciting [the prayer] *nishmat kol ḥai* during the daytime Shabbat [service]. I said [the words] *yishtabaḥ shimkha* ['may Your name be praised'] . . . and I suddenly saw [וראיתי פתאום] that the word . . . *yishtabaḥ* hints at [the *sefirah*] *Keter*, and [the word] *shimkha* hints at *Tif'eret*."[34]
3. "I was praying seated, and I was saying [the words][35] 'they are all

33. Isaac of Akko, *'Oẓar Ḥayyim*, fol. 38a. She (*Shekhinah*) is the seventh cosmic day, the Sabbath into which all the other days flow.

34. Ibid., fols. 42a–42b. Issac then goes on to explain the special correlation that exist between these two *sefirot*. Because the flow of divine emanation moves so powerfully upward from *Tif'eret* to *Keter*, and then down again, the channels (*ẓinorot*) between these two *sefirot* of the central column remain direct and open, and they are filled with the flow of *raḥamim* (compassion, grace, and love [ישרים ופתוחים ומתמלאים שפע רחמים]). The liturgical phrase ישתבך שמך (may Your name be praised) is therefore read in the following symbolic (and dynamic) manner: the devotee intends that the *sefirah Tif'eret* (which is symbolically correlated to the divine name—שמך) be elevated in praise (ישתבח) all the way up to the highest *sefirah* (*Keter*). It is important to emphasize that this theological insight and contemplative consciousness is attained *through the enactment* of the devotional ritual, thus binding the exegetical insight to the performative act and process of liturgical prayer.

35. Here Isaac refers to the words used to characterize the celestial angels, a passage recited during the morning service shortly before the recitation of the *Shema*.

beloved, they are all pure, they are all mighty' [כלם אהובים כולם ברורים כלם גבורים]. I saw that the word אהובים [beloved] hints at [the *sefirah*] *Gedulah*, insofar as they [the angels] are a chariot for the *gedulah* [the greatness] of the seed of Abraham, 'My beloved.'"[36]

4. "While I was in the synagogue reciting the mishnah *'elu devarim she-'ein lahem shi'ur* [בעודי קורא בבית הכנסת משנת אלו דברים שאין להם שיעור] . . . [37] I saw in these ten[38] the secret of the ten *sefirot belimah* [ראיתי בעשרה אלה סוד עס"ב]."[39]
5. "While I was in the synagogue reciting the *'Aleinu le-shabeiaḥ* [prayer], I saw in it a meaning according to the way of truth that was correct in my eyes . . . [עוד ואני קורא בבית הכנסת עלינו לשבח ראיתי בו פירוש על דרך האמת ישר בעיני]."[40]
6. "While I was still sitting at the table, and while I was still reciting the blessing after the meal [ברכת המזון], I saw a secret in [the words] 'blessed is He and blessed is His name' [ראיתי סוד בברוך הוא וברוך שמו] . . . [41] [And that secret] is that the first [mention of the word] ברוך [signifies] a fountain, like a wellspring of flowing living waters that never runs dry. . . . [42] The second [mention of the word] ברוך . . . hints at the drawing down of the flow of blessing [ברכה] from the first blessing [ברוך]."[43]

---

36. Ibid., fol. 43a. Though scholars of this literature may recognize the underlying symbolic nuances here, I shall unpack the density of this language for the nonspecialist reader. In the lexicon of kabbalistic symbolism, the word *'ahavah* (love) correlates to the *sefirah Ḥesed/Gedulah* (the Right Side of the inner divine balance, the force of love and compassion vis-à-vis the lower realms), which in turn corresponds to the biblical figure Abraham. These angels are a "chariot" (i.e., a receiver, a vessel) for the emanational flow extending from the divine *sefirah Ḥesed*. Isaac reads the term *berurim* as a cognomen for *Tif'eret*—the balance point between *Ḥesed* and *Gevurah*, and the apparent symbolic reason for its position between the phrases *'ahuvim* and *gibborim*. The three characterizations of the angels thus correlate to the second triad of the sefirotic structure (*'ahuvim* = *Ḥesed*; *berurim* = *Tif'eret*; *gibborim* = *Gevurah*) insofar as different sets of angels function as the "chariot" for different sefirotic forces.

37. M. *Pe'ah* 1: 1.

38. The ten ethical virtues listed in this *mishnah*.

39. Isaac of Akko, *'Oẓar Ḥayyim*, fol. 47a. The symbolic associations triggered by this recitation of the *'elu devarim* passage continue on for some length.

40. Ibid., fols. 47b–48a. As in other instances, the term דרך האמת (way of truth) is a standard reference to the exegetical application of sefirotic symbolism.

41. One of the opening lines of the blessing after the meal.

42. Isaac goes on to make it quite clear that this fountain of living waters is a symbol for the *'Ein-Sof*.

43. That is to say, the attraction of the flow of emanation (referred to as the "flow of bless-

7. "On that day I was sitting [attending a] *berit milah*, and I suddenly saw a secret [pertaining to that ritual], and my heart rejoiced greatly."[44]

Though there are a good many other such examples that could be adduced, these few instances will suffice to construct a portrait of a particular type of creative experience—a convergence between the performative dimension of ritual and the moment of hermeneutical clarity when the devotee passes from one state of knowing and understanding to another, when the hidden divine meaning suddenly becomes visible in the mind's eye. Isaac's representation of himself to the reader—a glimpse of autobiographical construction—is partially fashioned through a recounting of those moments when ritual enactment provides the stimulus for the unveiling of the secret to the interpreter's gaze. Through the confessional rhetoric of these passages, we are able to see the manner in which this kabbalist experienced his regular practice of the *miẓvot* (and particularly the devotional ritual of prayer) with close attentive regard to the deeper divine meanings understood to be latent within the liturgical text. Through such textual evidence, we further appreciate the degree of self-awareness and testimonial reflection that this kabbalist maintained with respect to his daily life as a mystic in perpetual search for the concealed secrets of divine truth.

Encounters with the Natural World

Let me now highlight one final modality of the relation between creative process and autobiographical construction in *'Oẓar Ḥayyim*. In addition to the stimulative power associated with waking from sleep and ritual practice, Isaac of Akko frequently frames new interpretive insight as the

---

ing," the שפע ברכה) from *'Ein-Sof* down through the *sefirot*. See Isaac of Akko, *'Oẓar Ḥayyim*, fols. 57a–57b. It may be noted here that earlier kabbalistic sources fashion a play on the words ברכה (blessing) and בריכה (pool of water), thereby underscoring a figuration of Blessing as an ontological flow of divine emanation—one that is conflated with the metonym of water, of the rush of spring streams and their ultimate collection in the lower pool that receives. See the articulation of this theme in ʿAzriel of Gerona, *Perush ha-'Aggadot*, pp. 39–40.

44. Isaac of Akko, *'Oẓar Ḥayyim*, fol. 124a. Isaac then continues to offer a kabbalistic-symbolic interpretation of the ritual of circumcision.

product of an encounter with the natural world—thereby viewing the created realm as alive with symbolic traces of the divine, as filled with hidden markers of the truths of metaphysical reality. The sight of the physical eyes, engaged with the phenomena of the natural world, reads earthly reality as a symbolic text, an interpretive cipher for the deep structures of the divine.[45] It is in this manner that the kabbalist also "sees the secret" of the *sefirot* from out of his physical experience, and his discourse of autobiographical reflection and self-representation is structured accordingly. Consider the following evidence from *'Oẓar Ḥayyim*:

> עוד ביום זה נסמכתי על גדר גן נאה וראיתי לפני אילן פרחים לבנים אשר ריחם נודף טוב. יקראו שמם באל ערבי אל יאסמין, ידמו לעלה ורדים שושנים לבנים אלא שמספר עלי השושן שהוא הורד ששה ושל יאסמין חמשה. וכשם שאמ' המקובל ר' עזרא שהורד נקרא שושן ע"ש ששה, כך אני אומר שאל יאסמין נקרא בלשון הקדש חבצלת ע"ש חמשה שראשית מלת חמשה ח"ת וראשית מלת חבצלת ח"ת. השתכלתי במהות צבעו ובמהות עלי בדיו, ר"ל ענפיו, וראיתי בהם רמז לעס"ב.

> On that same day, I was leaning against the fence of a beautiful garden, and I saw before me a tree of white flowers that gave off a pleasant smell. In Arabic [these flowers] are called by the name *al-yasmin* [jasmine], and they resemble the petals of white lilies, except for the fact that the number of petals on a lily are six, and the jasmine [flower] has [only] five. And just as the kabbalist Rabbi Ezra said that the lily is called *shoshan* because of its six [*shishah*] petals,[46] so too I say that *al-yasmin* is called *ḥavaẓelet* in the holy language because of its five petals. For the word *hamishah* [five] begins with the letter *het*, and the word *ḥavaẓelet* begins with the letter *het*. I contemplated the essence of its color and the essence of its petals, and I saw in them a hint to the ten *sefirot belimah*.[47]

---

45. This problem has also been analyzed in the recent work of Elliot Wolfson, with particular attention to the manner in which medieval kabbalists viewed the physical-natural world through the prism of a pervasively androcentric gender paradigm. See Wolfson, "Mirror of Nature Reflected in the Symbolism of Medieval Kabbalah."

46. This is undoubtedly a reference to Rabbi Ezra of Gerona's *Commentary on the Song of Songs* (see *Kitvei Ramban*, 2: 489). It is fairly certain that Ezra defines the word *shoshanah* as lily, a flower that has six petals in correspondence to the six sides of *Shekhinah*. Ezra states that the *shoshanah* is a plant called by the vernacular name לידה, though it is highly probable that Chavel's edition here preserves a scribal error in which the *dalet* has mistakenly replaced a *resh* (given the fact that the medieval Catalan word for lily is *liri*).

47. Isaac of Akko, *'Oẓar Ḥayyim*, fol. 99a.

The sight of the flower leads the kabbalist directly to a theological association; the traces of inner divine Being are embedded in the varieties of natural phenomena that he encounters. It is the lived experience of such encounters—the pleasures of absorbing natural beauty through the physical senses—that opens the doors of metaphysical insight to the ruminating kabbalist. The autobiographical character of this report is indicative of the degree to which Isaac of Akko links the deciphering of divine meaning to a very human *Sitz im Leben*. This-worldly reality is ultimately understood to be a clear portal onto the deep structures of the divine Self, and the mystical life is rendered meaningful as an enduring process of discovering those interpretive openings. As we find elsewhere in *'Oẓar Ḥayyim*:[48]

> I was contemplating [or gazing at] a tall mountain [עוד אני משתכל בהר גבוה] and I saw a secret in the color blue [וראיתי סוד בצבע התכלת]. [The secret] is that you should know [the word] *tekhelet* [literally, blue] is the language of completion and perfection [לשון תכלית ושלימות].[49] And *tekhelet* is also the language of yearning [חמדה]. . . . [As it is written

48. Ibid., fols. 181a–181b.

49. The Hebrew phrase "A is the language of [לשון] B" is an idiom rather resistant to direct and concise English translation. The phrase is used ubiquitously by Jewish exegetes to establish a phonetic play on similar sounding words, with the aim of using such correlations to ground fresh interpretive insight. In this instance, Isaac of Akko reads תכלת (blue) as תכלית (completion or perfection). This exegetical play—reading the phonetic correlation between תכלת and תכלית as (among other things) an allusion to *Shekhinah's* relationship to the other *sefirot*—was also developed by several kabbalists prior to Isaac of Akko. Given the general interpretive posture adopted by Isaac vis-à-vis Moses Naḥmanides, the words of the latter (*Perush ha-RaMBaN 'al ha-Torah*, 2: 254 [RaMBaN on Num. 15:38]) on this exegetical correlation are particularly telling: הזכרון הוא בחוט התכלת, שרומז למדה הכוללת הכל שהיא בכל והיא תכלית הכל, ולכן אמר וראיתם אתו וזכרתם את כל מצות ה' (Remembrance [of the *mizvah*] arises from the thread of blue [*tekhelet*]. This blue hints to the attribute [the *middah* or *sefirah*] that contains [or is inclusive of] all [the other *sefirot*]. For She is in all [of them], and She is the completion of them all [*takhlit ha-kol*]. Thus it is said [Num. 15:39]: "look at it and remember all the commandments"). To anyone who is familiar with the enigmatic symbolic rhetoric of Naḥmanides, it will be clear that his allusion here is to the *sefirah Shekhinah*, and that this symbolism is underscored by a play on the words תכלת and תכלית. What is more, the correlation of the blue thread to the specific act of remembrance appears to build consciously upon a well-known passage in BT *Menaḥot* 43b. The RaMBaN plays quite skillfully on four similar sounding words (תכלת, כוללת, כל, תכלית) to a powerful hermeneutic effect; he implicitly links all four words through the recurring presence of the letters כ and ל—overtly correlating them all to that attribute that holds and includes all of the sefirotic dimensions within herself (*Shekhinah*). It should further be noted that this exegetical association is also found in the zoharic literature. See, e.g., *Zohar* 3:175b and 3:226b (*Ra'aya Meheimana'*). It is also quite

(Ps. 84:3)]: "I long, I yearn for the courts of YHVH" [נכספה וגם כלתה ... נפשי]. That is to say [my soul yearns for the *sefirah* called] Perfection [תכלית], which includes all the other colors within it [שכל הגוונים נכללים בו].[50] And therefore, the eighth thread [of the *ẓiẓit*] that binds together and includes [or embraces] the seven other white threads [ועל כן הפתיל השמיני הכורך את הז' הפתילים הלבנים וכוללם] hints at [the *sefirah*] *Ḥokhmah*, for She[51] is the Divine Wisdom that includes [or embraces] the seven branches of the Pure Candelabrum [המנורה הטהורה]—*Gedulah*, *Paḥad*, *Tif'eret*, *Neẓaḥ*, *Hod*, *Ẓaddiq*, *'Atarah*—and this is according to the way of Proper Truth [וזהו על דרך האמת הנכונה]. And indeed by the way of Truth [על דרך האמת], this blue eighth thread hints at *'Atarah*, and the seven white [threads] hint at Meṭaṭron and . . . the six supernal angels.

The association to Meṭaṭron and the six angels implies the "way of *Sod*" in Isaac's exegetical method (though this phrase is uncharacteristically absent from the passage). This reading strategy is the second rung of interpretation on an ascending model (despite the fact that the usual order is inverted in this particular case—here starting with the highest and progressing to the lowest).[52] The first level focuses on the nature of human psychology, mind, and soul (דרך הנסתר)—a reading that follows in the text shortly after the close of the above-cited passage; the second

---

plausible that the *yod* of the word תכלית has further stimulated this interpretive move: the תכלת holds all ten (*yod*) divine potencies within itself.

50. The manuscript reading is תכלית and not תכלת (blue), but the context would indicate that Isaac is implying both usages simultaneously. This sefirotic dimension is the completion and perfection that includes all the other dimensions, and it is also represented by the color blue, which contains the other colors. Isaac's reading of the word תכלת as yearning or desire is grounded in a phonetic play on the word כלתה of כלתה נפשי לחצרות ה'. A reasonable reading of the manuscript might also be: "my soul longs to reach the תכלת [the *sefirah* called Blue], which includes all the other colors [שכל הגוונים נכללים בו]."

51. Despite the fact that *Ḥokhmah* is typically considered to be male vis-à-vis female *Binah* in the predominantly heterosexual gender paradigm of kabbalistic theology, the gendered nature of Hebrew—in which the word חכמה possesses a feminine ending—causes the otherwise male *sefirah Ḥokhmah* to be characterized in feminine terms (i.e., as "She"). The larger phenomenon of gender transposition and inversion in kabbalistic metaphysics and anthropology has been studied in the extensive analyses of Elliot R. Wolfson. See, e.g., Wolfson, "On Becoming Female: Crossing Gender Boundaries in Kabbalistic Ritual and Myth." A far more expansive discussion of these issues has now been included in Wolfson, *Language, Eros, Being: Kabbalistic Hermeneutics and Poetic Imagination*.

52. See the extended analysis of this exegetical technique in Huss, "NiSAN—The Wife of the Infinite."

on Meṭaṭron and the angelic realm (דרך הסוד); the third correlates to the lower *sefirot* (דרך האמת); and the fourth expounds upon the highest *sefirot* (דרך האמת הנכונה). Offering his layered reading of the word תכלת in reverse order as he does, Isaac culminates his exegesis with a correlation of that word to the wisdom of the mind that resides in the soul of the speaking creature. It is in this respect that תכלת as divine wisdom is read into the successive rungs of cosmic reality, and symmetry is established between the interpretive schema and the structure of Being. First explained as the *sefirah Ḥokhmah* who embraces and binds all the subsequent *sefirot*, תכלת is then read as *Shekhinah*—often characterized in kabbalistic literature as the lower dimension of divine wisdom that parallels *Ḥokhmah*.[53] This same force of divine wisdom is then correlated to the intellect that dwells in the soul.

All in all, every stage of metaphysical reality—from the intellect that dwells in the human soul to the highest dimensions of intradivine Being—is understood to be exegetically refracted in the word תכלת. Most notable for our present purposes, the wheels of this multilayered and intricate hermeneutic are first set in motion by the kabbalist's experience of תכלת in the natural world. The outward physical sight of the mountain and its color serves as a direct stimulus for the symbolic imagination; the kabbalist reads Nature as a text permeated with allusion and reflection, an array of markers of deeper divine truth. To see the color blue embedded in a natural phenomenon immediately leads Isaac of Akko to "see the secret" of metaphysical reality encoded therein. What is more, that correlation between a sensory perception and a divine truth is further linked to the meaning of symbolic ritual action (the wearing of the *ẓiẓit* garment with seven white threads and one thread of blue). The hermeneutical process of the kabbalist flows from the natural image to the ritual object to the very structure of the cosmos. All three exist along one continuum of truth; they are connected together in a web of meaning through intersecting symbolic lines, and they are unified within the mind and experience of the kabbalist. The external sight of the eye opens the interior vision of interpretive creativity; the hues of natural form are a prism for the symbolic texture of ritual and divine being.

---

53. See Scholem, "*Shekhinah*: The Feminine Element in Divinity," in id., *On the Mystical Shape of the Godhead*, pp. 143–144.

I conclude with one final example of this experiential and exegetical phenomenon—an anecdote that further reveals Isaac as a mystic closely attentive and drawn to the natural world, to the symbolic meaning he believed to be encoded therein:

> On that day I went out to the field, and I saw and contemplated a single blade of grass [עוד ביום זה יצאתי השדה וראיתי והשתכלתי בעשב אחד]. I saw that all vegetation points toward the perfection of [the four worlds of] *'Aẓilut*, *Beri'ah*, *Yeẓirah*, and *'Asiyah*. This includes all the existing creatures [כולל כל הנמצאים המחודשים].[54]

Whether it is the jasmine flower, the mountain colors, or the spear of grass, the phenomena of the natural realm are viewed with an eye to the cosmic meaning they reflect. Isaac of Akko testifies to a deep engagement with the natural world, and his autobiographical rhetoric reveals a man in search of meaningful correlations between his lived experience of daily sensation and the larger structure of cosmic Being. As with waking from sleep and ritual performance, Isaac's sensory encounters with the world of nature function as the sparks of symbolic creativity, the stimulus for the hermeneutical imagination seeking to understand an otherwise hidden divine reality. The embodied character of life leads the mystic to see the secret in a new way, and the moments of such experience crystallize a process of individual creativity—a construction of meaning that sharply contrasts with the transmission of received wisdom. It is through the ordinary and daily patterns of lived experience that the kabbalist arrives at the threshold of innovative insight, thereby affirming a model of authenticity and legitimacy that is predicated on the ability of the individual mystic to uncover and to create.

---

54. Isaac of Akko, *'Oẓar Ḥayyim*, fol. 118b.

Part Three *Contemplative Practice, Mystical Experience*

Six Contemplation, Theurgical Action, and the Presence of God

Theurgy—the power of human action and intention to affect the divine realm—is one of the main defining components of medieval Kabbalah, and it is central to Isaac of Akko's writings.[1] Isaac's approach to the contemplative life is rooted in the framework of prayer and other related paradigms of devotion. His prescriptive method of writing thus frequently returns to a symbolic interpretive reading of the liturgical text according to ontological categories and models. Discussion of the act of prayer emerges as the forum par excellence for the expression of advice on contemplative practice, as well as reflection on the ontological and cosmic implications of mystical practice and the enactment of liturgical text and ritual. In this respect, Isaac participated in a larger medieval genre. Kabbalistic approaches to the liturgy and the event of prayer were an integral feature of early Kabbalah, beginning as early as the traditions concerning devotional intention attributed to Jacob the Nazirite, Abraham ben David (the RABaD),[2] Judah ben Yaqar,[3] and

1. The subject of theurgy has been researched quite extensively in recent years. See, e.g., Idel, *Kabbalah: New Perspectives*, pp. 156–199; id., *Hasidism: Between Ecstasy and Magic*, pp. 147–207; Mopsik, *Les grands textes de la Cabale: Les rites qui font Dieu*; Wolfson, "Mystical-Theurgical Dimensions of Prayer in *Sefer ha-Rimmon*"; id., *Abraham Abulafia—Kabbalist and Prophet*, pp. 186–228; Brody, "Human Hands Dwell in Heavenly Heights: Worship and Mystical Experience in Thirteenth-Century Kabbalah," esp. pp. 218–236, 446–471, 631–671; Garb, *Manifestations of Power in Jewish Mysticism: From Rabbinic Literature to Safedian Kabbalah*; Hecker, *Mystical Bodies, Mystical Meals*, pp. 142–178.

2. See G. Scholem, *Reishit ha-Kabbalah*, p. 73 n. 2, and id., *Origins of the Kabbalah*, pp. 199–248.

3. See Judah ben Yaqar, *Perush ha-tefillot ve-ha-berakhot*. This text bears the traces of early kabbalistic thinking and practice with regard to the liturgy. The particular significance of this

Isaac the Blind,[4] and continuing unabated through the works of ʿAzriel of Gerona,[5] Joseph Gikatilla,[6] Moses de Leon,[7] Menaḥem Recanati,[8] and many others. In addition to kabbalistic sources, the esoteric spirituality of the Rhineland Pietists (*ḥasidei ʾashkenaz*) also contributed a great deal to this phenomenon, as is particularly evident from the writings of Eleazar of Worms and their possible impact on thirteenth-century kabbalists.[9]

In classical and medieval Jewish sources, the term *kavvanah* (intention) serves as an orienting rhetorical axis through which the complex dynamics of contemplation—as well as its theurgical underpinnings—may be understood. For medieval Jewish thinkers, as was true mutatis mutandis for their ancient rabbinic forebears, the relationship between external action and internal intention was the issue of paramount concern in prescribing religious practice and in understanding the meaning of human ritual.[10] The act of *kavvanah* is a process of mental orientation

---

scholar in the history of medieval Jewish mysticism is mostly related to his role as teacher of the great Moses Naḥmanides.

4. On the question of *kavvanah* in the thought and practice of Isaac the Blind, see Idel, "On Isaac the Blind's Intentions for the Eighteen Benedictions."

5. See "R. ʿAzriel mi-Gerona," ed. M. Gavarin.

6. Most notably in his classic work *Shaʿarei ʾOrah*.

7. Among this kabbalist's many writings on the subject of prayer, see "Sefer Maskiyot Kesef," ed. Wijnhoven, pp. 6–31; *Sefer ha-Rimmon*, ed. Wolfson, pp. 32–88.

8. Recanati, *Perush ha-Tefillot* in his *Sefer Taʿamei ha-Miẓvot*, pp. 27b–43b.

9. See Dan, *Jewish Mysticism*, vol. 2: *The Middle Ages*, pp. 221–311; Wolfson, *Through a Speculum That Shines*, pp. 188–269; id., "Sacred Space and Mental Iconography"; and Idel, "Intention in Prayer in Early Kabbalah," pp. 5–14.

10. It is important to note the larger literary legacy of this binary tension in sacred ritual. The question of whether ritual acts require intention in order to be fulfilled properly was already well developed in classical rabbinic literature. Perhaps the locus classicus for this issue is BT *Berakhot*, fols. 13a–b (and see the famous use of this ritual dialectic in Maimonides' *Mishneh Torah*, *Hilkhot tefillah*, 4). Also paradigmatic in this regard is M. *Berakhot* 5:1, which tells of the חסידים ראשונים, the pious men of old, who would wait an hour before saying the Eighteen Benedictions so as to first achieve the requisite *kavvanah*, to align their hearts with the deity. For a succinct discussion of this issue of *kavvanah* in classical rabbinic thought, see Urbach, *The Sages: Their Concepts and Beliefs*, pp. 396–399. Cf. Eilberg-Schwartz, *The Human Will in Judaism: The Mishnah's Philosophy of Intention*, esp. pp. 50–64, and Wolfson, "Iconic Visualization and the Imaginal Body of God: The Role of Intention in the Rabbinic Conception of Prayer," esp. pp. 4–14 and notes. For reflections on the influence of such classical notions upon medieval kabbalists, see Garb, "Power and Kavvanah in the Kabbalah," pp. 56, 65–66, and Fine, *Physician of the Soul, Healer of the Cosmos: Isaac Luria and His Kabbalistic Fel-*

and focus predicated on established symbolic correlations between the words of liturgical recitation (or other ritual performance) and the divine object of devotional concern. Thus, behind the idea of devotional intention is a highly defined and specific conception of *inward* ritual enactment. What the individual devotee thinks in the hidden depths of his own mind is just as important as the proper performance of the external forms of devotional ritual. To put it a different way: the instructor in kabbalistic matters of devotion views his own task as the regulation and prescription of human thought in the act of prayer and contemplation. Proper performance of kabbalistic devotion involves a certain well-defined mental condition—a specific adherence to a symbol-determined mental direction vis-à-vis the Divine.

Unification and Restoration

The underlying metaphysical drama of kabbalistic discourse may be broadly defined as the dialectic between separation and unification within divine reality. For despite the insistence that cosmic Being is one at its essence, and that all apparent separation and multiplicity are ultimately to be disregarded as the limited perception of the finite human mind,[11] a central feature of the kabbalistic enterprise is the attempt to unify and restore that which has been separated above. To be sure, that very separation is attributed to the sins of human beings in the lower world, and it is therefore incumbent upon the kabbalistic adept to exercise his cosmic power in the reunification of the divine Whole. This theurgic task was first articulated in the Provençal school of Isaac the Blind and that of his younger colleagues in the Aragonese town of Gerona.[12] The *Zohar,* too, composed a generation later in Castile, brims with a similar restorative and unitive conception.[13] Isaac of Akko's repeated emphasis on the unitive consequences of devotion

---

lowship, pp. 220–225. It perhaps goes without saying that this dialectic also lies at the heart of Baḥya Ibn Paquda's thought. See the recent analysis in Lobel, *A Sufi-Jewish Dialogue: Philosophy and Mysticim in Bahya Ibn Paquda's Duties of the Heart*, chap. 7.

11. See E. Fishbane, "Mystical Contemplation and the Limits of the Mind."

12. See Pedayah, "Flaw and Repair," pp. 157–285.

13. This dialectic appears on virtually every page of the *Zohar*. See, e.g., *Zohar* 2:213b, 2:256b.

and contemplation must therefore be understood as part of an underlying and orienting structure in medieval kabbalistic thought.

Consider the following representative passage. After underscoring the fact that liturgical prayer came to replace the devotion of the sacrificial cult, thus indicating that sacrifice and prayer are to be viewed as two manifestations of the same devotional phenomenon, Isaac states:[14]

> עיקר אמונתינו לייחד השם יתברך ר"ל לייחד המדות. מדות הגבורה עם מדות החסד כלומר כל מיני דין עם כל מיני רחמים. ובהתחבר זאת המדה שהיא אמונה עם אמת שהוא הקו המקבל מן החסד וממה אשר למעלה הימנו והקו משפיע ליסוד המשפיע לאמונה. והתפלה היא ליסוד הבנין שהיא הבינה שהוא המלך ונכנסת לו דרך אמונה שהיא שער לדברים.

> The essence of our faith is to unify the Blessed Name [i.e., God]; that is to say, to unify the Attributes[15]—the Attributes of Strength [*Gevurah*] with the Attributes of Love [*Ḥesed*], which is to say, [the unification of] all kinds of judgment with all kinds of compassion. [This unification also includes] the joining of the Attribute called "Faith" [*'Emunah*] with the Attribute called "Truth." Truth is the channel that receives from Love [*Ḥesed*] and from that which is above *Ḥesed*. And the channel sends the flow to *Yesod* [Foundation], which sends the flow to Faith [*'Emunah*]. And prayer should be directed to the foundation [*Yesod*] of the structure, which is *Binah* [Understanding]. *Binah* is the King, and [the prayer] enters before Him through Faith [*'Emunah*], which is the gateway to the other entities.

Isaac asserts in no uncertain terms how he perceives the fundamental kabbalistic task of unifying the various components of the metaphysical world and resolving the apparent polarities in the sefirotic realm. It is the act of prayer here that is endowed with this tremendous theurgical power to unify the two sides of the sefirotic structure—right and left, Compassion and Judgment, male and female, *Tif'eret* and *Shekhinah*. This unification is expressed through three verbs that signify a dynamic relationship between *sefirot*: לייחד (to unify), מקבל מ (receives from), and

14. Isaac of Akko, *Me'irat 'Einayim*, p. 94.

15. The structure of the deity is at times described as the unified four-letter Name of God (Tetragrammaton), and at times as the unity of disparate Attributes. Both of these characterizations symbolize the unity of the ten *sefirot* of Divinity.

משפיע ל (flows to). The movement of the divine *shefa*, and the reception of energy from one *sefirah* to another, reflects the process of dynamic unification caused by human action in the lower world. When the human supplicant in devotion directs his mind to *Binah*, the deep foundation of sefirotic structure, the dynamic force of flow and unification between different *sefirot* is stimulated. It is also important to note here that as *Binah* becomes the subject of contemplative prayer, her gender becomes inverted, and she is called "King," instead of her usual characterization as Upper Queen and Mother, the female force of the highest sefirotic triad, the lover of the male dimension *Ḥokhmah*. Thus we encounter an example of the remarkable kabbalistic tendency toward metaphysical gender transposition and inversion, one that reflects symbolic fluidity in the construction of theology. Mental intention toward *Binah* is a recurrent prescription in Isaac's writings—a contemplative technique that will be explored at length in the next chapter.

The act of unification by the human devotee is a response of correction or rectification to an inner-divine flaw directly caused by a human sin. The theurgic power of devotional intention is able to correct this metaphysical separation, thus endowing the human being with the power to alter the cosmos and Divinity both for the bad and for the good. Consider the following case:[16]

> ואדם כשראה העטרה שהיא מפרנסת כל העולם והנהגת הכל על ידה, נמשך אחריה לבדה וקצץ בנטיעות. ועל כן נטרד, ואחר כן עשה והקריב שור פר כי הקרבן מקרב הכחות. ועל ידי קרבן זה ייחד הכחות דו פרצופין . . . ייחוד שלם ואמתי.

> When Adam saw *'Atarah*—She that nourishes and rules the entire world—he was drawn to Her alone, and he [therefore] cut the shoots. Because of this he was expelled. Afterward, he sacrificed an ox, for sacrifice [*qorban*] draws [*meqarev*] the supernal forces together. Through this sacrifice he unified the forces of the Two Faces [*du-parẓufin*] . . . a complete and true unity.

Here we have an example of the contemplative sin of singling out *'Atarah* for devotion at the expense of the other *sefirot*. Adam's heresy, one that causes a supernal separation within Divinity, is found in his

16. Isaac of Akko, *Me'irat 'Einayim*, pp. 30–31.

mental posture toward the celestial realm.[17] The event of devotion—here represented paradigmatically by sacrifice—has the power to alter metaphysical reality dramatically. The sin of worshipping *'Atarah* is cosmically rectified through the devotional act of sacrifice, which serves to reconnect elements of the divine Being that were separated by the human heresy. The very fact that Adam adopted a theological posture exclusively oriented to the tenth *sefirah* resulted in the *ontological* separation of that female tenth *sefirah* from the male other half of her complete being. More precisely, the single androgynous dimension of God, characterized as the *du-parẓufin*, is restored to its original state of unity in which a single metaphysical body possesses both the male and female faces of the divine self.[18] In this sense, the human mind is able to will metaphysical change simply by orienting consciousness in a certain way, or by engaging in a cosmically potent ritual (i.e., sacrifice or prayer). Building upon earlier kabbalistic traditions, Isaac of Akko plays upon the homonymic relationship between the words קרבן and מקרב/קרוב to assert that the devotional act of sacrifice (and by extension, prayer) has the power to restore the wholeness of Divinity.[19]

Compare this with a related formulation found subsequently in *Me'irat 'Einayim*:[20]

וקטרת מלשון קשירה . . . ועשן הקטרת עם כונת הכהן היה קושר ומיחד דו פרצופין . . . דע כי כונת הקטרת אל העטרה שתתעלה ותתיחד אל התפארת.

The incense sacrifice should be understood as "a binding." . . .[21] The

---

17. This explanation of Adam's sin is traceable to the kabbalists of Gerona. See Scholem, *The Kabbalah in Gerona*, pp. 374–380; cf. id., "*Sitra Aḥra*," pp. 65–68.

18. In regard to this pervasive dimension of kabbalistic theology and gender construction, see Wolfson, *Language, Eros, Being: Kabbalistic Hermeneutics and Poetic Imagination*, pp. 142–189, 488–513. In Wolfson's assessment, this restoration is centered upon the reintegration of the female side back into the male. Within this conception, the primal perfection of the divine androgyne is essentially male, even as it subsumes the female within itself.

19. This particular usage—הקרבן מקרב הכחות—is traceable to the *Bahir*. See *Bahir*, p. 165: ואמאי אקרי קרבן, אלא על שם שמקרב הכחות הקדושות (Why is sacrifice called *qorban*? It is because sacrifice draws the holy powers closer to one another). Isaac of Akko is quite explicit about his indebtedness to the *Bahir* in this regard. See *Me'irat 'Einayim*, p. 144. For another early textual witness to this idea, see the passage by 'Azriel of Gerona cited in "Perush ha-Tefillah," ed. M. Gavarin, § 3, p. 54, n. 141. Cf. Garb, "Power and Kavvanah in the Kabbalah," p. 107.

20. Isaac of Akko, *Me'irat 'Einayim*, p. 127.

21. This interpretation of the word קטרת is predicated on an existing meaning of the root

smoke of the incense offering, along with the intention of the priest, would bind together and unify the Two Faces [*du-parẓufin*] . . . Know that the intention of the incense offering was directed toward *ʿAtarah*, so that She would ascend to, and become unified with *Tifʾeret*.

The purpose and consequence of devotional ritual is the *reunification* of the primal androgyne. The physical fact of the ritual (the sacrificial smoke) and the mental intent of the priest combine to engender a powerful theurgic effect.[22] Note again the technical use of the term לייחד (to unify), this time combined with the term לקשר (to bind). The kabbalist's vision of the cosmos is one predicated on the constant dialectic between separation and unity—a process dependent upon the devotional action of the human being (represented paradigmatically by the priest) in ritual. Indeed, the very use of these two terms implies a certain degree of initial *separation* within Divinity, for only something that is separated requires unification. In order to bind or to unify, one requires a minimum of two entities. Thus the ritual act of *yiḥud-qeshirah* implies an a priori flaw (since multiplicity is necessarily a flaw for the unitive theologian) within the divine Being, one that seems to have resulted from the sins of human beings. In this sense, the unitive type of devotional theurgy should be characterized as a fundamentally *restorative* model, insofar as the ritual act seeks to restore Divinity to its original perfect state of unity.

In understanding theurgical power as the foundational element of kabbalistic contemplation, we can clearly observe the manner in which the contemplative/mental term *kavvanah* interfaces with the human transformation of the cosmos.[23] It is the act of mental intention in ritual that is considered to have theurgic force. Yet it is not only the mental intention side of ritual that has the theurgic power to unify the sefirotic

---

קטר in classical Jewish sources. According to the lexical work of Marcus Jastrow, קטר was frequently used in ancient Hebrew and Aramaic sources in the sense of "to tie" or "to wreathe." See Jastrow, *A Dictionary of the Targumim, the Talmud Babli and Yerushalmi, and the Midrashic Literature*, pp. 1352–1353. This point has been noted in an analysis of the associations of the words קטר, קשר, and כתר by Green in his *Keter: The Crown of God in Early Jewish Mysticism*, p. 51.

22. For a remarkable precedent on the theurgic power of the sacrificial smoke, see *Zohar* 2:130a.

23. As has been noted, the association of *kavvanah* and cosmic power is analyzed at length in Garb, "Power and Kavvanah in the Kabbalah" and *Manifestations of Power in Jewish Mysticism*.

world. This is manifestly discernable from the foregoing text, in which the physical smoke of the incense offering is considered to join with devotional intention in the restoration of the primal androgyne. The theurgical power of the physical element of devotion is reinforced elsewhere in *Me'irat 'Einayim* from a different angle:

כי כונת הקרבן לקרב הכחות ליחד דו פרצופין להביא עלינו הברכה ממקום הקדש בדרך אמת ואמונה. ואם תשתכל בטבע הנר הידוע תראה בעיניך מופת חזק על סוד הקרבן ותדע כי באמת צריך אדם להשמיע דברי תפלתו לאזניו, ובודאי כי תפלות כנגד תמידין תקנום והכל אחד כשהתפלה יוצאת מפה קדוש והבן זה עד מאד.

> The intention in sacrifice is to draw the forces near to each other, to unify the Two Faces [*du-parzufin*], so as to draw the [flow of] blessing onto ourselves from the Holy Place through the way of truth and faith. And if you contemplate the nature of a candle flame, you will see with your own eyes a strong proof of the secret of sacrifice. And you will know that a person must definitely pronounce the words of his prayer so that his ears can hear them. For [our Sages] established that prayers replace sacrifices, and everything becomes one[24] when the prayer leaves a holy mouth. Understand this very well.[25]

In this passage we see a similar rhetoric of drawing the powers near to one another, as well as the act of unifying them through devotional ritual, oriented once again around the technical terms *leqarev* and *leyaḥed*. What is most remarkable about this particular text, however, is the emphasis on the vocalized words of prayer as a theurgical stimulus for metaphysical unification. By implication, Isaac asserts that the sound of the human voice in prayer functions in a parallel fashion to the physical smoke of ancient sacrifice. Thus we encounter an embedded *prescription* on Isaac's part as to the method of prayer instructed to his reader, and we gain a glimpse into some of the practical implications of kabbalistic theory. The classical Jewish legal stipulation that prayer be vocalized to the point of audibility[26]

---

24. Or "they are identical" (i.e., prayer and sacrifice).

25. Isaac of Akko, *Me'irat 'Einayim*, p. 153.

26. See BT *Soṭah*, fol. 32b; *Megillah*, fol. 20a. While the importance of audibility *is* stipulated and encouraged in this talmudic text, the final legal conclusion is that a person who has not performed the *Shema* prayer to the point of audibility is nevertheless considered to have fulfilled his religious obligation. Cf. Maimonides, *Mishneh Torah*, *Hilkhot keri'at shema*, 2;

is here transformed into a theurgically charged event, which directly correlates to the physical elements of the sacrificial ritual. As such, the paradigm of sacrifice has been transposed to a separate devotional plane, thereby creating a substitute ritual for the kabbalistic devotee. The human being must audibly vocalize his prayer, not only because of nomian strictures, but because his act of prayer reenacts the lost sacrificial ritual, and the restoration and reunification of the divine cosmos consequently hangs in the balance.

In this image, the human voice is given physical form as a prayer breath in resemblance to the sacrificial smoke; as the words of devotion are vocalized, that corporealized sound ascends to the supernal world to unify the separated divine Self. Once again we encounter the combination of inward mental power (intention) with the external physical power of ritual. The smoke and the corporeal substance of the human voice reach up into the heavens and stimulate the unifying flow of blessing. With regard to the phrase להביא עלינו הברכה (so as to draw the flow of blessing onto ourselves), we see a model of theurgy that extends the flow of divine energy into the human world, thus completing the cosmic circle whose stimulus is effected by human action.[27]

The theurgical act of unification in devotional ritual is given its most elaborate treatment in the framework of the *Shema* prayer, the paradigmatic declaration of theological unity. Here Isaac of Akko again emphasizes a dynamic process of unification, which seeks to maintain the complete indivisibility of *'Atarah* and *Tif'eret*—the two sides of the androgynous divine face (*du-parzufin*). The restoration and maintenance of this metaphysical condition is the ultimate purpose of sacred ritual in general, and of devotional ritual in particular. Other forms of theurgic unification, which are only directed to one side of the *du-parzufin*, are necessarily inadequate, for the proper contemplative method in devotion must seek to restore the unity of the androgynous face in its

---

Abraham ben Natan ha-Yarḥi, *Sefer ha-Manhig*, 1: 73–74 (pagination refers to text, not editor's Introduction). See also the relevant citation in affirmation of this practice from the prayerbook of Rav 'Amram Ga'on, as quoted in *Siddur ha-Ge'onim ve-ha-Mequbalim*, ed. Weinstock, p. 456, n. 4. The fact that a person is still designated as *yoẓe'* (having fulfilled his religious obligation) does not serve to undermine the previously stipulated instruction; it merely reflects the tenuous balance between ritual ideals and the implementation of those ideals.

27. See discussion of the model of "drawing down" later in this chapter.

entirety. Such is the premise, Isaac argues, behind the specific form of the liturgical text of the *Shema*:[28]

לא היה ייחוד גמור גמור שלא היה משמע הייחוד רק לאחד מהדו פרצופין. אבל עכשו שאמר אחד לתפארת ואחד לעטרה הרי זה ייחוד אמתי ושלם. ייחוד ראשון וייחוד שני כייחוד שמייחדים ישראל להב"ה בכל יום פעמים באהבה שמע ישראל י"י אלהינו י"י אחד שהוא ייחוד ראשון על התפארת ממעלה למטה ואחר כן ייחוד שני על העטרה ממטה למעלה והוא בשכמל"ו.

It was not a complete unity, for the unification was only directed to one of the Two Faces [*du-parzufin*]. But now, when the word "One" is directed to *Tif'eret*, and the [second] "One" is directed to *'Atarah*,[29] there is a true and complete unity. A first unification and a second unification, just like the unification that Israel unifies for the Holy One, blessed be He, twice daily in love [Deut. 6:4]: "Hear O Israel, the Lord our God, the Lord is One." This [line] is the first unification, through *Tif'eret*, from above to below. After this is the second unification, through *'Atarah*, from below to above. This [second unification occurs] through the line "Blessed is the name of the glory of his Kingdom for ever and ever."[30]

The act of recitation in devotional ritual thus carries the power to perform necessary restoration and unification within the divine Being. This mode of theurgical influence functions along two distinct axes: the gravitational model (stimulating the flow of unity from above to below)[31] and the countergravitational model, or the model of theurgical elevation. The dynamic of unification may therefore be characterized as bimodal, and is not a unidirectional force moving from upper to lower metaphysical dimensions. The human act of divine restoration begins either with the stimulation of the male dimension (*Tif'eret*) or with that

---

28. Isaac of Akko, *Me'irat 'Einayim*, p. 100. See n. 32 below for earlier kabbalistic treatments of סוד קריאת שמע.

29. This "second One" refers to the unification that takes place through recitation of the words . . . ברוך שם כבוד

30. See Green, *Keter: The Crown of God in Early Jewish Mysticism*, p. 46, n. 18, for comments on the early provenance of this line in classical rabbinic literature. Green also notes the numerous studies on this topic in modern scholarship.

31. On the development of this "katabatic" type (drawing down from above to below) in Jewish mysticism, see Idel, *Hasidism*, pp. 103–207; Garb, "Power and Kavvanah in the Kabbalah," pp. 101–108.

of the female dimension (*'Atarah*). Both recitative acts are needed for the maintenance of cosmic harmony and emanational efflux.[32]

A related teaching in *Me'irat 'Einayim* elaborates further on this theurgical conception.[33] In line with his self-perception as a conduit of culture, an individual whose task it is to report on all ideas he has received from reliable masters, Isaac of Akko transmits a passage that he attributes to Shem Ṭov Ibn Ga'on. However, this passage seems to be only a paraphrastic reworking of a portion of Ibn Ga'on's *Keter Shem Ṭov*[34]—a usage that is emblematic of the fluid and loose medieval conception of intellectual property.[35] The reference is thus built on the words of Ibn Ga'on, but is nevertheless blended with Isaac of Akko's own rhetoric and distinctive style.

> ענין הייחוד הראשון והייחוד השני . . . הייחוד הראשון שמע ישראל וגו'. י"י שלש עליונות, אלהינו הגדולה והגבורה, י"י התפארת עד הצדיק, אחד מייחד כל אלו שהזכרנו. והדל"ת רומזת לעטרה שהיא דלה . . . הרי ייחוד ממעלה למטה. והייחוד השני בלחש בשכמל"ו. שם העטרה, כבוד התפארת . . . מלכותו התשובה . . . לעולם ועד הוא התפארת שהוא העולם. ועד העטרה, הרי השפע בא מהתשובה לתפארת ולעטרה שהוא ממטה למעלה.

> This is the matter concerning the first unification and the second unification. The first unification occurs through the line "Hear O Israel, the Lord our God, the Lord is One" [*shema' yisra'el YHVH 'Eloheinu YHVH 'eḥad*]. [The first] *YHVH* [unifies] the three supernal [*sefirot*], *'Eloheinu* [unifies the *sefirot*] *Gedulah* [Greatness] and *Gevurah* [Strength], [the second] *YHVH* [unifies the *sefirot*] from *Tif'eret* to *Ẓaddiq*, the word *'eḥad* then unifies all [the *sefirot*] we have mentioned. The letter *dalet* alludes to *'Atarah*, for she is poor [*dalah*]. . . . This is the unification from above to below. The second unification occurs

32. The idea that two distinct modes of unification occur in the *Shema* prayer (one through the line שמע ישראל itself, and the other through the line ברוך שם כבוד) appears to be rooted in a passage from Jacob ben Sheshet's *Sefer ha-'Emunah ve-ha-Biṭaḥon*, pp. 360–361. A more expanded (and imaginatively rich) version of this tradition is found in *Zohar* 1:18b. Of course, the latter text too predates *Me'irat 'Einayim*, and may very well have also influenced Isaac of Akko's formulation of the matter.

33. Isaac of Akko, *Me'irat 'Einayim*, p. 211.

34. See the passage published in *Ma'or va-Shemesh*, pp. 50b–51a.

35. See Part II of the present study for extended reflection on the intersecting problems of reception, transmission, and authorship.

> through the whispering of the line "Blessed is the name of the glory of His Kingdom for ever and ever." (ברוך שם כבוד מלכותו לעולם ועד) [The word] *shem* [name] [alludes] to *'Atarah*, [the word] *kevod* [glory] [alludes] to *Tif'eret*, [the word] *malkhuto* [His Kingdom] [alludes] to *Teshuvah* [*Binah*]. . . . [The words] *le-'olam va-'ed* [for ever and ever] [allude] to *Tif'eret*, for *Tif'eret* is called *'olam* [world]. [The word] *va-'ed* [alludes] to *'Atarah*. The flow then comes from *Teshuvah* to *Tif'eret* and *'Atarah*, which is [the unification] from below to above.

Recitation of the liturgy thus functions as a performative rite, the goal of which is the restoration of cosmic unity. As each word of the *Shema'* is spoken, the various elements of the inner-divine world come into alignment and unity—a state of cosmic perfection that was lacking prior to the skillful performance of devotional ritual by the human being. As in the text preceding this one, the effects of unification in sacred ritual move in both the gravitational and the elevational modes, depending only on the specific liturgical text being recited by the human supplicant. In the second unification, the tenth *sefirah* (*'Atarah*) is stimulated by the devotee, causing the upward rise of divine energy, which subsequently returns gravitationally back from *Binah* to *'Atarah*. The restoration of primal unity is accomplished by the human being simply through the all-powerful acts of recitative performance and proper mental intention. The prescriptive and performative nature of this text is expanded even further in the continuation of the passage, in which a gaonic legal injunction is infused with a mystical-cosmic meaning:[36]

> ולפי שהייחוד הראשון שהוא אחד מלמעלה למטה והדל"ת רומזת על ייחוד העטרה ממטה למעלה על כן כתבו הגאונים ז"ל שצריך להאריך תולתא בחי"ת ותרי תולתי בדל"ת. כי החי"ת הוא ייחוד ממעלה למטה כאשר נכתוב, על כן אין צריך כונה יתירה כי מהרה יכוין אדם הייחוד ממעלה למטה בלא עמל. אבל ייחוד הדל"ת הוא ממטה למעלה וצריך בו כונה ועמל יתר לכוין מאין סוף לאין סוף ממטה למעלה ויכוין בלבו שהכל מיוחד באין סוף.

> Because the first unification takes place from above to below, and the letter *dalet* alludes to the unification of *'Atarah* from below to above, the *Ge'onim* of blessed memory wrote that one must lengthen one's pronunciation of the letter *ḥet* by a third, and lengthen pronunciation

---

36. Isaac of Akko, *Me'irat 'Einayim*, p. 211.

> of the letter *dalet* by two thirds.[37] Pronunciation of the *ḥet* is the unification from above to below. . . . For this reason, additional intention is not necessary, since a person can rapidly intend the unification from above to below without any labor. However, the unification that takes place through the *dalet* is from below to above. One requires additional intention and labor to intend the unification from Infinity to Infinity [מאין סוף לאין סוף][38] from below to above. One must intend in his heart that everything is unified in *'Ein-Sof.*

Just as the legal requirement regarding audibility in prayer was infused with theurgical and mystical power in an earlier example, here too Isaac of Akko offers a theurgically charged interpretation of the ancient ritual injunction to lengthen pronunciation of the letters of the word אחד (one) at the end of the *Shema*.[39] The vocalized sound of the *dalet* must be lengthened so as to lend extra vigor and power to the elevational mode of theurgy. Presumably this is needed precisely because this theurgical dynamic is countergravitational, thus moving against the natural stream of cosmic energy, and requiring greater strength and force to overcome it. Indeed, vocalization alone is viewed to be insufficient; an extra measure of contemplative focus is required to attain the needed level of cosmic empowerment. To center the mind on the Infinity that binds all of the *sefirot* together (and to fuse such concentration with the ritual act of utterance) this itself emerges as a technique for the transcendence of the ordinary workings of cosmic law. The kabbalist in possession of such potent mental techniques

37. An examination of the *Siddur ha-Ge'onim ve-ha-Mequbalim* and *Oẓar ha-Ge'onim le-Masekhet Berakhot* has not yielded the location of this exact formulation (i.e., including the word תולתא). So far as I can tell, the word also does not appear in this connection in talmudic sources. However, the tradition that the *dalet* must be lengthened in vocalization to a *greater degree* than the *ḥet* is well established in classical and medieval sources. See BT *Berakhot*, fol. 13b; Moses Maimonides, *Mishneh Torah*, *Hilkhot keri'at shema*, 2: 9; *Siddur ha-Ge'onim ve-ha-Mequbalim*, ed. Weinstock, pp. 469–470.

38. This term appears numerous times in Isaac of Akko's work; it seems to indicate the belief that *'Ein-Sof* extends from one end of the cosmos to the other, as opposed to a vertical configuration located directly above the *sefirot*. *'Ein-Sof* extends from both ends of the sefirotic system; it is ultimately the very essence of the cosmos that becomes manifest through the ten *sefirot*.

39. This ideal is also represented paradigmatically through the martyrological legend of Rabbi Akiva, in which the ancient sage lengthened his vocalization of the word *eḥad* just as his spirit left his body in the moment of death. See BT *Berakhot*, fol. 61b.

will succeed, the author asserts, in a reversal of the typical direction of divine energies. Such an intention well demonstrates the perceived power of human consciousness and empowered ritual over the normal functioning of the divine world, and further underscores the manner in which interior (*kavvanah*) and exterior (vocalization) modalities of ritual are understood to have transformative effects upon the life of God.

It is clear that the ultimate task of the supplicant is the restoration of divine unity, a repair of the broken divine self. Whether this is accomplished by stimulating metaphysical gravity or countergravity, unification is still the goal. As Isaac states in a different context:[40]

> שמור את יום השבת–שמור לעטרה, יום השבת לצדיק. אם כן דבור זכור רומז המשכת הצדיק בעטרה, ודבור שמור רומז התעלות העטרה בצדיק. וזהו הסלם שמלאכי אלהים עולים ויורדים בו. זכור ושמור בדבור אחד נאמרו, רמז לייחוד העטרה בצדיק, שזה מיוחד בזה וזה מיוחד בזה שלא נחללהו . . . השפע בא מהצדיק על ידי החסיד היודע להמשיך באמרו באי כלה באי כלה, ובכונתו ההגונה לתת בו נפש יתירה מתוך המשכת רוח קדש זה ממעין הקדש מיסוד הבינה בדרך אמת ואמונה בגוף חסיד זה.

> "Keep the Sabbath day"[41]—"keep" corresponds to *'Atarah*, "Sabbath day" corresponds to *Ẓaddiq*. Thus the word "remember" [*zakhor*] alludes to the drawing forth of *Ẓaddiq* onto *'Atarah*,[42] and the word "keep" alludes to the elevation of *'Atarah* to *Ẓaddiq*. This is the ladder upon which God's angels ascend and descend. The words "remember" and "keep" were uttered as one[43]—this is an allusion to the unification of *'Atarah* with *Ẓaddiq*, for each one is unified in the other, such that we do not profane Him. . . . The flow comes forth from *Ẓaddiq* through the [action] of the pious individual who knows how to draw

---

40. Isaac of Akko, *Me'irat 'Einayim*, p. 106.

41. Deut. 5:12.

42. The underlying logic of this interpretive association is the homonymic relationship between the words *zakhor* (of the biblical verse) and *zakhar* (masculine—correlated to *Ẓaddiq/Yesod*). This exegetical and symbolic play is first found in *Bahir*, p. 207 (§ 123), and it was further developed in *Zohar* 1:32a (*Tosefta*). The zoharic passage states the matter clearly and concisely: דתרין דרגין אינון מילה ופריעה, זכור ושמור, צדיק וצדק, דכר ונוקבא. אות ברית דא יוסף וברית דא רחל, ואצטריך לחברא לון (These two rungs are the cut and the folding back [of circumcision], *zakhor* and *shamor* [remembrance and keeping], *Ẓaddiq* and *Ẓedeq*, male and female. The sign [or mark] of the covenant [i.e., the mark of circumcision] is Joseph, and the covenant is Rachel, and one must join them together). On this convergence between memory and masculinity, between remembrance and gender construction, see Wolfson, "Re/membering the Covenant: Memory, Forgetfulness, and the Construction of History in the Zohar."

43. BT *Rosh ha-Shanah*, fol. 27a.

> forth [the flow] through uttering the words "Come, O Bride, Come, O Bride,"[44] and through his proper intention to give himself an additional soul through the drawing forth of this holy spirit from the holy wellspring, from the foundation of *Binah*, by the way of truth and faith, into the body of this pious individual.

Here again Isaac frames the unitive act through two parallel, and yet inverse, models of action: the gravitational attraction of drawing down, and the countergravitational model of elevation (התעלות)—a polarity that might also be characterized as katabatic versus anabatic effect.[45] In the context of this type, the event of unification, clearly initiated by the human kabbalist (characterized here as *ḥasid*), either begins through a theurgic stimulation of the male *Ẓaddiq* (the *sefirah Tif'eret*, or possibly *Yesod*)—in which case the theurgical dynamic unfolds in a gravitationally descending model—or begins through an arousal and stimulus of *'Atarah*, such that She may rise upward to Her male lover. It is through the *external* action of ritual utterance and the essentially *internal* action of mental intention that the kabbalist (*ḥasid*) is able to perform the ultimate cosmic orchestration. In a fascinating conclusion to this revealing source, Isaac indicates that the final goal of such unitive theurgy is the attraction of divine energy into the physical body of the human being. The "extra soul" (an idea that is widespread in the zoharic literature)[46] functions as the embodiment of divine reality in the human self as it has been directed there by the kabbalist in ritual and contemplation. Such is the ultimate realization of both *shamor* and *zakhor 'et yom ha-shabbat* (keep and remember the Sabbath day)—the theurgic consequence of Sabbath ritual observance with cosmic intention. The extra soul that is associated with the Sabbath is ushered into the Jewish soul by way of the theurgic utterance of the initiated

---

44. This formulation is derived from BT *Shabbat*, fol. 119a.

45. Note also the parallel in *Me'irat 'Einayim*, p. 49: ומחמת כח הקרבן עם הכונה ההגונה של מקריב מסתלקים כלומר מתעלים המלאכים אל האצילות והאצילות מתעלה אל הסבה הראשונה ומקבלים שפע רצון זיו וזוהר חיים וברכה (And because of the power of the sacrifice combined with the proper intention of the sacrificer, the angels ascend to the Emanation, and the Emanation ascends to the First Cause, and they [the angels] receive the flow of Will, radiance, life, and blessing).

46. On the use of this idea in the zoharic corpus, see Tishby, *The Wisdom of the Zohar*, pp. 1230–1233; Ginsburg, *The Sabbath in the Classical Kabbalah*, pp. 121–136.

kabbalist—the "*ḥasid* who knows." The key terms of this type—*yiḥud*, *hamshakhah*, *hit'alut*, and *shefa'*—are all conflated to construct a model of theurgic unification that functions equally on the gravitational and elevational axes of cosmic movement.

The compatibility of these two models is summed up by Isaac[47] in his recognition of an important earlier kabbalistic source[48] for this idea:

וראיתי בספר האמונה והבטחון שאומר בין שהתחיל הייחוד מלמעלה למטה בין שהתכוין ממטה למעלה הרי זה ייחוד נכון אמתי.

> And I saw in the *Book of Faith and Trust* that whether one begins unification from above to below, or whether one intends [the unification] from below to above, it is a correct and true unification.

In sum, the paradigm of theurgic unification was a foundational feature of kabbalistic devotional theory and practice. The mystic was perpetually concerned with restoring Divinity to the perfection that antedated human sin and heresy. What is more, the model espoused by Isaac of Akko and a great many others in the High Middle Ages was profoundly influential in the shaping of subsequent Jewish esoteric thought and practice, particularly the *yiḥud*-oriented contemplative ritual of sixteenth-century Safedian Kabbalah.[49]

Augmentation and Maintenance

In another text, Isaac of Akko traverses beyond the unitive model of theurgy, and characterizes human action as endowed with the capacity to *augment* existing divine energy and vitality.[50] Like the unitive model, however, this type also seeks to return divine reality to a perfected state, characterized through several combined images of a cosmic ideal. Isaac

47. Isaac of Akko, *Me'irat 'Einayim*, p. 211.

48. See Jacob ben Sheshet, *Sefer ha-'Emunah ve-ha-Biṭaḥon*, pp. 360–361.

49. On this phenomenon among the disciples of Isaac Luria, see Fine, *Physician of the Soul, Healer of the Cosmos*, pp. 220–299.

50. This type has also been discussed by Moshe Idel in the context of other sources—both ancient and medieval. See Idel, *Kabbalah: New Perspectives*, pp. 157–166. And see also M. Fishbane, *Biblical Myth and Rabbinic Mythmaking*, pp. 177–182.

asserts that the tenth *sefirah* (*Malkhut/Shekhinah/ʿAtarah*) takes on either the character of Compassion (the embodiment of the *sefirah Ḥesed*) or that of Judgment (*middat ha-din*), depending on the actions of Israel below.[51] If the Jewish people behave in a manner that is pleasing to God, then *Shekhinah* assumes the properties of *Ḥesed*, and if the people violate the will of God, then *Shekhinah* becomes the harsh judge of the lower world. To use the analogy provided by Isaac of Akko (and ultimately rooted in Plato's *Phaedrus*), the tenth *sefirah* functions as the passive horse to the direction of the Rider above. Whichever Rider (either *Ḥesed* or *Din*) is more dominant at a given moment in time determines the movement of the horse, which in turn affects the lower world. Nevertheless, it is clear that the direction given by that supernal Rider corresponds directly to human action below, thus de facto endowing the human being with the ultimate power over the cosmos, and positing a circular character to the universe. The action initiated in the physical world rises to affect the supernal realm—a consequence that then cycles back to the lower world either as compassion or judgment in the relationship of the deity to humanity. With this in mind, consider the following passage:[52]

> וכשאנו עושין רצונו של מקום אנו מוסיפין כח וגבורה ושפע וברכה והצלחה והרוחה עליה, שנ' ועתה יגדל נא כח י"י. וכל השפע בא אליה בלי פירוד, ואז ישראל עולים למעלה ומתגברים על כל העולם. וכל הספירות נאחזות ונקשרות ביסוד, ויסוד קשור על מלכות. ואז כל העולמות בשלוה ובהשקט. וזהו שכתוב ונתתי שלום בארץ . . . ונתתי שלום שהוא יסוד בארץ שהיא מלכות. ואזי כל העולם בשובע גדול ובברכה.

> When we do the Will of God we add power,[53] strength, flow, blessing, success, and relief onto Her [*ʿAtarah*]. As it is written [Num. 14:17]: "Let the power of *'Adonai* be great."[54] And all of the flow comes to Her without any separation. Then Israel ascend above and overpower

51. This notion is by no means original to Isaac of Akko; it is characteristic of a widespread conception of *Shekhinah* as the passive receiver of energy from the upper *sefirot*. For an example of this model of divine receptivity and passivity in an earlier kabbalistic source (one that also relates to theurgical influence from below), see Joseph Gikatilla, *Shaʿarei 'Orah*, pp. 59–60.

52. Isaac of Akko, *Me'irat ʿEinayim*, p. 7.

53. This phraseology is a direct reuse and reworking of an earlier midrashic tradition. See *Midrash Eikhah Rabbah*, 1: 33; *Pesiqta' de-Rav Kahana*, 25: 1. Abraham Joshua Heschel has discussed the place and significance of this issue in rabbinic literature. See his *Torah min ha-Shamayim be-'Aspeqlaria shel ha-Dorot*, 1: 74–75.

54. The term used for God in this biblical verse is אדני, but has been preserved in *Me'irat ʿEinayim* as י"י.

> the entire world. All of the *sefirot* grasp onto, and are bound to *Yesod*, and *Yesod* becomes bound to *Malkhut*. Then all of the worlds are in a state of calm and quiet. And this is the meaning of what is written [Lev. 26:6]: "I have made peace in the land . . ." "I have made *peace*"—that is *Yesod*. "In the land"—that is *Malkhut*. Then all the world is in a state of great satiation and blessing.

Several different theurgical images are combined in this text. The proper action of human beings yields an *augmentation* of numerous cosmic energies, phrased through the fascinating term of action *'anu mosifin* (we add). The actions of Israel below *increase* the force of *Shekhinah* to a manifestly greater degree than She would have without them. In this respect, the human being serves a unique function in the orchestration of the cosmos—a revealing aspect of the kabbalist's own self-perception as one whose actions are critical to the dynamic life of God. Moreover, Isaac explicitly claims that this theurgical act empowers the Jew over all the world (presumably over the natural world, as well as over his medieval gentile oppressors). It is not hard to see the manner in which cosmic power comes to substitute for earthly powerlessness in this instance; the Jew who is unable to overpower his worldly adversaries on the mundane level is able to overpower them at the cosmic level instead. By doing God's Will, and thus augmenting the divine energy above, he is elevated to a new status of empowerment vis-à-vis the rest of creation.

Embedded within this augmentory model is a further image of cosmic influence. Jewish action is ultimately aimed at a state of cosmic tranquility—calm and quiet within the divine life. For as humans bring *Yesod* and *Malkhut* into a restored binding, a reunification of male and female (ויסוד קשור על מלכות), all cosmic life (that is to say, all *divine* life) is brought to the great calm of alignment, the peace in which everything is as it should be, unified without any separation (*beli peirud*). As we have seen in previous examples, this perfection of the divine self by human action is expressed through the dynamic of *shefa'*, the living flow of divine energy. We may characterize this type as the model of cosmic tranquility and harmony induced by human action—a type that shares in the deep orienting feature of kabbalistic theurgy: stimulation of divine energy and emanatory flow.

This conflation of maintenance, unification, and "drawing down" (*hamshakhah*) is also well represented by Isaac's conception of the *tefilin* ritual. By virtue of the inextricability of this ritual from the event of devotion, remaining aware of the theurgical force of wearing the *tefilin* emerges as a mode of mental intention on the part of the supplicant. Put another way, the act of binding *tefilin* serves as a framework for discussing the larger issues involved in the proper *kavvanah* for prayer. In a noteworthy passage,[55] Isaac begins by establishing a symbolic correlation between the *tefilin* as they are placed on the head and arm of the human being in prayer and the theosophical processes of divine emanation as they exist in the realm above.[56] Thus the *tefilin* of the head corresponds to the upper six *sefirot*. The scroll box that lies on the human forehead signifies the very highest *sefirot*, the black leather straps represent the flow of energy through the rest of the upper six, and *Tif'eret*, which is itself the sixth, is symbolized by the knot tied at the back of the head. As Isaac states, this *qesher shel tefilin* corresponds to *Tif'eret*[57] since that is the dimension that Moses saw when he viewed the back of God.[58] The lower four *sefirot* are represented by the *tefilah* of the arm,

55. Isaac of Akko, *Me'irat 'Einayim*, pp. 79–80.

56. The meaning of the ritual of *tefilin* is widely discussed in kabbalistic literature, and Isaac of Akko was therefore building upon a significant foundation of earlier traditions and writings on the subject. For zoharic and other kabbalistic discussions of *tefilin*, see Tishby, *Wisdom of the Zohar*, pp. 1186–1188. Two notable sources from Geronese Kabbalah pertaining to the mystical meaning of the *tefilin* ritual are mentioned by Tishby in his critical edition of 'Azriel of Gerona's *Perush ha-'Aggadot*, pp. 4–6. Other zoharic texts not mentioned by Tishby that touch upon the ontological implications of the ritual of *tefilin* include *Zohar* 1:13b, 3:54b, 3:71a, and many others. As already discussed earlier in this study, both the Catalonian (Gerona, Barcelona, etc.) and the Castilian (*Zohar* and related literature) kabbalistic traditions were highly influential in Isaac of Akko's thought (the impact of the *Zohar* is most visible in *'Oẓar Ḥayyim*), and thus both must be considered in understanding his place in the history of kabbalistic ideas and practices.

57. The kabbalistic idea that the *tefilah* of the head corresponds symbolically to *Tif'eret*, and that the *tefilah* of the arm corresponds to *'Atarah/Shekhinah* is to be found in earlier and contemporaneous kabbalistic sources (including *Zohar Ḥadash* and the writings of Joseph of Hamadan). In these texts, the two components of the *tefilin* are also explicitly associated with the respective male and female character of *Tif'eret* and *'Atarah*. See the remarks and sources cited by Wolfson in his edition of Moses de Leon's *Sefer ha-Rimmon* (Hebrew text section), p. 239, notes to line 2. Of perhaps even more immediate importance for the development of Isaac of Akko's formulation are the remarks of Shem Ṭov Ibn Ga'on in *Keter Shem Ṭov*, fol. 34b. In that context, Ibn Ga'on also correlates the קשר של תפילין with *Tif'eret*.

58. This tradition is clearly based on the classical rabbinic *'aggadah* that Moses saw the back knot of God's own *tefilin*, a notion extended from the rabbinic claim that God Himself wears *tefilin*. See BT *Berakhot*, fol. 7a. This midrashic move is built upon Exod. 33:23–34:7, in

and the scroll box tied to the arm signifies *'Atarah*, insofar as She is the dimension that gathers and includes all the others. Thus the metaphysical symbolism latent in the donning of the *tefilin* reflects the paradigm of emanation from above to below, and does not reflect the actual order of their placement on the human body.

The ritual act of wearing *tefilin* therefore emerges as a human reenactment of the divine structure, and must be seen as part of the kabbalistic conception that the physical human body is a microcosmic reflection of the sefirotic world. Within that view, which has been characterized recently by Jonathan Garb as "isomorphic power"[59] and by Antoine Faivre as "symbolic correspondences" or "the principle of universal interdependence,"[60] the fact that the body is perceived to be a mirror of supernal reality endows it with tremendous theurgic force, and many kabbalists argued that the spiritual and ethical perfection of the body has a profound effect upon the life of the *sefirot*.[61] In similar fashion, due to its reflection of divine Being (owing to its placement on the microcosmic structure of the physical body), the *tefilin* ritual becomes charged with a theurgical element as well. This view is primarily formulated by Isaac in the pejorative terms of potential separation in the sefirotic domain. Using the legal prohibition against speaking between the donning of the head *tefilin* and the arm *tefilin* as his starting point,[62] Isaac remarks that separating these two acts in the lower world by speaking is itself tantamount to causing division above among the *sefirot*. Because the *tefilah* of the head extends down to the knot as *Tif'eret*, from whence the divine

---

which Moses is described as having viewed the back of God. This root idea is representative of the larger rabbinic attempt to project the elements and objects of human Jewish ritual and sacred study onto the divine persona. Arthur Green has examined the relationship between the divine *tefilin* and the development of crown symbolism in Jewish mysticism. The *tefilin* that God wears above is a symbolic correlate of the divine crown inscribed with the name of the people Israel. See Green, *Keter: The Crown of God in Early Jewish Mysticism*, pp. 49–57.

59. Garb, "Power and Kavvanah," pp. 153–162.

60. Faivre, *Access to Western Esotericism*, pp. 10–11. On the human embodiment of the divine, see also Wolfson, *Through a Speculum That Shines;* id., *Language, Eros, Being*; Hecker, *Mystical Bodies, Mystical Meals*; id., "Eating Gestures and the Ritualized Body in Medieval Jewish Mysticism"; Abrams, *The Female Body of God*.

61. See Joseph Gikatilla, *Sha'arei 'Orah*, 1:45–51; Joseph ben Shalom 'Ashkenazi (Pseudo-RABaD), *Perush Sefer Yeẓirah*, fols. 13a–15a.

62. See BT *Menaḥot*, fol. 36a.

energy (in the kabbalistic interpretation) flows into the *tefilah* of the arm through the scroll box as *'Atarah*, to make a separation within the earthly ritual directly causes a separation between the metaphysical male and female lovers *Tif'eret* and *'Atarah*. However, this form of negative theurgy is ultimately predicated on a more positive idea. For if separating the *tefilin* through speech effects a rupture in the cosmic unity, then the ideal of achieving an unbroken continuum in the devotional ritual serves as an act of cosmic maintenance, and the supplicant thereby sustains the complete unity of the sefirotic structure. In the words of Isaac of Akko:[63]

> קבלתי כי תפלה של ראש רומז לתפארת ושל יד לעטרה ולפיכך אמרו כל השח בין תפלה לתפלה עבירה היא . . . שקצץ בנטיעות שהיה לו לייחד דו פרצופין בהנחת תפליו והפריד בשחתו.

> I received that the phylactery of the head alludes to *Tif'eret*, and the phylactery of the arm alludes to *'Atarah*. This is why [our sages] stated that whosoever speaks between [the donning of] one phylactery and the other has committed a sin. . . . For he has cut the shoots, seeing as how he was supposed to unify the *du-parzufin* in the act of donning his phylacteries, and instead he separated [the *du-parzufin*] through his conversation.

Thus, the prescribed intention is for the kabbalist to actively establish and maintain the unified harmony of the *sefirot*. In wearing the *tefilin* as he prays, ritually concretizing the universal interdependence of microcosm and macrocosm, the individual mystic must keep this awesome cosmic responsibility present in mind. When the performative character of the *tefilin* ritual is ruptured by the act of ordinary speech (thus allowing the intrusion of the profane into the holy), the very Being of Divinity reaps the consequences. In this way a tight ontological link is posited between proper performance of the sacred rite and maintenance of the desired wholeness of God's own self. The formal gestures of ritual—conceived as composing an integrated whole—mirror the very unity and completeness of the *sefirot*. It is this refraction of supernal forms within earthly ritual that endows Jewish devotion with ultimate significance.

---

63. Isaac of Akko, *Me'irat 'Einayim*, p. 80.

Drawing Forth the Cosmic Flow

The key words of kabbalistic discourse represent highly defined mentalities and modalities of praxis—the underlying structures and premises of the Jewish mystical imagination.[64] The term המשכה (drawing forth or attraction) is one of the more common such cases in medieval Kabbalah—a representation of the cosmic reverberations believed to be stimulated through ritual performance.[65] The connotation of this word is generally that of downward movement (i.e., *katabatic* attraction), but the underlying phenomenon (human stimulation of the divine flow) is not considered to be unidirectional, and sometimes manifests itself as the *elevation* of inner-divine flux (or *anabatic* force).[66] As we observed at the close of the foregoing section, the "drawing forth" model also serves to illustrate the concept of isomorphic power, or universal interdependence:

> בנין האדם נעשה על צורת בנין העליון . . . מלת הלשון רומז לתפארת שהוא מכריע ראשון ובמלת המעור הוא ברית מילה רומז לצדיק שהוא מכריע שני כטעם נשיאות כפים שהוא כדי להמשיך אצילות הברכה מהעשרה.
>
> The structure of the human being was made according to the form of the supernal structure. . . . The speech of the tongue alludes to *Tif'eret*, for He is the first Mediator. The circumcision of the foreskin, which is called *berit milah*, alludes to *Ẓaddiq*, for He is the second Mediator. This is similar to the purpose of raising the hands [in priestly blessing], which is enacted so as to draw forth the emanation of blessing from the Ten.[67]

It is thus the *structural correspondence* between the human and divine forms that allows for theurgical influence.[68] Building upon the paradig-

---

64. On the significance of key words and verses as markers within zoharic textuality, see Hellner-Eshed, "The Language of Mystical Experience in the Zohar," pp. 16–47.

65. On the use of this term in medieval Kabbalah, see Idel, "On Isaac the Blind's Intentions," pp. 36–42.

66. See Isaac of Akko, *Me'irat 'Einayim*, p. 100.

67. Ibid., p. 131.

68. Consider a parallel articulation of this principle of structural correspondence in Isaac's later work *'Oẓar Ḥayyim*, fol. 145a: עוד ראיתי בבנין האדם שהוא עולם קטן רמז לעשרת הדברים (With respect to the structure of a man, I further observed that he is a miniature world [a microcosm], an allusion to the Ten Utterances [the ten *sefirot*]).

matic rhetoric of *Sefer Yeẓirah*,[69] Isaac notes specific correspondences between the two forms—symbolic correlations that were commonplace in medieval kabbalistic thought. What is particularly noteworthy here is the manner in which a specific devotional gesture (the raising of hands in the priestly benediction) is constructed as a ritual action designed to draw out the emanatory energy of the ten *sefirot* so that the cosmos may be enriched.[70] It is precisely because of the symbolic isomorphic correlation between the ten fingers of the human hands and the ten dimensions of Divinity that the earthly ritual is able to have such a dramatic cosmic effect. This passage must be compared with a different tradition preserved in *Me'irat 'Einayim* regarding the isomorphic power (universal interdependence) of raised hands in the priestly benediction, and the manner in which it reflects the "drawing forth" (המשכה) type.[71] This particular passage is presented by Isaac as part of the traditions he attributes to *qabbalat saporta*, a group of manuscript traditions (most probably of Catalonian origin) whose influential impact on Isaac of Akko has been considered by Amos Goldreich.[72]

> ענין נשיאות כפים הוא לפי שהאדם כלול מן העליונים, וכשהוא מרים ידיו ומכוין בכונת לבו לרום השמים שמורה על אמתת העולמים ושהוא מעמיד הכל, מיד ישראל נענין לפי שפעולתן היא במחשבה. וכמו שרום בחול"ם מריק לכלם כך רום בשורו"ק מריק לכלם, כמו חוט השדרה. ברכת כהנים גם כן רומז לזה שממשיך הברכה עד למטה.[73]

> The meaning of [the ritual act of] raised hands [in priestly benediction] is as follows. Because the human being is composed of [the same

69. *Sefer Yeẓirah* 6:4. The play of that text, which influenced medieval Kabbalah, focuses upon the homonymic correlation between *millah* as "word" (i.e., of the mouth) and *milah* as circumcision (of the penis). On the correlation between ברית הלשון and ברית המעור as modes of human creativity that parallel divine creativity, see Yehudah Liebes, *Ars Poetica in Sefer Yeẓirah*, p. 101.

70. On this image, see Brody, "Human Hands Dwell in Heavenly Heights: Worship and Mystical Experience in Thirteenth-Century Kabbalah," pp. 446–502, and "Human Hands Dwell in Heavenly Heights: Contemplative Ascent and Theurgic Power in Thirteenth-Century Kabbalah."

71. Cf. also the isomorphic correspondence in Isaac of Akko, *Me'irat 'Einayim*, pp. 27, 99, 105.

72. On *qabbalat saporta* as a source of influence for Isaac of Akko, see Goldreich, "Introductory Study to *Me'irat 'Einayim*" (separate pagination from the critical edition of the text), pp. 76–89.

73. Isaac of Akko, *Me'irat 'Einayim*, p. 98.

> structure] as the supernal world, when he raises his hands and focuses with the intention of his mind/heart on the "Apex of the Heavens"—which points to the "Truth of the Worlds" that supports everything—then Israel are immediately answered, since their action impacts "Thought." Just as *Rom* [apex], vocalized with a *ḥolam* vowel, flows forth to them all, so too *Rum* [apex], vocalized with a *shuruq* vowel, flows forth to them all, just like the spinal column.[74] The priestly blessing also alludes to this, since it draws the blessing downward.

רום vocalized as *Rom* refers to *Keter*,[75] while רום vocalized as *Rum* correlates to *Yesod* as it receives the seed through the spinal column. Accordingly, concentration and ritual gesture on the part of the human being in prayer, which is directed to the highest of divine dimensions [*Keter*] (and to the flow of emanation that goes forth from there), will yield a powerful theurgic result.[76] These two modes of theurgical stimulus (*kavvanah* and *nesi'ut* [or *nesi'at*] *kapayim*, concentration and ritual gesture) thus serve to produce two dramatic consequences. The first is a seemingly coerced and immediate answer to the prayers and supplications of the Jewish people. The human being, by virtue of his isomorphic correspondence to the divine form, is able to expedite the divine answer to earthly supplication. Nevertheless, it would seem that the use here of the generic term *'adam* is not meant to extend the power of such action to all human beings (a universalist position), but must be viewed within the context of the *nesi'ut kapayim* ritual action, which is restricted to the *kohen* (priest).[77] At most, the action of *nesi'ut kapayim*

---

74. That is to say, just as the spinal column brings down the seed of life from the brain to the phallus.

75. See Green, *Keter: The Crown of God in Early Jewish Mysticism*, p. 154.

76. The physical act of נשיאת כפים in the priestly benediction was widely reflected upon in kabbalistic sources. See, e.g., *Bahir*, p. 181 (§ 95), as well as the famous *Yanuqa'* passage in *Zohar* 3:186a–188a. In his study of this particular gesture mentioned above, Seth Brody offers many further examples from early kabbalistic literature. Extensive documentation of this phenomenon in the Provençal and Geronese schools of Kabbalah is provided and analyzed in Pedayah, *Name and Sanctuary in the Thought of Rabbi Isaac the Blind*, pp. 116–128.

77. As Elliot Wolfson has argued, in much of kabbalistic literature the term *'adam* generally does not refer to humanity at large, but rather connotes the circumcised Jew, who alone is considered to embody the supernal paradigm. For examples in support of this claim, see Wolfson, "Ontology, Alterity, and Ethics in Kabbalistic Anthropology," pp. 138–139, and *Venturing Beyond: Law and Morality in Kabbalistic Mysticism*, pp. 42–57.

as a theurgical event can be extended to the elite kabbalist, as we shall see in a subsequent case.

The second theurgical result is that of the downward attraction of the divine flow toward the lower *sefirot* and the mundane world. Here, too, it is the "principle of universal interdependence" between the upper and lower forms of the cosmos that endows the human being with the power to stimulate the katabatic movement of emanation. This correspondence of forms, which allows the microcosmic structure to alter and affect the macrocosmic, is further underlined by the allusion to the relationship in symbolic metaphor between the human spinal column and the interconnected flow within the metaphysical world. Just as the spinal column connects the brain to the physical sensation of the body and, according to medieval biology, transfers the seminal seed of life from the brain of the male to the sexual conduit of progenation (the phallus), so, too, divine energy is sent from *Keter* down through *Tif'eret* to the entire sefirotic structure. As the text states quite clearly, it is because the human being physically embodies (or is composed of) the divine structure (לפי שהאדם כלול מן העליונים)—what has been aptly called "theomorphism," as opposed to "anthropomorphism"[78]—that his physical action in ritual (*nesi'ut kapayim*) is so powerful. Thus the use of the human body in a dramatic ritual gesture serves to stimulate the flow of life and energy through the divine world, likened as it is to the spinal column.

It should also be observed that we once again witness what would seem to be an underlying archetype of the mystical conception of ritual: external action (represented by the physical gesture of raising the hands) and internal intention (expressed through the phrase מכוין בכונת לבו). This repeating conceptual pair may be viewed as indicative of the deep structure of spiritually oriented religious practice—one in which the enactor of sacred ritual simultaneously undergoes two intertwined modalities of sacred action, one conducted on the outward plane of the body and the other on the inner plane of the mind and consciousness. Both of these modes of ritual action are considered to have tremendous power over the workings of the divine cosmos, and they indicate

78. Wolfson, *Through a Speculum That Shines*, pp. 16–24.

the fundamentally dual nature of spiritual action and experience. The kabbalist (or other religious person of a spiritualist orientation) forever experiences ritual on these two planes of enactment. Considered more broadly, it may be argued that human action in general constantly balances the mental event, which is internal at its essence, and the physical event, which is commonly visible and capable of joint and collective experience with other ritual participants.

Despite the fundamentally theocentric character of religion, *homo religiosus* is forever involved in the definition and redefinition of the *human* role in relationship to the deity. Both implicitly and explicitly, the religious author offers insight into a particular conception of human nature—a state of being that is defined *in relationship to* the divine focus of worship. The kabbalist participates in this general human tendency. For despite the fact that the main topic of speculation and reflection is Divinity, *homo kabbalisticus* can hardly express himself without conscious and unconscious reflection on how he *as a human being* (and for the kabbalist this means a *Jewish* human being) fits into the world of the sacred and affects the deity to whom he relates. Thus, as we make a transition into an analysis of a second subtype of *hamshakhah*—the role of a purified mental state in the act of "drawing forth" the emanatory flow—we shall encounter an explicit articulation of something that has been *implicit* all along: the human role vis-à-vis the divine cosmos as the ultimate meaning of human life. Consider the following remarks that serve as a kind of preamble to Isaac's reflections on purified consciousness:

> סוד הענין כי האדם תכלית כונת הבראו בעולם הזה אינה להנאת עצמו, כלומר גופו ולטובתו בלבד בעולם הזה, אלא לדעת את בוראו. וגם חכמי המחקר מודים לזה. וסוד הידיעה מלשון הכתוב וידע אלהים, מלשון וידע אדם, שהוא המשכת שפע ברכה אל העטרה.

> The secret of the matter is that the ultimate purpose of the creation of the human being in this world is not for his own pleasure—that is to say, [the pleasure of] his body and his enjoyment in this world—but rather in order that he might know [contemplate] his Creator. The philosophers also acknowledge this. The secret of knowledge can be

derived from the scriptural phrase "*'Elohim* knew" [Exod. 2:25],[79] and from the phrase "the man ['Adam] knew" [Gen. 4:25]—which means the drawing forth of blessing flow onto *'Atarah*.[80]

This construction of the meaning and purpose of human life (the contemplation and knowledge of God) is based on the classic formulation of the issue by Moses Maimonides in his *Mishneh Torah* and *Guide of the Perplexed*.[81] This is most certainly the root of the allusion to *ḥakhmei ha-meḥqar* (the sages of investigation), a phrase commonly used to refer to medieval Jewish philosophers.[82] Moreover, the Maimonidean contemplative ideal was highly influential among kabbalists who preceded Isaac of Akko, perhaps most prominently so in the Hebrew writings of Moses de Leon.[83] Yet what is most significant about these lines for present purposes is the theurgical issue that it exemplifies—a use of וידע that clearly demarcates the difference between philosophical and kabbalistic notions of contemplation. In defining the meaning of earthly human life as embodied in the act of *yedi'ah* (knowledge) directed toward the divine realm, Isaac of Akko sets up the exegetical basis for his subsequent assertion that the final meaning of human life is the maintenance of the cosmos, the theurgical act of drawing forth the flow of divine energy through the contemplative act of *yedi'ah*. The kabbalist's discussion of theurgical processes is thus simultaneously an introspective reflection on the purpose of his own human life within the framework of the larger divine cosmos. As we shall now see, this transformative contemplation is marked by an ideal of purity and clarity in the consciousness of the mystic:

כי בכח צדיקי ישראל היודעים סוד הייחוד, ובכח מעשיהם הטובים, בקרבנות ובתפלה, דתפילות כנגד תמידין תקנום, ובכונתם ההגונה הזכה והטהורה, ובמחשבתם הצלולה הקשורה למעלה למעלה מכל הברכות, נמשך ומשתלשל כח רצון חיים וברכה

79. The verse is being interpreted here in such a way that *'Elohim* is the object *as well as* the subject of the sentence.

80. Isaac of Akko, *Me'irat 'Einayim*, p. 125.

81. Moses Maimonides, *Mishneh Torah*, *Hilkhot De'ot*, 3: 3; id., *Guide of the Perplexed*, trans. Pines, 3: 51.

82. See Ben Yehuda, *Dictionary and Thesaurus of the Hebrew Language*, 4: 2930.

83. On this phenomenon in de Leon's *Sheqel ha-Qodesh*, see E. Fishbane, "Mystical Contemplation and the Limits of the Mind."

אור בהיר צח ומזהיר מסבת הסבות על העטרה, וממנה לכל באי עולם. וזהו שאנו אומרים שהנהגת העולם הזה על פיה. וזש"ה ישראל אשר בך אתפאר. העטרה אומרת, ישראל אשר על ידך וכונתך הזכה והטהורה וידיעתך להמשיך הברכה, אתפאר אתלבש ואתעטר ואכלל ברחמים בכח התפארת.

By the power of the righteous ones of Israel—those who know the secret of unification—through the power of their good deeds, through sacrifice or through prayer, for prayer was established in the place of sacrifice, through their proper and pure intention, and through their clear mind bound above, above all the blessings–[from all this] the power of will, life, blessing, bright, clear, and radiant light, is drawn forth and descends from the Cause of Causes onto *'Atarah*, and from Her to all the inhabitants of the world. This is what is meant when we say that She conducts the [functioning of the] world. As it is written [Is. 49:3]: "Israel, in whom I will be glorified" [*yisra'el 'asher bekha 'etpa'ar*]. *'Atarah* says: 'Israel, by your hand, and by your pure intention, and through your knowledge of the ability to draw forth the blessing, I will become glorified, robed, and crowned, and I will be included in Compassion, in the power of *Tif'eret*.[84]

The structure of this text, anchored as it is in a succession of key terms, should be viewed as paradigmatic. The theurgic power of the elite (the *ẓadiqei yisra'el*), which directly results in the efflux of cosmic energy, is manifested through five (seemingly) distinct modes of action: (1) knowledge of the secret of unity; (2) good deeds (the larger question of ethics and mysticism will be treated subsequently); (3) the external performance of devotional ritual (represented through the interchangeable models of sacrifice and verbal prayer); (4) proper and pure intention (*kavvanah*); and (5) clear mind and thought. The act of *yedi'ah* (knowledge), clearly asserted to be the ultimate purpose of human existence, is here considered to be a kind of devotional *contemplation*; it is the act of contemplative knowing that exercises such force in the cosmos. Insofar as these lines directly follow the immediately aforecited passage (כי האדם תכלית כונת הבראו בעולם הזה . . .), it is clear that the human being ultimately was created to be the orchestrator of cosmic energy, to stimulate the ebb and flow of intradivine existence. This is the true meaning and *telos* of

84. Isaac of Akko, *Me'irat 'Einayim*, p. 126.

Jewish life. What is more, the implication of this passage is that types 1, 4, and 5 are conflated, such that the act of *yedi'ah* prescribes a state of human consciousness characterized as *kavvanah ṭehorah* and *maḥshavah ẓelulah* (pure intention and clear mind).[85] In my view, these images are far from arbitrary characterizations, and they reflect a specific model of culmination in the mystical experience. The elite kabbalistic practitioner seeks to attain a mode of consciousness removed from the complexities of, and the obscurities caused by, ordinary intellectual activity. What is more, the phrase *maḥshavah qeshurah le-ma'alah* has much the same meaning as the conception of *maḥshavah deveqah*—the characterization of contemplative ecstasy and *unio mystica* that was widespread among the Geronese kabbalists of the earlier part of the thirteenth century.[86]

The invocation of the images of *purity* and *clarity* with respect to mental experience is not dissimilar to other constructions of the contemplative ideal by mystics of different religions, and thus points toward a certain archetypal tendency.[87] For Isaac of Akko, the mental ideal for the Jewish mystic is that of a high state of purity, which I

---

85. This notion of purity in consciousness as a contemplative ideal is also illustrated by an earlier kabbalistic text, noted by Scholem in his "The Concept of Kavvanah," p. 178, n. 38, and cited from MS Berlin 833, fol. 98a. In the context of depicting a fiery experience of elevated consciousness on the part of the *ẓadiqim ve-ha-ḥasidim* (righteous and pious individuals), their state of *maḥshavah ṭehorah* (pure thought/mind) is characterized as the stimulus for the unification of the *sefirot*. Of interest to us as well is the fact that the term *mitbodedim* (meditators [in solitude?]) is also used in this passage (I discuss the importance of this term in Chapter 8). This text is also referred to and discussed in Tishby, *Mishnat ha-Zohar* (Hebrew edition), 2: 255. For further uses of the phrase *maḥshavah ṭehorah* in kabbalistic literature, see Idel, *R. Menaḥem Recanati the Kabbalist*, p. 132 (in which he compares relevant passages from Recanati's *Ta'amei ha-Mizvot* and Jacob ben Sheshet's *Sefer ha-Emunah ve-ha-Biṭaḥon*) and p. 258, n. 40. A state of purity (and sanctity) of heart at the moment of prayer is also represented as an ideal state in parts of the *Heikhalot* literature. See, e.g., *Synopse zur Hekhalot Literatur*, ed. Schäfer, §544 N8128 (p. 202).

86. Seth Brody has also treated this central issue in his "Human Hands Dwell in Heavenly Heights: Worship and Mystical Experience in Thirteenth-Century Kabbalah."

87. Buddhist notions of mental emptiness and "non-thinking" particularly come to mind as an example of the contemplative desire to achieve a refined and sharpened state of consciousness (see Bielefeldt, *Dōgen's Manuals of Zen Meditation*, pp. 133–160). Perhaps of even greater comparative relevance, Indian Yogic piety asserts the need for a process of both physical and psychic purification in preparation for, and experience of, contemplative mind (see Eliade, *Yoga: Immortality and Freedom*, pp. 50–52). And see also the studies assembled in Forman, ed., *The Problem of Pure Consciousness*, and the analysis in Forman, *Mysticism, Mind, Consciousness*, pp. 11–51, 81–107. Indeed, I submit that it would not be an overstatement to count the purification of consciousness as one of the deep cross-cultural structures of the human religious imagination.

believe should be defined as a state of spiritual lucidity and purity of focus in consciousness. Implicit in Isaac's characterization is a distinction between the kabbalist who has achieved this level of supreme purity of thought and all those whose minds are impure, insofar as purity as a concept and a condition is ultimately defined according to what it is *not*. In this respect, the state of purity may ultimately be defined as the lack of any contaminating element—an impurity that would likely encompass both a less refined state of contemplation (i.e., a lack of spiritual lucidity) and a profane mode of thought, considered ritually inadmissible. In this sense, the rhetoric of "pure intention and thought" is designed to *distinguish the kabbalist* from other individuals in keeping with the extreme degree of kabbalistic social elitism. By attaining this paradigmatic condition of a clear (*ẓelulah*) and purified (*ṭehorah*) mind (once again the characterization of an *internal* spiritual performance), and by combining that mode of consciousness with the *external* act of ritual devotion (*be-qorbanot 'o-be-tefilah*—in sacrifices or in prayer), the elite kabbalist is able to direct the flow of emanatory energy onto the tenth *sefirah*, and finally to the lower world of human existence as well (וממנה לכל באי עולם). This particular phrase reveals a distinctly nonexclusive conception of the filtration of divine energy to the lower world. That is to say, *all persons* of the earthly world receive their vitality from the flux of the sefirotic universe; Isaac does not limit this continuum of life to the Jewish people (could לכל באי עולם really be read as particularistic?), as he certainly does with respect to the theurgic power of cosmic stimulation. That power, according to Isaac, rests solely with the Jew, and even then such power is restricted to the esoteric knowledge of elite kabbalistic sages (כי בכח צדיקי ישראל היודעים סוד הייחוד).

The *sefirot* (channeled through *'Atarah/Shekhinah*) are the source of life and vitality for the lower worlds; in this respect, the cosmos functions as a continuous living organism.[88] The purpose of human existence is the act of drawing forth living energy through the *sefirot* (a cosmos-sustaining act) and the delivery of cosmic life to the entirety of earthly existence. That is the function of the kabbalist's esoteric act of *yedi'ah*,

---

88. On the notion of the cosmic continuum, and its relationship to the theurgic power of the human being, see Garb, "Power and Kavvanah," pp. 98–99, and *Manifestations of Power*, pp. 72–73. Garb characterizes this idea as the רציפה המרחבית (spatial continuum).

and therefore is the purpose of his creation by God (for, as noted above, the meaning of human life is explicitly linked to the act of *yedi'ah*). Articulation of theology and theurgy thus emerges as a prominent mode of *self-understanding* on the part of the human kabbalist; his conception of metaphysical dynamics is entirely oriented by his definition of human purpose and responsibility. In this respect, the divine cosmos is not self-sustaining (at least inasmuch as it has been damaged by improper human action). It requires the intervention and power of the human being as he acts in sacred ritual, both internally (through *kavvanah*) and externally (through the physical ritual of prayer). This is the force of Isaac's use of the verse from Isaiah—*yisra'el 'asher bekha 'etpa'ar*.[89] In this intentional kabbalistic misreading of the original biblical text (an interpretive play that serves a dynamic symbolic function), the tenth *sefirah* (*'Atarah/Shekhinah*) acknowledges the power of Israel (i.e., the Jewish kabbalist in devotional contemplation) to draw forth the flow of emanatory blessing, and to thereby cause *'Atarah* to be bound up in the energy of *Tif'eret*. More precisely, the actions of Israel below cause *'Atarah* to become *Tif'eret*-ized (*'etpa'ar*), crowned and unified with *Tif'eret*—a brilliant hermeneutical play on the two words תפארת and אתפאר. Such a transformation of the sefirotic domain ultimately has the larger cosmic result of sending down the flow of life to the inhabitants of the earth.

Two additional text cases will serve to further explore the use of this type in Isaac's writing. The first of these may also function as intriguing testimony to ecumenical religious conversation in the Middle Ages:

> ושמעתי מפי חכם מקובל שיום אחד נתלוו יהודי וגוי חכמים גדולים לדבר בחכמות. אמר הגוי ליהודי רואה אני באמת כי אלהיכם אלהי אמת ותורתיכם תורת אמת ומעשי אבותיכם נביאי האמת וכהניכם בעבודת מקדשכם שהיא עבודת הקרבנות אמת. כי על כל פנים כחות עליון אע"פ שהכל ביד עליון מכל מקום צריכים ממשיך להמשיכם לפרנס התחתונים בקרבנות ובתפלה ובשיר נעים ובכונת לב זך וטהור ונקי קשורה בעליונים. כי השם ית' נתן כח ביד האדם לעשות כל רצונו, ולפי מעשיו ימשיך עליו כח עליון. אם בטובה ימשיך עליו כח הטוב, ואם בהיפך היפך. הכל ביד האדם.

> I heard from the mouth of a wise kabbalist that one day a Jew and a Gentile—both great sages—came together to discuss matters of

89. This verse was widely used in kabbalistic literature to infer mystical meaning regarding the *sefirot*. For a usage that foreshadows Isaac of Akko's interpretation of the verse as a symbolic allusion to the interconnected nature of *Tif'eret* and *'Atarah*, see *Zohar* 2:74a.

> wisdom. The Gentile said to the Jew: I truly see that your God is a true God, your Torah [or "your teachings"] is a Torah of truth, the deeds of your forefathers—the prophets of truth—and that of your priests in the service of your Temple, which is the service of sacrifices, were true. For with regard to the supernal powers, even though everything is in the hands of the Supernal, nevertheless the powers need a drawer [*mamshikh*] to draw them forth, in order to nourish the [inhabitants of the] lower world, through sacrifices, prayer, pleasant song, and a pure and clean intention of the mind/heart bound to the supernal [powers]. For God, may He be blessed, gave the human being the power to do all of His Will, and by way of his [the human's] actions, *he will draw onto himself supernal power.* If he acts for the good, he will draw onto himself good power, and if he acts in the opposite manner, then he will receive the opposite consequence. All is in the hands of the human being.[90]

It is not clear whether this anecdote is to be taken as historical, or if the tradition preserved by Isaac of Akko has simply procured a fictionally agreeable Gentile to legitimate Jewish religion vis-à-vis the other religions of the world. The very idea, however, that sages of different faiths would meet to discuss matters of wisdom in an implicitly ecumenical fashion—whether that image be historical or fictional—is remarkable testimony to the spiritual and social outlook of the times.[91] Yet the issues that are discussed in this report—which are asserted to be essential tenets of the Jewish faith—are even more intriguing to my mind. Indeed, despite the fact that a pious caveat is posited to the effect that "all is in the hands of heaven," the passage makes amply clear that the center of universal power lies in the actions of the human being, and that the divine domain is actually in a *state of dependency* on the human. This radical position is stated quite clearly: מכל מקום צריכים ממשיך להמשיכם לפרנס התחתונים (nevertheless the powers

---

90. Isaac of Akko, *Me'irat 'Einayim*, p. 143.

91. The argument in this regard has tended to claim that Muslims were far less inclined to attack Jews *on theological grounds* than were their Christian counterparts in the Middle Ages. See Lewis, *The Jews of Islam*, p. 85; M. R. Cohen, *Under Crescent and Cross: The Jews in the Middle Ages*, p. xviii. We may recall, in some contrast, that Isaac of Akko (at least by the time of the writing of *'Oẓar Ḥayyim*) had a more fearful outlook toward Muslims, and a more optimistic attitude toward the greeting of his Christian neighbors. See Chapter 2 above.

need a drawer [*mamshikh]* to draw them forth, in order to nourish the [inhabitants of the] lower world). The use of the term צריכים is highly provocative indeed, and quite blatantly demonstrates the *self-conception* of the kabbalist with respect to the larger divine cosmos. As a kabbalist, in his ritual actions and his mental intentions, he possesses the key to cosmic power and divine transformation. This particular worldview is unequivocally reinforced by the basic subversion of the original caveat that "all is in the hands of the Supernal." For Isaac concludes the reflection by stating in no uncertain terms that הכל ביד האדם (all is in the hands of the human being). Thus, this passage, like those noted above, is fundamentally anthropocentric, and oriented toward a deeper understanding of the place of the human in the larger scheme of the cosmos and the divine Self. The ultimate assertion is that the cosmos depends entirely upon the actions and intentions of the human being.[92]

As was also the case with the earlier example, the event of *hamshakhah* takes place as a consequence of both the external physical act of ritual and the internal mental event of *kavvanah*. This state of *kavvanah* is once again constructed as a modality of mind predicated on the attainment of purification within human consciousness—here supplemented by the further image of a "clean" (*naqi*) state of intention or consciousness. While the precise meaning of the word "clean" (i.e., what state of mind and intention is in fact considered to be clean) remains ambiguous in this passage, the use of this word would seem to underscore the need to *prepare* for contemplative ascent by ridding one's mind of all impure and profane thoughts.[93] My assumption (and this must remain hypothesis, due to the laconic nature of the text), given the likely connection of these practices to the ideal of detachment from physicality (a theme to be dealt with more extensively in Chapter 8), is that the

---

92. Regarding this text, the reader should also consider the remarks of Dov Schwartz, in which the passage is deemed to bear the "unmistakable traits of the magical-astral explanation of sacrifice." See Schwartz, "From Theurgy to Magic: The Evolution of the Magical-Talismanic Justification of Sacrifice in the Circle of Nahmanides and His Interpreters," pp. 194–195.

93. This assumption accords well with the fact that the image of a cleansed mind was a dominant feature of Sufi mysticism—a stream of religious thought and praxis that seems to have been formative for Isaac of Akko. I thank Prof. Lenn Goodman for affirming this point for me with regard to Islamic religion.

elite mystic was expected to cleanse and purify his consciousness of all association with the profane world of corporeal existence. Only then would his directed consciousness become theurgically empowered. The kabbalistic conception of cosmic dependence on the human (at least as far as *hamshakhah* is concerned), framed here through a typology of purified mind and the event of drawing forth, may be further reinforced by one final passage:

> ואמרנו שהתפארת שמח בה וכועס עליה כל זה משל כי לשפע ברכת רחמים בה בזכות הצדיקים ובמחשבתם הזכה שהם ברי לבב שעליהם נאמר מי יעלה בהר י"י ומי יקום במקום קדשו נקי כפים ובר לבב. כנו שמחה ואורה וכיוצא באלו ולסלוקם ממנה בעון הדור כנו כעס ועצבון וכיוצא בהן. והכל משל כדי לתת למשכילים בינה להבין ענין שפע רחמים אל בני העולם על ידה וסלוקם מהם בעשותה בהם פורענות כמעשיהם.

> We have said that [the image of] *Tif'eret* rejoicing in Her [*'Atarah*] and becoming angered with Her is all a parable for the flow of Compassion's [= *Tif'eret*'s] blessing onto Her, by virtue of the righteous ones and their pure minds. For they are pure of heart [or mind], as it has been written of them [Ps. 24:4]: "Who may ascend the mountain of YHVH? Who may stand in His holy place?—He who has clean hands and a pure heart." [This effect] has been called joy and happiness, and the like. The withdrawal of these from Her [*'Atarah*] through the sin of a generation has been called anger and sadness, and the like. This is all a parable [provided] so as to give the wise ones the understanding to understand the matter of the efflux of Compassion to the people of the world through Her [*'Atarah*], and the withdrawal of that Compassion from them when She visits punishment upon them in accordance with their actions.[94]

Although classical midrashic texts frequently use the term *mashal* in the process of manipulating a worldly image or interaction to teach some greater truth about the theological realm,[95] *mashal* is used here by the kabbalist to neutralize anthropomorphism. Isaac of Akko asserts that all such anthropic imagery regarding the relationship between

---

94. Isaac of Akko, *Me'irat 'Einayim*, p. 132.

95. See David Stern, *Parables in Midrash*, pp. 11–12, where the *mashal* is understood to be a narrative or image that points beyond itself.

Tif'eret and *'Atarah* (rejoicing or becoming angered) ultimately refers to the theurgically stimulated flow of emanation through the cosmos. It is in this context that we once again encounter the significance of mental purity—a condition of consciousness that has the immense power to draw forth the cosmic energies. The universe functions through dynamic movements of flow (*shefa'*) and withdrawal (*siluq*), both of which are ultimately dependent upon the actions and *state of mind* cultivated by the "righteous ones"—code for the elite kabbalist who maintains and sustains the world. It is the kabbalist who enables *'Atarah*, and ultimately all the inhabitants of the earth, to receive the *shefa'*. As Isaac states quite clearly: כל זה משל כי לשפע ברכת רחמים בה בזכות הצדיקים ([This] is all a parable for the flow of Compassion's [= *Tif'eret*'s] blessing onto Her, by virtue of the righteous ones). The use of the biblical terms *naqi kapayim* (of clean hands) and *bar levav* (pure of heart) in this passage serve to further represent the centrality of the juxtaposition of an external physical condition with an internal state of being—the two fundamental poles of human experience. Physical ritual purity is represented by the term "clean hands," while Isaac clearly correlates internal purity with an exalted mystical consciousness (i.e., בר לבב [pure of heart] is correlated with מחשבתם הזכה [their pure thought]). Furthermore, just as purity of heart and hands are the prerequisites for passage into the sacred space (the ascension of God's mountain in the biblical discourse), so too the mystic who will ascend the metaphysical divine mountain in contemplation and intention must function in a state of purified and rarefied consciousness. As in earlier examples, Isaac of Akko makes it clear that the kabbalist is to understand his role in the cosmos (and by extension, his purpose in life) as the stimulation and facilitation of the flow of Divinity through the *sefirot* and down to the earthly world. The ideal religious type manifested here is that of a physical body and a mental existence unsullied by any impurity.

Another subtype of the *hamshakhah* theurgical model in Isaac's *Me'irat 'Einayim,* which should further enrich our understanding of kabbalistic ritual enactment, may be termed the *vocalization* type. This issue was briefly anticipated earlier in this chapter with respect to the unitive model of theurgy. My primary concern here, however, is the intersection of vocalization and the enactment of katabatic attraction ("drawing down"). This subtype places the emphasis on the external pole of human devotional behavior (that is, the sound that emerges physically from the human mouth and is audible externally to the human ears), and, as we saw in the case cited earlier in this chapter, it lends insight into Isaac of Akko's *esotericization* of a normative legal requirement (a kabbalistic interpretation of the talmudic stipulation that prayer be audible). Theurgical power, expressed through the key word *hamshakhah*, is associated with the ritual act of audibly vocalizing the liturgical text of prayer. Isaac of Akko begins with an analogy regarding sacrifice, transmitted from one of his numerous oral sources, which he uses to set the stage for his assertion with respect to vocal power in the devotional ritual of prayer.

עוד אמר אלי ראיה חזקה ומופת מופלא נראה לעין שעשן הקרבנות סבה להמשיך שפע ברכה וחיים ורצון לעולם השפל מהעולם העליון. קח לך נר של שעוה או נר אחר וכבה אותו וטרם כלות עשנו שימהו מכוון תחת נר דולק ותראה שהעשן ימשיך להבת הנר העליון מלמעלה למטה היפך טבע האש והנר התחתון ידלק.

> He also told me of a strong and wondrous proof, visible to the eye, that the smoke of sacrifices is the cause for the drawing down of the flow of blessing, life, and will to the lower world from the upper world. Take for yourself a wax candle, or a different kind of candle. Extinguish it, and before its smoke ceases place it directly beneath a burning candle, and you will see that the smoke will draw down the flame of the upper candle, from above to below, the opposite of the [ordinary] nature of fire, and the lower candle will be ignited.[96]

As we have noted in numerous cases, the kabbalist believed that the phenomena of the mundane world replicated deep cosmic patterns and structures. This passage reveals the profoundly *physical* nature of theurgic action; external corporeal deeds that are performed in the earthly world are thought to result in physio-spatial changes in the Being of the cosmos. Here it is clear that the kabbalistic conception of cosmology is not entirely metaphorical or figuratively constructed. On the contrary, this text displays the high degree of physical literalism inherent in these

---

96. Isaac of Akko, *Me'irat 'Einayim*, p. 143.

ontological speculations about the workings of the universe. What is discernable in the functioning of natural law may be applied to larger cosmic dynamics and paradigms. Just as smoke has the power to invert the natural *upward* movement of the earthly flame, so, too, the smoke of mundane sacrifice (as a physical manifestation of sacred devotion) has the power to bring Divinity into the lower world. The focus of this transmission is on the physical power of the devotional action; the realities of natural law are enlisted to bolster this idea. It is in this respect that the conclusion regarding sacrificial smoke is extended to the theurgic power of the human voice in prayer:

> ויה"ב שנ"ר דעת"ו אומ' כי הואיל ותפלות כנגד תמידין תקנום צריך על כל פנים למתפלל להוציא הבל הדברים בפיו כדי להמשיך שפע ברכה ואין כונת הלב לבדו מספיק להוציא מלב מחשבת תועי רוח המזלזלים בתפלה רחמנא ליצלן מדעתיהו.

> And I, Isaac . . . of Akko, . . . say that since prayer was established as a substitute for sacrifice, the supplicant must send out the breath of his words through his mouth, so as to draw forth the flow of blessing. And the intention of the mind alone is not sufficient. [Such a view] should be removed from the minds of the flawed of spirit, who deride prayer—Heaven forefend![97]

The assertion regarding the physical power of sacrificial smoke is thus employed as the basis for a more applicable proposition: the physical power of human breath in the vocal act of liturgical prayer.[98] As noted earlier, this theurgical statement builds on the normative legal requirement that prayer be audibly vocalized.[99] Yet the reason for this ritual standard in the kabbalistic mentality is one of cosmic empowerment and the human calling to draw forth the emanational flow of Being. The polemic of Isaac's remarks is clearly directed toward the philosophers of his time, some of whom argued that the nomian structures of ritual (in this case, prayer) were unnecessary in light of the philosopher's ability to substitute inner intention for the external

97. Ibid., p. 143.

98. To be sure, and among other sources, the language of Psalm 141:2 stands in the background of this conception (תִּכּוֹן תְּפִלָּתִי קְטֹרֶת לְפָנֶיךָ [Take my prayer as an offering of incense]).

99. The case cited earlier uses the candle analogy with similar implication, and the two passages should be read in conjunction with one another.

performance of the commandments. Numerous kabbalists, among them, Moses de Leon, attacked this philosophical position precisely on the grounds that the *external* act itself was endowed with tremendous cosmic power to affect Divinity, and thus could not under any circumstances be disregarded.[100] As we have seen in several cases, Isaac of Akko, like many kabbalists before him, was deeply taken with the problems posed by the internal-external dialectic of ritual, and he asserts on more than one occasion that both of these poles of action serve powerful functions in the restoration and maintenance of divine reality. In this respect, the construction of theurgical power viewed here is a manifestly *physical* one. The corporeal substance of sacrificial smoke results in a physical transformation of cosmic Being, and in a like manner, the breath released in the speech of human prayer has a physical consequence in the divine realm—here articulated in the image of *hamshakhah*. For Isaac of Akko (as for Kabbalah in general), the devotional paradigms of sacrifice and prayer are essentially fluid images in mystical reflection on the contemplative and theurgical processes. Implied in Isaac's remarks is the notion that these two historically determined modalities reflect one and the same devotional phenomenon, and thus may be treated as identical in the search for paradigms of devotional theurgical action. Needless to say, this position emerges naturally out of the classical rabbinic assertion that prayer substitutes for sacrifice ("כי הואיל ותפלות כנגד תמידין תקנום").[101]

Let us consider one final topos that falls under the rubric of theurgy (and katabatic attraction, in particular) in *Me'irat 'Einayim*: the cosmic power of moral integrity and proper behavior. Indeed, I would suggest that this belief (and implicit prescription) functions as a foundational element both for Isaac's general conception of theurgy and for the question of contemplative experience. In setting out to understand the place of morality in Isaac of Akko's kabbalistic thought, the deeply *particularistic* character of ethical construction in medieval Jewish religion must be emphasized. For with regard to behavior,

---

100. See Matt, "The Mystic and the *Mizwot*," esp. p. 375; Wolfson, "Mystical Rationalization of the Commandments in *Sefer ha-Rimmon*."

101. See BT *Berakhot*, fol. 26b.

the medieval kabbalist did not think in the categories of a universalist ethic, of a standard of moral action that might be applicable to all peoples irrespective of culture and religion. This neo-Kantian view was the furthest thing possible from the kabbalistic mentality in the Middle Ages.[102] Instead, we should apply the root question of ethics to Kabbalah (adapted, of course, to a highly particularist mentality), as it has been formulated by philosophers from Plato to the present: What is the proper way to conduct a life,[103] and what are the larger implications of that behavior? What is the good—which is to say, what are the ideals that define us as human beings and that define the essence of our particular culture? For the kabbalist, "the good" (and, as we shall see, the Hebrew correlate of this very term is in fact used) is ultimately defined as action that accords with the Will of God. To conduct one's life with moral integrity is therefore inescapably shaped by a highly ritualistic conception of right action and conversely oriented by the pervasive rhetoric of sin. This dominant construction is occasionally supplemented by glimpses of what might be called a universalist ethical intuition, albeit one always framed within the boundaries of specific cultural norms. An example of this view of good action or behavior (which admittedly remains vague as to the precise content of "the good") may be culled from a passage cited earlier in this chapter with different emphasis:

כי בכח צדיקי ישראל היודעים סוד הייחוד, ובכח מעשיהם הטובים . . . נמשך ומשתלשל כח רצון חיים וברכה אור בהיר צח ומזהיר . . .

> It is from the power of the righteous ones of Israel, those who know the secret of unification, *through the power of their good deeds* . . . [that] the power of will, life, blessing, bright, clear, and radiant light, is drawn forth and descends . . .[104]

Despite the fact that we, as moderns, might be tempted to read the phrase "good deeds" along the lines of a universalist ethic of conduct, it is not entirely clear if this is Isaac's intention, or if a more particularist conception is implied here—one based on a divinely ordained (thus

---

102. See Wolfson, "Ontology, Alterity, and Ethics in Kabbalistic Anthropology," p. 131.

103. See Williams, *Ethics and the Limits of Philosophy*, pp. 1–21.

104. Isaac of Akko, *Me'irat 'Einayim*, p. 126.

automatically binding) and culturally specific code of conduct. Compare, therefore, this usage of *ṭov*/good (and its intersection with the ideals of behavior) with a different passage, which also illustrates the powerful interface between "good" conduct and theurgical implication:[105]

אתה יודע כי התחתונים נזונים מן העליונים, והעליונים נקשרים בעליונים מקבלים כח ושפע בעשותנו הטוב והישר בעיני אלהינו ומוסיפים שפע וקיום. ויש בנו כח לתת כח למעלה וחס ושלום פגם אלא שאנו פוסקים הטוב והשפע . . . בעשותינו הטוב יורד השפע דרך צנורות רוחניות, ובעשות הרע יורד דרך אחרת לצד אחר ונפסק הטוב לעליונים ואינו בא דרך ישר מספירה לספירה ונשארת הספירה יבשה מכל טוב. ונמצא כי בעונותינו נחסרה מכל ואין לה פגם גדול מזה. הנה הדבר ברור ונכון כי יש כח בעליונים להשפיע לתחתונים, ויש כח בתחתונים לסייע לעליונים ולקיימם.

You know that the lower [world] is nourished by the supernal, and that the supernal dimensions—bound to [further] supernal dimensions—receive power and flow when we do what is good and right in the eyes of our God,[106] and we add flow and firmness [to the supernal dimensions]. *We have the power to bestow power above*, and, Heaven forbid, [to bestow] flaw as well if we stop the good and the flow [above]. . . . When we do good the flow descends through spiritual channels, and when we do bad, it descends through a different way, to another side,[107] and the flow of good is stopped [from reaching] the supernal dimensions. Then it does not come forth in a straight path from *sefirah* to *sefirah*, and the *sefirah* remains dryly bereft of all good. It follows that it is through our sins that She lacks for everything, and there is no flaw in Her greater than this. It is indeed clear and true that the supernal

105. Ibid., p. 158. Regarding the theurgical impact of *ṭov* in earlier kabbalistic literature, see the usage in *Bahir*, p. 169 (§ 82). Cf. Garb, "Power and Kavvanah," p. 99.

106. This phrase is derived from Deut. 6:18, widely used in Jewish sources to refer to general standards of ethical conduct that are not specifically indicated in halakhic prescription. In Naḥmanides' commentary to this verse, the master states that the words טוב וישר point toward those actions that extend beyond the letter of the law (לפנים משורת הדין). See Naḥmanides, *Perush ha-Ramban ʿal ha-Torah*, 2: 376. Cf. Green, "Judaism and the Good," pp. 129–130.

107. This correlation of evil to צד אחר (another side) is no doubt a reverberation of the Castilian conception of evil, most prominently expressed in the *Zohar* as סטרא אחרא (the Other Side). For general overviews of this theme, see Scholem, "*Sitra Aḥra*: Good and Evil in the Kabbalah," pp. 56–87; Tishby, *The Wisdom of the Zohar*, pp. 447–528. It is noteworthy that this idea appears in *Meʾirat ʿEinayim*, inasmuch as it reflects familiarity with Castilian ideas that were integrated by Isaac in the first decade of the fourteenth century.

> dimensions have the power to flow to the lower dimensions, and it is [also true] that the lower dimensions have the power to support and to maintain the supernal dimensions.

This passage posits an unequivocally binary conception of human action (divided between clearly demarcated boundaries of good and bad), which has a correlative effect upon the state of the divine cosmos. Here, as we saw in earlier cases, the human being wields a tremendous power over the divine, enabling a nourishing flow of emanation, on the one hand (here constructed as *katabatic* attraction—note the recurrent use of the rhetoric of *descent*), and causing obstruction, desiccation, and flaw on the other. Indeed, Isaac of Akko does not shy away from the bold implications of these assertions. On the contrary, he builds upon them to reach an understanding of the purpose and power of the human being that understands the meaning of human life in relationship to its powerful cosmic role. As he states quite explicitly: יש בנו כח לתת כח למעלה וחס ושלום פגם (we have the power to bestow power above, and—heaven forefend—[to bring about] a flaw), and ברור ונכון כי יש כח בעליונים להשפיע לתחתונים, ויש כח בתחתונים לסייע לעליונים ולקיימם (It is indeed clear and true that the supernal dimensions have the power to flow to the lower dimensions, and it is [also true] that the lower dimensions have the power to support and to maintain the supernal dimensions). The use of the word *ṭov* (good) in this text remains rather ambiguous, and only assuredly implies the ability to accord earthly behavior with a celestial divine Will. The "good" that is embodied or absent in worldly behavior correlates directly to an ontological force of "the good" within God's own perpetually emanating self. Negative action results in a *sefirah* parched from the withdrawal of the nourishing waters of "the good," and the word *ṭov* becomes synonymous with the array of other metaphors employed to refer to the divine flow of energy, the emanation of cosmic life. Much as the word *berakhah* (blessing) is used ubiquitously in kabbalistic literature to refer to the divine flow and to a human utterance (thus implying a direct correlation between ritual performance and divine reality), the enactment of virtue assumes a macrocosmic reverberation and refraction as well. We may further note that upright action is polarized with behavior characterized as sin (עונותינו)—a deeply ritualistic conception of proper and improper action. In this respect, the ethical ideal is inextricably linked to the fulfillment of tradition-specific, divinely sanctioned behavior; morality is defined as the ideals of action determined by a particular sociocultural configuration, and not by a universalist conception of justice and the good. Consider the following parallels from *Me'irat 'Einayim* that make my point clear:

בזמן שישראל עושין רצונו של הב"ה העטרה אצל התפארת כמו הכלה אצל החתן. והכתר עליהם כמו גג החופה על החתן והכלה, והחכמה והבינה סביבותיהם כמו כתלי החופה סביבות החתן והכלה, ומקבלים שפע ברכה חיים ורצון.

> When the people of Israel do the Will of the Holy One, blessed be He, *'Atarah* is with *Tif'eret* like the bride is with the groom. And *Keter* is over them like the roof of the wedding canopy over the groom and the bride. *Ḥokhmah* and *Binah* surround them like the walls of the *Ḥuppah* around the groom and the bride, and they [all] receive the flow of blessing, life, and Will.[108]

Compare this with the very similar rhetoric found elsewhere in this treatise:

כשישראל עושין רצונו של מקום אז הוא אומר שמי בקרבו, כלומר שמשפיע פנים המאירים, פנים של רחמים בקרב העטרה. אבל בשעת כעס הם פנים של זעם.

> When Israel do the Will of God,[109] then He says [Exod. 23:21] "My Name is in him," which is to say that He sends forth the flow of radiant countenance, the face of *Raḥamim* [Compassion = *Tif'eret*] onto *'Atarah*. But when He is angry, this is a countenance of fury.[110]

In this configuration, ideal conduct is that which accords with the will of God—a Will that prescribes a culturally specific mode of behavior. Upright action is unambiguously identified with adherence and obedience to a heavenly decree (the divine *razon*)—not to some universalist ethic, abstractly conceived. If the people of Israel behave

---

108. Isaac of Akko, *Me'irat 'Einayim*, p. 119.

109. This is directly based on several talmudic versions of a classical idea that Israel will be protected by God if it does the will of God. See, e.g., BT *Sukkah*, fol. 29a; *Ketubbot*, fol. 66b.

110. Isaac of Akko, *Me'irat 'Einayim*, p. 134.

in this manner, the sefirotic world will be transformed for the better, whether that theurgy is expressed generally as a romantic *hieros gamos* or particularly as the flow of light from the face of *Tif'eret* to *'Atarah*. Moreover, to turn away from sin in penitence, to transform one's actions to conform to the ideal of righteous action, is a mode of behavior that reverberates in the cosmos:

כשיעשו ישראל תשובה ויהיו צדיקים גמורים, אז יהיה הייחוד שלם והשפע מתברך ומתעלה השכינה ותתברך ויהיו דו הפרצופין כחתן וכלה.

> When Israel repent and are completely righteous, then the unity will be complete. The flow will bless and elevate the *Shekhinah*, and the Two Faces [*du-parzufin*] will be as groom and bride.[111]

The restoration/unification of Divinity, the transformation of the sefirotic world into a perfected condition, is fully linked to the *human* process of self-perfection. As noted earlier, it is the penitential process that paves the way to a state of spiritual completion of the human self, a condition that is mirrored in the conjugal unity of male and female above. Righteousness as an ethical ideal—tied as it is to the undoing of sin—is not merely a human event, but a cosmic-divine one as well.

Make Me a Sanctuary of the Soul: Katabatic Theurgy and Divine Presence in *'Ozar Ḥayyim*

Having assessed the extensive evidence in *Me'irat 'Einayim*, we must now consider (albeit more briefly) the place of theurgical empowerment in Isaac's later work. As in the earlier writings, *'Ozar Ḥayyim* displays a significant concern with the cosmic drama of katabatic theurgy (drawing down the *shefa'*). But the later ruminations reflect a different emphasis—the assertion that the skilled kabbalist not only draws down the cosmic flow of energy through the divine world of the *sefirot*, but also channels that force into this lower world, a process that culminates in the indwelling of divine presence in his human soul. While we did observe elements of this view in the *Me'irat 'Einayim*

111. Ibid., p. 112.

sources (recall the texts considered above under the "purified consciousness" model), *'Oẓar Ḥayyim* is marked by a greater focus on this feature of the theurgic enterprise, as well as a rather unique depiction of the indwelling presence of Divinity in the human soul.[112] In this manner, the human self is constructed and represented as a chamber for the divine energies in the earthly realm—even as a lower sanctuary for the otherwise supernal deity. Borrowing and adapting from the philosophical discourse of his day, Isaac of Akko framed this experience of contemplative intimacy with the deity as an indwelling of the divine mind and life force within the intellect and soul of the human devotee.[113] In parallel fashion to his ruminations on ascent and union (to be discussed later), we can identify numerous cases in *'Oẓar Ḥayyim* that depict a relation to the deity in which the limitations of distance are effaced, and the human being is transformed into a sanctuary for the divine presence. Like the architectural space constructed in a geographic locale, the person is construed to contain an interior sacred topography that is uniquely suited to the descent and dwelling of the divine life force. This indwelling, which transforms the human self from a purely mundane creature to a vessel of the sacred, turns on the axis of katabatic theurgy; the earthly infusion of supernal energies is tied directly to the attraction of divine *shefa'* from above to below, thereby positing a continuum of energy from the divine world into the mundane human self. To be sure, this line of connection is associated with the human *soul* (the immortal entity that derives directly from Divinity), but that supernal soul nevertheless provides an anchor for the divine life force in the earthly realm. My analysis of the *'Oẓar Ḥayyim* material on this subject will proceed in two stages. We shall first consider a series of textual cases from which we may extrapolate the underlying type of katabatic theurgy directed into the human soul—a form of theurgical activity that culminates in a state of illumination or heightened intimacy with the deity. While the phenomenon

112. Also noted in Gottlieb, "Illumination, *Devequt*, and Prophecy in R. Isaac of Akko's *Sefer 'Oẓar Ḥayyim*," p. 245.

113. One of the most prominent examples of this idea is found in Moses Maimonides' *Guide of the Perplexed*, 3: 51. In that classic section, the overflow of the supernal Active Intellect onto the intellect of the cultivated philosopher is correlated to the event of *devequt* and union with the divine.

is certainly more widespread in *'Oẓar Ḥayyim* than the evidence to be surveyed, we shall limit ourselves to a few key instances that may be taken as paradigmatic and representative. This evidence established and interpreted, we shall call particular attention to the manner in which this theurgically driven indwelling is further characterized by Isaac as a (re)construction of the divine Sanctuary (*miqdash*) within the human self.

In two instances in *'Oẓar Ḥayyim* Isaac of Akko looks to models from the prophetic books of the Hebrew Bible—figures that are implicitly utilized as ideal paradigms for the theurgical action undertaken by latter-day kabbalists. In the first of these, Isaac reflects on the theurgic power of a somewhat unexpected figure—Binayahu ben Yehoyada, one of the triumphant commanders of King David's armed forces mentioned in 2 Samuel 23.[114] This Binayahu, Isaac asserts, was endowed with a special degree of esoteric knowledge, a remarkable capacity to grasp the secrets of the divine name—the secrets that compose the mysterious reality of all existence from the depths of the earth to the heights of the heavens.[115] His very name—יה"ו-ידע (the one who knew YHV, representative of the divine Tetragrammaton)—is understood to mark this talent (וכן ביהוידע יה"ו ירמוז זה שאיש זה חננו האל רוחניות יתירה לדעת ולהבין ולהשכיל בסתרי יה"ו הרומז לסתרי המציאות שזהו סודו מתהומא דארעא ועד רומיה דרקיעא עילאה). Implicit in this discussion is the striking claim that it was because of this unique contemplative power (this ability to manipulate the potent divine names) that Binayahu ben Yehoyada showed himself to be such a brave and victorious warrior—a fascinating convergence of religious beliefs about human empowerment vis-à-vis the divine universe, about the cosmic forces that stand behind strength and triumph. Having made this assertion, Isaac proceeds to unpack the various symbolic associations considered to be latent in the four-letter name of God (YHVH), arguing therein for a direct line of connection between the divine world of the *sefirot* and the intellective soul that dwells in the mind of the human being. The realms above and world below are all symbolically represented by the mysterious Tetra-

114. Isaac of Akko, *'Oẓar Ḥayyim*, fol. 17a.

115. Precedent for such a kabbalistic conception of Binayahu ben Yehoyada can be found in several zoharic passages. See, e.g., *Zohar* 1:6a, 9a, 132a, 3:182b.

grammaton, and all of these disparate meanings are ultimately rooted in the great Source of all Sources, the transcendent and infinite *'Ein-Sof*. It lies in the hands of the kabbalistic adept in drawing forth the empowering energies that run through this continuum. As Isaac goes on to assert:

> בכל זה היה בניהו בן יהוידע יודע ומבין ומשכיל להמשיך שלשלת שפעי אל עליון בע'. איש חי אשר נפשו מלובשת רוח אלהים חיים, שכל נפש אשר לא נחה עליו הרוח האלהי אינו חי, ואם הוא חי הרי הוא כח בלתי מדבר, אין לו יתרון על החי הבלתי מדבר רק הדבור לבד . . . ורב פעלים, אין בכל הנמצאים מי שיוכל לפעול מתוך כח עצמו לבדו מאומה רק מתוך כח השפע האלהי, וזהו סוד לא בחיל ולא בכח כי אם ברוחי וגומ'. ומלת פעלים תרמוז לריבוי השפעים האלהיים אשר בניהו זה ממשיך בע' שהוא כנס' ישר'. שלזה ירמוז מקבצאל, קבוץ אל כנס' ישראל מקום כניסת שפעי האל.

In regard to all of this, Binayahu ben Yehoyada knew and understood how to draw forth the chain of divine flow onto himself.[116] He was an *'ish ḥai* [a living man],[117] in that his soul was garbed in the spirit of the living God [*ruaḥ 'Elohim Ḥayyim*]. For every soul that has not received the indwelling of the divine spirit is not alive [*'eino ḥai*], and if it lives, it is a life force that does not speak [*koaḥ bilti medabber*]. A person's only superiority over the unspeaking creature [or life form] is that of speech. And [the meaning of the phrase] "who performed great deeds" [*rav pe'alim*] is thus: there is no [creature] from among all the existents [of the world] who can act by its own force alone. Only through the force of the divine flow [is it able to act]. This is the secret of [the verse] [Zech. 4:6]: "Not by might, nor by power, but by My spirit—said

---

116. To be sure, this abbreviation in the manuscript (בע') could certainly be read as "onto *'Atarah*" (i.e., onto *Shekhinah*). That is the way this abbreviation is used in the vast majority of cases in the Ginsburg manuscript of *'Oẓar Ḥayyim* (MS M-G 775). However, the sequence of his argument in this passage, and the logic of his remarks, works far better if בע' is read as בעצמו (onto himself). As the reader may note, there is a clear usage of בע' a bit later in the passage that does unquestionably refer to *'Atarah/Shekhinah*. The fact, however, that the first usage appears in the context of the claim that the human soul is animated and infused by the efflux of the divine spirit leads me to assume a reading of בע' as בעצמו.

117. The phrase איש חי (a living man) is the recorded *ketiv* (written tradition) of the masoretic biblical text, but the transmitted vocalization of the phrase (*qri*) is איש חיל (man of strength)—a meaning that accords far better with the plain sense context in II Samuel 23 in which Binayahu is portrayed as a strong and triumphant warrior. While there is little doubt that Isaac of Akko knew the proper vocalization of the text, he chose to utilize the *ketiv* meaning, insofar as it accords better with his kabbalistic insight and argument.

YHVH." The word *pe'alim* [deeds] hints at the abundance [*ribui*][118] of divine flow that this Binayahu would draw onto *'Atarah*, who is [also called] *Kenesset Yisra'el* [the Assembly of Israel]. For it is to this [process] that [the word] *miqavze'el* hints—the ingathering [*qibuz*] [of the divine flow] into *Kenesset Yisra'el*, the place of the gathering together [or assembly] of the divine flow.[119]

With a playful attentiveness characteristic of a midrashic exegete, Isaac of Akko parses Binayahu's name and place of origin as signifiers of a theurgic power to draw down the divine *shefa'* through the *sefirot*, and ultimately into human souls below. For while the prophetic text records Binayahu as originating from the place called *Qavze'el*, Isaac reads this word in a far more active sense—as the one who gathers together the flowing energies of the divine in *'Atarah*, the tenth *sefirah* [מקבץ-אל]. The divine life force is characterized as *ruaḥ*, as the spirit-breath that descends from the Infinite realm to the world below, giving vitality to the cosmos as the human body is sustained by the intake of breath. As in a variety of early kabbalistic sources, Isaac depicts the presence of God as manifest in *ruaḥ*,[120] and an unbroken line of connection is posited between the world of the *sefirot* and the human intellective soul—a crucial link in the great chain of Being. It is this influx that bestows the flow of life onto the human self; it is only by receiving the *ruaḥ 'Elohim Ḥayyim* that the human being merits the status of a speaking, thinking creature. This is the final goal of Binayahu's theurgical action—to draw down and channel the *shefa'* through the *sefirot* into his soul below (and thereby achieve heightened empowerment).

The anchoring of this theurgic dynamic (particularly the link between *'Atarah* and the human soul) in a biblical paradigm is further manifest in a separate passage.[121] In this instance, Isaac of Akko interprets the model of the prophets Elijah and Elisha, centering his attention on the transfer of a divine *ruaḥ* from master to disciple. The cloak (אדרת) that Elijah

118. This is a direct interpretive play on the phrase *rav pe'alim*.

119. Isaac of Akko, *'Ozar Ḥayyim*, fol. 17a.

120. This correlation is particularly prominent in the early kabbalistic commentaries to *Sefer Yeẓirah*.

121. Isaac of Akko, *'Ozar Ḥayyim*, fols. 10a–10b.

leaves with his student Elisha[122] is read by Isaac to be a symbolic representation of the divine spirit (תרמוז אדרת זו לרוח האלהות), a channeling of the divine sefirotic energies down from *'Ein-Sof*, ultimately entering the human soul as Presence. According to Isaac's exegesis, in transferring the cloak to Elisha, Elijah engaged in an act of katabatic theurgy, an attraction of efflux from the *sefirot* to the lower world. He sought, "through his own power, to properly draw down [the flow] through the ten *sefirot*, from attribute to attribute, all the way to *'Atarah*, and from *'Atarah* into his soul [להמשיכו מכחו המשכה נכונה בעס"ב ממדה למדה עד עט' ומהע' בנפשו]." As further documented above, the human soul is the next step in the emanation of efflux through the divine self—to send the powerful force of *ruaḥ* into oneself or another, the prophet (or kabbalist) must first engage in the skilled act of cosmic *hamshakhah*. Implicit in these passages about empowerment and katabatic theurgy is the underlying ontological belief that the human being and the deity are not separated by some unbridgeable chasm of transcendence—on the contrary, the gathered energies of *'Atarah* are channeled directly into (and thereby connected to) the soul.

Beyond the biblical paradigms—which (I would suggest) frequently serve for medieval kabbalists as vicarious and nontestimonial ways of depicting their own mystical beliefs and experiences—Isaac offers an articulation of the issue that is far more explicit as to the implications and prescriptions for the active life of the kabbalist. In the following case, the theurgical intention is also located directly in a liturgical-ritual framework:[123]

> וכל זה להמשיך שפע מהאדון היחיד הוא הר"ב ר' אב"א (הראשון בלי ראשית, אחרון בלי אחרית) בשכמל"ו בע', שלע' הוא סוד נפילת אפים. ונפילתינו זו על פנינו הוא להמשיך בנפשנו שפע מהע' מהשפע אשר המשכנו בע'. ואחר כל זה אנחנו קוראים סדר יומא בפסוקים ובקשה לבקש רחמים שהשפע אשר המשכנו מאין סוף בשמו הגדול והקדוש הע', ומהע' בנפשנו, יצא לנו מן הכח אל הפועל. וזהו סוד פסוק ובא לציון גואל וגו'. מלת גואל תרמוז לשפע הנזכר, לציון ירמוז לנפשות הצדיקים המצויינים בתורה וחכמה וקדושה ותפלה ומצות ומעשים טובים.

All this is to draw forth the flow [*lehamshikh shefa'*] from the Singular Master—the First without beginning, and the Last without

122. See 2 Kings 2:8–15.

123. Isaac of Akko, *'Oẓar Ḥayyim*, fol. 44b.

end [*HRBR ABA*],[124] blessed be the name of his glorious kingdom forever and ever—onto *ʿAtarah*. For [a *kavvanah* directed] to *ʿAtarah* is the secret of *nefillat ʾappayim* [the ritual gesture of falling on one's face]. This falling upon our faces is meant to draw into our souls the flow from *ʿAtarah*, from the flow that we have already drawn into *ʿAtarah* [from *ʾEin-Sof*]. And after all this, we read the *seder yomaʾ* in verses and petition to request compassion, that the flow we have drawn down from *ʾEin-Sof* into *ʿAtarah*, His great and holy name, and from *ʿAtarah* into our souls, will go out from potentiality into actuality [*yeẓeʾ lanu min ha-koaḥ ʾel ha-poʿal*]. And this is the secret of the verse [Is. 59:20], "and a redeemer shall come to Zion" [*u-vaʾ le-Ẓiyon goʾel*]. The word *goʾel* [redeemer] hints at the abovementioned flow [*shefaʿ*]; [the word] *le-ẓiyon* [to Zion] hints at the souls of the righteous who excel in Torah, wisdom, holiness, prayer, *miẓvot*, and good deeds [*maʿasim Ṭovim*].

The physical gesture of the *taḥanun* ritual is thus interpreted as a performative rite designed to channel the flow of divine energy from the uppermost reaches of infinite emanation into the lower domain of the human soul. A chain of connection, a line of influx, is posited between *ʾEin-Sof* itself and the soul of an individual person. The universal and the individual dimensions converge, and the human self is placed directly within the circle of cosmic power. And yet we may observe a conceptual thread that does not appear in the earlier cases of katabatic theurgy. For while the mystic aims to receive the flow of divine energy from above, Isaac is quite clear that such soul-reception is performed with the ultimate goal of *reactivation and influence*. The hope of the kabbalist is that he will merit the ability to retransmit the received divine energies, to actualize that which has been encased in concealment within his own soul. In this way, the individual ritual participant becomes a conduit for the recycling and reissuance of the cosmic life force in the world; the human self (in devotional enactment) serves as a cor-

124. My thanks to Boaz Huss for his counsel in clarifying this term. And see Gottlieb, "Illumination, *Devequt*, and Prophecy in R. Isaac of Akko's *Sefer ʾOẓar Ḥayyim*," p. 231. For a different usage of the phrase *ʾadon yaḥid*—one in which the term connotes the "First Cause" of the unfolding divine unity, the *sefirah Keter*—see Isaac's formulation in his *Perush le-Sefer Yeẓirah* (ed. Scholem, "Perusho shel R. Yiẓḥaq de-min-ʿAkko le-Pereq Riʾshon shel Sefer Yeẓirah"), p. 391, lines 16, 25–27, 32–33.

ridor of transformation and redistribution of divine vitality. This function of the soul gives the individual self of the kabbalist a heightened and clarified status. Cosmic empowerment at a remove (implicit in katabatic theurgy)[125] here morphs into a state of action in which the forces of divine emanation course through the human soul, to be harnessed and brought back into actuality.[126]

As intimated above, the indwelling of divine *shefa*ʿ in the soul recasts the very status of the human persona, the very nature of the self. The individual receiver of these energies is reconstructed as hallowed ground; the human soul is reconceived as sanctuary and divine abode. It is to this remarkable trope of thought and imagination that we now shift our attention.

Reflecting on the divine promise located in Ezekiel's prophecy (Ezek. 36:26), "רוח חדשה אתן בקרבכם" ("I will place a new spirit in your midst"), Isaac interprets this "new spirit" to be the purifying and transformative force of Divinity that infuses the human soul—an influx of supernal life that washes away the existing impurities of demonic beings that have sullied the human soul with evil urges and unimpeded desires.[127] The human being is transformed and cleansed through his function as a vessel and dwelling-place for the divine רוח; intimacy between devotee and deity is framed as an event of purification and transcendence of physical desire:

> ואמנם המים הטהורים המטהרים את הנפש ירמזו לשפעי המדות האלהיות ולמש"ה ולכח השכל האמתי וליצר הטוב. ואת רוחי אתן בקרבכם ירמוז אל הת' רוח אלהים

---

125. See Garb, *Manifestations of Power*, pp. 113–141.

126. In the manuscript pages preceding the above-cited passage, this same idea is formulated separately, and it is worthwhile for the reader to compare the two usages so as to clarify the significance and intentionality of the trope. Reflecting on the difference between uttering the *shema*ʿ in a standing position as opposed to a sitting position, Isaac remarks (fols. 43b-44a): כי סוד מעשינו זה לתת לנפשנו כח להתעלות אל מקור השפע ולעורר אותו לכח כל ששת ימי החול ולשכון בתוך נפש להתלבש בו ואמנם קוראנו אותו בישיבה בשוכבנו ובקומינו הוא להוציא שפע זה שבתוך נפשנו מן הכח אל הפועל (For the secret of this action [uttering the *shema*ʿ in a standing position] is to give our souls the power to ascend to the source of the flow, to arouse [that Source] to power all during the six days of the week, and to have it dwell in the soul, that it may be garbed [in the soul]. On the other hand, our recitation of the *shema*ʿ while seated, when we lie down and when we arise, is to bring out this flow within our souls from potentiality to actuality).

127. Isaac of Akko, *ʾOẓar Ḥayyim*, fol. 8a.

חיים ומלת בקרבכם תרמוז לשכל הקנוי השוכן תוך הנפש המדברת ובקרב פנימיותיה.
שישכון עליו שפע השכל האלהי הוא מה שאמ' הכתוב ועשו לי מקדש ושכנתי בתוכם.

> And indeed the pure waters that purify the soul hint to the flow of the divine attributes, to Meṭaṭron, Prince of the Face, to the force of the true Intellect, and to the good inclination [*yeẓer ha-ṭov*]. [The statement] "I will place my spirit in your midst" [*ve-'et ruḥi 'eten be-qirbekhem*][128] hints at *Tif'eret*, the spirit [*ruaḥ*] of the living God. The word *be-qirbekhem* [in your midst] hints at the acquired intellect [*sekhel ha-qanui*] that dwells within the speaking soul, in its inner regions. For when the flow of the Divine Intellect dwells upon [that human acquired intellect], it is as it is written [in Exod. 25:8]: "Make me a Sanctuary that I may dwell among them."[129]

Most remarkable here is the correlation between the sacred space of the ancient Sanctuary (framed in the biblical world as that of the mobile Tabernacle—משכן—and the stable Temple in Jerusalem—בית המקדש) and the interior space of the human mind-soul in contemplation of Divinity. The exhortation of the deity (in Exod. 25:8) to "make Me a Sanctuary" is clearly adapted to refer to the proper cultivation of human contemplation and knowledge of the divine *muskalot* (intellective-spiritual dimensions). Once having prepared the mind sufficiently, the mystic will have fulfilled the injunction to construct a holy dwelling into which the divine Presence may descend—a (con)templation whereby the human mind functions as a temple of God on earth.[130] Such a conception reveals a partially immanentist theological orientation—one in which the deity does not remain in the transcendent remove of the highest heavens, but instead descends to the human world to dwell within the work of Creation. This immanentist model is taken a step further here through the assertion that the human self is transformed into the very house of divine Being, a sacred space for the earthly indwelling of God. In some accord with the medieval reception of Aristotelian metaphysics, the human mind becomes the locus for the manifestation of the divine mind and emanational vitality in the lower world.

---

128. A reference to Ezek. 36:27.

129. Isaac of Akko, *'Oẓar Ḥayyim*, fol. 8a.

130. Cf. Corbin, *Temple and Contemplation*; Wolfson, "Sacred Space and Mental Iconography: *Imago Templi* and Contemplation in Rhineland Jewish Pietism."

Let us compare the usage of these motifs in a parallel passage. In the context of elaborating upon an ethical ideal that requires the rigorous subjugation of anger and pride for the sake of attachment to the divine *muskalot*, Isaac reflects on the wording of Psalm 74 and its relation to the contemplative matters at hand:

> האבות והנבונים החכמים והחסידים . . . יהיה להם כאשר היה לחנוך ואליהו ז"ל וכל זה רמוז בפסוק . . . אל ישב דך נכלם עני ואביון יהללו שמך. שכן דך ירמוז לנפש המשכלת שהקב"ה מצפה ממנה תשובה הגונה ע"ד דכדוכה מהיכלה. כי כל עוד היותה כלואה בהיכלה צריכה להיות מדוכדכת ושפלת רוח כי היא משכן לשמו של הקב"ה . . . הכח הזה שהוא הנפש המדברת אשר הוא משכן וכסא לכבודך.

> The patriarchs and the wise ones, the sages and the pious ones . . . it shall be for them as it was for Enoch and Elijah of blessed memory. And all of this is hinted at in the verse [Ps. 74:21] . . . "Let not the downtrodden turn away disappointed; let the poor and needy praise Your name." For [the word] "downtrodden" [*dakh*] hints at the intellective soul from which the Holy One expects proper repentance, in the sense that [the soul] is downtrodden and oppressed on account of the chamber [in which it resides]. For all the while that she [the intellective soul] is imprisoned in her chamber, she must be downtrodden and of humble spirit. This is because she is a sanctuary [and dwelling-place] for the name of the Holy One, blessed be He. This force—the speaking soul [*ha-nefesh ha-medabberet*]—is the sanctuary and throne for [the divine] Glory.[131]

As with our first case, the kabbalist portrays the contemplative mind as temple and sanctuary for the divine presence—a holy space that is modeled on the ancient Sanctuary of Jerusalem, and at the same time serves (by implication) in its place. The lament of the psalmist, invoked by Isaac of Akko, bemoans the ruined Temple of God, the desecration of the visible monument to the Israelite covenant with YHVH: שלחו באש מקדשך לארץ חללו משכן שמך—(They made Your sanctuary go up in flames . . .). And that dirge follows with the affirmation of the downtrodden people in their quest for the divine presence, the exhortation of the humbled and the poor to praise the name of God: אל ישב דך נכלם עני ואביון יהללו שמך (Let not the downtrodden turn away disappointed; let

131. Isaac of Akko, *'Oẓar Ḥayyim*, fol. 19a.

the poor and needy praise Your name). Indeed, our kabbalist moves to assert that the devotee must cultivate a state of downtrodden humility in order to replicate the broken condition of the geographic Sanctuary and the dispossessed people. It is precisely this humility and brokenness that is required for the intellective soul to serve as the dwelling-place for the divine name. The architectural locus of the ancient Temple has been destroyed, the name of God has been defiled and reviled by the foes of Israel (Ps. 74:3–11, 18). But this physical displacement has been reborn and internalized within the sacred place of the contemplative mind. Through the preparation of the intellective soul, by way of rigorous moral cultivation, the descent of the divine presence is able to *take place* again in the earthly realm. Like the imperative to reject the corporeal trappings of pride and passion in favor of the divine *muskalot*, the mystic prepares to receive the divine presence through the penitential posture of humility. The effacement of pride, the affirmation of a downtrodden brokenness, builds the new sacred chambers of divine indwelling—the internalization of divine vitality within the deepest spiritual corridors of the human self.

Seven Techniques of Mystical Contemplation

Kavvanah and Devotional Experience

For the medieval kabbalist, both the external, physical enactment of ritual and the internal event of consciousness that takes place concurrently were endowed with great theurgical power in the transformation and maintenance of the divine cosmos. Both the event of the mind and the event of the body were construed to be modalities of practice and action. As such, the kabbalistic view rejects the notion, often asserted in anthropological and sociological theory, that thought and action are fundamentally distinct modalities of human existence;[1] that action is necessarily correlated to the external sphere of being (as manifest through bodily action); and that the inner workings of the mind do not fall within the realm of behavior. Such a separation is also the premise of some modern philosophies of mind, in which behavior is first and foremost considered to be decidedly *nonmental*, and is fundamentally defined as "publicly observable" conduct.[2] What we have described as the external-physical pole of behavior is characterized as action that can be perceived by other human beings. By contrast, the internal workings of consciousness, in this view, are defined as a mode of being that is essentially inaccessible to outside observers. In diverse writings, many kabbalists also articulate such existential distinctions, but for them thought itself is considered to

1. A classic formulation of this dichotomy is to be found in Durkheim, *Elementary Forms of Religious Life*, p. 34. Also see the consideration of this problem (and the assessment of a variety of ritual theories) in Bell, *Ritual Theory, Ritual Practice*, pp. 19–37, 57–61, 69–93. Portions of Bell's discussion of a thought-action divide in conceptions of ritual (particularly as found in the work of theorists such as Lévi-Strauss, Durkheim, and Geertz) have also been reprinted in Grimes, ed., *Readings in Ritual Studies*, pp. 22–28.

2. See Strawson, *Mental Reality*, pp. 25–29. Strawson seeks to qualify the strictures of this division, but nevertheless maintains the general structure.

be a mode of practice and action that has metaphysical reverberations. Thus sacred action frequently occurs along a *mental* axis, and as such, ritual practice cannot be purely limited to bodily behavior, symbolically laden with significance and visible to the public. Moreover, in the kabbalistic view, mental and nonmental modes of action function as one, and thus cannot be fully separated in the ritual act.[3]

The conduct of the mind is central to kabbalistic behavior, and thus the texts of medieval Kabbalah display a marked emphasis on concrete instruction and prescription to that end.[4] As might be expected, given Isaac of Akko's indebtedness to the meditative posture of eastern Kabbalah, this characterization is highly applicable to *Me'irat 'Einayim* and *'Oẓar Ḥayyim*. In a great many instances, Isaac adopts a dialogical mode of written expression in which his comments are explicitly addressed in the second-person form to his reader, with a clearly didactic intention. In these passages, Isaac seeks to instruct his reader in the ways of mystical practice as he himself has received them, and as he understands them. What emerges from this attempt is a distinct genre of Jewish mystical literature (by no means restricted to Isaac), which may be characterized as *the rhetoric of prescription*.[5] While not quite the same

---

3. In one instance (*'Oẓar Ḥayyim*, fol. 113b), Isaac invokes and affirms the rabbinic dictum (BT *Yoma'*, fol. 29a) that the thought of a forbidden action is even more destructive than the forbidden act itself. Nevertheless, the kabbalistic conception of the ritual significance and force of intention stands in marked contrast to the dominant Amoraic view as preserved in the Babylonian Talmud. Recorded in the name of Rava, the *gemara* in tractate *Rosh ha-Shanah*, fol. 28b, asserts that the performance of *miẓvot* does not require accompanying *kavvanah* in order to fulfill the individual's religious obligation. Discussion of these same matters may be found in Garb, *Manifestations of Power in Jewish Mysticism*, pp. 30–36.

4. In framing thought as a mode of sacred action—one prescribed and regulated by the revered master—we might note the parallel nature of Maimonides' discourse in his *Hilkhot Yesodei ha-Torah* (within *Sefer ha-Mada'* of the *Mishneh Torah*). For it is in that context that the great philosopher-jurist sought to situate proper theological belief within the framework of the prescribed and prohibited actions of the religious life (מצוות עשה ולא תעשה). Indeed, the RaMBaM is unequivocal in his assertion that correct belief (and the avoidance of *incorrect* belief) are the very roots and foundation for the life of *miẓvot*—a claim that explicitly seeks to legislate theological thought, and to conceive of such thought as a mode of sacred behavior. This point is underscored by the very formal fact that these principles of theological belief are characterized as הלכות and situated within a legal code designed for the broader Jewish community. For more extensive analysis of this issue, and the relationship between philosophy and *halakhah*, see Twersky, *Introduction to the Code of Maimonides*, pp. 61–92, 356–374. Such a conception of interior practice also structures the thinking of Baḥya Ibn Paquda.

5. On rhetoric as textual genre, see Booth, *Rhetoric of Fiction*, pp. xiii–xiv.

as a mystical manual (for a manual implies a continuous and systematic work aimed at such instruction),[6] the fragments of such prescription, scattered throughout Isaac's writings (and especially in *Me'irat 'Einayim*), are part of the same instructional genre.[7] For the most part, the advice offered by Isaac in this forum is contemplative in orientation—a mode of practice that seeks to center the meditative mind on divine reality, to experience that reality in the performance of sacred ritual. In this manner, contemplation implies a certain mental orientation in which the human being seeks to experience the divine through the media of knowledge and precisely directed consciousness. Isaac of Akko aims to guide his reader in the kabbalistic attempt to contemplate Divinity; an effort directed toward the achievement of a heightened state of spiritual consciousness and intimate encounter with God.[8]

As also observed in the foregoing chapter, the contemplative orientation in Isaac's writing is primarily expressed in the context of reflection on devotional ritual and the performance of liturgically based prayer. Within this frame, the prescriptive rhetoric for the enactment of mystical contemplation revolves around the term *kavvanah* (intention) in its various forms,[9] and the mystic is instructed on how he might best direct his contemplative focus in response to the symbolism of the liturgy. These instructions regarding *kavvanah* are meant to guide and regulate the individual in his performance of interior mental practice, a mode of action hidden from the public's observation. It is in this sense that I wish to nuance the conception of *practice* as it was integrated by Isaac of

6. For a comparative perspective on the use of mystical manuals and the instructional genre, see Bielefeldt, *Dōgen's Manuals of Zen Meditation*, pp. 15–106.

7. It should be noted that the prescriptive/instructional method of writing was also characteristic of kabbalists such as Abraham Abulafia, the author of *Sha'arei Ẓedeq* (now identified by Moshe Idel as Natan ben Sa'adya Harar), and Judah al-Botini.

8. We might gain some comparative perspective on this methodological question by observing the manner in which Bernard McGinn has characterized the contemplative approach in Christian mysticism. Reflecting on the thought of Gregory the Great, McGinn (building upon the terminology of David Hurst) shows contemplation to be a mode of attentive regard for Divinity, a cultivation of intimacy between devotee and deity that is anchored in both ocular and auditory modes of religious experience. See B. McGinn, *Growth of Mysticism*, p. 55. In his history of Christian mysticism, McGinn surveys the development of the concept of *contemplatio* from its Greek origins through its widespread usage in medieval Christian piety (ibid., pp. 50–79).

9. As noted earlier, in this respect, Isaac of Akko participates in a larger genre of Kabbalah concerned with the mystical meaning and enactment of the liturgy.

Akko and many of his fellow kabbalists. Indeed, the complex processes of the mind associated with ritual performance are themselves considered to be prescribed modes of sacred ritual action.

In this chapter I shall set out to present a typology of contemplative practice as I discern it to be manifest in *Me'irat 'Einayim* and *'Ozar Ḥayyim*, structured by the following phenomena and devotional techniques:[10] (1) the movement, journey, and pilgrimage of consciousness through the divine *sefirot*; (2) binary concentration and the nature of fixed intention; (3) visualization of the sefirotic realm and contemplation of the divine name.

The Journey of Consciousness

The act of directly experiencing the divine realm through the medium of consciousness involves a journey of the mystic's mind from its ordinary physical environment to the metaphysical space of God, manifested to consciousness through the system of the ten *sefirot*. It is in this respect that the kabbalist traverses a demarcated boundary in cosmic reality, ultimately moving through the metaphysical map of God's inner self. In *Me'irat 'Einayim*, for example, Isaac of Akko elaborates on the mystical meaning of the enigmatic ancient rabbinic dictum לעולם יכנס אדם שני פתחים ואחר כך יתפלל (a person should always first enter two openings, and afterward commence his prayer). This statement, which appears to originate in BT *Berakhot*, fol. 8a, is somewhat unclear in its talmudic context, but seems to require the devotee to enter a certain physical distance into the synagogue before beginning to pray. This literal meaning was dramatically transformed by the earliest kabbalists of the Middle Ages, upon whose insights Isaac of Akko attempts to build. Already in Jacob ben Sheshet's *Sefer ha-'Emunah ve-ha-Biṭaḥon*

10. While the study of Jewish mystical techniques has been relatively underdeveloped in modern scholarship (in contrast to the more extensive examination of ideas and concepts characteristic of intellectual history), there have been several important advances in this area that must be noted here. See the following representative works, listed in the chronological order of their publication: Fine, "Techniques of Mystical Meditation"; Idel, *Kabbalah: New Perspectives*, pp. 74–111; id., *Mystical Experience in Abraham Abulafia*, pp. 13–52; Fine, *Physician of the Soul* (a monograph largely devoted to the rituals and techniques cultivated in Luria's fellowship); Idel, *Enchanted Chains: Techniques and Rituals in Jewish Mysticism*.

this rabbinic dictum is interpreted in a contemplative vein, outlining the preliminary meditative stages that the supplicant must pass through in order to attain higher states of consciousness and draw down divine energy.[11] Referring to Todros Abulafia's *'Ozar ha-Kavod*, a treatise composed several decades after ben Sheshet's text, Isaac of Akko situates his own approach among those kabbalists who understood the "two openings" of the talmudic dictum to connote not physical space, but *metaphysical* space as constructed in the inner eye of contemplation. In this view, the two openings correspond to two dimensions of the supernal divine world, the *sefirot Gedulah* and *Paḥad* (Greatness and Fear), alternatively called *Ḥesed* and *Din* (Love and Judgment).[12] Thus manipulating a paradigmatic text from antiquity to serve the interpretive needs of the present (though they most certainly believed these ideas to be the intended meaning of the rabbinic sources), several medieval kabbalists argued that the supplicant in devotion is required to pass through two initial divine pathways before reaching his ultimate meditative goal of the higher (or deeper) *sefirot*.

In this view, the human mind is meant to cross the threshold of divine reality, to enter deep within God's own self. The final point of ascension for that earthly consciousness is the *sefirah Binah*, the third highest of the divine dimensions, and the Palace that houses the seeds of all subsequent Being. This is the ultimate devotional goal for the mystic, and true prayer can only take place once the mind has reached that divine summit.[13] Isaac opens an extensive discourse on this subject with the following preliminary remarks:

וכדי שתבין בשכלך סוד כניסת שני פתחים הללו, להראות לך הדרך ולהאיר עיני שכלך למען יראו הדרך אשר ילכו בה ואת המעשה אשר יעשון לפתוח הפתחים לפני שכלך . . . כי אנחנו פתחנו לך השערים אשר בהם יבא גוי צדיק, אצייר לך צורת

---

11. See Jacob ben Sheshet, *Sefer ha-'Emunah ve-ha-Biṭaḥon* in *Kitvei RaMBaN*, 2: 366. 'Azriel of Gerona also interprets the talmudic dictum as a statement about metaphysical divine reality (and thus the object of entrance by the human contemplative mind). See *Perush ha-'Aggadot le-Rabbi 'Azri'el*, p. 11.

12. Moshe Idel has also touched on this image in his discussion of an extended passage from Isaac's *'Ozar Ḥayyim*. See Idel, *Absorbing Perfections: Kabbalah and Interpretation*, pp. 450–451.

13. Moshe Idel has shown that this emphasis on *Binah* as the primary object of devotional contemplation is indebted to the teachings of Isaac the Blind. See Idel, "On Isaac the Blind's Intentions for the Eighteen Benedictions," pp. 25–52.

תבנית עשרה גלגלים למען יראו עיני בשרך וישמחו עיני לבך בהכנס שכלך אל האפיריון . . . הוא בית י"י העליון.

> So that you will understand in your mind the secret of entering these two openings . . . to show you the way, and to illumine the eyes of your mind, so that they will see the path to go on, and the practice that they must enact in order to open the openings before your mind . . . we have opened the gates for you through which a righteous individual may pass. . . . I will draw for you a diagram of ten circles [or spheres] so that your physical eyes will see and the eyes of your heart will rejoice when your mind enters the Palace [אפריון][14] . . . the Supernal House of God [בית י"י העליון].[15]

The diagram of ten circles mentioned here, and inserted as a graphic image in the text, serves an instructional function for the contemplative mystic in his prayer and meditation. Drawn as ten concentric circles, the inner point of which represents the earthly world, and the outer ring of which corresponds to the highest *sefirah Keter*, the diagram clearly bears the influence of Aristotelian (geocentric) and Neoplatonic conceptions of cosmic structure.[16] What is more, as an object

---

14. This term is derived from Song 3:9. With respect to its usage as a symbol for *Binah* in kabbalistic literature, there appears to be precedent in 'Ezra of Gerona's *Perush le-Shir ha-Shirim*, p. 493, though this correlation is only implicit: "[Song 3:9] 'King Solomon made himself a palanquin [אפריון—lit., a portable throne] from the wood of Lebanon.' This is to say, from the efflux of *Ḥokhmah* [משפע החכמה], and from her bright radiance, that light [comes forth], and it emanates from [*Ḥokhmah*]. This is what was said in *Genesis Rabbah* [3:4], 'from where was the light created? The Holy One, blessed be He, wrapped Himself [in that light as one would with] a robe, and He radiated its light from one end of the world to the other.' The robe is the summoning forth of the emanation of *Ḥokhmah,* which surrounds everything." It would indeed seem that the אפריון in this exegesis corresponds to the *sefirah Binah*, insofar as 'Ezra's interpretive phrase משפע החכמה parallels the biblical phrase מעצי הלבנון, thus implying that the sefirotic dimension that emerges directly from the *sefirah Ḥokhmah* is to be associated with the אפריון (and *Binah* directly follows *Ḥokhmah* in the sefirotic chain). The original biblical word refers to a palanquin (used as a portable throne for the king), but the word already functioned as a metonym for a larger "space" (with the further implication of the king's palace) in the earliest rabbinic midrashim in our possession. Thus we find in *Pesiqta de-Rav Kahana*, p. 3: "'King Solomon made himself an *'Apiryon.*' *'Apiryon* is the Tent of Meeting." Apparently following the symbolic association recorded by 'Ezra of Gerona, the *Zohar* also correlates the word אפריון to *Binah*. See *Zohar* 2:127a.

15. Isaac of Akko, *Me'irat 'Einayim*, p. 88.

16. See MacKenna, "Appendix I: A Suggestive Outline of Plotinian Metaphysics," in id., ed. and trans., *Plotinus: The Enneads*, pp. 711–737. On the Jewish philosophical appropriation of these ideas, see Guttmann, *Philosophies of Judaism*, p. 189.

of devotional contemplation, the image is strikingly similar to the mandala form used in Hindu religion, and other circular diagrams of contemplation in Jewish mysticism.[17] Indeed, contemplation of a circular image as a focal point for meditative consciousness is a deeply cross-cultural topos, a fact that prompted Carl Jung to characterize it as one of the underlying archetypes of the human imagination as reflected in dream consciousness.[18] It is clear from Isaac of Akko's remarks that this image was meant to guide the meditative gaze, aiding the devotee in his contemplative progression through ever-higher layers of cosmic reality.[19] The task of the supplicant in prayer is to achieve nothing less than a *mental entrance* into the divine world, moving through the initial openings to higher planes of Being and consciousness.

The ultimate meditative goal of the mystic is to reach the dimension of divine reality called "the Supernal House of God" (בית י"י עליון), which is unequivocally identified with the *sefirah* of *Binah* in the lines that immediately precede the passage cited above.[20] In fact, the supplicant is directed to enter into the supernal sacred space of *Binah* (characterized in the familiar symbolic terms of Palace or Shrine, and thus metaphysical sacred space). As such, the contemplative mind engages in a topographi-

---

17. See Idel, *Kabbalah: New Perspectives*, pp. 63, 107. Idel has shown that the visualization of circles was an established part of kabbalistic practice, inasmuch as it is reflected in the writings of David ben Yehudah he-Ḥasid and Joseph ben Shalom 'Ashkenazi (both of whom were likely connected in some way to the production of the zoharic literature. See Liebes, "How the Zohar Was Written," pp. 93–95, 126–134). In manuscript fragments attributable to these kabbalists and their fellows, concentrically circular diagrams are found in which each *sefirah* is correlated with the color by which it is to be imagined in consciousness. In a separate study, Idel also shows how contemplation of the circle image is central to Abraham Abulafia's mystical practice. See Idel, *Mystical Experience in Abraham Abulafia*, pp. 109–116.

18. See C. G. Jung, *Dreams*, pp. 169–297.

19. The technical terminology that is used to characterize the meditative act is also quite revealing. The experience is manifestly ocular and imaginative—a sensory mode achieved through the interior eyes of the mind, in contrast (or perhaps in complement) to the eyes of the flesh. This sensory distinction, a well-established trope of experiential discourse in medieval Jewish mysticism, is found influentially in the writings of Yehudah ha-Levi and has been considered in depth in Wolfson, *Through a Speculum That Shines*, pp. 160–187. It was through the unique perception available to the inner eyes of the imagination (alternatively called עין הלב and עין השכל), to spiritual sight, that the mystic sought to attain a visual revelation of the divine *sefirot*. That sight, impossible for the eyes of the body, became possible through the inner vision of spiritual consciousness.

20. Isaac of Akko, *Me'irat 'Einayim*, p. 88.

cal or spatial experience of the divine, an event in consciousness in which the mind crosses the perceived boundaries between the physical and divine realms and enters a defined "space" within Divinity.[21] Indeed, the human being inescapably constructs the image of his intimate encounter with Divinity in spatial terms, owing to the fact that the forms and structures of the physical/natural life inevitably shape our human images of the supernatural.[22] Thus the paradigmatic sacred space of the physical world (the earthly Temple, or House of God) becomes projected onto the topography of metaphysical reality, and the divine structure is conceived to be the idealized macrocosm of the human world.[23] Upon his ascent to the divine realm, the devotee encounters the parallel image of his earthly shrine, and his prayer is consequently oriented by that ideal form in much the same way that his earthly prayer is oriented by a *physical* sacred space. In this sense, the process of contemplative ascent to the divine may be characterized as a pilgrimage to the ideal sacred center. The depictions of entrance from one domain to another, of the kabbalist crossing the boundaries that divide the physical and the metaphysical, indicate that this journey is a liminal passage between the profanity of the mundane and the sacrality of the cosmic center.[24]

---

21. Elliot Wolfson has analyzed this phenomenon with regard to the contemplative orientation of the *Ḥasidei 'Ashkenaz* and has demonstrated the use of sacred space imagery and *imago templi* in the construction of contemplative images. See Wolfson, "Sacred Space and Mental Iconography: *Imago Templi* and Contemplation in Rhineland Jewish Pietism," pp. 593–634 (in this study Wolfson also reflects upon the larger question of *kavvanah,* which lies at the center of my present work). In this respect, Wolfson's work (as well as my own analysis in this chapter) builds upon the foundational study by the Islamicist Henry Corbin, *Temple and Contemplation*. Through comparative analysis of religious texts depicting the presence and absence of the sacred Shrine, Corbin argued that the act of contemplation is deeply connected to the image of the celestial Sanctuary that replaces the ruined earthly Temple. See, in particular, *Temple and Contemplation*, pp. 263–390.

22. Interestingly enough, the same assumption that I have made here (in a very different intellectual framework) underlies the interpretive posture of medieval philosophers such as Sa'adia Gaon and Moses Maimonides. For those thinkers, the physicality of the human imagination comes to explain why the Torah characterizes the deity in anthropomorphic terms. The Torah speaks in the language of human beings because that is the only way in which the finite human consciousness can understand divine reality.

23. On the shift of concern from the earthly to the celestial shrine among ancient Jewish mystics, see Elior, *The Three Temples: On the Emergence of Jewish Mysticism*, pp. 63–81.

24. I have adapted this religious type from the writings of Victor Turner on the subject. Turner likens pilgrimage to "passage rites" in the sense that they both exhibit a liminal dimension in the transformation from one state of being to another through a religious process and

This prescription for the entrance of the mind through two openings in divine reality is taken up again in Isaac's later work.[25] In that instance, contemplation is trained upon *Tif'eret*, the *sefirah* through which the devotee will ultimately arrive at the two divine "openings" of *Ḥesed* and *Din*.[26] Engaging in a highly creative meaning-play, Isaac reads the word *le-'olam* (from the phrase . . . לעולם יכנס אדם) as a reference to *Tif'eret*—thus underscoring the path of progression and ascent from *Tif'eret* to the upper *sefirot*. In offering this exegesis, Isaac radically deconstructs the straightforward meaning of the phrase, parsing *le-'olam* as "in/to the world" (called *Tif'eret*), instead of its literal meaning of "always" or "forever." The attention of consciousness is to be directed away from this corporeal world (*'olam*), and redirected to the divine world (*'olam*) of *Tif'eret*. Isaac once again argues that the true rabbinic intention behind "enter two openings" was kabbalistic and contemplative, and *not* physical-spatial in its prescription (שעיקר כוונת רז"ל אינו במורגש גופני שהם פתחי בתים מורגשים . . . אבל אמרו שיעור יכנס במחשבת שכלו שיעור שני פתחים אלהיים). Thus, in addition to again constructing the ancient sages as kabbalists (a common move among medieval kabbalists), Isaac reinforces the motif of *mental journey and passage* from one dimension to another as a key component of the contemplative experience in prayer.[27] In his quest for intimacy and en-

ordeal. See V. Turner and E. Turner, *Image and Pilgrimage in Christian Culture*, pp. 33–35. Turner's reflections on the relationship between pilgrimage and mysticism are worth citing here, insofar as they directly relate to the phenomenon of interior mental journeys: "Pilgrimage may be thought of as extroverted mysticism, just as mysticism is introverted pilgrimage. The pilgrim physically traverses a mystical way; the mystic sets forth on an interior spiritual pilgrimage. For the former, concreteness and historicity dominate; for the latter, a phased interior process leads to a goal beyond conceptualization." Indeed, Turner recognizes the essential feature of mystical pilgrimage to be an internalization of an event that also takes place on the physical-historical plane. The mystic adapts the image of a sacred center in the given religion and transposes that object of pilgrimage from the realm of the body to the realm of the spiritual imagination.

25. Isaac of Akko, *'Oẓar Ḥayyim*, fol. 129b.

26. Isaac underscores the imperative to maintain focus on *Tif'eret* all the day long, even while it is still critical to keep the mind connected to *'Ein-Sof*. It is for this reason that *Tif'eret* functions as the necessary contemplative threshold before the entrance into the open pathways of *Ḥesed* and *Din*. On the instruction to bring the mind back to contemplative alignment with *Tif'eret*, compare Isaac's remarks in his *Perush le-Sefer Yeẓirah* (Scholem, ed., "Perusho shel R. Yiẓḥaq de-min-'Akko le-Pereq Ri'shon shel Sefer Yeẓirah"), p. 392, lines 13–15.

27. In his *Perush le-Sefer Yeẓirah* (which seeks to adapt and expand upon the earlier com-

counter with the divine presence, the mystic ascends in mind through a series of defined passageways and thresholds within the very being of God. The kabbalist sets out on a contemplative pilgrimage—the path of a journey whose steps correspond directly to specific words and stages in the devotional liturgy.

Consider a more elaborate prescription for this contemplative practice of mental ascent and sojourn—one that Isaac offers in conjunction with the central standing prayer (the *ʿAmidah*):[28]

ראיתי לכתוב כונת פסוק י"י שפתי תפתח ופי יגיד תהלתך עד"ה [על דרך האמת] לפי מיעוט שכל שבי. כבר ידעת כי בכל מקום שם אל"ף דל"ת רומז לעטרה, ומפני שהעטרה שערי תפלה, ר"ל בית שער ליכנס משם לפנים ומלפנים לפני לפנים עד בית י"י עליון, תקנו רבותינו ז"ל פסוק זה לומרו בתחלת התפלה. וראוי שבעוד שיאמר הבא להתפלל אדני שיכון אל העטרה. שפתי תפתח, כלומר תפתח לי שערי רחמים למען אכנס לפני לפנים אל מקום התהלה העליונה שהוא הבינה. ופי יגיד תהלתך, כלומר אמשיך בך שפע ברכה מתהלתך שהוא הבינה. ומיד תכנס דרך ישר במחשבתך הנכונה מהעטרה דרך הקו האמצעי עד תוך בית י"י העליון ואמור ברוך, ואתה כורע ותכון בכל מלה המקובל בה . . . אם תרגיל עצמך בשעת התפלה לכוין בפסוק אדני שפתי תפתח מה שכתבתי בו, שתוסיף ברכה וטובה כאלו אתה מייחד בקריאת דל"ת דאחד [בק"ש]. ולא עוד אלא מה שגזרו חכמים ליכנס שיעור ב' פתחים, תכנס אתה שיעור ששה פתחים ושכרך הרבה מאד.

I have seen fit to write down the proper intention for the verse [Ps. 51:17] "Lord open my lips, and my mouth will speak your praises" by the Way of Truth [*ʿal derekh ha-ʾemet*][29] with the small amount

---

mentary of Isaac the Blind), Isaac of Akko underscores the principle that contemplation of the upper dimensions occurs by way of the lower rungs. In that context, Isaac emphasizes the elusiveness of the upper divine light, despite the quest and attempts of the devotee. Through the lower emanations, however, an indirect glimpse of the supernal becomes possible. See *Perush le- Sefer Yeẓirah* (Scholem, ed., "Perusho shel R. Yiẓḥaq de-min-ʿAkko le-Pereq Riʾshon shel Sefer Yeẓirah"), p. 381, lines 13–21.

28. Isaac of Akko, *Meʾirat ʿEinayim*, p. 89.

29. As is well known, this phrase was the technical term used by Naḥmanides and his interpreters to indicate the introduction of kabbalistic meaning into the context of multiple modes of exegesis. In Naḥmanides' own writings, this phrase introduces relatively enigmatic and laconic kabbalistic interpretations designed to be understood only by the initiated mystical reader, and these are juxtaposed with exoteric meaning. On this particular question of the enigmatic and initiatory character of this rhetoric, as well as the desire to keep kabbalistic secrets from the larger populace, see Naḥmanides' own Introduction to his *Commentary on the Torah* in *Perush ha Ramban ʿal ha-Torah*, 1: 7–8. See also Wolfson, "By Way of Truth: Aspects of Nahmanides' Kabbalistic Hermeneutic," pp. 103–104; Idel, "Nahmanides: Kabbalah, Halakhah, and Spiritual Leadership," p. 38; Pedayah, *Nahmanides: Cyclical Time and Holy Text*, pp. 120–157;

of intellect that I possess. You already know that the divine name *'Adonai*[30] always alludes to *'Atarah*. Because *'Atarah* is the gate for prayer—that is to say, a gatehouse by which to enter inward,[31] and then further inward,[32] all the way to the Supernal House of God, our Sages established[33] that this verse should be uttered at the beginning of the Standing Prayer.[34] While the supplicant utters the word *'Adonai*, he should direct his intention toward *'Atarah*. [The subsequent words of the verse] "open my lips" are to say: "open the gates of compassion for me, so that I may enter inward to the place of Supernal Praise, which is *Binah*." "And my mouth will speak your praises" [ופי יגיד תהלתך].

Halbertal, *By Way of Truth: Nahmanides and the Creation of Tradition*, pp. 297–333. According to the analysis of Boaz Huss, the use of this phrase by Isaac of Akko is actually meant in an even more precise sense than its general usage in the Naḥmanidean corpus. As mentioned earlier, Huss argues that Isaac of Akko outlined a hermeneutical system meant to stand in hierarchical superiority to the standard fourfold system of PaRDeS exegesis, which Isaac termed NiSAN. See Huss, "NiSAN—The Wife of the Infinite: The Mystical Hermeneutics of Rabbi Isaac of Acre," pp. 155–181.

30. Literally, "the *'Alef Dalet* name." This commences his kabbalistic interpretation of Ps. 51:17, which begins with the name אדני—the divine name consistently associated with the tenth *sefirah* in medieval kabbalistic symbolism.

31. Isaac here employs the rhetoric of an *inward* journey to the most exalted points of sefirotic Being, a terminology that is frequently interchangeable in medieval kabbalistic literature with the rhetoric of hierarchy and ascension, and is specifically traceable to the rhetorical constructions of Isaac the Blind and his school. See, e.g., Isaac the Blind's *Perush le-Sefer Yeẓirah*, p. 1, line 15. On the use of this term in early Kabbalah, see Pedayah, "Flaw and Repair," p. 166 n. 35; Sendor, "Emergence of Provençal Kabbalah," 2: 152, n. 34.

32. The phrase "Supernal House of God" (בית י"י העליון) reinforces my suggestion that contemplation here involves a mental journey to a substitute Temple, an intradivine sacred space. This is so precisely because of the connotation of לפני ולפנים in classical rabbinic literature, which is that of a crossing into the Shrine by the high priest for the purpose of offering incense. The locus classicus for this association, but by no means the exclusive such source, is BT *Berakhot*, fol. 7a: תניא אמר רבי ישמעאל בן אלישע פעם אחת נכנסתי להקטיר קטורת לפני ולפנים וראיתי אכתריאל יה ה' צבאות שהוא יושב על כסא רם ונשא ואמר לי ... (It has been taught: Rabbi Yishm'a'el ben 'Elisha' said—"one time I entered within [לפני ולפנים] to offer incense, and I saw 'Akatri'el yah, the Lord of Hosts, who was sitting on a high and exalted throne, and He said to me . . . "). Clearly a tannaitic tradition (as determined from the use of the word תניא, combined with the use of Hebrew), this source provides one of the earliest usages of the phrase to connote an entrance associated with the Temple and the priest. Modeled on this rabbinic paradigm, the quoted text from *Me'irat 'Einayim* presents the human kabbalist as a priest who acts in the metaphysical Temple, the Palace of *Binah*.

33. See the talmudic discussion in BT *Berakhot*, fol. 4b.

34. I.e., the prayer of the Eighteen Benedictions, referred to in early rabbinic literature simply as התפילה. See, e.g., BT *Sukkah*, fol. 26a.

This is to say, I will draw down[35] onto you [or within you] the flow of blessing from your Praise, which is *Binah*. You shall then immediately enter in a straight path, through your properly directed thought, from *'Atarah* through the Central Line [הקו האמצעי] until you reach the Supernal House of God, and then you shall say "*Barukh*," and bow, and direct your intention toward each word according to its received kabbalistic meaning. . . . If you train yourself during prayer to intend the verse "*'Adonai* open my lips" as I have written of it, you will increase blessing and goodness as you do during the recitation of the *dalet* of the word *'eḥad* [of the *Shema'*]. Moreover, whereas the Sages decreed that one must enter two openings, you shall enter six openings,[36] and your reward will be very great.

In this instruction, the performance of liturgical recitation is presented as the stimulus and framework for contemplative consciousness. As he utters the words of the benediction, the supplicant is to enter into the sefirotic realm in meditative mind, to penetrate deeply into the hiddenmost dimensions of divine Being. The structure of the *sefirot* provides a map for human consciousness in its contemplative progression, and it is in this sense that we may understand the enactment of symbolic reading by the kabbalist—particularly with respect to the text of prayer. Each word of the benediction corresponds symbolically to a specific sefirotic dimension, a hermeneutical approach that is characteristic of the broader kabbalistic posture vis-à-vis the canonical texts of

35. Here the word יגיד has been interpreted by Isaac in the sense of the Aramaic word נגד—which means "to draw forth" or "to flow." We find use of this word already in the biblical book of Daniel 7:10, and the early kabbalists made this association in depicting the theurgic attraction of the divine flow. See the tradition preserved by Jacob ben Sheshet (a mystic who was privy to direct oral contact with Isaac the Blind) in his *Sefer ha-'Emunah ve-ha-Biṭaḥon*, p. 368. The *Zohar* too makes considerable use of this Aramaic word in conjunction with the dynamic of attraction and sefirotic flow. Given our knowledge of Isaac of Akko's deep affinity for the zoharic literature (and his physical pursuit thereof)—despite the fact that he does not directly integrate a great deal of zoharic material into *Me'irat 'Einayim*—the evidence from the *Zohar* itself is certainly noteworthy. In *Zohar* 2:260b we find a passage that asserts that the words אדני שפתי תפתח should be understood as a prescription for the ascent of the human mind/will to the high reaches of the sefirotic universe and the consequent drawing down of energy into the cosmos.

36. These six openings refer to the six sefirotic dimensions of the Central Line (הקו האמצעי). They are (in the reverse order that the devotee must traverse in his upward contemplative journey): *Yesod*, *Hod*, *Neẓaḥ*, *Tif'eret*, *Gevurah*, and *Ḥesed*. After crossing through these six openings, the supplicant is then able to begin his recitation of the benediction from within *Binah*.

the tradition.[37] As such, the recitation of those words in the act of ritual performance becomes a guide in the meditative movement of consciousness, the symbolic significance of the text a marker in the mystic quest for divine encounter. Each word of the sacred text points to a supernal reality, and thus the interpretive event of reading is a pathway to contemplation of Divinity.[38] In the frame of this prescription, the kabbalist is to use the preface line to the Eighteen Benedictions (אדני

---

37. This model accords well with other recent scholarship to the effect that kabbalistic mystical experience most often arises out of the exegetical act (see M. Fishbane, *The Exegetical Imagination: On Jewish Thought and Theology*, pp. 105–122; Wolfson, *Through a Speculum That Shines*, pp. 383–392). For given the fact that the Torah was considered by kabbalists to be a *corpus symbolicum*, whose very structure and meaning reflected the inner life of God, to read the sacred text as a kabbalist was to engage in mystical vision and illuminatory experience of the deity. Each word of the sacred text points to a supernal reality, and thus the interpretive event of reading is a pathway to contemplation of Divinity. This characterization of kabbalistic meditative experience is all the more applicable to Isaac of Akko's approach to prayer, insofar as the contemplative implications are made explicit through a detailed rhetoric of prescription.

38. This phenomenological type—the experiential correlation between recitative ritual performance and a graded contemplative journey through the divine dimensions—is also well attested in another text from Isaac's *Me'irat 'Einayim* (p. 93): "When you say [the word] 'Blessed' [ברוך], intend towards *Keter*, for He is the source of all blessings. 'You.' When you say [the word] 'You' [אתה], begin to intend toward *Ḥokhmah*. And in your intention of the word 'You' to *Ḥokhmah*, interpret in your mind [lit., heart] the word אתה in the sense of אתא [come forth]. Then draw your thought forth from *Ḥokhmah* to *Tif'eret*, and when you reach *Tif'eret*, interpret in your thought [the word] אתה in the literal sense of אתה [You], which is the second-person form. Then draw your thought forth to *'Atarah*. All of this must be intended [when you recite] the word אתה. When you say *YY* [י"י], intend toward *Teshuvah* [i.e., *Binah*]. [When you say] *'Eloheinu* [our God], [intend] toward the Arms of the world [a symbolic allusion to the *sefirot Ḥesed* and *Gevurah*], which is to say: to *Teshuvah* with the Arms. [When you say] 'King,' [intend] toward *Teshuvah*. [When you say] 'the world,' [intend] toward *Tif'eret*, for *Teshuvah* is king of the World to Come, which is *Tif'eret* [a somewhat surprising symbolic association, given the fact that "the world to come" is often a symbol used to refer directly to *Teshuvah/Binah*—see *Zohar* 1:32a; 1:168a; 1:207a; 1:242b; 2:162a; 2:185a]. And *Tif'eret* is king over the ruler of this world, who is *'Atarah*. *'Atarah* is king over this lower world. [When you say] 'Who has sanctified us,' 'Who has made for us,' or 'Who has given us life,' [intend] toward *Tif'eret*." It should be noted that while several words of the benediction correspond each to only one point in the sefirotic domain—one stop in the progressive movement of human consciousness through Divinity—Isaac's prescription for the performance of the word אתה is far more lengthy and complicated. While remaining focused on the single word אתה, the supplicant is instructed to inaugurate his concentration on the supernal *sefirah Ḥokhmah*, then drawing his mental direction downward through the sefirotic structure, from *Ḥokhmah* to *Tif'eret*, and from *Tif'eret* down to the tenth *sefirah 'Atarah*. The fact that the mind must undergo such an involved journey during the recitation of only one liturgical word seems to point toward a mechanics of ritual enactment in which vocalization may have been drawn out either in lengthy sounds or long pauses after the utterance of the word in question had taken place.

שפתי תפתח) as a contemplative entry point into his experience of the divine world in prayer.[39] The word אדני corresponds symbolically to the lowest *sefirah* (*ʿAtarah/Shekhinah*), and thus this line is directed to that dimension, as though to say: "*ʿAtarah*, open the way for me, so that I may ascend upward through the *sefirot* to reach my contemplative goal of *Binah*." The first word of the benediction itself—*Barukh*—can only be uttered once the kabbalist has reached the summit of his contemplative aspiration. *Binah* is the metaphysical sacred space for which the human mind yearns. Transcending the *physical* sacred space in which his devotion occurs, the supplicant finds a substitute space within Divinity that may serve as the structure for his mind's prayer. It is in this respect that Isaac of Akko seeks to guide and regulate inner mental practice. His prescriptive words aim to structure the conduct of the mind as a ritual action in and of itself.

The supplicant seeks to attain an intimate encounter with Divinity by entering into and journeying through the metaphysical space of God—a mental sojourn that responds directly to a hermeneutics of the liturgical text. To read and recite the words of prayer is to stimulate a correlated experience of metaphysical reality. It should also be observed at this point that the contemplative progression of the human mind in prayer is necessarily *gradual* and graded according to specific sefirotic stages. Before the supplicant can engage in the ultimate meditative goal of his devotion (prayer within *Binah*), he must pass through an initial mental preparation, which begins with his direct beseechment of *ʿAtarah*, and follows with his upward movement through the *sefirot* between *ʿAtarah* and *Binah*. The implication of the pre-benedictory practice (אדני שפתי תפתח) is that human consciousness requires a gradual ascent; it cannot make an immediate transition from earthly consciousness to *Binah* consciousness. Taken as a whole,

---

39. In a similar vein, commenting on the tenth *sefirah*, Joseph Gikatilla states: ולפי שאין לכל נברא בעולם דרך להיכנס לשם יתברך אלא על ידו, וכל שאלה ותחנונים ובקשה אינם נכנסים אלא על-ידי אדנ"י, הוצרכו לקבוע בראש כל התפילות: 'אדנ"י שפתי תפתח' . . . ועל-ידי שם זה נכנסות התפילות לפני יהו"ה יתברך (And because no creature in the world possesses any way to enter into God, be He blessed, other than through *ʾAdonai* [i.e., *Shekhinah*], and [because] every question, supplication, and request [from humans] only enter through *ʾAdonai*, [the Sages] found it necessary to establish [the words] "*ʾAdonai*, open my lips" at the beginning of the [standing] prayer. . . . It is through this name [*ʾAdonai*] that the prayers enter before YHVH, be He blessed [*Tifʾeret*]). See Joseph Gikatilla, *Shaʿarei ʾOrah*, p. 58.

this passage displays a series of rhetorical tropes that characterize and nuance the contemplative experience. Beginning with an emphasis on *opening* and *entrance* as features of devotional action, the kabbalist constructs a portrait of the divine world that is characterized by progressive inwardness, as constituted by increasingly deeper dimensions into which the devotee must penetrate with a concentrated mind. The drama of contemplative ascent is thereby merged with the *rhetoric of entrance* into the interiority of divinity; in the ritual process of devotion, the human being (or at least his mind) enters into the deepest recesses of God's being.

A prescription for contemplative sojourn that is offered by Isaac with regard to the recitation of the *Shema'* prayer embodies an additional feature of the ritual instruction and enactment—an emphasis placed on a *physical* aspect of the ritual-contemplative performance. The practice outlined here stipulates that the devotee is to circumscribe a lengthy and complex mental journey within the boundaries of a single breath and sound. Like the prescriptions offered for the recitation of the standard benedictory formula (. . . ברוך אתה י"י),[40] this practice would seem to require an unusual lived framework for its implementation—indeed, it is quite likely that the kabbalists who practiced such methods in prayer cultivated separate devotional fraternities for their enactment. For it is highly dubious that such lengthy performances of ritual were cultivated in ordinary (or larger) communal settings in which the pace of recitation would inevitably have been faster. This hypothesis finds support in the historical fact that Aragonese Jewish communities during this period were frequently composed of numerous different prayer quorums, which functioned side by side.[41] Furthermore, in the case cited below, we observe a self-conscious awareness of the challenge and difficulty posed by such devotional-mystical practices, and of the consequent need for powerful discipline and training in the aspiration toward a proper enactment. I cite this

40. See n. 38 above in which I cite and discuss Isaac's contemplative practice for the word אתה—a technique that he apparently utilized for the opening benediction of the *'Amidah* prayer.

41. See Assis, *Golden Age of Aragonese Jewry: Community and Society in the Crown of Aragon, 1213–1327*, pp. 325–326.

passage at considerable length in view of its special status as one of the most extraordinary articulations of contemplative ritual practice in all of Isaac's writings:[42]

[A] הנה לך כונה נכונה ואמתית לכוין בסוד שמע ישראל י"י אלהינו י"י אחד שקבלתי והיא קבלה חשובה על אריכות דל"ת דאחד, וחייב כל בר ישראל לכוין כן תמיד.

[B] ואכתוב לך הכונה אשר תכוין משמע עד דל"ת דאחד. שמע לעטרה, תכוין שהיא כניסת הכל מלשון וישמע שאול. ישראל רומז לעדת ישראל. י"י לתפארת עם שש קצוות. אלהינו לזרועות עולם. י"י לשלש עליונות. אחד. האל"ף רומז לכתר. החי"ת צריך שתאריך בחי"ת עד שתמשיך במחשבתך הנכונה הזכה וההגונה שפע הברכה מן החכמה אל הבינה, ומזו לזו ומזו לזו עד הצדיק, שהם שמונה כמספר החי"ת.

[C] וכשתגיע לדל"ת דאחד שהיא רבתי צריך שבעוד שתהיה עומד בדל"ת שתאריך בה עד שתיחד העטרה שהדל"ת רומז לה בצדיק. ותחשב בלבך שהכל, כלומר כל העשרה, כלולים בצדיק. ואחרי כן תעלה מחשבתך בהוד, ותחשב שההוד כלול מכל העשרה. וכן לנצח וכן לתפארת וכן לפחד וכן לגדולה וכן לבינה וכן לחכמה וכן לכתר עד אין סוף. בכל אחת צריך שתחשב שהיא כלולה מכלם וכלם באין סוף מאין סוף לאין סוף. וכל זה בנשימה אחת. ולא יהיה פלא בעיניך כי ההרגל על כל דבר שלטון ומן השמים יסיעוך כי הבא ליטהר מסייעין אותו.

[D] ושמעתי מפי מקובל משכיל כי הייחוד הנכון בכונת דל"ת דאחד הוא שיכוין כן שבכל אחת כלולים כל העשרה ומיוחדים בה. כן בכל אחת ואחת מהעטרה ועד הכתר וליחד הכל באין סוף. ודע באמת ובאמונה . . . כי כונתי במלת אחד שאני מכוין תמיד זו היא. באל"ף ובחי"ת אני מכוין כאשר כתבתי, ובדל"ת כונתי ומחשבתי כן היא הצדק בצדיק הכל מיוחד בצדק, הכל מיוחד בצדיק, הכל מיוחד בהוד, הכל מיוחד בנצח, הכל מיוחד בתפארת, עם שש קצוות, הכל מיוחד בפחד, הכל מיוחד בגדולה, הכל מיוחד בבינה, הכל מיוחד בחכמה, הכל מיוחד בכתר כשלהבת הקשורה בגחלת, והכל מיוחד באין סוף מאין סוף לאין סוף, הוא אחד ומיוחד בכל שש קצוות . . . מהאל"ף דאחד עד תשלום כל זה בדל"ת דאחד בנשימה אחת.

[A] Here [lit., for you] is a proper and true intention to employ for the secret of [the prayer] "Hear, O Israel, the Lord our God, the Lord is One," that I have received.[43] It is an important tradition regarding

---

42. Isaac of Akko, *Me'irat 'Einayim*, p. 213.

43. On earlier roots of the idea that recitation of the word *'eḥad* in the *Shema'* must be accompanied by a contemplation of the entire sefirotic structure, see Idel, "*Sefirot* Above the *Sefirot*," pp. 278–280. Cf. id., "On Isaac the Blind's Intentions," p. 45, n. 118.

the lengthening of [the letter] *dalet* of the [word] *'eḥad* [One], and every Jew is required to intend according to [its method].

[B] And I will write for you the intention which you must intend from the word *shema'* through the letter *dalet* of the word *'eḥad*. The word *shema'* should be intended toward *'Atarah*. Intend that She is the Assembly of All [or the Gathering Together of All (כניסת הכל)] in the sense of [I Samuel 23:8] "Saul summoned all the troops" [וישמע שאול]. *Yisra'el* alludes to the people of Israel. *YY* [*YHVH*] [is to be intended toward] *Tif'eret* with the Six Directions.[44] *'Eloheinu* [is to be intended toward] the Arms of the World.[45] *YY* (*YHVH*) [is to be intended toward] the upper three [*sefirot*]. *'Eḥad*. The *'alef* of the word *'eḥad* alludes to *Keter*. *Ḥet*. You must lengthen [pronunciation of the] *ḥet* [for as long as it takes] to draw, through your proper and pure thought, the flow of blessing from *Ḥokhmah* to *Binah*, from this one to that one, and from that one to this one, all the way down to *Ẓaddiq*,[46] for they are eight like the [numeric value of the letter] *ḥet*.

[C] When you reach the letter *dalet* of the word *'eḥad*, which is [written] large, it is necessary that while you are still [pronouncing] the *dalet* that you lengthen it until *'Atarah*, to which the *dalet* alludes, becomes unified with the *Ẓaddiq*. Think in your mind that the All, which is to say all of the ten, are included within *Ẓaddiq*. After that, raise your mind to *Hod*, and think that *Hod* is made up of all ten. Do the same for *Neẓaḥ*, the same for *Tif'eret*, the same for *Paḥad*, the same for *Gedulah*, the same for *Binah*, the same for *Ḥokhmah*, the same for *Keter*, until *'Ein Sof*. With each one you must think that it is made up of all of them, and all of them are included within *'Ein Sof*, from Infinity to Infinity. *All this [must be accomplished] in one breath*. Do not be surprised by this, for regularity [enables] control over all things, and Heaven will help you—for help is given to the one who comes to purify himself [כי הבא ליטהר מסייעין אותו].[47]

---

44. The "six directions" (שש קצוות) correspond to the middle six *sefirot* that stand between the upper three (*Keter*, *Ḥokhmah*, *Binah*) and the tenth (*'Atarah*).

45. As noted earlier, the "Arms of the World" correspond to the fourth and fifth *sefirot*, *Ḥesed* and *Gevurah*.

46. A further cognomen for the ninth *sefirah*—*Yesod*.

47. This is a classic talmudic formulation. See BT *Yoma'*, fol. 38b; *'Avodah Zarah*, fol. 55a; *Menaḥot*, fol. 29b.

> [D] I heard from the mouth of a wise kabbalist that the proper unification in the intention for the letter *dalet* of the word *'eḥad* is that [the supplicant] intend that each one includes all ten, and that they are unified in that One. Such should be done for each and every one [of the *sefirot*], from *'Atarah* to *Keter*, and [one must] unify all of them in *'Ein Sof*. Know in truth that this is always the way I intend with respect to the word *'eḥad*. On the *'alef* and the *ḥet* I intend as I have written of it, and on the *dalet* my intention and my thought are directed toward the unification of *Ẓedeq* (*'Atarah*) and *Ẓaddiq* (*Tif'eret*). Everything is unified in *Ẓedeq*, everything is unified in *Ẓaddiq*, everything is unified in *Hod*, everything is unified in *Neẓaḥ*, everything is unified in *Tif'eret* with the Six Directions, everything is unified in *Paḥad*, everything is unified in *Gedulah*, everything is unified in *Binah*, everything is unified in *Ḥokhmah*, everything is unified in *Keter*, like the flame is bound to the coal,[48] and everything is unified in *'Ein Sof*, from Infinity to Infinity. It is One and unified in all Six Directions . . . From the *'alef* of [the word] *'eḥad* until the conclusion in the *dalet* of *'eḥad*, [this must be accomplished] *in one breath*.

The recitation of the *Shema'* thus entails two general stages, the second of which is far more complex than the first. The first five words of the line compose the initial unit, one in which the mind of the devotee moves in an upward progression from the lowest *sefirah* (*'Atarah*) all the way up to the supernal sefirotic triad (*Keter*, *Ḥokhmah*, *Binah*). The stage of mental ascent leads into the *descent*, which occurs with considerable complexity in the utterance of the word *'eḥad*. As such, the contemplative experience of prayer is one of dialectical movement between upward and downward mental progression through the intradivine system, which unfolds through a distinctively performative ritual drama.

With respect to the remarkable practice of lengthened breath and vocalization, what is implicit in other cases (e.g., with regard to the word אתה in the benedictory formula ... ברוך אתה) has here become an explicit prescription ("All this [must be accomplished] in one breath"). The contemplative progression of the mind through the meditative map of the *sefirot* is inextricably linked to a breath technique and mode

48. A standard image for the indivisibility of the *sefirot* from *'Ein-Sof* in early Kabbalah, which originates in *Sefer Yeẓirah* 1:7.

of articulation not unlike those cultivated by other meditational systems.[49] The fact that the human mind must undergo a complex and focused journey from *sefirah* to *sefirah*, all during the vocalization of the word *'eḥad*, and all in one single breath, explicitly correlates the mental process to the physical process—the sustainment of a unified vocalized breath as the external-physical reflection and *enabler* of the internal event in consciousness. The prescribed performance of this technique breaks up the individual sounds correlated with the letters of the word א-ח-ד as stages in the mental contemplation of Divinity, while still requiring that these stages function contiguously without any cessation in the outflow of breath. The mystic must achieve a single flow of vocal sound as it emerges from a unified breath, but that interwoven sound is nevertheless clearly composed of the different shapes of sound associated with the three letters—*'alef*, *ḥet*, and *dalet*. As the distinct sounds are uttered (flowing contiguously into one another), the mind of the supplicant moves in a correlated fashion from the top of the sefirotic structure down to the tenth *sefirah*. The unbroken breath is also clearly meant to influence and reflect the complete unity of the *sefirot*, as well as

---

49. This would seem to apply particularly to the breath-centered orientation of Yogic spirituality (see Eliade, *Yoga: Immortality and Freedom*, pp. 53–65) and that of various streams within Buddhist meditative practice (see Bielefeldt, *Dōgen's Manuals of Zen Meditation*, pp. 63–65, 113–115, 180–183; Harvey, *An Introduction to Buddhism*, pp. 246–255, 270, 277). Indeed, the practice of lengthening the breath, sometimes further characterized as a pause or suspension of respiration between the in-breath and the out-breath (or vice versa), was an integral feature of Yogic meditational practice, and this method is also detectable in the writings of Abraham Abulafia, who, along with direct or indirect Sufi impact, was a likely influence on Isaac of Akko. On Abulafia's use of breathing and vocalization techniques, see Idel, *Mystical Experience in Abraham Abulafia* (English version), pp. 13–52, esp. pp. 24–28. It would seem that the text I have cited above by Isaac of Akko is related to a root idea and practice found in Abulafia's *Sefer Mafteaḥ ha-Shemot*, as cited in Idel, *Mystical Experience in Abraham Abulafia* (Hebrew version), p. 26: צריך שיקח כל אות ואות מאותיותיו של שם המפורש ויניענה בתנועת נשימתו ארוכות (!) שלא ינשום בין שתי אותיות כי אם נשימה אחת ארוכה כפי מה שיוכל לסבלה באריכות ואחר כך ינוח בשיעור נשימה אחת צריך (He must take each of the letters of the Ineffable Name and pronounce their vowels in one long breath, such that he should not breathe in between two of the letters—only one long breath, according to what he can tolerate in length. After this, he should rest for the measure of one breath [my translation]). It is quite probable that Abulafia received instruction in these practices from his teacher, Barukh Togarmi, who appears to have originated in the Far East. What is more, the existence of robust trade routes between Egypt and India as early as the eleventh century makes it possible to speculate that these practices were learned by visiting traders and brought back to their home contexts. On the connection between this trade and the Maimonides family (whose relation to Sufi piety is well known), see Goitein and Friedman, *India Traders of the Middle Ages*, p. 117.

the contemplative necessity of traversing the *entirety* of that metaphysical structure. All this is presented to the reader as a clear and structured guided meditation; Isaac speaks to his audience as a master contemplator leading the novice through the cosmic labyrinth in consciousness, through the experiential interstices of breath, utterance, and mind.

In describing this meditative technique, and in instructing his reader in its implementation during prayer, Isaac of Akko acknowledges the initial difficulty and challenge in performing this practice—an awareness that highlights Isaac's own self-perception of his pedagogical purpose in writing. The counsel that he offers in this regard is deeply revealing of the manner in which adept kabbalists understood the nature of mystical practice. True progression in the arts of mystical contemplation requires discipline and a *regularity of performance*. Such disciplined practice enables the supplicant to break through to new levels of ability in mental contemplation and its necessary correlate in the regulation of lengthened breath. For despite the acknowledged difficulty of such a breathing/vocal and contemplative exercise, Isaac of Akko assures his novice reader that repeated practice will ease the initial challenge, and that discipline—combined with a little help from Above—has the power to conquer ordinary obstacles to spiritual fulfillment: כי ההרגל על כל דבר שלטון ומן השמים יסיעוך (for regularity [enables] control over all things, and Heaven will help you). In this respect, the ordinary human condition would not appear to be conducive to such a meditative-physiological feat; the devotee instead requires a means to transcend the regular state of nature. This process of overcoming the limitations of human ability is facilitated by training, on the one hand (a human accomplishment that is enabled through practice), and by divine or heavenly intervention, on the other. As such, the ideal form of devotion is a meeting and a fusion of human and divine intention. Furthermore, as a master speaking to the less initiated, Isaac offers a confessional testimony to his own implementation and successful use of this challenging exercise. Thus the teacher inspires confidence in the student through his own example, and through the reassurance that success in such difficult matters is possible and worth the challenging road to its attainment.[50]

---

50. Consider the following additional example of the "journey of consciousness" model as it relates to the mystical enactment of the *Shema*ʿ. This experience rises directly from a

The meditative exercise outlined in this text also involves a further component that shapes the journey of consciousness in contemplation. In keeping with the widespread kabbalistic idea that each one of the ten *sefirot* is itself composed of the entire decadic structure—thus invoking an image of an infinite series of concentric sefirotic systems—Isaac presents the meditative process as a recurrence of virtually identical structures, each oriented under a nominally different rubric.[51] As the mystic's mind moves from one *sefirah* to the next, each focal point emerges as an orienting axis for all ten *sefirot*, and as a smaller-scale representation of the larger-scale pattern of ten. The meditative experience is therefore constantly structured by the decadic model and its unity, even as the mind contemplates individual *sefirot*. Each step in the mind's pathway through the metaphysical map stimulates a dialectical movement between the specific point of focus and the larger pattern of ten represented repeatedly on a smaller scale.

The dynamic relationship between the rhythms of the physical self and the contemplative journey of the mind in prayer is taken up again in Isaac's later work, in an equally extraordinary passage.[52] Centered as before on the proper recitation of the *Shema*ʿ, Isaac articulates a direct correlation between an embodied ritual practice and a contemplative ascent to the highest (and most recondite) dimensions of God. He begins by boldly asserting the supremacy of a contemplative technique that

---

symbolic performance of the sacred text, and calls for an all-encompassing contemplation of the entire sefirotic structure through the word *'eḥad*. As Isaac states in *Me'irat ʿEinayim*, p. 210:

> All ten *sefirot* are alluded to in this verse in a single unity. Therefore, one's intention must be directed to the overall unity [of the *sefirot*]. When [the individual] utters the [first] Divine Name [YHVH], he must first intend toward *Keter*, *Ḥokhmah*, and *Binah*. When he utters [the Name] *'Eloheinu*, [he must intend] toward *Gedulah* and *Paḥad*. When he utters the second Divine Name (YHVH) [he must intend] toward the Six Directions. And when he utters [the word] *'eḥad*, he must return and intend the *'alef* toward *Keter*, the *ḥet* to the [middle] eight *sefirot* [since ח has the numerical value of 8], the *dalet* to *Malkhut*, which is the last [*sefirah*]. He must lengthen [the *dalet*], and intend toward Her [*Malkhut*] that all these Attributes [*sefirot*] are all One, and that their end is bound to their beginning, and their beginning to their end [*Sefer Yeẓirah* 1:7]. And he must intend as though he can gather them all back into *Keter*, from whence they emanated.

51. See discussion of this and related themes in Idel, "*Sefirot* Above the *Sefirot*," pp. 239–280.

52. Isaac of Akko, *'Oẓar Ḥayyim*, fols. 39b–40a. Also see the analysis of Huss, "NiSAN—The Wife of the Infinite," pp. 167–168.

he came to realize in the course of his own ritual practice and recitation (בעודי קורא פסוק שמע ישראל בתפלת שחרית ואני מתכוין בדלת דאח"ד ראיתי כוונה בפסוק זה ישרה בעיני מאד מכל דברי המקובלים אשר ראיתי ואשר שמעתי)—a method that first instructs the devotee to "scatter [or spread] the focus of his contemplation" to the full distance of the world, so as to bind together and elevate all the souls of Israel above, to be harnessed within the force of the supernal angel Meṭaṭron.[53] It is the utterance of the words *Shema' Yisra'el* that frames this first focus on the elevation of Israelite (or Jewish) souls. This expansion and spreading out of consciousness—the preliminary act of devotional concentration—leads directly to the journey of ascent into the web of nested pathways contained within the divine self. For upon reciting the subsequent triad of words—*YHVH 'Eloheinu YHVH*—the supplicant in prayer is instructed to train contemplation on the infinite dimension of Divinity (*'Ein-Sof*—referred to here as: "The First Without Beginning/The Last Without End"), and the ten *sefirot* that flow forth from—and manifest—that mystery. It is here that Isaac frames the sojourn into God's deepest being as a continuous ascent upward on the rungs of a supernal ladder—one that is to be perpetually envisioned atop the head of the mystic, an emanational continuity established between the mind/soul of the kabbalist and the sefirotic dimensions of the divine. As Isaac formulates the practice: והוא שתמיד יומם ולילה יראה עס"ב [=עשר ספירות בלימה] על ראשו בעמוד או סולם מוצב על ראשו שרגל סולם זה על ראשו וראשו של סולם זה למעלה משלשת העולמים עם הר"ב ר' אב"א [=הראשון בלי ראשית אחרון בלי אחרית] (Constantly, day and night, he should envision the ten *sefirot* atop his head, in a column or ladder set upon his head, such that the bottom of this ladder is upon his head, and the top of the ladder is higher than the three worlds with The

53. This fascinating rhetoric might be considered in relationship to the forms discussed in earlier chapters on reception, transmission, and creativity. In this brief statement, Isaac has revealed his own willingness to overturn the authority of reception in favor of an interpretive and performative insight that he has reached on his own. The exegesis and practice that he outlines here are presented as the product of an individual epiphany attained through his own performance of the *Shema'* ritual, and immediately deemed to be superior to *all other interpretations and methods* that he has received (whether they be textual or oral). Thus the creativity of sudden insight—a hermeneutics that flows directly from the process of ritual performance—is understood to replace and supersede the otherwise authoritative traditions transmitted from reliable masters. This move is deeply telling of the attitude toward individual kabbalistic interpretation and creativity adopted by Isaac in his later writing.

First Without Beginning/The Last Without End [*'Ein-Sof*]). Isaac thus conjures up an image with a vertical trajectory—a contemplative state that situates the mind of the supplicant in direct continuum with the descending hierarchy of the *sefirot*. Within this cosmic and meditative frame, the rhythms of utterance structure a contemplative performance of the nomian ritual; the ascent of consciousness through the *sefirot* realizes the perceived subsurface meaning of the ritual drama:

שכאשר יאמר יי' יתן למחשבת שכלו התעלות מהע' [=עטרה] שעל ראשו ודרך הת' [=תפארת] והשאר בכללו עד שיגיע לר"ב ר' אב"א בשכמל"ו [=ברוך שם כבוד מלכותו לעולם ועד] ולא יפריד מחשבת שכלו ממנה מהרה כי עמידתה בו היא היא השתחויה הנכונה על כל ההשתחויות.

וכשיאמר אלהינו ימשיך מחשבת שכלו ממנה עד הע' [=עטרה] ועד ראש עצמו. וכאשר יאמר י"י יתן עוד שנית התעלות למחשבת שכלו מראשו והע' עד הר"ב ר' אב"א . . . וכאשר יאמר אחד ימשיך עוד מחשבת שכלו מהר"ב ר' אב"א עד הע' . . . בעודו אומ' הח"ת של אחד תהיה המשכה זו, ובעודו אומ' הדל"ת של אחד יתן עוד שלישית למחשבת שכלו התעלות מהע' השוכנת בראשו, ר"ל תוך נפש שכלו עד הר"ב ר' אב"א. ובעוד מחשבת שכלו עולה דרך הקו האמצעי והוא מאריך בדלת [ד]אח"ד ראש לשונו דבק בשיניו אשר מספר שיניו ל"ב כמספר ל"ב נתיבות.

When he utters [the divine name] *YY* [*YHVH*], he should elevate the thought of his mind from [the *sefirah*] *'Atarah* that is atop his head, through *Tif'eret* and the other [*sefirot*], until he arrives at "The First Without Beginning/The Last Without End" [*'Ein-Sof*], blessed is the name of the glory of His kingdom forever and ever. And he should not separate the thought of his mind from [*'Ein-Sof*] quickly, for [the mind's act of] standing in [*'Ein-Sof*][54] is a [mode of] devotion more proper than all other [modes of] devotion.

And when he says *'Eloheinu*, he should draw forth the thought of his mind from Her (*'Ein-Sof*) down to *'Atarah*, and then down to his own head [*ve-'ad ro'sh 'aẓmo*]. And when he says *YY* [*YHVH*], he should elevate the thought of his mind a second time, from his head and *'Atarah* up to "The First Without Beginning/The Last Without End" [*'Ein-Sof*). . . . And when he says *'eḥad* [one], he should again draw forth the thought of his mind from "The First Without

54. This phrase does not translate easily—*'amidatah bo* might also be loosely rendered as: "her [the mind] remaining anchored in, and connected in *kavvanah* to *'Ein-Sof*."

> Beginning / The Last Without End" [*'Ein-Sof*] down to *'Atarah*. . . . While uttering the *ḥet* of [the word] *'eḥad*, [he should engage in] this drawing forth, and while uttering the *dalet* of *'eḥad*, he should give an extra third of a measure[55] to elevate the thought of his mind from *'Atarah*, who dwells in his head—that is to say, within the soul of his mind [*tokh nefesh sikhlo*][56]—all the way up to "The First Without Beginning / The Last Without End" [*'Ein-Sof*]. While the thought of his mind is ascending through the Central Line, and while he is lengthening the *dalet* of *'eḥad*, the tip of his tongue cleaves to his teeth—for the number of his teeth is thirty-two, like the number of the thirty-two Paths [of Supernal Wisdom].

As with the passage from *Me'irat 'Einayim*, the very physical process of utterance characterized in this text is linked to the contemplative journey of the mind through the *sefirot*. With tongue pressed against teeth, the *dalet* is lengthened—a depiction of enunciation that runs parallel to the prescription for breath-elongation observed in the previous passage (as well as in the prescriptions for a theurgically charged utterance of the *dalet*, examined in Chapter 6). The number of teeth in the mouth of the devotee is correlated to the thirty-two paths of supernal wisdom, paths that the mind will traverse in its sojourn through the sefirotic dimensions of divine being.[57] Thus physical enactment is tied intimately to the contemplative drama, and there exists a taut relationship between the bodily nature of ritual speech—the performative gesture of ritual action—and the state of *kavannah* cultivated in consciousness. Put differently still: the contours of *recitation as a ritual act* both mirror and stimulate the elaborate journey of the mind into God. Consonant with other prescriptions in Isaac's writing, the mystic is instructed to ascend all the way to *'Ein-Sof* itself, the targeted locale of the contemplative mind. Building upon this attainment, the devotee then seeks to fashion a continuous path of meditative movement and

55. The reader may recall that this prescription for uttering the *dalet* with an extra measure of enunciation was discussed above in Chapter 6.

56. This is a rather unusual phrase. It may be an allusion to the "intellective soul," which is the locus of prophetic contemplation in the human mind.

57. This correlation between the ten *sefirot* and the thirty-two paths of wisdom is a direct allusion to the text of *Sefer Yeẓirah* 1:1.

passage from the heights of Infinity down into his own mind. In this conception, a line of connection is posited between the mystic's consciousness (his *sekhel*), the *sefirot* that sit atop his head (and which presumably send forth divine energy into the devotee), and the wellspring of *'Ein-Sof* that stands supreme. Such is the meaning of the envisioned sefirotic ladder atop the mystic's head—he is instructed to ascend and descend the rungs of Divinity, all the while retaining an awareness of the manner in which his own self (embodied in the head, the mind of contemplation) is linked to the continuous chain of divine energy. He ascends from below to the summit of Infinity, and, by necessity, he returns to himself (via the lower *sefirot*) once again. Indeed, *'Ein-Sof* is the ultimate goal of the contemplative journey—an assertion that would seem to undermine the highly apophatic rhetoric that usually accompanies kabbalistic reflections on *'Ein-Sof* and its unattainability.[58] It is therefore all the more striking that the devotee seeks to cultivate a line of unbroken connection between his individual consciousness and that infinity—a continuity that posits an ontological chain between person and deity, a prescribed experience of Divinity dwelling atop and within the head of the mystic.[59] At the same time, this state functions as an ocular meditation that is to be evoked in the devotional experience. In this mode of contemplation, all other points of focus are nullified and shut out, and *'Ein-Sof* occupies the entirety of the mystic's meditative attention. As Isaac formulates the matter in a different passage:

> ההשתחויה הנכונה . . . למקובל האמתי . . . היא העלאת מחשבת השכל לאין סוף אל האדון היחיד הר"ב ר' אב"א בשכמל"ו ודבוקה בו . . . העלאת מחשבת השכל אל המקום הזה שהוא הוא המקום הודאי מקום לכל מקום זו היא הדרך הנכונה האמיתית . . . ואמנם סוד הדבר הנכון הוא שלילת כל נברא . . . ממחשבה זכה נכונה שלא יהיה בה דבר בעולם בלתי מקום זה הנזכר ואצילותו עמו.

> The proper devotion . . . for the true kabbalist . . . is the elevation of the thought of the mind to *'Ein-Sof*—to the Singular Master, "The First Without Beginning / The Last Without End," blessed is the name

58. See, e.g., *Zohar* 2:239a; Tishby, *Wisdom of the Zohar,* 1: 229–255, esp. p. 234.

59. Elements of this motif are also examined in Wolfson, *Through a Speculum That Shines*, pp. 357, 363, 367.

> of the glory of His kingdom forever and ever—and to be cleaved to Him. . . . The elevation of the thought of the mind to this Place—the real (or true) Place, the Place of every place [*maqom le-khol maqom*]—this is the proper and true way. . . . And indeed, the correct secret of the matter [*sod ha-davar ha-nakhon*] is the negation of every creature . . . from the thought that is pure and sound [*mi-maḥshavah zakhah nekhonah*]—that there should not be in [that thought] anything of the world, except for this aforementioned Place and Its emanation.[60]

Not only is the devotee believed to be able to reach *'Ein-Sof* in contemplative concentration, but all other thoughts are to be removed from the scope of *kavvanah*. Only then is the purified mind filled with the Place that contains all, only then can the mind rise on its anabatic journey through Divinity. This-worldly consciousness is considered to be an inhibitor of ultimate devotional consciousness, and the mind is *prepared* through an act of nullification and expulsion. Put differently: to realize the ultimate heights of meditative ascent and *devequt*, the mystic is first called upon to engage in an erasure of earthly consciousness—a state of no-thought that enables the attainment of ideal thought.[61] Focusing on *'Ein-Sof* is considered to be the one true contemplation, the one true subject of devotional intention. In so prescribing the contemplative ideal, Isaac of Akko defines the parameters of center and periphery in devotional mind.

Divided Consciousness and the Anchors of Intention

From the literary inception of Kabbalah in Provence, the mystical authors struggled to reject the potential polytheistic implications of their decadic mode of theology, and they sought to defend sefirotic thinking as a fundamentally unitive and monotheistic worldview. It may be argued that the famous criticisms leveled by Meir ben Shimon

---

60. Isaac of Akko, *'Oẓar Ḥayyim*, fol. 29b.

61. Such an act of clearing the mind of all worldly thoughts for the sake of attaining a higher, spiritual state of consciousness has much in common with meditative prescriptions found in other religious traditions. See, e.g., Bielefeldt, *Dōgen's Manuals of Zen Meditation*, pp. 133–160. This text also bears phenomenological correlation to the motif of contemplative purification discussed in Chapter 6.

of Narbonne[62] cast a long shadow over early Kabbalah, and numerous mystical writers set out to compose *apologia* for the basic Oneness of the sefirotic system.[63] Thus was born the fundamental tension of kabbalistic thought in general, and of devotional mysticism in particular, between the need to posit and discuss individual *sefirot* and to insist simultaneously that there is no real individuation, only total and undivided Infinity. Within the contemplative context of prayer, the kabbalists were constantly caught between an emphasis upon specific sefirotic points of intention, in which the mystic directs his mind to the *sefirah* best suited to a given time of day or piece of the liturgy, and the underlying axiom that these specific points should never be entirely divorced from the united totality. What emerges from this ongoing dialectic is a prescription for a kind of divided consciousness—one in which the supplicant is instructed to focus simultaneously upon a particular *sefirah*, and to keep his mind connected to the structure of unity and its higher source (often to the monistic flux of *'Ein-Sof* itself). From this perspective, the Infinite sefirotic totality is the ultimate focus of the mystic's contemplation, but the human mind nevertheless requires specific mental anchors with which to guide the meditative consciousness. Each point of intention is thus only a configuration for the finite mind insofar as it cannot directly apprehend the totality of Infinity. For Isaac of Akko, the aforementioned tension rises to particular centrality, and a detailed analysis of his view on the matter is necessary in order to fully appreciate the contours of his devotional-contemplative mysticism. In *Me'irat 'Einayim*, we read:

באי זו דרך שתאחז בכונת הברכות והתפלה הזהר מאד שלא תקצץ בנטיעות לחשב באחת מהן בלבד. אלא תמיד תהיה מחשבתך קשורה בכלן יחד מאין סוף לאין סוף

---

62. See discussion of these matters, with particular attention to the sources of the polemic, in Scholem, "New Documentary Witness to the Origins of Kabbalah," pp. 7–38.

63. This seems to have been the underlying purpose of the first major systematic work of kabbalistic theology, R. 'Asher ben David's *Sefer ha-Yiḥud*. In that book, R. 'Asher sets out to elaborately develop the terse kabbalistic teachings of his uncle and master R. Isaac the Blind, and is clearly concerned with demonstrating the fundamental unity and monotheism of sefirotic thought. This effort seems to have the character of an apologetic response, and would appear to be partly aimed at the critique of Meir b. Shimon. Indeed, the content of this defense of sefirotic unity is also reflected in the very title of the treatise. See E. Fishbane, "The Speech of Being, The Voice of God: Phonetic Mysticism in the Kabbalah of Asher ben David and His Contemporaries," p. 488. For a critical edition of this text, see *R. Asher ben David: His Complete Works and Studies in His Kabbalistic Thought*, ed. Abrams.

בכל ששת קצוותיהן. ובעוד שתהיה מחשבתך מיוחדת באין סוף, תפשט ותמשיך ענף ממחשבתך אל ההויה אשר תצטרך לכוין אליה. אבל מכל מקום תמיד יהיה שרש כונתך קשור ומיוחד בכלן בכלל אין סוף כשלהבת הקשורה בגחלת וכענבים באשכל כן יהיו כל עשר ספירות מיוחדות במחשבתך מאין סוף לאין סוף. ומה שכתבתי למעלה שברכת אתה חונן לחכמה, השיבנו לתשובה, סלח לנו לחסד וכן כלם, זה יש לך לכוין–שרש מחשבתך יהיה קשור באין סוף.

Whichever path you adopt in the intention for blessings and prayer, be very careful not to cut the shoots by contemplating only one of them [the *sefirot*] alone. Instead, always have your mind bound to all of them together, from Infinity to Infinity, on all six of their sides. And while your mind is still united with *'Ein-Sof*, draw forth a branch from your mind [i.e., the place where your mind is] to the dimension [lit., being] that you need to intend toward. Yet you should nevertheless always keep the root of your intention bound and united to all of them, included within *'Ein-Sof*. Like the flame that is bound to the coal, and like the grapes in a cluster, so too all ten *sefirot* should be united in your mind from Infinity to Infinity. And with respect to what I wrote above, that the benediction *'atah ḥonen* [is to be intended] toward *Ḥokhmah*, [the benediction] *hashiveinu* toward *Teshuvah*, [the benediction] *selaḥ lanu* toward *Ḥesed*, and in a similar fashion for the rest of [the *sefirot*],[64] you should intend in the following way: the root of your consciousness should be bound to *'Ein-Sof*.[65]

This passage clearly exhibits an affirmation of *'Ein-Sof* as the ultimate and primary destination of the contemplative mind—as a dimension that can and must be attained in devotional concentration.[66] Indeed,

---

64. For the textual antecedents of such a symbolic and performative reading of the Eighteen Benedictions, see Idel, "On Isaac the Blind's Intentions," pp. 28–30; "R. 'Azri'el mi-Gerona—Perush ha-Tefillah," ed. M. Gavarin, § 9: 4, pp. 36–46.

65. Isaac of Akko, *Me'irat 'Einayim*, p. 92.

66. By way of parallel, consider the following example taken from one of the more famous texts on *kavvanah* associated with the early kabbalists (see Scholem, "Concept of Kavvanah in the Early Kabbalah," p. 172): והמתעלה בכח כוונתו מדבר לדבר עד הגיעו לאין סוף (And he who ascends through the power of his *kavvanah* from rung to rung [lit., from entity to entity] until he arrives at *'Ein-Sof*). See also the text by Joseph Gikatilla cited by Scholem, ibid., p. 178, n. 50: שאדם צריך להתכוון בתפלתו ולעלות מספירה לספירה ומחפץ לחפץ עד שיגיע בלבו למקור החפץ העליון הנקרא אין סוף . . . ממעמקים קראתיך כלומר מאת המקור העליון הנקרא אין סוף (A person must direct [his mind] in his prayer and he must ascend from *sefirah* to *sefirah*, and from entity to entity, until he arrives in his heart [mind] at the source of the highest entity, which is called *'Ein-Sof* . . . [Ps. 130:1] 'From the depths I have called out to You,' which is to say, from the

speaking as a master of mystical instruction and prescription, Isaac advises his reader to keep the entire sefirotic unity and the energizing force of *'Ein-Sof* present in mind throughout the mystical enactment of liturgical prayer. All intention that moves toward individual *sefirot* for particular needs and moments is acceptable and even necessary, but only if the supplicant maintains a conscious connection between the specific *sefirah* of mental focus and the larger inseparable flow of Infinity. Concentrating the mind on a particular *sefirah* thus emerges as an extension of the mind's connection to the Infinite source. This conception is expressed in the above-cited passage through the richly evocative phrases *shoresh kavvanatkha* and *shoresh maḥshavatkha* ("the root of your intention" and "the root of your consciousness/thought")—images that invoke a mental experience of duality, of simultaneous points of focus held concurrently in consciousness. The alternation in emphasis between them establishes the *boundaries* of mental concentration, of periphery and center in the mind's attention toward the divine objects it contemplates. The "root" may retreat to the background, or to the periphery of consciousness, while the specific point of focus rises to the center of mental visibility. Nevertheless, Isaac adamantly requires the supplicant to maintain a connection between his state of focus and that all-important root. And as the life of a tree is organically bound to and nourished by its subterranean roots, so too the meditative gaze must mirror the ontological condition of particular *sefirot* vis-à-vis their infinite ground of being.

---

supernal source that is called *'Ein-Sof*). In my estimation, these sources attest well to the fact that kabbalists treated *'Ein-Sof* as a metaphysical locale that may be contemplated (and reached) by the human mind. How else are we to explain the blunt rhetoric found in these lines? It is, of course, true that this positive approach was constantly undermined in the process of apophatic speech and mystical unsaying. Nevertheless, many kabbalists were clearly inclined to view *'Ein-Sof* as the object of ultimate devotion. Oddly enough, despite Scholem's citation of the text from Gikatilla, he nevertheless makes the following broad claim ("Concept of Kavvanah," p. 166): "Needless to say, an unmediated and explicit kavvanah directed to Ein-Sof itself, in the stricter meaning of the concept, *does not exist for Isaac [the Blind] nor the entire early Kabbalah that came after him*" (emphasis added). As I hope is demonstrated by the texts examined in this study, such a conclusion is dubious at best, and overtly undermined in a good number of cases. A related argument (on the notion that certain early kabbalists affirmed the possibility of contemplating *'Ein-Sof*, and the consequent interplay of apophatic and kataphatic speech) is advanced in Wolfson, "Negative Theology and Positive Assertion in the Early Kabbalah," pp. v–xxii. Also see the discussion of this dialectical in E. Fishbane, "Mystical Contemplation and the Limits of the Mind."

According to Isaac's thinking, to direct consciousness only to one *sefirah* without realizing its dependency on and inextricability from *'Ein-Sof* is to commit the ultimate heresy of separation above and engagement in polytheistic worship—a theurgical rupture that is caused by the error in intention, and that is aligned in terminology with the paradigmatic heresy of Elisha ben Abuya (*qiẓeẓ ba-neṭi'ot*—cut/uprooted the plants/shoots).[67] Yet Isaac's point is not only that a focus on a specific *sefirah* must maintain awareness of, and devotional attunement to, the Infinite source. Quite remarkably, Isaac exhorts his reader to first *unite* his mind with *'Ein-Sof* itself and then to draw that exalted consciousness down to the particular *sefirah* relevant to the given moment. Assuming that mental attachment to the Infinite domain is the highest goal imaginable for the supplicant, and given the fact that it is clearly not presented as a theurgical act (i.e., the drawing down of emanation), what then is the purpose of drawing a "branch from your mind" (i.e., from the place where your mind is) to a particular *sefirah*? Would not that seem to be a *descent* from the heights of consciousness? What we learn from Isaac's prescriptive rhetoric is that the mystic must seek to attain an *all-encompassing* consciousness of Divinity. The mind must be firmly rooted in the totality of *'Ein-Sof* and the sefirotic structure as a whole.[68] In experiential terms, the process might be likened to the lens of a camera through which the eye of the viewer may alternate between the blurred nature of a panoramic view and the sharpness of particulars that emerges when the lens is in focus. The specific *sefirot* that come into focus for the mystic in meditation are ultimately only sharper points of orientation in the larger panorama of *'Ein-Sof*.[69]

---

67. See discussions of this conception of heresy in rabbinic theology in Segal, *Two Powers in Heaven*, particularly pp. 60–73; Liebes, *Sin of Elisha*, pp. 29–50; Rubenstein, *Talmudic Stories*, pp. 64–104. An alternate reading of the tannaitic sources of this representation (and its transformation in amoraic retellings) is suggested in A. Goshen-Gottstein, *Sinner and the Amnesiac*, pp. 47–61, which reassesses the key phrases involved and raises new doubts about our ability to discern a clear historical picture of Elisha ben Abuya, as well as the perception of him in rabbinic sources; see *ibid.*, pp. 225–229. Either way, however, Elisha ben Abuya was certainly perceived as the paradigmatic divider and heretic in medieval kabbalistic sources.

68. The emphasis on directing devotion to the totality of the sefirotic structure has roots in earlier Provençal Kabbalah. See Idel, "Prayer in Provençal Kabbalah," pp. 279–280.

69. In one instance in *'Oẓar Ḥayyim* (fol. 73a), Isaac adopts classic Neoplatonic terminology to underscore his view of this relationship between *'Ein-Sof* and the *sefirot*. *'Ein-Sof*

This conception of *'Ein-Sof*—contemplative anchor vis-à-vis the other *sefirot*—is maintained and developed in *'Oẓar Ḥayyim*. The devotee is instructed never to waver in his focus on *'Ein-Sof*, even while fulfilling an intention directed to a lower *sefirah*. Let us consider two related texts in this work that exemplify such a continuous strain in Isaac's devotional thinking. In the first of these passages, Isaac opens with high praise for those kabbalists of his generation who have discovered and preserved the intentions for prayer according to the secret symbolism of the ten *sefirot*. Despite this exuberant affirmation of the chain of tradition, however, Isaac does see fit to sharpen the contemplative prescription as he believes it to have been originally transmitted:

> דע כי המקום אשר הזכירוהו המקובלים שיתכוין בו המברך והמתפלל או המתחנן או המשבח ומזמר לאל חי בשכמל"ו [=ברוך שם כבוד מלכותו לעולם ועד] הענין הנכון אשר יעשה והמחשבה הנכונה אשר יחשוב . . . הוא שיחשוב בלבו כי שהמקום ההוא ספר שכולו אש לבנה והאותיות והמלות והדברים אשר הוא קורא כתובים עליו באש שחורה ובעודו קורא יהיו עיני בשרו בו ועיני לבו באדון היחיד בשכמל"ו הוא אין סוף.

> Know that [with respect to] the place mentioned by the kabbalists [as the desired locus] of intention for the one who blesses and the one who prays, for the one who petitions, the one who praises, and the one who sings to the Living God [*'El Ḥai*]—the proper conduct that he should enact and the proper thought that he should think . . . [is the following]: He should think in his heart [mind] that this place is a book that is entirely white fire, and the letters and words that he reads are written upon it in black fire. And while he is still reading, his physical eyes should be [directed to this fire], and the eyes of his heart [mind] should be [directed to] the Singular Master (*ba-'adon ha-yaḥid*)—blessed is the name of the glory of his Kingdom for ever and ever—Who is *'Ein-Sof*.[70]

It is well established in both the Naḥmanidean and the zoharic tradi-

---

(referred to as *ha-adon ha-yaḥid*—one of Isaac's terms of choice to characterize the Infinite) is said to be utterly one and simple (בתכלית הפשיטות, האחד היחיד), and the different names of the *sefirot* are not considered to reflect any change or multiplicity within the deity. They are only distinct from the perspective of creaturely consciousness.

70. Isaac of Akko, *'Oẓar Ḥayyim*, fol. 70b. See Huss, "NiSAN—The Wife of the Infinite," p. 179, in which the centrality of *'Ein-Sof* for Isaac's theory of *kavvanah* and prophecy is underscored, and cf. Gottlieb, "Illumination, *Devequt*, and Prophecy in R. Isaac of Akko's *Sefer 'Oẓar Ḥayyim*," pp. 236–238 (esp. the summative conclusion on p. 238), in which Isaac's conception of complete contemplative union with *'Ein-Sof* is observed.

tions that the white fire of this conception symbolizes the *sefirah Tif'eret*, while the black fire represents *'Atarah/Shekhinah*.[71] These symbolic correlations proceed from the notion that the tenth *sefirah*—*'Atarah/Shekhinah*—is the revealed female dimension of Divinity that makes the concealed bright light of the masculine visible and manifest. As the letters of black fire make the underlying white fire discernable and meaningful to the human mind, *'Atarah/Shekhinah* reveals the truth of *Tif'eret* through a veil of disclosure, funneling into manifestation an otherwise undifferentiated light. This symbolism also accords well with the reference to *'El Ḥai* as the focal point of prayer, insofar as this divine cognomen is most often associated with the lower masculine within the deity—particularly its extension in *Yesod*.[72] Thus, the *kavvanah* that Isaac first reports in the name of revered kabbalists is most probably an instruction to center devotional concentration on the *sefirah Tif'eret*—a tradition preserved explicitly earlier in *'Oẓar Ḥayyim* as well.[73] Here the mystic is encouraged to envision Divinity as a metaphysical text—as a book set open before the contemplative gaze of the devotee (שיחשוב בלבו כי שהמקום ההוא ספר שכולו אש לבנה).[74] In this way, the liturgical text that is read during the ritual performance of prayer is to be accompanied by an intention directed to the divine page above—the text of inner divine reality—one that appears to the mystic's contemplative eye as radiant white flame. Given the rabbinic and other kabbalistic associations of the white fire / black fire motif,[75] this envisioned supernal book is also certainly the cosmic Torah—the Logos that is the spiritual source of earthly Scripture, the divine word through which the lower world came into being.

All of these interpretative observations, however, are but a prelude to further understanding the devotional motif and practice of binary

71. See, e.g., *Ma'arekhet ha-'Elohut*, end of chap. 12, and *Zohar* 2:84a.

72. See Joseph Gikatilla, *Sha'arei 'Orah*, ed. Ben-Shlomo, 1: 93 (beginning of chap. 2).

73. See fol. 65a.

74. The contemplative visualization of Divinity as a metaphysical text is studied at length (with particular attention to the interstices of language, body, and gender) in Wolfson, *Through a Speculum That Shines*, and more recently in id., *Language, Eros, Being*.

75. While this motif is rather widespread in the literature, the following cases are representative: JT *Sheqalim*, fol. 25b; *Tanḥuma'*, *Berei'shit*, 1; Naḥmanides, *Perush ha-RaMBaN 'al ha-Torah*, ed. Chavel, 1: 7; *Zohar* 3:132a. The contours of this topos have been explored in Idel, *Absorbing Perfections*, pp. 45–79.

concentration. At the end of the passage, a consciousness of split intention is prescribed that orients the devotee toward a distinction between the sight of the physical eyes (*'einei besaro*) and the deeper internal vision of the heart-mind (*'einei libbo*).[76] The practitioner is instructed to direct his physical eyes to this inner, divine book of fire (even if this vision also correlates to the experience of reading the liturgical text of this world), thus implying that the lower *sefirot* can in fact be visualized through the corporeal sense of sight. Alternatively, Isaac may be employing the phrase *'einei besaro* in a broader sense—as a characterization of the lower (or more external) mode of contemplative perception, and not necessarily as limited to that which the physical organ of sight can perceive. Either way, the kabbalist is instructed to maintain a simultaneous state of split vision and concentration between the more accessible and external dimension of *Tif'eret* (as envisioned through the black fire of *'Atarah/Shekhinah*) and the deeper, more interior realm of *'Ein-Sof*. In this manner, *'Ein-Sof* is once again portrayed as the necessary foundation and anchor for other specific points of sefirotic focus in prayer.

This practice is borne out in a parallel passage, lines in which our author overtly prescribes a sustained contemplation of the *sefirah Tif'eret*. The kabbalistic devotee is instructed to remove all thoughts of the ordinary world from his consciousness, centering his mind instead upon the supernal World of *Tif'eret* (וכל אדם ירא אלהים חייב לשלול מלבו כל עניני העולם, שהת' סוד העולם).[77] Here the divine world substitutes for the mun-

---

76. As noted earlier in this study, this polarity was central to the thought of Yehudah ha-Levi on religious experience—a phenomenon and terminology examined extensively in the work of Elliot Wolfson. See Wolfson, "Merkavah Traditions in Philosophical Garb: Judah Halevi Reconsidered," pp. 215–235; id., *Through a Speculum That Shines*, pp. 163–181.

77. As mentioned earlier in this chapter, the exegetical correlation of *'olam* to *Tif'eret* functions in the context of a kabbalistic interpretation of the rabbinic dictum *le-'olam yikanes 'adam shnei petaḥim, ve-aḥar kakh yitpalel*. In reading *le-'olam* as "in/to the world of *Tif'eret*" (as opposed to "always"), Isaac formulates the following *kavvanah*: "a person must enter into the two openings of the *sefirot Ḥesed* and *Gevurah* through *Tif'eret*, who is called *'olam*." The motif of removing all mundane thoughts, and focusing exclusively on the deity, is notably related to the Maimonidean prescription for proper *kavvanah*. Interestingly, the *sefirah Tif'eret* is mentioned in Isaac of Akko's formulation (based, to be sure, on the tradition ascribed to Naḥmanides—see Idel, "On Isaac the Blind's Intentions," p. 30, line 20), despite the fact that Maimonides utilized the term *Shekhinah* to characterize the subject of exclusive focus (though it goes without saying that Maimonides used this terminology in its classical sense—as a generic term for the divine Presence). See Moses Maimonides, *Mishneh Torah, Hilkhot Tefilah*, 4:16: כיצד היא הכוונה שיפנה את לבו מכל המחשבות ויראה עצמו כאלו הוא עומד לפני השכינה (How

dane world in the contemplative mind, and *Tif'eret* is presented as the constant object of meditative focus (note the relatedness of this practice to the one observed at the end of the last section—a prescription in which all earthly thought was to be nullified before contemplation of *'Ein-Sof*). Nevertheless (and here is the key point), Isaac constructs true contemplation as that state of mind in which intention is directed *simultaneously* to *'Ein-Sof* and *Tif'eret*: דע שעם כל מה שצריך אדם לתת למחשבת שכלו דיבוק באדון היחיד תמיד צריך הוא לשים לנגד עיניו מדת הת' כל היום וכל הלילה (Know that along with the requirement of a person to cleave the thought of his mind to the Unique Master [*ba-'adon ha-yaḥid*], he must always place the Attribute of *Tif'eret* before his eyes, all day and all night).[78] Both *'Ein-Sof* and *Tif'eret* are to be maintained in the devotional mind with thoroughgoing constancy—there appears to be no moment when *Tif'eret* is not to be contemplated by the kabbalist, a state of consciousness that is accompanied by *devequt* with *'Ein-Sof*.

This ideal of a divided consciousness is not restricted by Isaac to the role of *'Ein-Sof*; it is also formulated as the dialectic between *Binah*—cosmic womb of all sefirotic Being—and her lower progeny in the form of *Tif'eret* and *'Atarah*.[79] These lower dimensions are frequently the prescribed mental anchors for contemplative focus, but Isaac insists that the supplicant never isolate them from the sefirotic totality, and that one must keep one's intention bound to *Teshuvah* (*Binah*) itself. Indeed, this contemplative requirement is so stringent that an isolation of *'Atarah* or *Tif'eret* from their source in *Teshuvah* is considered to be tantamount to idolatry. This prescription understands the *sefirah Binah* to be a root anchor in mystical contemplation, a division in concentration that is phenomenologically parallel to what we have seen with regard to *'Ein-Sof*.

The conception of a duality in consciousness (what has alternatively been called "binarism")[80] between *Binah* and a lower *sefirah*

---

is intention [to be practiced]? He should empty his mind of all thoughts, and see himself as though he were standing before the *Shekhinah*).

78. Isaac of Akko, *'Oẓar Ḥayyim*, fol. 129a.

79. Evidence for this latter type is drawn primarily from *Me'irat 'Einayim*, and does not manifest significantly in *'Oẓar Ḥayyim*. As we have seen above, the latter text emphasizes the contemplation of *'Ein-Sof* and the retention of *'Ein-Sof* as an anchor of intention.

80. See Idel, "Prayer in Provençal Kabbalah," pp. 268–272.

is deeply rooted in earlier kabbalistic traditions from the Provençal school—the use of which is one of the most prominent examples of Isaac of Akko's eclectic and anthological method. The core idea—that the supplicant must maintain mental focus on *Binah* even while contemplating the lower *sefirot*—seems to have originated in that form in the school of Isaac the Blind (who was in turn indebted to the traditions of his father, the RABaD),[81] and his view subsequently

---

81. The background to this issue is somewhat complex, but it should be reviewed in detail in order to appreciate Isaac of Akko's place in the history of kabbalistic ideas and practices. The presence of such antecedent traditions stemming from the earliest kabbalists known to us was first noted by Scholem in his *Rei'shit ha-Qabbalah*, p. 73 n. 2, which cites fragments from two important manuscript witnesses (MS JTS 838, fol. 48a and MS British Museum 755, fol. 85b) that mention the views of Ya'aqov ha-Nazir and 'Avraham ben David (the RABaD) on the details of *kavvanah* for the Eighteen Benedictions. In those cases, Jacob ha-Nazir was credited with the view that *Binah* was the primary object of devotional contemplation (balanced, that is, in binary tension with *Tif'eret*), while the RABaD was said to have argued for a rather different practice, primarily directed toward the highest *sefirah* in the chain of Being (*'Ilat ha-'ilot*, or *Keter*), but which also functioned in a binary relationship with a lower metaphysical (inner divine) entity called *Yoẓer Berei'shit* (a name used prominently in the *Hekhalot* literature of Late Antiquity; see Scholem, *Major Trends*, p. 65). The text cited by Scholem in *Rei'shit ha-Qabbalah* (p. 73 n. 2) reads as follows: קבלת ר' יעקב הנזיר שלש ראשונות ושלש אחרונות לבינה והאמצעיות ביום לתפארת ובלילה כולם לבינה. וקבלת הרב ר' אברהם ז"ל שלש ראשונות ושלש אחרונות לעלת העלות והאמצעיות ליוצר בראשית (The tradition of R. Ya'aqov ha-Nazir is that the three initial benedictions [of the Eighteen Benedictions] and the three concluding benedictions [are to be intended] toward *Binah*. The middle benedictions during the day [are to be intended] toward *Tif'eret*, and at night all [of the benedictions are to be intended] toward *Binah*. The tradition of the Rav, R. 'Avraham of blessed memory, is that the three initial benedictions and the three concluding benedictions [are to be intended] toward the Cause of Causes [*Keter*], and the middle benedictions [are to be intended] toward *Yoẓer Berei'shit*). The R. 'Avraham mentioned in this passage is none other than R. 'Avraham ben David (RABaD), the noted talmudist and father of Isaac the Blind. Idel, "Prayer in Provençal Kabbalah" and "On Isaac the Blind's Intentions," makes a convincing case for correcting this particular attribution, however, providing separate manuscript evidence to support the claim that the *Binah*-directed *kavvanah* (i.e., the tradition attributed to Ya'aqov ha-Nazir in the texts cited by Scholem) was preserved in the name of Isaac the Blind (the RABaD's son), and indeed seems to be authentic. Idel published this terse text from MS Jerusalem JNUL 4° 6246, fol. 2a. Moreover, Idel has provided an additional manuscript witness that in fact preserves the attribution of the *Binah*-directed *kavvanah* to the RABaD himself and attributes the other *kavvanah* (i.e., to *'Ilat ha-'ilot*) to Ya'aqov ha-Nazir (Idel, "Prayer in Provençal Kabbalah," pp. 266–267; the text is cited from MS Oxford 1646, fol. 116b): קבלת ר' יעקב הנזיר ז"ל שלש ראשונות ושלש אחרונות לעלה שבעלות ואמצעיות ליוצר בראשית. קבלת הר"ר אברהם ז"ל שלש ראשונות ושלש אחרונות לבינה ואמצעיות ביום לתפארת בלילה לבינה כלם (The tradition of R. Ya'aqov ha-Nazir of blessed memory is that the three initial benedictions and the three concluding benedictions [are to be intended] toward the Cause of Causes, and the middle benedictions [are to be intended] toward *Yoẓer Berei'shit*. The tradition of the Rav, R. 'Avraham of blessed memory, is that the three initial benedictions and the three concluding benedictions

influenced the thought of other early kabbalists, most notably ʿAzriʾel of Gerona.[82]

Yet as recent scholarship has demonstrated, the origins of this model do not end there. Indeed, the binary mentality (or the model of divided consciousness) was also a basic structure of the devotional thought of the *Ḥasidei ʾAshkenaz*, and it appears that the root of this central kabbalistic conception is to be found in the writings of these German Pietists.[83] For several of these *ḥasidim*, and for Eleazar of Worms in particular, the divide in devotional concentration was made between the lower *kavod* (Glory) and the transcendent dimension of Divinity, which cannot be accessed by the human mind. In his view, the human being in prayer directs one part of his focus to the lower dimension (the *kavod*) and directs the deeper core of his intention to the transcendent deity.[84] While

---

[are to be intended] toward *Binah*, and the middle benedictions during the day [are to be intended] toward *Tifʾeret*. At night, all [of the benedictions are to be intended] toward *Binah*). Thus the two manuscript witnesses reflect inverse attributions of the separate *kavvanot*. Given these facts, and further postulating that the son was more likely to have preserved the tradition of his father than that of Yaʿaqov ha-Nazir, Idel concludes that the *Binah*-directed *kavvanah* should be attributed to the RABaD and Isaac the Blind, and not to Yaʿaqov ha-Nazir.

While all this is important in order to understand Isaac of Akko's views, it is particularly significant to underline the binary (or dual) character of these *kavvanot*. For, as Idel notes, both the tradition attributed to the RABaD and that attributed to Yaʿaqov ha-Nazir are of a binary nature. The one divides devotional concentration between *Binah* and *Tifʾeret*, and the other divides it between *ʿIlat ha-ʿilot* and *Yoẓer Bereʾshit*. See Idel's comments on the use of the term *Yoẓer Bereʾshit* in "Prayer in Provençal Kabbalah," p. 284. In both traditions, the divide is made between a more transcendent dimension and a more accessible one. At a basic structural level, therefore, the two traditions reflect a similar idea regarding binary contemplation that is divided between a higher and a lower sefirotic dimension.

82. The scope and details of this Provençal influence on ʿAzriʾel of Gerona is documented and analyzed in "R. ʿAzriʾel mi-Gerona—Perush ha-Tefillah," ed. Martel Gavarin, who gives particular attention to the manuscript variances from the Provençal circle that emphasize the significance of directing one's focus to *Binah* and the sefirotic structure as a whole—textual traditions (however directly transmitted) that very clearly influenced Isaac of Akko (this point is *not* noted by Gavarin). See ibid., § 1, pp. 41–46, 59, 65.

83. See Idel, "Prayer in Provençal Kabbalah," pp. 271, 277; id., "Between Ashkenaz and Provence," pp. 5–14; Abrams, "*Sefer Shaqod* of R. Shemuel ben R. Kalonimus and the Doctrine of the *Kavod* According to a Disciple of R. Eleazar of Worms," p. 220.

84. The central problem of the *kavod* in medieval German pietism has been dealt with by several scholars. Among these studies, see Dan, *Esoteric Theology of Ashkenazi Ḥasidism*, pp. 104–170; Wolfson, *Through a Speculum That Shines*, pp. 195–269; id., *Along the Path*, pp. 1–62 (and notes, pp. 111–187); and Abrams, "Secret of All Secrets: The Idea of the Glory and Intention for Prayer in the Writings of R. Eleazar of Worms," pp. 61–81. On the specific subject of a dialectic between an upper *kavod* and a lower *kavod*—constructed as the interplay of hidden and revealed

this idea was certainly shaped by the earlier view of Saʿadya Gaon,[85] it differs considerably from it insofar as Saʿadya limited the idea of revelation to the created Glory (*kavod nivra'*), and Eleazar argued for a deeper stratum of intention directed to the purportedly *transcendent* dimension of God.[86] As has been intimated in the studies of Moshe Idel, Elliot Wolfson, and Daniel Abrams, this issue was articulated through exegesis of a well-known talmudic statement: המתפלל צריך שיתן עיניו למטה ולבו למעלה (The person in prayer must direct his eyes downward, and his heart upward).[87] While the literal meaning of this talmudic remark seeks to caution the supplicant against visual distraction during prayer, as well as to encourage a posture of humility,[88] Eleazar of Worms interpreted it to mean that while the external-physical enactment of the prayer ritual should be directed to the *kavod* (שיתן עיניו למטה)—the lower dimension of divine manifestation—the inner intention of the heart-mind was to be directed to the higher, transcendent dimension of Divinity (לבו למעלה). As Abrams has demonstrated, Eleazar asserted that the devotee should in fact bow to the *kavod*, but direct his deeper mental intention to the upper region of Divinity, configured as the Tetragrammaton.[89] In this respect, there was to be a distinction between the external and

---

dimensions in the divine realm—see Dan, "The Hidden *Kavod*," pp. 71–78; Wolfson, *Along the Path*, p. 3 (this reference summarizes Wolfson's argument; in truth, the entire essay addresses this underlying question); Abrams, "*Sefer Shaqod* of R. Shemuel ben R. Kalonimus and the Doctrine of the *Kavod* According to a Disciple of R. Eleazar of Worms," p. 223.

85. See Altmann, "Saadya's Theory of Revelation: Its Origin and Background," pp. 140–160.

86. It should also be noted, of course, that a separate circle of German Pietists cultivated a different mode of intention, one whose lower focus of intention was directed to the cherub located on the divine throne. For those Pietists, the *kavod* was considered to be part of the transcendent realm of emanated divinity (thus devoid of all anthropomorphism), and the human object of devotion was the form of the "special cherub," as opposed to the intention directed to the lower *kavod* in the writings of Eleazar of Worms. See Abrams, "Secret of All Secrets," p. 74; id., "The Evolution of the Intention of Prayer to the Special Cherub," pp. 1–26; id., "From Divine Shape to Angelic Being: The Career of Akatriel in Jewish Literature," p. 54; id., "The Boundaries of Divine Ontology: The Inclusion and Exclusion of Meṭaṭron in the Godhead," pp. 307–309; Dan, *"Unique Cherub" Circle*, pp. 101–124.

87. BT *Yevamot*, fol. 105b.

88. The comment of RaShI to this phrase in BT *Yevamot*, fol. 105b, articulates yet another interpretation. The French exegete claims that "eyes downward" refers to a direction of the eyes toward the Land of Israel, since that is the place where the *Shekhinah* dwells.

89. Abrams, "Secret of All Secrets," p. 71.

internal performance of ritual. In the estimation of Wolfson, Eleazar's use of this talmudic remark reflects the view on the part of the Ashkenazic sage that the *Shekhinah* cannot be gazed at directly,[90] and must instead be visualized through the imaginative faculty, which is implied through the use of the technical term *lev*.[91] It does in fact seem that the binary orientation of devotion in German pietism was a key influence on the shaping of the kabbalistic conception of a consciousness divided between *Binah* and *Tif'eret/'Atarah*—a view that is directly linked to a new application of the talmudic dictum. In fact, this specific connection is overtly reflected in a significant manuscript fragment that preserves a tradition from the school of Solomon Ibn Adret: המתפלל צריך ליתן עיניו למטה לע' . . . ולבו למעלה לתש' כדי להמשיך לתפ' ומן התפ' לע' (The person in prayer must direct his eyes downward to *'Atarah* . . . and [he must direct] his heart upward toward *Teshuvah* in order to draw down [efflux] to *Tif'eret*, and from *Tif'eret* to *'Atarah*).[92]

It is clear that Isaac of Akko's view on these matters is heavily indebted to the earlier Provençal and Barcelonese traditions—an influence that further reveals Isaac's function as a collector and transmitter of received traditions. As he states (clearly acknowledging a similar preservation in Shem Ṭov Ibn Ga'on's *Keter Shem Ṭov*):[93]

כשיתפלל אדם שמונה עשרה, השלש ראשונות והשלש אחרונות לתשובה, והאמצעיות לתפארת. ואע"פ שאמרנו לתפארת יזהר שלא יזיז כונתו מהתשובה. והדיבור בכונה

---

90. The fact that the *Shekhinah/Kavod* is meant to be the object of devotion in Eleazar's thought is based on the pietist's application of the talmudic prescription (BT *Sanhedrin*, fol. 22a) that the devotee envision the *Shekhinah* before his eyes as he prays: אמר ר' שמעון חסידא המתפלל צריך שיראה עצמו כאילו שכינה כנגדו שנאמר שויתי ה' לנגדי תמיד (Rabbi Shimon the Pious said: the one who prays must see himself as though the *Shekhinah* were in front of him. As it says [Ps. 16:8]: "I set YHVH before me always"). This talmudic dictum, and its use in *Sefer Ḥasidim*, has also been discussed in Wolfson, "Sacred Space and Mental Iconography," pp. 603, 623.

91. Wolfson, "Sacred Space and Mental Iconography," p. 623. Related issues are also discussed at length in id., *Through a Speculum That Shines*, pp. 188–269.

92. MS Parma 1221, fol. 10b; cited in Abrams, "Secret of All Secrets," p. 69, n. 40. Abrams also notes that this text should be compared with *Ma'arekhet ha-'Elohut*, fol. 114a. I would add that although the exact formulation is not present in this passage from *Ma'arekhet ha-'Elohut*, the citation of the talmudic dictum in the context of the problematics of visualizing the *Shekhinah* is in fact in evidence.

93. Isaac of Akko, *Me'irat 'Einayim*, p. 84. Isaac explicitly refers to *Keter Shem Ṭov* here, as he does in many other cases in *Me'irat 'Einayim*. See Shem Ṭov Ibn Ga'on's text as printed in *Ma'or va-Shemesh*, p. 35b. The two texts are not identical, but they transmit essentially the same idea.

יהיה לתפארת, ועיקר כונתו לתשובה. ובכל החתימות יכוין אל התשובה בכלל הכל מאין סוף לאין סוף.

When a person prays the Eighteen Benedictions, the first three and the last three [benedictions are to be intended] toward *Teshuvah*, and the middle [benedictions are to be intended] toward *Tif'eret*. And even though we have said that [these benedictions are to be intended] toward *Tif'eret*, [a person] should be careful not to move his intention from *Teshuvah*. The intention for the utterance should be to *Tif'eret*, and the essence of his intention should be toward *Teshuvah*. For all the conclusions [to each benediction] he should intend toward *Teshuvah* in the totality of the All,[94] from Infinity to Infinity.

In the foregoing, the phrase עיקר כונתו (essence of his intention) functions with the same connotation as the phrases שרש כונתך (root of your intention) and שרש מחשבתך (root of your thought) considered earlier. The mystical supplicant is instructed to maintain a dual mode of consciousness in his contemplation of Divinity as it emerges directly from his symbolic performance of the liturgical text. Even as he must intend toward *Tif'eret* for certain benedictions and components of benedictions, the deeper foundation of his meditative consciousness must be connected to *Binah* (*Teshuvah*). Indeed, the kabbalist is instructed to achieve a mode of contemplation in which multiple dimensions can be the subjects of concurrent concentration—a state of consciousness that in all likelihood depicts an advanced state of meditation (יזהר שלא יזיז כונתו מהתשובה).[95] What is more, a root concentration on *Binah* here also implies a mental connection to the entirety of the sefirotic structure (יכוין אל התשובה בכלל הכל),[96] an orientation that further invokes the image of Infinity encountered earlier ("from *'Ein-Sof* to *'Ein-Sof*").

This meditative process of remaining focused on *Binah*, while simultaneously directing consciousness to the *sefirah* that correlates sym-

---

94. This phrase seems to refer to the entirety of the ten *sefirot*.

95. This line is a direct reuse of the older kabbalistic tradition from Provence and Gerona. See "R. 'Azri'el mi-Gerona—Perush ha-Tefillah," ed. M. Gavarin, § 1, pp. 41–46; Idel, "On Isaac the Blind's Intentions," p. 35 (where this phrasing is traced to Isaac the Blind, owing to the fact that variations on it are found in traditions transmitted by 'Ezra of Gerona and 'Avraham ha-Ḥazan), 37, 38 (see in particular n. 83 on that page). Cf. the text cited by Idel on p. 45.

96. I discuss the Provençal roots of this idea above.

bolically to the given word or benediction in question, is underscored through the rhythmic return to *Binah* during the conclusion to each benediction (ובכל החתימות יכוין אל התשובה). This prescription is explained more clearly in a subsequent passage. Referring to the opening benedictions of the *'Amidah* prayer, Isaac states:[97]

חתימת ברכה ראשונה אל התשובה על מדת אברהם. חתימת ברכה שניה אל התשובה על מדת יצחק. חתימת ברכה שלישית אל התשובה על מדת יעקב, ויראה לי דהוא הדין לכל שאר הברכות שיחתום על זו הדרך שאמרנו בייחוד כלל אין סוף.

> The conclusion[98] of the first benediction [is to be intended] toward *Teshuvah*, according to the Attribute of Abraham (the *sefirah Ḥesed*). The conclusion of the second benediction [is to be intended] toward *Teshuvah*, according to the Attribute of Isaac [*Din*]. The conclusion of the third benediction [is to be intended] toward *Teshuvah*, according to the Attribute of Jacob [*Tif'eret*]. And it seems to me that this is the case for all the rest of the benedictions,[99] that one should conclude [each benediction] in this manner as we have stated it, in the unity of the principle of *'Ein-Sof*.

These lines too are a retransmission of a tradition attributed to Isaac the Blind, further supporting Isaac of Akko's profile as a collector and conduit of earlier traditions.[100] But this reusage should not be dismissed simply as diachronically derivative. For as discussed earlier, eclecticism and the penchant for the anthologization of traditions is itself a form of literary creativity—a method that reveals the author's awareness of himself as a valid link in the chain of authoritative transmission and that illuminates our understanding of his place in the larger history and development of medieval Kabbalah. All this said, however, markers of overtly original thinking are in evidence in the closing lines of this passage. Applying an established kabbalistic tradition, Isaac clearly asserts his own voice with respect to other relevant benedictions—adding his signature emphasis on the need to retain awareness of, and inclusion within, the domain of *'Ein-Sof*.

---

97. Isaac of Akko, *Me'irat 'Einayim*, p. 86.

98. The term חתימת ברכה refers to the . . . ברוך אתה י"י sequence that concludes a particular benediction.

99. Of the Eighteen Benedictions prayer.

100. See the lines of text published in Idel, "On Isaac the Blind's Intentions," p. 30.

The *Du-Parẓufin* and Binary Contemplation

The theological ideal outlined above is presented by Isaac as an essential kabbalistic tenet, and the failure to enact this devotional ideal is characterized as idolatry and heresy. Thus, as Moshe Halbertal and Avishai Margalit have observed, what is considered to be idolatrous represents the direct inverse of the highest theological ideal in a particular religious culture.[101] The fact that kabbalists considered the isolation of a particular *sefirah* in contemplation to be the essence of theological heresy is a strong indication (conversely constructed) of their most deeply held belief. Aside from the frequent call to maintain concentration on *Binah* and the decad as a whole, there is another recurring refrain on this subject in Isaac's writing (primarily in the earlier *Me'irat 'Einayim*). This refrain emphasizes the theological heresy involved in the isolated contemplation of the tenth *sefirah* (*'Atarah/Shekhinah*) by itself, and instructs the devotee instead to fix the meditative mind on the androgynous unity of *'Atarah* and *Tif'eret*—otherwise known as the *du-parẓufin*.[102] In these cases, this androgynous dimension of Divinity is presented as the primary object of mystical contemplation, and ultimately serves as a metonym for the larger unity of the sefirotic structure.[103] It is

---

101. Halbertal and Margalit, *Idolatry*, pp. 1–8.

102. As is well known, the development of the ontological conception of the *du-parẓufin* in kabbalistic thought ultimately derives from the ancient midrashic tradition that the first human was created as one androgynous being, a single organism with both male and female faces (which in turn appears to be indebted to Platonic mythic motifs). See *Midrash Bereishit Rabbah*, 8:1; BT *Berakhot*, fol. 61a; Margaliot, ed., *Midrash Vayiqra' Rabbah*, 14:1. Cf. *Midrash Tanḥuma' parashat Tazria'*, ed. S. Buber, § 2. This tradition regarding the androgynous nature of the primal human was transposed onto the metaphysical structure of Divinity by medieval thinkers (see next note).

103. The binary tendency in contemplation, as it is specifically reflected in the unified androgyne of *Tif'eret* and *'Atarah*, also emerges out of a development of theological ideas from the *Ḥasidei 'Ashkenaz*, who in turn received even earlier traditions from late antiquity. For, as Moshe Idel has observed, the metaphysical duality between the angel Meṭaṭron and *Qadosh Barukh Hu'* (the Holy One, blessed be He), and their respective roles as receivers of human prayer in antiquity (on this theme, see Green, *Keter: The Crown of God in Early Jewish Mysticism*, pp. 33–41), functioned as a precursor and foundational idea for the Ashkenazic notion of binarism in devotion, and subsequently, for that of the kabbalists (Idel, "Prayer in Provençal Kabbalah," pp. 270, 277–278). Indeed, we may say that the very notion of a *divinized* Meṭaṭron, and his relationship to the more supernal dimension of God (*Qadosh Barukh Hu'*), provided the basic structure for the conception of two objects of devotion in

the divine realm for medieval kabbalists (on the divinization of Meṭaṭron, see my references below). The notion that the isolation of the tenth *sefirah* (which is symbolically correlated to Meṭaṭron) is the ultimate theological heresy certainly builds upon the paradigmatic example of heresy in antiquity: the sin of Elisha ben Abuyah in rabbinic literature (see the study of the sources pertaining to this topic, as well as an analysis of its meaning in talmudic mysticism, in Liebes, *Sin of Elisha*, pp. 11–50, as well as in the studies of Segal, Rubenstein, and Goshen-Gottstein cited above). As discussed earlier, that talmudic heretic was characterized as having "cut the shoots" (*qiẓeẓ ba-neṭi'ot*) precisely for his assumption that there were two powers in heaven (*shtei reshuyot ba-shamayim*) upon encountering the angel Meṭaṭron during his celestial ascent with Rabbi Aqiva (see, among other works, Segal, *Two Powers in Heaven*, p. 61, and Abrams, "From Divine Shape to Angelic Being: The Career of Akatriel in Jewish Literature," p. 49). The frequent invocation of the technical phrase קצץ בנטיעות by Isaac of Akko and other kabbalists (for an earlier example of this usage in medieval Spanish Kabbalah, see 'Azri'el of Gerona, *Derekh ha-'Emunah u-Derekh ha-Kefirah* in Scholem, "*Seridim Ḥadashim*," p. 209), as well as the specific focus upon not isolating *'Atarah* (which correlates directly to Meṭaṭron, the focal point of theological sin by Elisha ben Abuya), seems to indicate that the classical image was formative in the medieval kabbalistic (and 'Ashkenazi Ḥasidic) construction of positive and negative theological extremes. The recurring emphasis in kabbalistic literature that the ten powers of the divine structure are in fact only one Being (and the corresponding identification of a multiplicitous conception of Divinity with the heretical act of *qiẓuẓ ba-neṭi'ot*) is clearly modeled on the content of the classical sin of Elisha ben Abuya.

The other important element in the eventual evolution of this idea into the kabbalist's *du-parẓufin* was the binary character of the *kavod nivra'* (created Glory) and the transcendent God (*Qadosh Barukh Hu'*) as it was formulated in the medieval philosophical discourse on religious experience in the writings of Sa'adya Gaon and Moses Maimonides. On this idea in the writings of Sa'adya Gaon, see Altmann, "Saadya's Theory of Revelation"; for an example of this idea in Maimonides' thought, see *Guide*, 1: 19. Furthermore, as Elliot Wolfson has shown (Wolfson, "Secret of the Garment in Naḥmanides," p. xxxiii), for Naḥmanides and the kabbalists who continued his line of thought, the fundamental secret of the angelic garment (the *sod ha-malbush*, also characterized as the *kavod nivra' ba-mal'akhim*), shown to prophets in their revelatory experiences, was that the angelic garment itself was *identical* with the *Shekhinah*, or the anthropic embodiment of the tenth sefirotic emanation (the commonly accepted axis of revelation). In other words, the *kavod*, which is a divinized angel in anthropic form, is the embodiment of the tenth emanation (the *Shekhinah*). Given this fact, I would emphasize, directing prayer to this angel become divine (conceived as Meṭaṭron) was essentially the same as directing prayer to the lowest divine dimension, the *Shekhinah* (*'Atarah*). See the observations and textual considerations in Scholem, *Origins of the Kabbalah*, p. 187. This very correlation (and indeed *identification*) between Meṭaṭron and *Shekhinah* has been established even more overtly by Wolfson in a separate study of the *Ḥasidei 'Ashkenaz* (*Through a Speculum That Shines*, pp. 224–226, 256–263) as the embodiment of the *kavod*. And cf. Wolfson, "Meṭaṭron and Shi'ur Qomah in the Writings of Ḥaside 'Ashkenaz," pp. 67, 69–71, 73–76, 79–81, which adduces a number of texts to support the claim that the 'Ashkenazi Pietists considered such an identification between Meṭaṭron and *Shekhinah* to be one of their most profound secrets. On Meṭaṭron as the embodiment of the *Shekhinah* in her angelic garment (the *sod ha-malbush*), a conclusion that follows from his earlier article on the subject mentioned above, see Wolfson, *Through a Speculum That Shines*, pp. 312–313; and see also mention of a parallel kabbalistic tradition in ibid., p. 184, n. 247. This connection between (and indeed frequent identification of) Meṭaṭron, the *Kavod*, and the *Shekhinah* has also been examined in depth by Daniel

my contention, therefore, that Isaac advocates two main modes of devotional contemplation—one centered on *Binah*, and the other on the *du-parẓufin*. As has been demonstrated above (and as Idel and Gavarin have shown), the former is derived primarily from the school of Isaac the Blind. In exhorting his reader to the second model, however (viz., concentration on the unified *du-parẓufin*), Isaac of Akko was building upon the legacy of Naḥmanidean Kabbalah,[104] primarily as it was developed and expanded in the circle of Solomon Ibn Adret (the RaShBA).[105] The prescription for both of these focal points, however, rests on the notion that a foundational mental connection to the sefirotic *totality* must be maintained at the root of consciousness. In this manner, the eclectic and itinerant kabbalist weaves together varied traditions that stem from separate schools and tradition complexes—an act of harmonization that itself constructs a new conceptual frame for transmission. To exemplify this matter, let us return to a portion of a passage dealt with earlier in Chapter 6. There Isaac employs rhetoric similar to that

---

Abrams in several studies (with special attention to the 'Ashkenazic literature). See Abrams, "Boundaries of Divine Ontology: The Inclusion and Exclusion of Meṭaṭron in the Godhead," esp. pp. 308–315; id., "From Divine Shape to Angelic Being: The Career of Akatriel in Jewish Literature," pp. 53, 56, 60–61; id., "The *Shekhinah* Prays Before the Holy One Blessed Be He: A New Source for a Theosophical Conception Among the German Pietists and Their Conception of the Transmission of Secrets," pp. 515, 517.

It would appear that the female half of the *du-parẓufin* (*'Atarah*) came to serve the same devotional function of a lower divine entity (coupled with the more transcendent male dimension) that Meṭaṭron had served for earlier Jewish thinkers in their binaric construction of Meṭaṭron and *Qadosh Barukh Hu'* as foci of human prayer. The fact that the *Ḥasidei 'Ashkenaz* conceived of the upper *kavod* and the lower *kavod* as male and female dimensions of Divinity (see the summary conclusions in Wolfson, "Image of Jacob," in *Along the Path*, pp. 60–61) further strengthens this hypothesis. It would therefore seem that the devotional binarism between Meṭaṭron and *Qadosh Barukh Hu'* evolved (combined with the Sa'adyanic conception, and building upon its midrashic roots) into the male-female androgynous pole of devotional focus in medieval Kabbalah (the *du-parẓufin*). As such, there are two binary configurations to which the kabbalist must intend—the first is between *Binah* and *Tif'eret*, and the second is between *Tif'eret* and *'Atarah* (the *du-parẓufin*). Both cases embody concentration directed toward an accessible dimension and a transcendent dimension simultaneously. Consequently, in each case the devotee must take care not to isolate one part of the object of intention from the other; both elements must be maintained in consciousness.

104. For an example of the use of this term in Naḥmanides' own pentateuchal commentary, see *Perush ha-RaMBaN 'al ha-Torah*, 1: 38. In his commentary to this particular verse (Gen. 2:18), Naḥmanides was building on the presence of the *du-parẓufin* tradition in BT *Berakhot*, fol. 61a.

105. See Idel, "On Isaac the Blind's Intentions," p. 49.

used in connection with the maintenance of a root concentration on *Binah*. In this case, however, the foci are different.[106]

ואע"פ שכונת הקטרת אל העטרה, אין הכהן רשאי לזוז מחשבתו מן התפארת, שעיקר הקטרת והקרבנות אל השם הגדול, להמשיך הברכה והשפע מן התפארת אל העטרה וממנה אל העולם השפל.

> Even though the intention of the incense offering [should be directed] toward *ʿAtarah*, the priest is not permitted to move his consciousness from *Tif'eret*, for the essence of [the intention for] the incense offering and the sacrifices is to the Great Name,[107] to draw forth blessing and flow from *Tif'eret* to *ʿAtarah*, and from Her to the lower world.

In a fashion similar to teachings regarding *Binah*, the supplicant here is advised to maintain a dual focus on both *ʿAtarah* and *Tif'eret*. Although the fact of unity was undoubtedly implied in the assertions regarding *Binah* as well, here it is clear that *ʿAtarah* and *Tif'eret* must be contemplated as an indivisible unity, and not as separate entities in the divine world. As explained in the previous chapter, this mental act of contemplation is aimed at the stimulation of a cosmos-energizing flow from the sefirotic world to the physical world below. This point, though implied in the above-cited passage, is stated explicitly elsewhere in Isaac's text:[108] כונת המקטיר צריך שתהיה לדו פרצופין בייחוד שלם (The intention of the one who makes an incense offering must be directed toward the Two Faces [*du-parẓufin*] in a complete unity). And further:[109] כי כונת הקרבנות לדו פרצופין כאחד ובכלל דו פרצופין שבעה ההויות שהם לשלש עליונות וכונת הקרבנות הוא להמשיך שפע לעטרה (The intention for the sacrifices is [to be directed] toward the Two Faces [*du-parẓufin*] as one. Included in the *du-parẓufin* are the seven

106. Isaac of Akko, *Me'irat ʿEinayim*, p. 127.

107. A cognomen for *Tif'eret*.

108. Isaac of Akko, *Me'irat ʿEinayim*, p. 151.

109. Ibid., p. 111. It may be argued that in a culture so concerned with legitimation through reception (which was frequently constructed through *orality* as opposed to *textuality*), greater attention should be given to the kabbalist as a manifestation of the broader concerns of his contemporaries, and less emphasis placed on the complex (and often dubious) matter of originality in the matrix of reception and transmission. Indeed, in Isaac of Akko's articulation of the contemplative concern with the *du-parẓufin*, he refers, in at least one place (ibid., p. 30), to a similar formulation by Shem Ṭov Ibn Ga'on.

beings, which are a name for the three supernal [*sefirot*].[110] The intention for the sacrifices is to draw forth the flow to *'Atarah*). In these two examples, the focal point for devotional consciousness is the combination of *'Atarah* and *Tif'eret*—the dual-faced androgynous dimension of Divinity. In the second passage, Isaac indicates that the larger sefirotic system becomes concentrated in the *du-parẓufin*, and the energies of the higher *sefirot* are channeled into that lower unity of male and female. In this sense, the devotee meditates on the entirety of the sefirotic system *through* the contemplative prism and channel of the *du-parẓufin*. As anticipated above, this positive ideal of devotional contemplation is implied in Isaac's understanding of theological heresy, wherein idolatry is defined as the devotion directed to one half of the *du-parẓufin* without the other. Any contemplation of *'Atarah* that does not view her as the indivisible half of an androgynous whole is considered to be tantamount to idolatrous worship. The mystic must focus his devotional concentration on the oneness of divine reality that subsumes the two genders in a single ontic structure. Isaac of Akko defines this notion of contemplative heresy, and the positive ideal that underlies it, in *Me'irat 'Einayim*:[111]

ואני אומר שראוי לשאול כיון שאסור לנו להרהר בלילה במידת לילה שהוא העטרה, הואיל והלילה מיוחדת לה, פן יקחנה אדם לבדה במחשבתו והיה נרגן מפריד ולא יכון ביום כי אם למדת היום ולא למדת הלילה. ואני נותן טעם בזה כי הואיל ורוב החוטאים והמקצצים אינו אלא בעטרה מפני שהנהגת העולם הנגלה הזה על פיה.

I say that it is proper to ask [the following]: Since it is forbidden for us at night to contemplate the Attribute of Night, which is *'Atarah* [given the fact that night is unique to Her, so that a person will not contemplate Her alone in his consciousness and thereby be a mischief-making separator [of the *sefirot*],[112] why during the day are we supposed to in-

110. This is a rather enigmatic correlation.

111. Isaac of Akko, *Me'irat 'Einayim*, p. 85.

112. This phrase (*nirgan mafrid*) is clearly derived from its usage in Prov. 16:28, along with the interpretive transformations that were recorded in subsequent midrashic and kabbalistic exegesis. In the original biblical context, the phrase ונרגן מפריד אלוף may be translated as "a querulous man alienates his friend"—the word *'aluf* meaning "friend" (on this meaning of the word, see Ben-Yehudah, *Complete Dictionary and Thesaurus of the Hebrew Language*, 1: 239, and see the NJPS translation, ad loc.). But what was a depiction of ethical interhuman alienation in the biblical idiom is given a rather different twist in rabbinic Midrash. In this later literature, the word *'aluf* is considered to be a reference to the deity—characterized as *'alufo shel 'olam*, the Supreme One of the world. The act of one charged as a *nirgan mafrid* is that of the primordial snake in Eden, whose misrepresentation of the divine command and deception of

> tend toward the Attribute of Day, and not to the Attribute of Night?[113] And I hereby give an explanation for this. Most of the sinners and the separators [i.e., heretics] commit their sin with regard to *'Atarah*, for She rules this revealed world.

The primary concern for the kabbalist is that the supplicant not pray exclusively to *'Atarah* as if She alone were the divine Being. This mistake is frequently made, Isaac asserts, given the fact that *'Atarah* is the dimension of divine reality most accessible to the human being. Since She is the ruler of the earthly world, it might easily be thought that She alone is God. For this reason, a greater degree of conservative caution is taken with respect to intentions directed toward *'Atarah* than with those directed to *Tif'eret*.[114] Undoubtedly, this cautious rhetoric, which is found numerous times in *Me'irat 'Einayim*, was due in part to the offensive launched by critics such as Me'ir ben Shimon of Narbonne in the early days of kabbalistic literary creativity.[115]

Eve results in the separation of the Supreme One of the world (though it is unclear precisely what is meant by this separation, we may assume an allusion to the rabbinic charge of heresy in presuming any duality in the divine Being). For this exegetical move, see *Midrash Bereishit Rabbah*, ed. Theodor and Albeck, 1: 182 (§20:2). The theological use of this phrase is then laced with kabbalistic meaning in a number of zoharic passages. In a manner that provides direct precedent for Isaac of Akko's usage (i.e., that the separation of the Supreme One involves a rupture of the *sefirot*, a sin that creates imbalance in the divine cosmos), the *Zohar* expands significantly on the original midrashic twist. See, e.g., *Zohar* 3:12a.

113. That is to say, should not the same inversion for the sake of theological caution be applicable to *Tif'eret*? If the Attribute of Day must be contemplated at night, Isaac asks, why not contemplate the Attribute of Night during the day? In the logic of kabbalistic metaphysics, however, male and female within Divinity were not considered equal potencies, either with respect to their ontology or with regard to their status in the subjective perception of human consciousness. Instead, medieval kabbalistic discourse (particularly as embodied in the zoharic literature) asserted that the female side of divinity (often symbolically correlated with the Left Side, or the demonic) was subsumed and included within the male dimension (or the Right Side). This complex and important topic, particularly with respect to the construction of gender, has been treated at length in recent years by Elliot Wolfson, and his work has concluded that the kabbalistic mentality was prone to an androcentric view of the cosmos, in which the female force is ontically subsumed and restored to a primal male state of perfection. See the following representative (if highly selective) articulations of this issue in Wolfson's work: "Left Contained in the Right: A Study in Zoharic Hermeneutics," pp. 27–52; *Through a Speculum That Shines*, pp. 270–397; *Language, Eros, Being*, pp. 142–189, 488–513.

114. It might also be suggested (particularly from a modern feminist perspective) that attributing independent power to the female force was not considered to be legitimate by medieval kabbalists *precisely because of her femininity*. Given the androcentric character of kabbalistic theology (despite the bold proposition that the divine contains a female dimension) and Jewish religion more broadly, the mystic could hardly conceive of an *independent* female deity.

115. See n. 61 above on the texts of this polemic.

In order to appreciate the degree to which this issue permeates Isaac of Akko's treatment of contemplative matters, let us look again at several other parallels:[116]

ויה"ב שנ"ר דעת"ו אומר במיעוט שכל שבי כי כל עצמו של הרב הוא לרמוז בסוד לא יהיה לך אלהים אחרים על פני שלא לקצץ בנטיעות, שלא להפריד העטרה במחשבה, שלא לכוין אליה בקרבנות ותפלה בלבד, אלא בייחוד הבנין.

And I, Isaac, the young one, son of Samuel, may God protect him, from Akko—may it be rebuilt—say, with the small amount of intellect that I possess, that the essence of the Rabbi's[117] [intention] was to allude, with regard to the secret of [Exod. 20:3; Deut. 5:7] "You shall have no other gods but Me," that one must not cut the shoots by separating *'Atarah* in one's consciousness. One must not intend toward Her alone in sacrifices and in prayer. Instead, [one should intend toward Her unified] in the unity of the structure.[118]

This particular construction of idolatrous heresy is presented in *Me'irat 'Einayim* as the paradigmatic theological sin that is projected back into history by the kabbalists onto existing models of heresy in Israel's past. All other heresies (as found in the canonical biblical text and elsewhere) are subsumed within this one, and Isaac of Akko seeks to make the claim that all heretics ultimately reenact the eternally returning sin of isolating *'Atarah* in contemplation.[119] Isaac appears to imply that every instance of deviance committed by human beings with respect to their faith is,

---

116. Isaac of Akko, *Me'irat 'Einayim*, p. 105.

117. This allusion is typical of Isaac's method of reference to Naḥmanides. In this instance, Isaac is expanding significantly on the highly terse and enigmatic commentary of Naḥmanides to the words על פני in Exod. 20:3. For traces of the allusion that stimulated Isaac's deduction, see the section of Naḥmanides' *Perush ha-Ramban 'al ha-Torah*, ed. Chavel, beginning with the words ועל דרך האמת תבין סוד הפנים ממה שכתבנו (1: 391). Such traces are particularly visible in the master's mention of "the secret of the word *'aḥerim*," and his assertion that these forbidden "others" refer to all entities other than the *shem ha-nikhbad*—the Venerable Name—Naḥmanides' term of choice to invoke the *sefirah Tif'eret*. Nevertheless, there is a wide gap between Naḥmanides' mysterious words and the expanded exegesis of the metacommentator.

118. Use of the term בנין to refer to the larger structure of the *sefirot* is already present in the earliest sources of medieval Kabbalah. See, e.g., Isaac the Blind's *Perush le-Sefer Yeẓirah*, p. 2 (line 28). This usage seems to have been shaped to some extent by the writings of Solomon Ibn Gabirol. See Sendor, "Emergence of Provençal Kabbalah," 2: 19, n. 39.

119. Isaac of Akko was by no means alone among medieval kabbalists in expressing this view. As already observed, similar ideas can be found a good deal earlier in the well-known

in the final analysis, rooted in a single great flaw: the separation in consciousness of the *du-parzufin*. Such is the manner in which the sin of the golden calf—the climactic heresy of the biblical narrative—is explained:[120]

שחשבו עושי העגל לזבוח לאלהי ישראל. אלהי ישראל רומז לעטרה, ולפי שכונת הזביחה לתפארת ולעטרה, והם לא כונו אלא לעטרה בלבד, וקצצו בנטיעות וגרמו לרחמים שיסתלקו מהעטרה.

> For the makers of the [golden] calf thought to make their sacrifice to *'Elohei Yisra'el* [lit., the God of Israel]. *'Elohei Yisra'el* alludes to *'Atarah*, and because [the proper] intention for sacrifice is toward *Tif'eret* and *'Atarah*,[121] but they [the makers of the golden calf] intended toward *'Atarah* alone—they cut the shoots, and caused Compassion[122] to withdraw from *'Atarah*.

Thus the ultimate kabbalistic heresy has been grafted on to the paradigmatic sin of the Hebrew Bible. For the kabbalist, all events of idolatry and theological sin are nothing other than symbolic allusions to the one basic heresy of contemplating *'Atarah* as a separate entity. As such, the general kabbalistic hermeneutic of symbolic construction and the extrapolation of sefirotic meaning from seemingly mundane events and images is here applied to the biblical model of heresy as well. This remarkable projection, which reveals the kabbalistic propensity to subsume *all meanings* within the architecture of sefirotic metaphysics, is extended even further in the following instance:[123]

שלא יטעו בה בעטרה. כל אלו האזהרות הוא שלא נעשה מעשה אדם הראשון, ודור הפלגה, ונדב ואביהוא, ואלישע אחר, וכיוצא בהם, שלא נפרידנה במחשבתינו מהצדיק.

> So that people should not err regarding *'Atarah*. All of these warnings[124] are [designed] so that we will not [repeat] the action of the first man

---

text from the Gerona circle, "*Sod 'Ez ha-Da'at*," cited and discussed by Scholem in *The Kabbalah in Gerona*, pp. 374–380, and in "*Sitra Aḥra*," pp. 64–71.

120. Isaac of Akko, *Me'irat 'Einayim*, p. 133.

121. Which is to say: *Tif'eret* and *'Atarah* as one.

122. A standard cognomen for *Tif'eret*.

123. Isaac of Akko, *Me'irat 'Einayim*, p. 195.

124. The reference here is to the commandments of prohibition (*mizvot lo ta'aseh*), briefly discussed in the lines of *Me'irat 'Einayim* that precede the quoted passage.

> (Adam), the generation of the flood, Nadav and Avihu, Elisha *'aḥer*,[125] and the like—that we not separate Her from *Ẓaddiq* in our consciousness [lit., thought].

Here it is amply clear that *all theological heresies*—sins that are considerably different in their original literal contexts—are read by Isaac (building on earlier influences) to refer to a contemplative isolation of *'Atarah*. The mystic recasts earlier sins under the all-encompassing rubric of sefirotic meaning and the ideals of kabbalistic devotion. The fact that such a radical equalization of heresies is posited is a testament to the markedly central place that this contemplation of the *du-parẓufin* occupied for Isaac of Akko and other kabbalists. Authentic devotion and right belief are marked by an adherence to this particular unitary mode of intention and mental direction.

Visualization Techniques and Contemplation of the Divine Name

As Moshe Idel has shown, several kabbalists at the turn of the fourteenth century cultivated a contemplative approach that sought, as a mode of *kavvanah*, to visualize the *sefirot* as a divine name of variegated colors—in some instances configured as a circle.[126] In Idel's estimation,

---

125. The reference here is to Elisha ben Abuyah, the paradigmatic heretic of talmudic literature discussed above.

126. See Idel, *Kabbalah: New Perspectives*, pp. 103–111; id., "Intention and Colors: A Forgotten Kabbalistic Responsum," p. 6. The text that Idel cites in this second study (published with critical notes and variances from manuscript) instructs the devotee to envision the form of the Tetragrammaton (YHVH) before his eyes as he prays. As he intends toward each *sefirah* of the divine Being, he is to envision that four-letter name in the color that corresponds symbolically to that specific *sefirah*, in addition to vocalizing the visualized divine name in a different manner for each *sefirah* (as well as *visualizing* the different vowel notations). Upon directing the mind to the lowest of the ten emanations (*Shekhinah*), the supplicant is instructed to envision the Tetragrammaton in a color that includes all the other colors, insofar as *Shekhinah* is the *sefirah* that includes all the other *sefirot*: וכשמזכיר איזה דבר המורה על המלכות יצייר שם יהו"ה בין עיניו בגוון שכולל הגוונים כולם (When he recites any word that points toward *Malkhut* [i.e., *'Atarah/Shekhinah*], he should envision [lit., draw] the YHVH Name between his eyes in a color that includes all the colors). The fact that the term כשמזכיר is used is quite telling. It is in direct relationship to the act of liturgical recitation (and the corresponding hermeneutical deduction arising from the symbolic association of the word in question) that the devotee envisions the divine name in a particular manner. The visual experience that he must invoke is precisely linked to his interpretive performance of the text. When a word is recited that cor-

this use of colors served as a medium for the elevation of consciousness through the visual use of the imagination, and was employed in this manner by such well-known kabbalists as Joseph ben Shalom 'Ashkenazi and David ben Yehudah he-Ḥasid. While my consideration of Isaac of Akko's use of visualization practice will not relate directly to the contemplation of colors, Idel's remarks concerning the practice of visualizing the divine name in prayer are highly instructive for our purposes, and they set the context for our analysis of this subject in Isaac's writing.[127] The following queries posed by Idel are particularly pertinent: "Is concentration on the symbolic connotations of a given word the only mental operation that ensures the mystical elevation of thought? How does the linguistic medium, corporeal in both its written and its oral forms, enable human thought or soul to penetrate utterly spiritual dimensions of reality?"[128]

The questions posed by Idel are highly applicable to Isaac of Akko's mystical approach. For as we have seen above, kabbalistic devotional contemplation is deeply bound up with the symbolic associations of the liturgical text. As the mystic recites the liturgy, his mind is meant to move through the metaphysical map of Divinity in close and direct correlation to the sefirotic implications of the text being performed. In that framework, mystical experience of God is the direct result of an essentially *exegetical* enterprise. A mental contemplative encounter with Divinity follows from such a symbolic interpretation of the text intertwined with its performative recitation. In addition, this contemplative experience is both stimulated and guided by an *ocular* encounter with the letters of sacred language in general (the text of prayer) and the visualized letters of the divine name in particular. The visual object of devotional contemplation propels and directs the mystic toward an experience of God through an encounter with the *form* of language (i.e., its written manifestation to the eye) in a way that precedes a cognitive

---

relates symbolically to the *sefirah Malkhut* (*'Atarah/Shekhinah*), the interpretive deduction that follows from the recitative act correspondingly affects the color envisioned.

127. See Wolfson, *Through a Speculum That Shines*; id., "Circumcision, Vision of God, and Textual Interpretation," in *Circle in the Square*, pp. 29–48, 140–155; id., "Sacred Space and Mental Iconography."

128. Idel, *Kabbalah: New Perspectives*, p. 103.

interpretation of its *content* (i.e., the meanings invoked by a given word). It is in this respect that the two modes may be distinguished as contemplative processes—the form of sacred language itself serves as a meditative stimulus. However, as other scholars have demonstrated,[129] the sensory (particularly the ocular) experience also functions hermeneutically, insofar as the vision itself is shaped by and consequently further stimulates a symbolic association. The "linguistic medium" of the text thus provides a physical pathway to spiritual modes of consciousness, but one that turns on an exegetical axis.

Another manifestation of the polarity between inner and outer human action in the context of a sacred ritual performance can be seen in the relationship between the outward act of recitative vocalization and the inward visualization of the divine name. According to Isaac of Akko, the meditative practice of contemplating the vowel notations of the divine name in the enclosed realm of human consciousness functions to *substitute* for the kabbalist's inability (because of halakhic proscription) to vocalize that name. Living in a ritual world where such outward pronunciation is prohibited, the mystic internalizes an enactment of the divine name, transferring its performance to an interior plane of action. Indeed, in order to maintain the meditative and theurgical power of that holy name, ocular enactment provides a substitute for its vocal/auditory enactment. The following lengthy passage exemplifies this phenomenon in a decisive way:[130]

> ויה"ב שנ"ר דעת"ו ראיתי לכתוב קבלת כונת נקוד השם המיוחד אשר נאמר עליו בדברי רז"ל כל ההוגה את השם באותיותיו אין לו חלק לעולם הבא. ועל כן כל הקורא אותו בשפתיו בנקודו הרי הוא מחלל את השם וגדול עונו מנשוא מפני שאין כל העולם השפל הזה המלוכלך בלכלוכי בני אדם בעונותיהם ובמעשיהם כדאי שיצא אויר והבל הנקוד הקדוש מן השם המיוחד ולהתערב עם אויר העולם הנזכר. אמנם כל היודעו יחשב בלבו בנקודו כאלו הוא נקוד לפניו. ודע באמת כי מה שארז"ל מפני מה ישראל צועקים ואין נענין, מפני שאין יודעין להתפלל בשם. כונתם ז"ל לומר שאין יודעין להתפלל בנקוד השם המיוחד הראוי לאותו ענין שהוא צריך. כי לשם המיוחד נקוד לאלפים ולרבבות וכל נקוד ונקוד יש לו כח ידוע לענין ידוע, וחכמי ישראל קבלו מהם כל אחד לפי מה שזכהו השם ית' והיודע שמו של הב"ה בנקודו הפועל מה שהוא צריך בקבלה אמתית לא יצטרך להזכירו בפה בעת צרתו אלא לכוין בלבו בלבד

129. Wolfson, *Through a Speculum That Shines*, pp. 383–392.

130. Isaac of Akko, *Me'irat 'Einayim*, pp. 89–90.

באותו הנקוד ויקרא אל הב"ה בשפתיו באחד מכנויו ומיד יענהו ויהיה עמו בצרתו עד שיצילהו ממנה. וזש"ה כי ידע שמי יקראני ואענהו וגו'. ומי שאינו יודע שמו על דרך זה שאמרנו לא יענהו השם בתפלתו מחמת תפלתו אלא ברחמיו שרחמיו על כל מעשיו אלא א"כ יתפלל בדמעות, שאע"פ שמיום שחרב בית המקדש ננעלו שערי תפלה, שערי דמעות לא ננעלו כי בודאי המתפלל בכונת הלב ובדמעות מיד הוא נענה, ובלבד שלא יהיה במתפלל ההוא דבר מהדברים המעכבים את התפלה. וכונת נקוד השם המיוחד בברכות הוא כנקוד דְּבָרְךָ כמו שכתוב לעולם דברך י"י נצב בשמים וגו'. ובמקדש היה כהן גדול מזכיר שם של שתים עשרה בנקודו והיו כל ישראל עונין אחריו בשכמל"ו. ואל תקשה על מה שאמרתי למעלה מפני אויר העולם השפל הזה, כי אע"פ שהיה הכהן הגדול מזכירו לא היה הבל דבריו מתערב עם האויר כי היה הבית מלא כבוד השכינה והמשכיל יבין.

And I, Isaac . . . of Akko, . . . have seen fit to write down the tradition [concerning] intention toward the vowel notation[131] of the Special Name,[132] about which it has been said in the words of our Sages of blessed memory:[133] "whosoever pronounces the Name as it is spelled [lit., through its letters] has no share in the world to come." Thus, every [person] who utters that Name with its vowel notation with his lips desecrates the Name, and his sin is too great to bear.[134] For it is not proper that the holy air and breath of the [vocalized] vowel notation from the Special Name enter into this lower world, sullied with the filth of human beings in their sins and in their deeds. [It is not proper that the holy] air mix with the air of the world that has been mentioned. *However, every individual who knows [the Name], should contemplate it with its vowel notation in his heart, as though it were [actually] notated in front of his face*. And know for certain what our Rabbis of blessed memory have said:[135] "Why is it that Israel cry out and are not

---

131. While the Hebrew word ניקוד is generally translated as "vocalization," I have preferred the phrase vowel notation so as to avoid confusion with the act of vocal utterance—an act that forms the centerpiece of the mystical view expressed in these passages. In this context, therefore, the term "vocalization" does not refer to the vowel points beneath and above the letters, but rather to the external human act of speech in which those "vowel notations" (ניקוד) are uttered by the devotee.

132. The *shem ha-meyuḥad* is generally a reference to the Tetragrammaton (YHVH).

133. See *Mishnah Sanhedrin*, 10: 1; BT *Sanhedrin*, fol. 90a. Cf. *Midrash Tanḥuma' Yelamedeinu, Va'era'*, § 1.

134. The source of this phrase is in Gen. 4:13.

135. See *Pesiqta' Rabbati*, 22:12. In that rabbinic source we find the phrase מפני מה ישראל מתפללים ואינן נענים as opposed to the use of the word צועקים as it appears in the text cited above.

answered? Because they do not know how to pray through the Name."[136] Their intention (may their memory be blessed) was to say that those [who are not answered] do not know how to pray through the vowel notation of the Special Name that is appropriate for the given matter that [the individual] needs. For the Special Name has thousands and myriads of [possible] vowel notations,[137] and each individual vowel notation has a specific power for a specific matter.[138] And the wise ones of Israel[139] received [*qibblu*] [these Names], each individual according to the merit bestowed upon him by God. And he who knows the Name of the Holy One blessed be He in its vowel notation, who enacts what he needs through a true *qabbalah*, *he does not need to pronounce the Name with his mouth in his time of trouble, but only needs to focus in his heart on that same vowel notation*, and to call out to the Holy One blessed be He with his lips using one of [God's] cognomens.[140] [Upon doing this], he will immediately be answered [by God], and [God] will be with him in his time of trouble until he is saved from it.[141] And this is what Scripture has stated [Ps. 91:14-15]: 'For he has known My Name. He will call to Me, and I will answer him.'[142] And whosoever does not know [God's] Name in this way that we have stated [i.e., with vowel notation

---

136. A parallel use of this rabbinic tradition—along with particular instruction concerning the vowel notations to be envisioned—is found in Isaac of Akko, *'Oẓar Ḥayyim*, fol. 40b.

137. This conception is clearly derived from the Kabbalah of Abraham Abulafia. See Idel, *Mystical Experience in Abraham Abulafia*, pp. 14–52; id., *Language, Torah, and Hermeneutics in Abraham Abulafia*, pp. 1–28.

138. Literally, "a known power for a known matter."

139. This seems to be a reference to kabbalists.

140. I have used the word "cognomen" here in my translation to signify the different Hebrew term. Given the fact that the Special Name is visualized in the mind/heart of the kabbalist in lieu of vocalizing that Name, the use of the word כנויו clearly refers to the more exoteric appellations given to the deity. These cognomens are to be contrasted with the *esoteric* names that fall under the rubric of the *shem ha-meyuḥad* with its innumerable notated variations.

141. In connection with this idea (and the larger theurgical power of the recitation of divine names), it should be observed that contemporary scholars of religion have argued for a fresh understanding of the inextricable character of mystical and magical elements in the study of religious forms and practices. Particularly with respect to medieval kabbalistic religion, we must move beyond what was an artificial divide between two faces of the same beast. See Idel, *Hasidism: Between Ecstasy and Magic*, pp. 103–145. In keeping with this view, I do not seek to differentiate between mysticism and magic as they pertain to the theurgical use of divine names in Kabbalah.

142. For a parallel usage of this verse in the exhortation to contemplate and know God through the Name, see Isaac's *Perush le-Sefer Yeẓirah* (Scholem, ed., "Perusho shel R. Yiẓḥaq de-min-'Akko le-Pereq Ri'shon shel Sefer Yeẓirah"), p. 392, lines 5–7.

and internal visualization], God will not answer him in his prayer as a result of his prayer, but only through His compassion, for His compassion is [extended] to all of His creations. [The only way prayer will be answered by God without knowledge of the Name] is if the person prays with tears. For despite the fact that from the day the Temple was destroyed the gates of prayer were locked, the gates of tears were not locked.[143] For surely he who prays with intention of the heart and with tears is immediately answered, provided that this supplicant does not have in himself any of the things that obstruct prayer. The intention for the vowel notation of the Special Name in the benedictions is like the vowel notation for the word *devarkha*,[144] as it is written [Ps. 119:89]: "Forever Your word [*devarkha*] YHVH stands firm in the heavens."[145] In the Temple, the high priest would recite the twelve-letter Name with its vowel notation, and all of Israel would respond after him with the words: "Blessed be the Name of the Glory of His Kingship forever and ever."[146] Do not find difficulty [or contradiction between this] and what I said above with respect to the air of this lower world. For despite the fact that the high priest would recite [the Name], the breath of his words would not mix with the air [of this world], since the Temple was filled with the Glory of the *Shekhinah*. And the wise will understand.

The primary phenomenon exhibited in this passage is the internalization of a previously external ritual act. What was vocalized in ancient times by the high priest is now transfigured to the internal plane of consciousness, to a visual mode of enactment located in the human mind. As such, this idea further represents the deep structure of kabbalistic prescription, one that is aimed at the regulation and guidance of *internal* action and conduct. In the kabbalist's view, external utter-

143. See BT *Baba Meẓi'a'*, fol. 59a.

144. As Moshe Idel has shown, this tradition of visualizing the name notated like the word דְּבָרְךָ is derived from earlier manuscript traditions related to the visualization of the name in diverse color formations. See Idel, *Mystical Experience in Abraham Abulafia*, pp. 33–34; id., *Kabbalah: New Perspectives*, p. 106. Also consider the text cited by Idel in his "On Isaac the Blind's Intentions," p. 28. In addition to this passage in *Me'irat 'Einayim*, Isaac articulates this tradition in *'Oẓar Ḥayyim*, fol. 131a.

145. This is an example of citation by memory on the part of the kabbalist, in which the original biblical words are slightly misquoted. The biblical text reads: לעולם יהו"ה דברך נצב בשמים.

146. See BT *Yoma'*, fol. 35b, 39a, 41b; *Ta'anit*, fol. 16b.

ance of the divine name is prohibited precisely because the name itself is conceived to be an ontological entity of a wholly spiritual, even divine nature, while the world into which it is spoken (as breath released from the human mouth in the act of speech) is wholly corporeal, and thus at its essence profane. These two entities are entirely incompatible due to the fact that they embody opposite extremes in the order of Being. While the divine name is the ontic embodiment of the sacred, the corporeal nature of the created world is the embodiment of the profane. In the view of Isaac of Akko, the one repels the other.

This is the reason why the utterance of the high priest in the ancient Sanctuary is considered to be of a different order from that of the ordinary individual in devotion. In the case of the high priest, the spiritual/divine substance of the uttered name—released as an ontic entity through the breath of that priest—does not come into contact with profane corporeal reality, but rather with the ontic Presence of God, in the embodiment of the *kevod ha-Shekhinah* (the Glory of the *Shekhinah*) that filled the sacred space of the Sanctuary.[147] The ordinary supplicant, who does not offer his prayer in the *Shekhinah*-infused space of the Temple, must transfigure the vocal act into a visual event in the inner eye of his consciousness. This phenomenon is a remarkable example of a substitute ritual—one in which the substitution crosses the boundaries of two distinct realms of sense experience. The paradigmatic ritual—one that can no longer be performed due to the vicissitudes of history—is preserved in an internalized form, which is conceived to have equal power in the theurgic stimulation of Divinity and brings about a divine answer to human prayer. Indeed, the technique of visualization reflects a magical-theurgical orientation predicated on a precise knowledge of the notated divine name, and on the cultivated ability to conjure up the image of that name in the mind's eye. It is precisely because the internal visualization reenacts the lost ideal performance of the ritual (i.e., in the ancient Temple by the high priest) that such an audacious power is attributed to it. The kabbalist in the act of visualization is able to force an immediate divine answer to his prayer (ומיד יענהו) as a direct result of his role of substitution for the high priest of old. The kabbalist thus

147. The biblical root of this image is found in 1 Kings 8:11.

functions as the new priest,[148] and his ocular enactment of the ritual is a direct and intentional substitute for the vocal performance of the ritual in ancient times.[149] In articulating this mode of substitution and internalization, Isaac of Akko was building on already existing tradi-

---

148. This phenomenon has also been observed by two other scholars. See Brody, "Human Hands Dwell in Heavenly Heights: Worship and Mystical Experience in Thirteenth Century Kabbalah"; Pedayah, *Name and Sanctuary in the Thought of R. Isaac the Blind*, pp. 148–177.

149. The techniques of ritual internalization cited above are taken up again in Isaac of Akko's *'Oẓar Ḥayyim*, and several sources may be referenced from that corpus as well. With regard to the divine name, the act of external utterance is once again proscribed as taboo, and thus visualization of the vowel notations within the boundaries of consciousness is deemed a proper substitute (*'Oẓar Ḥayyim*, fols. 101a–101b): כי ההוגה השם הנכבד והנורא הזה באותיותיו אין לו חלק לעולם הבא, והדרך הזה אשר אתה צריך לצייר בשכל . . . היא . . . ואמנם הניקוד בכל אות במחשבת השכל כאשר אמרנו לא אוכל לפרש אמנם ארמוז כי כבר ידעת שהרוצה להגיע אל ראש הסולם צריך הוא להיות הולך ועולה הולך ועולה והמשכיל יבין (For one who utters this venerable and awesome name through its letters does not have a portion in the world to come. The way in which you must picture [this name] in your mind is [the following]. . . . And indeed, [with regard to] the vowel notation for each letter, [envisioned] in the thought of the mind as we have stated, I cannot interpret [explicitly], though I shall hint (*'omnam 'ermoz*). For you already know that one who wishes to reach the top of the ladder (*lehagia' 'el ro'sh ha-sulam*) needs to be one who proceeds and ascends, proceeds and ascends—and the sage will understand [*ve-ha-maskil yavin*]). Through usage of the same rabbinic tradition (*Mishnah Sanhedrin* 10:1) cited in *Me'irat 'Einayim* (ההוגה השם . . . באותיותיו אין לו חלק לעולם הבא), Isaac here further underscores the instruction to substitute the proscribed vocal act with a prescribed contemplative act. In this way, the perceived power of the vocalization is *preserved* (in contrast to the rabbinic prohibition against engaging the vowels directly, preferring instead the substitution of the name *'Adonai*), albeit transferred to the interior domain of contemplation. Envisionment of the divine name in consciousness is understood to be a meditative act that propels the devotee through the *sefirot*; the journey through the divine emanations represented by the ascent of the ladder. As was the case in the evidence drawn from *Me'irat 'Einayim*, a distinction is asserted in *'Oẓar Ḥayyim* between the ritual act performed externally (here prohibited and regarded as taboo) and that which is more exalted by virtue of its internalization and enclosure within the contemplative mind. In a parallel text in *'Oẓar Ḥayyim*, this distinction between externalized performance and inner contemplation (visual by implication) is characterized as a divide between *shimush* and *yedi'ah* (usage and knowledge). See *'Oẓar Ḥayyim*, fols. 82b–83a. To know (and presumably to visualize) the sacred name is not only a preferable alternative to the now forbidden act of enunciation—it is rewarded by the deity as a sign of great mystical attainment. In Isaac's words: אשר נפשו זכה ודביקה עם האל די לו הידיעה והשכל שנא' אשגבהו כי ידע שמי (The one whose soul is pure and cleaved to God, knowledge and mind are sufficient for him. As it is written [Ps. 91:14]: "I will lift him up [I will keep him safe], for he knows my name"). The kabbalist seeks to achieve a higher plane of ritual action (affirmed by the deity), the most profound level of which takes place within the mind. In this way, the enunciation obliterated by post-Temple proscription is reengaged in the contemplative consciousness. Through the act of internalization, a dormant dimension of ritual practice (the utterance of the ineffable name) is resurrected on a substitute plane of enactment. Voice is replaced by vision, and an echo of the lost priestly ritual survives in the inner eye of kabbalistic devotional practice.

tions. As Idel has shown, traces of this phenomenon can be found in the writings of several earlier Jewish thinkers, among them, Isaac Ibn Latif, Abraham Abulafia, and Joseph ben Shalom 'Ashkenazi. It seems highly probable that Abulafia was the prime influence in this regard.[150]

The practice of the foregoing visualization technique is highly complex. For although Isaac of Akko's account ostensibly provides a relatively simple visualization method (i.e., envisioning the Tetragrammaton according to the vowel notation of דְּבָרְךָ), Isaac's extended explanation of these matters on the next page of *Me'irat 'Einayim* reveals that a far more elaborate technique is involved.[151]

> גם קבלתי הרוצה להיות אהוב למעלה ונחמד למטה ושתהיה תפלתו נשמעת לאלתר יכון בלבו בהזכירו השם הנכבד לאותיות אלו עם נקודם המקובל והם אותיות השם המיוחד שתי פעמים ואחרי כל אחד אל"ף ונקודם הוא תחת היו"ד קמ"ץ ותחת הה"א שב"א ותחת הוא"ו קמ"ץ ותחת הה"א קבוץ שפתים והאל"ף נבלעת. וכן נקוד השם השני רק שהה"א האחרונה בחירי"ק וגם האל"ף נבלעת. ואחר שיכוין בנקודם זה יכון בלבו שעשר ספירות מיוחדות בו והכל מיוחד באין סוף. ולמעלה הזכרתיו במלת נבוב. וטעם הבלעת האל"ף מפני שהיא אל"ף של שם הנעלם והמבין יבין. ואם תחבר האל"ף של שם הנעלם עם כל אות בפני עצמו של שם המיוחד ותנקוד אותם בחמש נקודים שהם חמש הברות הדבור והם קמ"ץ וצר"י ושור"ק וחיר"ק וחול"ם בכל גלגוליהם האיפשרים להתגלגל שלא ידמה נקוד זה לנקוד חברו ואחר כן תמנה ההברות תמצאם אֶלֶף. וזהו סוד גדול כי כל דבר שב אל מקום עיקרו.

> I have also received that [a person] who wishes to be beloved above and precious below,[152] and that his prayer be heard above, should, when he recites the Venerable Name [*shem ha-nikhbad*], intend in his heart [*yekhaven be-libbo*] toward the following letters with their received vowel notations. They are the letters of the Special Name [*shem ha-meyuḥad*] [spelled out] two times [in a row]. And after each one[153] there is an *'alef.* The vowel notation [under the letters is as follows]: Under the *yod* a *qamaẓ*, under the *he'* a *sheva'*, under the *vav* a

150. See Idel, *Mystical Experience in Abraham Abulafia*, pp. 30–37. The larger phenomenon of envisioning the name as part of an imaginative enterprise (that is, the conjuring up of the image within the mind), aimed at a revelatory encounter with the textually embodied deity, is a focus of Wolfson, *Through a Speculum That Shines*.

151. Isaac of Akko, *Me'irat 'Einayim*, p. 91.

152. For early uses of this expression, see BT *Berakhot*, fol. 17a; BT *Qiddushin*, fol. 71a.

153. Of the two sequential four-letter divine names.

qamaẓ, under the *he'* a *qubbuẓ sefatayim*, and the *'alef* is silent.[154] The same goes for the vowel notation of the second name, except that the final *he'* [is notated] with a *ḥiriq*. [Here too] the *'alef* is silent. After he intends toward this vowel notation [of the letters], he should intend in his heart that the ten *sefirot* are united in it [the name], and all is united in *'Ein-Sof*. And I have mentioned this above with regard to the word N-B-V-B.[155] The reason for the silence of the *'alef* is that it is the *'alef* of the Hidden Name [*shem ha-ne'elam*], and he who understands will understand. And if you join the *'alef* of the Hidden Name with each letter of the Special Name [*shem ha-meyuḥad*] individually, and if you notate them with the five vowel notations, which are the five syllables of speech—and they are: *qamaẓ*, *ẓere*, *shuruq*, *ḥiriq*, and *ḥolam*—[and if you notate them] in all of their possible variations, such that the vowel notation of one will not resemble the vowel notation of another, when you count the syllables afterwards, you will find that they are one thousand [*'elef*].[156] And this is a great secret, for every entity returns to the place of its [original] root.

The methods of visualization and letter combination reflected in this passage are clearly rooted in the thought and practice of Abraham Abulafia. As Idel has noted, charts detailing similar practices are found in the writings of both Abulafia and the German pietist Eleazar of Worms.[157] Both of these two thinkers composed works devoted to the esoteric explication of the divine name and its myriad permutations, and both men exercised a considerable influence on their contemporaries and on subsequent Jewish intellectuals. Despite the fact that Isaac of Akko here recounts a complex practice concerning vowel notation of the divine name, the essential prescription still calls for an *internal* performance, and not an external, vocalized enactment. The supplicant is instructed to intend in his heart-mind (*yekhaven be-libbo*—the imaginative-visual dimension of mental activity) toward the elaborate sets of

154. Literally, "the *'alef* is subsumed [in the previous letter]."

155. On the previous page, Isaac uses the word נבוב as a model for the vowel notation of the four-letter divine name.

156. That is to say, the letter *'alef*, when conjoined with the other notated letters, is capable of one thousand (*'elef*) different permutations. Thus the hermeneutical play on the letters א-ל-ף.

157. Idel, *Mystical Experience in Abraham Abulafia*, pp. 22–24.

notated letters when he recites the "Venerable Name" during the utterance of ordinary benedictions. As such, the "Venerable Name" (*ha-shem ha-nikhbad*) is the divine name as it is encountered in the ordinary liturgical benediction (יהו"ה), vocalized as *'Adonai*, while the kabbalist must envision a different set of letters before his eyes as he enacts that very prayer. According to Isaac's description of the technique, the supplicant is to envision two sequential Tetragrammatons, each spelled out with an *'alef* at their conclusion, and each notated in a specific format. The name was therefore envisioned in the following manner:

יָ הְ וָ הֶ א יָ הְ וָ הִ א

The "Hidden Name," which is correlated to the *'alef*, is also based on Abulafian technique, and seems to allude to either of two possibilities: the name spelled אהו"י or that spelled אהי"ה.[158] In theosophical Kabbalah,[159] both of these names are associated with the *sefirah Keter* as it points toward *'Ein-Sof*. The association of the letter *'alef* with *Keter*, and of the subsequent four letters of the Tetragrammaton with the rest of the sefirotic structure, was quite common in early kabbalistic literature.[160] Thus, to contemplate the notated divine name was essentially

158. On the use of this in Abulafia's thought, see ibid., p. 22.

159. Admittedly, the distinction between ecstatic (prophetic kabbalah, utilizing divine names) and theosophic (sefirotic) kabbalah is not quite so clear. On the problematics involved in such categorizations see Wolfson, *Abraham Abulafia*, pp. 94–177.

160. Already in the *Bahir* we find the following passage: ומאי ניהו עשרה מאמרות א' כתר עליון ברוך ומבורך שמו ועמו ומי עמו ישראל שנא' דעו כי יי' הוא אלהים הוא עשנו ולא אנחנו להכיר ולידע אחד האחדים המיוחד בכל שמותיו (What are the ten utterances? The first is supreme crown [*keter 'elyon*], blessed, and blessed be its name and its people. And who are its people? Israel, as it is written: "Know that YY He is God. He has made us, *ve-lo' 'anaḥnu*" [figuratively, we belong to the *'alef*], so as to recognize and know the One of Ones, singular in all His names). See *Bahir*, p. 181 (§ 96). This passage from the *Bahir* is examined by Arthur Green in his discussion of the symbol of *Keter* in the early Kabbalah. Green notes that in the Munich manuscript of this text, the *'alef* of *ve-lo'* is highlighted by a small scribal mark above the letter (see *Bahir*, p. 180). It is clear that the text means to distinguish the *'alef* as a hypostatic entity of the cosmic structure, a significant departure from the crown symbolism and imagery of earlier Jewish literature. See Green, *Keter: The Crown of God in Early Jewish Mysticism*, pp. 134–136. I would also add that a parallel passage (and perhaps a conscious usage of the bahiric text) is to be found in 'Azri'el of Gerona's *Perush ha-'Aggadot*, p. 40 (manuscript variances to line 3 of the base text). Reflection on the metaphysical status of the *'alef*, along with the symbolic connotations of the Tetragrammaton was also undertaken by 'Asher ben David. See *R. Asher ben David*, ed. Abrams, pp. 104–105. For a more extended consideration, see E. Fishbane, "The Speech of Being, the Voice of God: Phonetic Mysticism in the Kabbalah of Asher ben David

to contemplate the entire sefirotic structure of Divinity. This identity is stated quite explicitly in the passage cited above: "After he intends toward this vowel notation [of the letters], he should intend in his heart that the ten *sefirot* are united in it [the name], and all is united in *'Ein-Sof.*" It should further be observed that the fusion of the "Kabbalah of names" (*qabbalat ha-shemot*) with the "Kabbalah of *sefirot*" reveals Isaac of Akko's unique position as a bridge between eastern and western kabbalistic approaches. For while the former was mainly represented in the writings of Abraham Abulafia (one of the main expositors of "eastern" Kabbalah), the latter was employed primarily in Aragon and Castile, but not to any substantial degree in the Kabbalah of the East.[161] In Isaac of Akko's writings, and in his personal testimony to his implementation of these practices in his own devotion, these twin legacies are combined. Indeed, it may be argued that to visualize the many permutations of the divine name was itself a contemplation (and visualization) of the innumerable interactions and dynamics between the various *sefirot* of divine Being. Given the fact that medieval kabbalists routinely correlated the Tetragrammatic letters to specific *sefirot*, and further given the fact that the Tetragrammaton as a whole was symbolically identified with the entirety of the sefirotic structure, visualization of the name clearly functioned as the linguistically embodied form of God to which the kabbalist directed his contemplative gaze.[162] To envision the conjunction of the letter *'alef* with all of the other possible linguistic variations

---

and His Contemporaries," pp. 490–502. While this is not the place to fully elaborate upon the symbolism of the *'alef* in medieval Kabbalah, one additional source should be mentioned in this context. In his study of the *ḥug ha-'iyun* texts, Mark Verman cited an important passage from the circle of mystics that also views the metaphysical *'alef* as the fountain and source for the emanation of all subsequent divine Being. See Verman, *Books of Contemplation*, pp. 54–55.

161. This assertion holds true with respect to the larger trends of kabbalistic thought and expression, but should nevertheless be qualified with the observation that the Naḥmanidean Kabbalah of *sefirot* did permeate the intellectual culture of Akko (as noted in Chapter 2), and Abulafia's writings also appear to employ certain key elements of sefirotic Kabbalah. With respect to the latter, see Wolfson, *Abraham Abulafia*, pp. 94–186.

162. Wolfson has argued that the kabbalists understood the divine body itself to be the paradigmatic sacred text, and thus to envision the letters of the Tetragrammaton was to envision the metaphysical body of God. See Wolfson, "Circumcision, Vision of God," pp. 29–48, 140–155; id., *Through a Speculum That Shines*, pp. 247–269; id., "Erasing the Erasure," 49–78, 155–195. Now see the extensive reflections on this theme in id., *Language, Eros, Being*, pp. 190–260, 513–545.

of the name was therefore to contemplate the variations and multiple channels of emanation in the efflux of divine energy from *Keter* into all the other lower *sefirot*. In this respect, sacred language functions as the physical medium for an experience of the divine.

Isaac of Akko was well aware of the practical difficulties that these elaborate techniques posed for the supplicant seeking to pray in a kabbalistic manner. As we saw earlier, he attempts to reassure his reader through personal testimony to his own successful implementation of the techniques. The example of the master thus serves to educate and to inspire the kabbalistic novice. In so doing, the correlation between visualization of the name and contemplation of the *sefirot* is further articulated:[163]

> וראוי לכל רודף אחר מדת החסידות לכוין בלבו בכל הנקודים אשר הזכרנו למעלה בהזכירו בפיו השם הנכבד . . . ובאמת אני רגיל לכון בלבי בנקודים הנזכרים . . . ועוד אני כולל כונה על השם המיוחד עם כונת הנקודים הנזכרים, והוא שאני מכוין בראותי בלבי תג של יו"ד של שם המיוחד, שהוא קוצו של יו"ד הנזכר בדברי רז"ל אל הכתר, וביו"ד עצמה אל החכמה, ובה"א אל התשובה ובוא"ו אל התפארת עם שש קצוות אשר הוא קיומם, ובה"א אחרונה אל העטרה עד אין סוף. וגלוי וידוע לפני מי שאמר והיה העולם שלא כתבתי דברי אלו לכבודי ולתפארתי כי אם לכבוד ולתפארת של מלך מלכי המלכים ית' למען ירגיל עצמו לעשות כן כל המעיין בספר זה, ויעשה רצון בוראו ית' וימצא חן ושכל טוב בעיני אלהים ואדם.

> It is proper for every person who is in pursuit of the attribute of piety [*middat ha-ḥasidut*] to intend in his heart [*lekhaven be-libbo*] toward all the vowel notations mentioned above when he utters the Venerable Name with his mouth. . . . And truthfully, I regularly intend in my heart toward [or, I am practiced in the intention of] the notations [of the name] mentioned above. . . . I also include an [additional] intention toward the Special Name [*shem ha-meyuḥad*] with the intention of the aforementioned vowel notations. When I envision in my heart the crownlet of the *yod* of the Special Name, which is the tip of the *yod* referred to in the sayings of our Rabbis of blessed memory,[164] [I intend] toward *Keter*, on the *yod* itself [I intend] toward *Ḥokhmah*, on the *he*' [I intend] toward *Teshuvah*, on the *vav* [I intend] toward *Tif'eret* with the six directions, for He [*Tif'eret*] is the foundation [of the six directions],

---

163. Isaac of Akko, *Me'irat 'Einayim*, p. 91.

164. See BT *Menaḥot*, fol. 29a.

> and on the final *he'* [I intend] toward *'Atarah*, all the way to *'Ein-Sof.*[165] And it is revealed and known to the One who spoke and the world came into being that I have not written these words for my honor and my glory, but rather for the honor and glory of the King of kings may He be blessed,[166] so that he who examines this book will [consequently] train himself (*yargil 'azmo*) [to pray in this manner],[167] and will [thereby] do the Will of his Creator, may He be blessed, and [Prov. 3:4] "will find favor and right knowledge in the eyes of God and man."

Here Isaac's prescriptive and propaedeutic endeavor is very much in evidence. The kabbalistic novice who wishes to attain the heights of ideal devotion must train and discipline himself in the contemplative arts; gaining mastery of this visionary practice will, Isaac assures, lead the devotee to the sought-after attribute of *ḥasidut* (the paradigmatic state of piety and the culmination of spiritual self-cultivation). This rhetoric of guidance and prescription is framed within a first-person testimonial—in reporting his own contemplative practice in a highly self-conscious and confessional manner, Isaac seeks to underscore the attainability of such complex meditations, to reassure the novice that such goals can in fact be reached through regular discipline and practice. In his testimony to his own practice of this technique, as in his remarks cited earlier in this chapter, Isaac of Akko makes clear that the visual concentration on the Tetragrammaton is itself a method of contemplation directed at the

---

165. The implication of this statement is that the infinite domain of *'Ein-Sof* extends from both ends of the sefirotic structure, not only from the top of the *sefirot* as a vertically transcendent dimension of God. This, I argue, is the way we should understand Isaac's frequent phrase *me-'ein-sof le-'ein-sof.* Indeed, as I demonstrated earlier through a remarkable passage from *Me'irat 'Einayim*, Isaac of Akko's underlying contemplative position was that the kabbalistic devotee ultimately only contemplates *'Ein-Sof* in his prayer, and that the separate *sefirot* are the particular configurations of that *'Ein-Sof* as it appears to the human being in the moment of prophetic/contemplative cognition. As such, *'Ein-Sof* is indeed a prescribed object of mental intention and concentration, but that object of human focus extends monistically from one end of the divine cosmic structure to the other and is not limited in its locale to the vertical summit that stands hierarchically above *Keter*. From this perspective, *'Ein-Sof* is the cosmic All, the totality of cosmic Being whose manifestation is seen in the *sefirot*.

166. This rhetoric of humility, directly connected to the act of articulating and transmitting esoteric matters, is also found in the narratives of the *Zohar*. See E. Fishbane, "Tears of Disclosure: The Role of Weeping in Zoharic Narrative," p. 32.

167. I have used the word "train" here for the sake of the felicity of the English sentence, and the reader need not distinguish this translation of the word *yargil* from my earlier rendering of the word as "practice."

sefirotic structure of Divinity (i.e., "When I envision in my heart the crownlet of the *yod* of the Special Name . . . [I intend] toward *Keter*, on the *yod* itself [I intend] toward *Ḥokhmah*," etc.). It should be observed, however, that the notated divine name (in all its variations) was not the only visual image used by Isaac in his prescriptions for the devotional encounter with Divinity. In a separate context within *Me'irat 'Einayim*, Isaac presents a series of linguistically based visual images of the sefirotic structure, including the widely used image of concentric circles (or layers of an onion).[168] In Isaac's rendition, the concentric *sefirot* are presented as

---

168. Isaac of Akko, *Me'irat 'Einayim*, pp. 118–120. Embedded within that series of passages is an exhortation that focuses on the pictorial-formal character of the sefirotic diagram to be envisioned: והנה לך צורת עשר ספירות על זה הדרך שאמרנו ואם תשתכל בצורת העמדתן ממש יתגלו לך סודות נפלאים אם קבלת (Here you have [a] diagram/picture of the ten *sefirot* according to the way that we have stated. And if you contemplate [or envision] the form of their arrangement, wondrous secrets will surely be revealed to you if indeed you have received [i.e., if you have received instruction in these matters from a reliable master]). For an example of the concentric circle image of Divinity as it is found in the writings of other kabbalists, see Joseph ben Shalom 'Ashkenazi, *Perush le-Sefer Yeẓirah*, p. 18a. It is clear from Isaac of Akko's diagrams, both those located on pp. 118–120 and that found on p. 88 of *Me'irat 'Einayim*, that he adhered to a model in which *Keter* was the outer ring, with each of the *sefirot* enclosed in progressively smaller concentric circles. Despite the fact that the diagram preserved in Joseph ben Shalom 'Ashkenazi's text places a *yod* at the small center of the concentric circles (a typical symbol for the *sefirah Ḥokhmah*), it seems from his analysis that this was meant to refer to the physical world within the sefirotic system, and thus need not be seen as the inverse model to that put forth by Isaac of Akko. The model accepted by Isaac is also reflected in a diagram preserved in a manuscript fragment from MS Milano-Ambrosiana 62, fol. 4a, which outlines the colors to be associated with the *sefirot*, and presents those associations in a concentric diagram. There too the outer rings are linked to the highest *sefirot*, whereas the inner circle is linked to *Malkhut*. Moshe Idel has argued that this particular manuscript fragment belongs to the thought of David ben Yehudah he-Ḥasid. See Idel's description of this manuscript in *Kabbalah: New Perspectives*, p. 106, and p. 326, n. 234. On this larger issue, and the association of an envisioned divine name of colors with both David ben Yehudah he-Ḥasid and Joseph ben Shalom 'Ashkenazi, also see Idel, "Intention and Colors," pp. 6–11. It would seem that this model of concentric sefirotic reality diverged from the thought of Isaac the Blind, who repeatedly likens the hierarchy of the sefirotic structure to progressively inner and deeper dimensions. See Isaac the Blind, *Perush le-Sefer Yeẓirah*, pp. 1 (line 19), 3 (lines 54–57), 6 (line 137), 7 (line 149), and 11 (lines 233–237). I readily acknowledge that the use of the words *penimi* and *penimiyut* in Isaac the Blind's text are somewhat ambiguous, and may in fact be synonymous with "elusive" or "transcendent." Indeed, Havivah Pedayah has argued that the term *penimi* in Isaac the Blind's writings generally refers either to transcendent ontic reality (as derived from medieval Jewish philosophy) or to an epistemological elusiveness—the dimension that eludes the grasp of the human mind. See Pedayah, "Flaw and Correction," p. 166, n. 35; id., *Name and Sanctuary*, p. 81, n. 40; Sendor, *Emergence of Provençal Kabbalah*, 2: 4–5, n. 12 (and the sources cited there), as well as 2: 152, n. 34. Asher ben David also uses the term *penimi* to describe the interrelationship between human epistemology and cosmic ontology. In Asher's schema, the *koaḥ ha-penimi* (the inner force) emerges from the depths of

the first letters of each of the *sefirot* enclosed one within the other, from the all-encompassing כ of *Keter* to the ע of *'Atarah* located at the smallest center of the diagram. The key issue, however, is Isaac's exhortation to his reader that the entirety of the sefirotic structure be visualized by the kabbalist at the moment of prayer:[169]

ואשר קבל דרך האמת באמרו שלום מכוין בעליון להמשיך הברכה והשלום מהסבה הראשונה עד הסבה האחרונה ויהיו עשר ספירות תמיד לנגד עיניו מיוחדות בייחוד האמתי על דרך אשר כתבתי בתבנית זו אשר קבלתי.

> He who has received by the way of truth, when he utters the word *shalom*[170] he intends [his mind] toward the Supernal in order to draw forth the blessing and the peace [*shalom*] from the First Cause to the Last Cause, *and the ten sefirot should always be before his eyes*, united in the true unity, according to the way that I have written, in the structure [or diagram] that I have received.

The act of contemplating Divinity in devotion, here represented by the technical phrase *mekhaven ba-'elyon*, is linked directly to a *visual* encounter with the sefirotic structure. The graphized diagrams of letters representing the Being of the *sefirot* are meant to function as focal points for mental concentration in prayer, a mode of focus that is performed through the internal eye of the imagination. Whether the anchor for envisionment is the notated divine name, or a concentrically configured picture of the first letters of the ten *sefirot*, the kabbalist in prayer is clearly meant to associate these envisioned letters with the structure and inner dynamics of the sefirotic system. This

---

the Infinite as the first palpable manifestation of the sefirotic emanation. *Penimi* does not necessarily connote transcendence and hierarchy in Asher's thought, but rather refers to the most primal dimension of the emanational chain that is progressively revealed through subsequent sefirot. See *R. Asher ben David*, ed. Abrams, p. 105. Note also Moshe Idel's discussion of this problem in "*Sefirot* Above the *Sefirot*." Idel attributes this idea (i.e., of *penimiyut*) to kabbalists including Isaac the Blind, 'Azri'el of Gerona, Isaac ha-Kohen, Moses of Burgos, David ben Yehudah he-Ḥasid, and members of the *'Iyyun* circle. In Idel's assessment, these kabbalists conceived of this inner reality of the sefirotic cosmos to be configured in anthropomorphic form, comprised of ten potencies. On this point, also see Idel, "Image of Adam Above the *Sefirot*," pp. 41–56. For further discussion and notation, see E. Fishbane, "The Speech of Being, the Voice of God," p. 493. For a sustained study of the notion of *penimiyut* in the history of Jewish spirituality, see Margolin, *Human Temple*.

169. Isaac of Akko, *Me'irat 'Einayim*, p. 121.

170. In the closing line of the Eighteen Benedictions.

act of visualizing Divinity—the dimensions of God placed before the eyes of the devotee—functions in tandem with the process of liturgical recitation ("when he utters the word *shalom* . . . the ten *sefirot* should always be before his eyes, united in the true unity"). In order for the ritual articulation of the benediction to be satisfactory from a kabbalistic perspective, the devotee must align a mental image of the *sefirot* (the visual anchor of his devotional concentration) with the external event of liturgical speech.

It is with this point in mind that we turn to the *locus classicus* of visualization practice in *Me'irat 'Einayim*:[171]

אני יה"ב שנ"ר דעת"ו אומר בין ליחידים בין להמון שהרוצה לידע סוד קשירת נפשו למעלה ודיבוק מחשבתו באל עליון, שיקנה באותה המחשבה התמידית בלי הפסק עולם הבא ויהיה תמיד השם עמו בזה ובבא, ישים לנגד עיני שכלו ומחשבתו אותיות שם המיוחד כאלו הם כתובים לפניו בספר כתיבה אשורית, ותהיה כל אות גדולה בעיניו בלי תכלית. רצוני לומר שכאשר תשים אותיות השם המיוחד ית' כנגד עיניך יהיו עיני שכלך בהם ומחשבת לבך באין סוף הכל יחד ההבטה והמחשבה שניהם כאחד. וזהו הדיבוק האמתי שאמ' הכתו' ולדבקה בו, ובו תדבק, ואתם הדבקים וגו'.

I, Isaac . . . of Akko, . . . say to the elite as well as to the masses, that he who wants to know the secret of binding his soul above and having his mind cleave to the Supernal God, such that through that constant and unceasing consciousness he will attain the world to come, such that God will be with him always in this [world] and the next, should place before the eyes of his intellect [*sikhlo*] and his consciousness [or thought (*maḥshavto*)] the letters of the Special Name [*shem ha-meyuḥad*] as if they were written before him in a book with Assyrian writing.[172] Each letter should be envisioned in an unendingly great size.[173] That is to say,

171. Isaac of Akko, *Me'irat 'Einayim*, p. 217. This passage is also discussed in Idel, *Kabbalah: New Perspectives*, p. 50.

172. The phrase כתיבה אשורית was used in antiquity to refer to a form of block Hebrew script that was deemed proper for sacred writing. See, e.g., BT *Shabbat*, fol. 115b; *Megillah*, fol. 8b, 18a; *Sanhedrin*, fol. 97b.

173. It would seem that Isaac's discussion of this visualization practice with regard to the divine name was also inspired by (or based on) Naḥmanides' own comments on Exod. 28:30. See *Perush ha-RaMBaN 'al ha-Torah*, 1: 474, where the RaMBaN argues that the priest of old would engage in a ritual that involved the envisionment of the letters of the divine name. During this visualization, the letters appeared illumined and radiant to the eyes of the priest (כאשר האותיות מאירות לעיני הכהן). What is more (and perhaps most significant), this ancient visualization practice was believed to result in a state of prophecy and elevated consciousness (וזאת מדרגה ממדרגות רוח הקדש היא למטה מן הנבואה ולמעלה מבת קו). It seems

> when you place the letters of the Special Name before your eyes, the eyes of your intellect [*'einei sikhlekha*] should be directed toward them, and the thought of your heart [*maḥshevet libbekha*] should be [directed] toward *'Ein-Sof.* It all [should be performed] together, the vision and the thought together as one. This is true cleaving, as Scripture has stated [Deut. 11:22; Deut. 30:20; Joshua 22:5]: "To cleave to Him"; [Deut. 10:20] "And to Him you will cleave"; [Deut. 4:4] "And you are the ones who cleave . . ."

This text reveals the ultimate goal of the visualization technique discussed thus far. In conjuring up the image of the Tetragrammaton within the mind, the mystic seeks to attain an entirely new state of consciousness—one that transcends his experience of the earthly world and breaks through to the World to Come. As such, the kabbalistic technique directly leads to the joining of the human mind with Divinity, an experience and ontic status characterized by several early kabbalists as *maḥshavah deveqah* (thought that cleaves to Divinity).[174] On further examination, this passage is more complex in its description of contemplative method than first appears, and thus requires closer attention to the terminology and to the assumptions that underlie the rhetoric.

Isaac of Akko clearly distinguishes between two separate modes of visual concentration: that performed with the "eyes of the intellect" (עיני שכלך) and that with the "thought of the heart" (מחשבת לבך). This distinction is notable in light of the fact that the two phrases were essentially synonymous in the earlier writings of Islamic-Jewish Neoplatonists.[175] For those thinkers, the fundamental distinction in the act of prophetic vision lay in the divide between the sense datum perceivable by the physical eyes and that which cannot be seen physically, but that *can* be seen through the spiritual sight of the mind. I have noted above, with particular reference to Elliot Wolfson's work,[176] that the term *lev*

---

clear that this tradition—preserved in Naḥmanides' *Commentary*—combined with the Abulafian Kabbalah of divine names, stands as the background for Isaac of Akko's remarks in *Me'irat 'Einayim*.

174. See Brody, "Human Hands Dwell in Heavenly Heights: Worship and Mystical Experience in Thirteenth Century Kabbalah," pp. 410–419.

175. See Wolfson, *Through a Speculum That Shines*, p. 171.

176. See Wolfson, "Merkavah Traditions in Philosophical Garb: Judah Halevi Reconsidered," pp. 203–235; id., *Through a Speculum That Shines*, pp. 174, 178, 294, 314. On p. 314,

most frequently connotes that aspect of perception and cognition associated with the human imaginative faculty (a connection that is prominently exemplified in the writings of Judah Halevi [ca. 1075–1141]). Yet regardless of whether Isaac of Akko is alluding specifically to the imagination, he is certainly asserting a hierarchy (or depth contrast) between that which is contemplated through the "eyes of the intellect" and that which is contemplated through the "thought of the heart." The mode of focus conducted through עיני שכלך is directed toward the four letters of the שם המיוחד (the Special Name), which in turn represent the structure of the sefirotic system from *Keter* to *'Atarah*. On the other hand, מחשבת לבך is employed to contemplate *'Ein-Sof*—the dimension of Divinity that transcends the Tetragrammatic structure of the *sefirot*. We therefore encounter a binarism similar to the texts of this type considered earlier. One part of the mind (*sekhel*) is directed toward the *sefirot*, while the other (presumably deeper) element of consciousness (*lev*) is to be focused on *'Ein-Sof* itself. In this manner, the kabbalist in contemplation seeks to maintain two differentiated states of focus—one explicitly more profound than the other. This text also provides us with a further component of the contemplative technique not expressed in the earlier cases cited. Here Isaac instructs the supplicant to visualize the Tetragrammaton in letter forms of infinite size—a prescription that clearly functioned as a method to break through from a lower state of consciousness to a more exalted mental connection to Divinity. It would seem that the very enormity of the letters was meant to function as a contemplative pathway into the nonfinite/nonphysical experience of divine reality.[177] To envision the letters in this manner was to envision the *sefirot* themselves—an interpretation confirmed both by name

---

Wolfson cites a zoharic text that conflates the two images—a distinction not maintained by Isaac of Akko. In the text cited by Wolfson (*Zohar* 3:280b), the authors of the *Zohar* use the phrase עין השכל דלבא (possibly rendered as "the intellectual eye of the heart" or "the eye of the mind in the heart").

177. It might even be suggested that this idea is descended from the giant-scale measurements of God found in the ancient שיעור קומה texts—a notion that seeks to convey an approximation of infinite size and the fundamental *Otherness* of Divinity through unimaginably large proportions. On the texts of this tradition, see Scholem, "*Shi'ur Komah:* The Mystical Shape of the Godhead," pp. 23–25. Compare this to the more recent assessments of Wolfson, *Through a Speculum That Shines*, pp. 86–87, and Green, *Keter: The Crown of God in Early Jewish Mysticism*, pp. 52–54, 88–89.

symbolism and by the fact that the instruction to contemplate *ʾEin-Sof* immediately follows.

In addition to the various texts cited in the notes (above and below), let me turn now more overtly to two representative sources from *ʾOẓar Ḥayyim* on this matter of contemplative visualization. Similar to the evidence observed in *Meʾirat ʿEinayim*, there is a continued correlation between envisionment of the name and meditation on the *sefirot*—a practice that culminates explicitly in the quest for *ʾEin-Sof*. The following passage—in which we again encounter the striking motif of the *sefirot* situated atop the head of the devotee in the form of a ladder—further clarifies the degree to which the divine name serves as a prism for the envisioned deity. The divine *sefirot* are manifest to the devotional eye through the textuality of the name:[178]

אהיד"ע משתכל באשר קבלתי מגדול דורו בענותנות ובחכמת הקבלה והפילוסופיא ובחכמת צירוף אותיות היה חזק מאד, לשוות תמיד לנגד פני עס"ב כדכתי' שויתי י"י לנגדי תמיד כי מימיני בל אמוט. וראיתים היום הזה על ראשי למעל ממנו כעמוד ורגליהם על ראשי וראשיהם למעלה למעלה מכל אבי"ע. רגל הסולם על ראשי וראשו למעלה מכל אבי"ע. וכל עוד היותי משתכל בסולם זה שהוא שמו של הקב"ה אני רואה את נפשי דביקה באין סוף.

I, . . . , Isaac . . . of Akko, was contemplating that which I received from the great one of his generation in humility and in the wisdom of Kabbalah and philosophy—and he was also very strong in the wisdom of letter combination [permutation].[179] [I received the instruction] to constantly place the ten *sefirot* before my face, as it is written [Ps. 16:8]: "I have placed YHVH before me always—He is at my right hand, I shall never be shaken." And I saw them this day—on my head, above it like a pillar. Their feet were upon my head, and their top (their head) was above [all of the four worlds—] *ʾAẓilut*, *Beriʾah*, *Yeẓirah*, *ʿAsiyah* [*ABYA*]. The foot of the ladder [*regel ha-sulam*] was upon my head, and the top

178. Isaac of Akko, *ʾOẓar Ḥayyim*, fol. 99a.

179. We cannot be certain of the identity of this personality, mentioned by Isaac with such great reverence. Note, however, the markers of authenticity and authority employed in the passage—indicators of the characteristics believed to mark the greatness of a transmitter of kabbalistic wisdom. The anonymous master is represented as one who has excelled in each of the major branches of wisdom in Isaac's day—the kabbalah of *sefirot*, philosophical knowledge, and the kabbalah of name permutations. These attainments in wisdom and learning are further authenticated through affirmation of the ultimate prerequisite for kabbalistic advancement: the great moral virtue of humility and the effacement of a prideful ego.

> [the head] [of the ladder] was above [the four worlds of] *ABYA*. And all the while that I gaze upon [or contemplate] this ladder—which is the name of the Holy One, blessed be He—I see my soul cleaved to *'Ein-Sof*.[180]

The last lines of this passage confirm what was observed in the texts from *Me'irat 'Einayim*, cited above. The visualization of the name is, in fact, a visualization of the *sefirot*—the name is ontologically identical with the deity as revealed to the devotional eye of the kabbalist. What is more, this act of envisionment culminates explicitly in the attachment (or is it union?) of the human soul to *'Ein-Sof* (a moment of *devequt*)—a bold assertion that is in keeping with the parallel passage in *Me'irat 'Einayim* (and, as we have seen, with texts found elsewhere in Isaac's kabbalistic corpus as well). Underscored through his use of Psalm 16:8 ("I have placed YHVH before me always"), the structure of the revealed divine presence is presented as textual in nature; the ladder of emanations—whose bottom end rests on the head of the devotee in seeming ontic continuum—is, in fact, "the name of the Holy One, blessed be He." To envision the divine name is to envision the divine Self.[181]

The other passage from *'Oẓar Ḥayyim* that I shall cite here offers an intriguing twist on this ocular practice, and also documents a convergence between the contemplative practice of visualization and the use of divine names (and their perceived cosmic power) for the writing of kabbalistic amulets:

> ישנתי ואחר חצי הלילה בעודי ישן שמעתי באומרים לי לבל אסיר מנגד מחשבת שכלי שם הגבורה בכל דברי תפלותי וברכותי לא יסור לעולם מנגד עיני בעיגוליו הנכונים. אני מתבונן בהם, בדברים האלה, וראיתי לפני על פי צורה זו וזהו אגלא. השתכלתי בו ושש לבי בקרבי מאד מפני שמצאתי מספר עיגוליו בסוד אהי"ה, אשר הרב הגדול העושה כחיו גדולות נוראות בכח שם זה כולל עמו תמיד אהי"ה אשר אהי"ה בקמיע שלו הקמיע המופלא.

> [A] I slept, and after half the night—while I was still sleeping—I heard [voices] telling me never to remove the Powerful Name [*shem ha-*

180. Compare this passage with parallel lines, located on fol. 193a: אני היד"ע השתכלתי בד' אותיות אהו"י הכוללות השם אהי"ה והשם יהו"ה וראיתי כי עס"ב כלולות בשם אהו"ה כמו בשם יהו"ה (I . . . Isaac . . . of Akko contemplated the four letters 'EHVY that include the name 'EHYH and the name YHVH, and I saw that the ten *sefirot belimah* are included within the name 'EHVH, just as they are in the name YHVH).

181. Cf. the remarks by Wolfson in *Language, Eros, Being*, pp. 208–209.

> *gevurah*] from [the gaze of] my mind, [to maintain this gaze] during all the words of my prayers and blessings. [The name], with all its correct circles, must never be removed from before my eyes.
>
> [B] I was contemplating these words, and I saw [the name] before me according to this form—'EGLE' [*drawn in the MS with a configuration of twenty-one circles on the letters*]. I contemplated it, and my heart rejoiced greatly within me—for I found that the number of its circles is the secret of [the name] 'EHYH.
>
> [C] [And such is the way] of the great rabbi, who conducts his great and awesome powers through the power of this name—he always includes [the words] *'EHYH 'asher 'EHYH* with it in his amulet, his wondrous amulet.[182]

Though the identities of the voices heard are left mysterious, the manner of this somnolent transmission is much the same as that observed in the earlier analysis in Chapter 5 of Isaac's creative process. The deepest insights into kabbalistic wisdom are received by Isaac in and around the sleeping state. The instruction to maintain visual contemplation of the divine name is, however, given a rather striking twist here—the power of the name 'EHYH (a frequent cognomen for the *sefirah Keter*) is discerned and harnessed through engagement with a cluster of twenty-one circles, a number that is reflected in the alphanumeric value of the name 'EHYH (the letters 'EGLE', graphized with the twenty-one circles, serve as a substitute form for the exalted divine name—an association that occurs elsewhere in Isaac's work as well).[183] As such, we may extrapolate that the kabbalist in prayer conjures up the image of the divine name 'EHYH—seen in a configuration of twenty-one circles—thereby connecting the mystic's mind to the elusive transcendence of *Keter* as he recites the benedictions. The ocular encounter with the name (as deduced through the symbolic valence of the twenty-one circles) progresses directly into an encounter with the *sefirot*. And as was the case with previous passages, the act of envisionment is considered to channel the efflux of divinity through the theurgic power of devotional ritual.

---

182. Isaac of Akko, *'Oẓar Ḥayyim*, fol. 96b.

183. See, e.g., ibid., fol. 40b.

Eight Asceticism, Prophecy, and Mystical Union

Given the manner in which Isaac of Akko sought out the divine meanings embedded within the natural world, occasionally even noting the pleasurable aspects of such sensation, it is a curious irony that we also find a very different recurring theme in Isaac's writing—an ideal that at first glance appears to be diametrically opposed to the powerful encounters with nature. Here I refer to Isaac's repeated emphasis on the need for the kabbalist to transcend the realm of physical sensation (המורגשות) for the sake of mental attachment to the intellective dimensions (המושכלות) of the spirit. These two opposing modalities (positive encounters with nature in search of divine symbolism, on the one hand, and complete detachment from the senses, on the other) are not fully reconciled by the author—at best we can say that the state of detachment from and negation of the physical senses was understood to be a higher mystical state of mind than that of the interpretive gaze fixed on the forms of nature. Isaac argues that the extrapolation of *muskalot* meaning from *murgashot* perception was part and parcel of a necessary transcendence of corporeal sensation, a transformation of mundane consciousness into contemplative mind. After a careful consideration of the sources, it becomes clear that (despite his inference of divine meaning from the physical world) this kabbalist experienced a deep state of anxiety and discomfort with his own embodied life—articulating an ideal of physical self-transcendence and a highly negative view of the body and its desires. Sensate experience, and the inevitable appetites that follow, is a condition of being that must be restrained, even harshly subjugated, for the sake of a pure attachment to the divine realm. Such disembodied contemplation is ultimately reached through the מושכלות (intellective dimensions)—a mode of mystical perception that replaces physical sensation with an interior, spiritualized vision of Being.[1] In this respect, Isaac of Akko's attitude toward physical existence and spiritual yearning stands within a vast historical matrix of like-minded thinkers, both within the history of Judaism and in the much broader panorama of philosophical and religious traditions. As numerous scholars have noted, the prevalence of such attitudes within the three Abrahamic traditions of the West (to say nothing yet of the widespread manifestations of this phenomenon in other religions of the world)[2] is ultimately indebted to Platonic and Neoplatonic conceptions of an existential tension between the eternal celestial soul and the mortal physical body.[3] In this, as in so many other aspects of intellectual history, the Greek and Roman legacy looms large over the subsequent development of Western religious thinking.

As Charles Taylor emphasizes, it was Plato who set the stage for much of the subsequent thinking on selfhood when he asserted that

---

1. Numerous medieval kabbalists (and especially in the circle of the *Zohar*) believed that the true mystic is required to transform his physical desire into a spiritual eros located in the contemplative consciousness. Comparing kabbalistic texts to Tantric Yoga on this score, Elliot Wolfson demonstrates how medieval biology—in which the semen of male desire and arousal originates as light in the brain, passing down through the spinal column to the male sexual organ—shaped this relationship between contemplation and eros. The kabbalistic adept was exhorted to achieve a symbolic state of celibacy and physical renunciation by elevating the semen of physical eros back to its state of light-seed in the brain of contemplative mind. In this way, Wolfson argues, carnal eros and desire was not to be repressed as much as it was to be elevated and transformed into the spiritual eros of contemplation and enlightenment. See Wolfson, *Language, Eros, Being*, pp. 307–324, 564–572.

2. For a representative range of recent scholarship on the subject, see the essays collected in Wimbush and Valantasis, eds., *Asceticism*. For a recent study of this problem in the formative period of Judaism, see Diamond, *Holy Men and Hunger Artists: Fasting and Asceticism in Rabbinic Culture*.

3. See discussion of these matters in Hadot, *Plotinus—or The Simplicity of Vision*, pp. 23–34. John Dillon has underscored the presence of two distinct views of the soul-body tension in the writings of Plato—a seeming contradiction that had significant implications for the reception-history of these ideas among Neoplatonic and other indirect inheritors of the Greek legacy. Dillon argues that while a relatively negative attitude toward the physical life does exist in the Platonic writings, the great sage appears to have held to the position that (despite its reluctance) the soul was ultimately responsible for the ongoing guardianship and refinement of the physical body—an imperative that was not to be abandoned. This core view stands in contrast to the more accepted notion that the soul could not be *freed* from its bodily prison. See Dillon, "Rejecting the Body, Refining the Body: Some Remarks on the Development of Platonist Asceticism," in Wimbush and Valantasis, eds., *Asceticism*, pp. 80–87.

reason would lead to the moral life of the good, insofar as it would prevent a person from being led blindly by desire and passion.[4] The appetites of physical desire required the control and centeredness of rationality. This Platonic binarism between reason and desire is ultimately reflected in medieval philosophical Hebrew through the juxtaposition of the מושכלות (intellective, rational aspects of perception and thinking) and the מורגשות (the sensate, physical dimensions). What is more, however, the מושכלות-מורגשות polarity was also a version of the Platonic distinction between the physical form as it manifests in this world and the Ideal form that exists in the divine realm.[5] To shut out and negate the forms of the sensate world was to contemplate the higher divine realities, much as the ancient Greek philosopher spoke of the contemplation of the Ideal form as a higher way of philosophical knowledge. It is this latter association that is most applicable to Isaac of Akko's use of these terms in articulating an ascetic imperative and a contemplative ideal. The world as perceived through the מורגשות had to be transcended for the sake of a greater mystical consciousness.

In considering Isaac of Akko's place in this major trope of Western religious discourse, we must first note the relevant research of Moshe Idel, in which the lines of connection between Platonic, Sufi, and kabbalistic sources on the question of physical detachment are explored in some detail.[6] Idel has demonstrated that Isaac of Akko was the recipient of such traditions (ultimately of Neoplatonic extraction) as they were transmitted from Sufi thinkers, first to Abraham Abulafia and his disciples, and then finally to Isaac himself. In all likelihood, Isaac received these matters from one Natan ben Sa'adyah—the close disciple of Abulafia who appears to have been the author of the fascinating text known as *Sha'arei Ẓedeq*, and who explicitly notes his awareness of certain ascetic practices of physical detachment as they were employed by

4. See Taylor, *Sources of the Self: The Making of the Modern Identity*, pp. 115–120.

5. See the sources and comments provided in Klatzkin, *Thesaurus Philosophicus*, 2: 286–288. In addition to the explication of other meanings and lexical associations, Klatzkin adduces the use of מושכל הראשון in the Tibbonide Hebrew rendition of Maimonides' *Guide* 3:51 as a cognomen for the Divine (2:288).

6. Three of these articles ("*Mundis Imaginalis* and *Likkutei HaRan*"; "Ecstatic Kabbalah and the Land of Israel"; "*Hitbodedut* as Concentration in Ecstatic Kabbalah") were published together in Idel, *Studies in Ecstatic Kabbalah*, pp. 73–169.

his Muslim contemporaries.[7] This connection is underscored by Idel through his identification of Isaac of Akko as the probable compiler and editor of *Liquṭei ha-RaN*—a collection of teachings attributed to the same Rabbi Natan, who is referenced frequently in Isaac of Akko's *Me'irat 'Einayim*.[8] Most recently, Idel has offered an extended analysis of Isaac's intellectual inheritance on this score—a reflection that centers upon an anecdote attributed to Isaac of Akko, preserved in the widely disseminated kabbalistic ethical treatise by Eliyahu de Vidas, *Rei'shit Ḥokhmah*.[9] In that text, an ordinary or "idle" man is utterly transformed into a great spiritual master—progressing from his lustful desire for a beautiful woman to a detachment from all corporeal sensation and desires. Once removed from these physical passions, the "idle man" is transfigured into a contemplative, a saint whose mind is completely bound to the spiritual dimensions of Divinity. What is most extraordinary about this process of self-transformation is that the man is only transported beyond the senses and the passions by first engaging in a direct and sustained contemplation of the woman's beautiful physical form. Concentrating on the particular corporeal image for a lengthy period of time is what ultimately leads to the transcendence of that very sensate consciousness. The ideal is clearly that of detachment from corporeality and physical desire, but the path to that transcendence is *not* one of repression and sublimation. Instead, it is one of *intense engagement* with the distracting lust, to the point where the concentrating mind is taken to a new level of meditative abstraction. In this piece, Idel puts forth the argument that this contemplative model is ultimately indebted to Platonic Greek traditions as they likely shaped a Sufi attitude toward the transformation of love and eros.[10] On the basis of a number of textual considerations explored

---

7. For reference to the ascetic practices of Muslim pietists in the text of *Sha'arei Ẓedeq*, see Natan ben Sa'adyah Har'ar, *Le porte della giustizia*, ed. Idel, p. 476, lines 31–32.

8. See ibid., pp. 52–62; Idel, *Studies in Ecstatic Kabbalah*, pp. 81–83.

9. *Rei'shit Ḥokhmah*, *Sha'ar ha-'Ahavah*, end of chap. 4. See Idel, "From Platonic to Hasidic Eros: Transformations of an Idle Man's Story" (now also published in Idel, *Kabbalah and Eros*, pp. 153–178). See further reflections on the question of asceticism in Jewish mysticism in Idel, *Kabbalah and Eros*, pp. 223–232.

10. Idel, "From Platonic to Hasidic Eros," pp. 224–226, 230–231.

elsewhere by Idel and Paul Fenton,[11] it is argued that Isaac of Akko may very well have received a version of these traditions from a Sufi source, or (perhaps more likely) from one of the several Sufi-inspired Jewish mystics with whom Isaac had direct contact. As mentioned above, this point of transmission was likely Natan ben Saʿadyah, author of *Shaʿarei Ẓedeq*, insofar as this text places great emphasis on detachment from the corporeal as a fundamental prerequisite for advancement in meditative practice. Regarding the progression from contemplation of the physical to an ultimate negation of sensate corporeality, I would like to suggest that such a view may help us resolve the seeming contradiction between Isaac's repeated sensory encounters with nature and his simultaneous insistence on sensory nullification. The kabbalist might indeed understand his intense focus on natural form as a pathway to the transcendence of such perception. Either way, however, a distinction in kind should certainly be made between sensation as it relates to natural phenomena, on the one hand, and sensation as it relates to erotic physical desire, on the other.

The degree to which Isaac of Akko's thought on this subject was shaped by Jewish-Sufi transmission (as it reverberated among the disciples of Abraham Abulafia) has been further explored by Idel and Fenton with respect to the meaning of the term *hitbodedut* (seclusion and/or meditative concentration) in several kabbalistic documents (among them, the writings of Isaac of Akko).[12] Clarifying the probable practice that is represented by the word *hitbodedut* (and the existing scholarship on it) will be a crucial step in our understanding of Isaac of Akko's views on asceticism, sensory nullification, and the contemplative life. The general conclusion of Idel and Fenton on this matter is that this mystical technique was modeled on an established Sufi practice that was in vogue at the time (mid to late thirteenth century) in the northern region of the Land of Israel, and in the Jewish communities of Egypt

---

11. Idel, "Ecstatic Kabbalah and the Land of Israel"; Fenton, "Solitary Meditation in Jewish and Islamic Mysticism in the Light of a Recent Archeological Discovery"; id., "La 'Hitbodedut' chez les premiers Qabbalistes en Orient et chez les Soufis."

12. See Idel, *Studies in Ecstatic Kabbalah*, pp. 73–169; Fenton, "Solitary Meditation in Jewish and Islamic Mysticism." This constellation of issues and terms was first studied in Ephraim Gottlieb, "Illumination, *Devequt*, and Prophecy in R. Isaac of Akko's *Sefer 'Oẓar Ḥayyim*," pp. 238–241.

(i.e., Alexandria and Cairo).[13] The final aim of this method was the attainment of prophecy, a condition considered in these circles to be the height of religious aspiration and experience. Through cultivation of an intense and disciplined control over one's emotional state of mind, and through an attitude of detachment from and indifference to the physical world, the mystic attempts to ascend ever higher in rarefied consciousness toward the ultimate goal of prophetic mind—a summit experience that was a highly characteristic pursuit in Abraham Abulafia's own mystical manuals. Discussion of this technique with respect to Isaac of Akko has centered upon two passages from *Me'irat 'Einayim* in very close proximity to each other. The first of these offers the most elaborate explanation of this prerequisite state of emotional equanimity and detachment from the physical world that we have in our possession. I shall cite the original text in full,[14] owing to the fact that it formed the cornerstone for the inquiries into the *hitbodedut* practice of both Idel and Fenton, and for the degree of insight that it offers into our larger concerns.

> [A] R. 'ABNeR said to me that a man who was a lover of wisdom came to one of the *mitbodedim* [hermits or meditators] and asked that he accept him so that he might become one of the *mitbodedim* [אמר לי הר' אבנ"ר כי בא איש אוהב חכמה לאחד המתבודדים ובקש ממנו שיקבלהו להיות מהמתבודדים].
>
> [B] The *mitboded* replied: My son, blessed are you unto the heavens [or by heaven], for your intention is good. But tell me, have you achieved equanimity or not [א"ל המתבודד: בני ברוך אתה לשמים כי כוונתך טובה היא אמנם הודיעני השתויתה או לא]?
>
> [C] [The man] replied: Master, explain your words [א"ל רבי באר דבריך].
>
> [D] He said to him: My son, if there are two men, and one of them honors you while the second one shames you, are they equal in your eyes or not [א"ל בני אם שני בני אדם האחד מהם מכבדך והאחד מבזך הם שוים בעיניך או לאו]?

13. Idel, *Studies in Ecstatic Kabbalah*, pp. 106–107; Fenton, "Solitary Meditation in Jewish and Islamic Mysticism." Cf. Fenton, "La 'Hitbodedut'"; id., "Judaeo-Arabic Mystical Writings," p. 101.

14. Isaac of Akko, *Me'irat 'Einayim*, p. 218.

> [E] The man replied: By the life of your soul, master, I would feel pleasure and satisfaction from the one who honors me, and sorrow from he who shames me, but I am nevertheless not vengeful or malicious [א"ל חי נפשך אדוני כי אני מרגיש הנאה ונחת רוח מהמכבד וצער מהמבזה אבל איני נוקם ונוטר].
>
> [F] [The master] said to him: My son, go in peace. For all the while that you have not achieved equanimity and your soul senses the shame that is done to you, you are not ready to have your mind connected to the supernal when you enact *hitbodedut*. Therefore go and humble your heart further with a true humility until you achieve equanimity and then you shall be able to engage in *hitbodedut* [א"ל בני לך לשלום כי כל זמן שלא השתויתה שתרגיש נפשך בבזיון הנעשה לך אינך מזומן להיות מחשבתך קשורה בעליון שתבא ותתבודד. אמנם לך ותכניע עוד לבבך הכנעה אמתית עד שתשתוה ואז תוכל להתבודד].
>
> [G] The cause of equanimity is the attachment of thoughts to God. This [attachment] causes the person not to feel the honor of people for him, nor the shame that they do unto him [וסבת ההשתוות הוא דבוק המחשבה בשם ית' הוא מסבב אל האיש ההוא שלא ירגיש בכבוד הבריות לו ולא בבזיון שעושים לו].

As Idel notes in his analysis of this text,[15] Isaac of Akko essentially transmits two differing perspectives on the order of the stages on the way to mystical experience, each of which directly contradicts the other. The first, which Idel concludes was likely the authentic position of R. 'ABNeR, is that a state of equanimity and detachment toward the physical world (especially with respect to interpersonal relationships) must precede any attempts at mystical meditation. It is only through the cultivation of emotional detachment from the ridicule and praise of other people (an imperative that seeks to negate the value of a prideful ego) that the spiritual adept will be able to attain true mystical connection with Divinity ("all the while that you have not achieved equanimity and your soul senses the shame that is done to you, you are not ready to have your mind connected to the supernal when you enact

15. Idel, *Studies in Ecstatic Kabbalah*, pp. 113–114. An earlier, albeit less extensive, version of this article was published in Green, ed., *Jewish Spirituality: From the Bible Through the Middle Ages*, pp. 405–438.

hitbodedut").[16] However, the passage concludes (section G) with an assertion of the exact opposite view! There the mystic adept must first seek to attach himself to the deity by means of *devequt* (ultimate attachment to God), and only thereafter will he be able to achieve emotional equanimity ("The cause of equanimity is the attachment of thoughts to God. This [attachment] causes the person not to feel the honor of people for him, nor the shame that they do unto him"). In other words, equanimity is possible precisely because the individual has transcended all earthly concerns and is in a state of unified attachment to the divine essence.[17] Idel argues that the second view is that of Isaac of Akko

---

16. It is quite clear that the phrase מחשבתך קשורה בעליון (your mind connected to the supernal) should be read interchangeably with the idea of *devequt*. As Seth Brody has shown, מחשבה דבקה was a ubiquitous image and practice in medieval Kabbalah, and connoted the state of human mental binding and union with Divinity. See Brody, "Human Hands Dwell in Heavenly Heights: Contemplative Ascent and Theurgic Power in Thirteenth-Century Kabbalah," pp. 123–158.

17. In articulating his own view on the matter (*Me'irat 'Einayim*, p. 218), Isaac of Akko also cites a passage from Naḥmanides' *Commentary on the Book of Job* (albeit with minor differences between Isaac's version and that preserved in the standard edition of Naḥmanides' commentary [*Perush le-Sefer 'Iyov* in *Kitvei Ramban* 1:108]) that underscores the relationship between *devequt* and the experience of physical existence. As noted earlier in this study, the interpretive acts of citation, paraphrase, and commentary frequently serve as the creative framework for Isaac's presentation—the threshold between reception and transmission to a new audience: וראיתי לחבר כאן דברי הר"ם ב"ן ז"ל בפי' איוב . . . כי החסיד הגמור הדבק באלהיו תמיד ולא יפריד הדבק מחשבתו בו ענין מעניני העולם יהיה נשמר תמיד מכל מקרה ופגע ואפי' ההווים בטבע וישתמר מהם ככה יעשה לו תמיד כאלו יחשב מכת העליונים אינם מבני ההויה וההפסד למקרי העתים וכפי קרבתו להדבק באלהיו ישתמר שמירה מעולה והרחוק מן האל ובמעשיו ואפי' לא יתחייב מיתה בחטאו אשר חטא והיה משולח ונעזב למקרים (I have seen fit to write here the words of RaMBaN of blessed memory in his commentary on Job. . . . For the completely pious individual who attaches himself to his God constantly, and who [does not allow] any worldly matter to separate his mind [from its state of cleaving to God], will constantly be protected from every accident and harm [on the term *miqreh*, see Klatzkin, *Thesaurus Philosophicus*, 2: 270–272]. He will even be protected from that which occurs in Nature. Thus it shall be for him always, as if he were considered to be one of the supernal beings—those [who are] not from among the children of earthly existence, not from among those who are abandoned to the accidents of time. And in accordance with his drawing close to God in order to be attached to Him, [the human being] will be protected with a supreme protection. [However], he who is distant from God, even if his actions do not make him liable to [the punishment of] death for the sin he has committed, he will be sent forth and abandoned to the accidents [*miqrim*] [of the natural world]). Let us first note that the phrase ההויה וההפסד was used in medieval Jewish philosophical literature, an example of which can be found in Maimonides' *Guide*, 1: 75. Cf. Klatzkin, *Thesaurus Philosophicus*, 1: 196–197. According to Klatzkin, the term הפסד generally connoted either destruction or the nullification of reality (בטול המציאות) in Jewish philosophy of the Middle Ages. In the cited passage from Maimonides' *Guide*, however, the term ההויה וההפסד is used in the context of explaining the ontic distinctions between lower matter and the heavenly spheres. According

himself, and that it was grafted on to the conclusion of the transmission from R. 'ABNeR. This point is primarily demonstrated by Isaac's additional formulation of the matter on the very same page of *Me'irat 'Einayim*:

> He who has merited the secret of attachment will merit the secret of equanimity [הזוכה לסוד ההתדבקות יזכה לסוד ההשתוות]. And if he merits the secret of equanimity, he will merit the secret of *hitbodedut* [ואם יזכה לסוד ההשתוות יזכה לסוד ההתבודדות]. Once he has merited the secret of *hitbodedut*, then he will merit the Holy Spirit, and from that he will reach prophecy, until he prophesies and foretells future events [ומאחר שזכה לסוד התבודדות הרי זה יזכה לרוח הקדש ומזה לנבואה עד שיתנבא ויאמר עתידות].

Here the ordering of matters is presented with greater clarity, if also with greater brevity. The stage of התדבקות (attachment/cleaving) is considered to be the first stage on the path to prophecy,[18] and di-

---

to Shlomo Pines (*Guide*, 1: 223), the term is to be translated (that is, from its Arabic original) as "generation and corruption," reflecting the role of accidental forces (מקרים) in the realm of lower matter that occur in the transition from the heavenly realm to the physical realm. In Naḥmanides' view, and by extension that of Isaac as well, *devequt* not only engenders a state of indifference to matters of this world, but also creates a physical *immunity* on the part of the human being to the events and occurrences of the natural world. It enables his participation in God's protective providence. What is more, in transcending the physical through mental union with Divinity, the kabbalist is veritably transformed into a member of the heavenly domain. That which would affect or harm any other mere mortal does not touch the mystic in the state of *devequt*. By virtue of his contemplative attainment, he receives supernatural protection from all "accidents" while still living in the natural world. In this respect, we find a remarkable instance of the ability of the spirit to overcome the vagaries and ordeals of physical existence. Indeed, the act of contemplative *devequt* (through the state of divine conjunction) creates an emotional *and* a corporeal detachment from the physical world. The mystical ideal is thus one of self-transcendence—a process of reaching beyond the human and natural realms to the transnatural, divine domain.

18. In this context it is important to note the presence of such a correlation (between *devequt* and prophecy) in Naḥmanides' *Perush 'al ha-Torah* itself. Strikingly, the usage there is also combined with a technical (and somewhat enigmatic) use of the term התבודדות—a parallel to the terminological cluster observed above. The following passage is to be found in *Perush ha-Ramban 'al ha-Torah*, 2: 404 (on Deut. 13:2): כי יקום בקרבך נביא . . . ויתכן שירמוז הכתוב למה שהוא אמת, כי בנפשות בקצת האנשים כח נבואי ידעו בו עתידות, לא ידע האיש מאין יבא בו אבל יתבודד ותבא בו רוח לאמר ככה יהיה לו לעתיד לבא בדבר פלוני . . . [ו]הדבר נתאמת לעיני רואים. אולי הנפש בחדודה תדבק בשכל הנבדל ותתכוין בו. והאיש הזה יקרא נביא כי מתנבא הוא ועל כן יבא האות והמופת אשר יאמר אליך ("If a prophet arises among you . . ." It seems that Scripture alludes to what is indeed true, for in the souls of a certain few people there is a prophetic power through which they can forecast future events. The person will not know from whence this

rectly precedes the rung of equanimity (השתוות). It is only thereafter that the devotee may proceed to התבודדות—a condition that Idel argues should be understood as intense meditative concentration, as opposed to the surface meaning of the word (i.e., seclusion). In contrast, the first passage clearly asserts that extreme humility is the fundamental basis for the sought-after state of equanimity, and that humility is the key to the attainment of exalted mystic/prophetic consciousness. Such an ethical posture serves as the prerequisite for initiation into the fraternity known as the מתבודדים—a term that seems to have had implicit meaning for both the transmitter and the receiver of this anecdote. As we shall see in subsequent discussion of passages from *'Oẓar Ḥayyim*, Isaac of Akko frequently makes reference to a social group called the מתבודדים—a group of individuals who were famed for their piety and powers of mystical achievement. From the transmission offered in the

---

[power] comes upon him, but he will meditate (and seclude himself?), and a spirit [or divine wind] will come upon him [inspiring him] to say: such and such will happen in the future in matter *x*. . . . And that thing [that he predicted] then becomes verified before the eyes of witnesses [lit., viewers]. Perhaps the soul [of that person] in its sharpness [or focus?] will become attached to the Separate Intellect, and will focus on it. And that man will be called a prophet, for he prophesizes, and the sign and proof that he speaks of will come to pass). In Naḥmanides' view, the ability to prophesize is a direct consequence of a state of cleaving to the supernal realm. By binding himself to the upper world (through the polyvalent act of התבודדות), the prophet receives divine inspiration in the palpable and ontic form of רוח. As noted earlier in this chapter, this conception of divine רוח as the source of prophetic insight (or רוח הקודש) was a major theme of interest and rumination in the writings of the earliest kabbalists of Provence and Gerona. The correlation between התבודדות, דבקות, רוח הקדש also has clear precedent in the earlier writings of 'Azri'el of Gerona (*Perush ha-'Aggadot le-Rabbi 'Azri'el*, p. 40), and it appears that Isaac of Akko was the recipient of a convergence of related traditions on this subject. Commenting on the well-known rabbinic tradition about Ben 'Azz'ai being encircled by fire as a physical representation of his having "descended to the Chariot" (*Midrash Vayiqra Rabbah* 16:4)—a paradigmatic moment of the mystical experience—R. 'Azri'el clearly argues that prophetic mind is attained directly through the condition of *devequt*. That *devequt* is in turn caused by a precise method of *hitbodedut* and *kavvanah*: מפני שהיה יושב ושונה ומדביק המחשבה למעלה היו חקוקים בלבו הדברים הנוראי', ומתוך האצילות ההיא ודבקות המחשבה ההיא היו הדברי' מתוספים ומתרבים ומתוך השמחה היו נגלים לו. וכענין זה היתה המשכת הנבואה שהיה הנביא מתבודד לו ומכוין לבו ומדביק מחשבתו למעלה, וכפי דבקות הנבואה היה הנביא צופה ויודע מה שעתיד להיות (Because he was sitting and learning and cleaving his thought [to the realm] above, the Awesome Entities [or Words] were engraved in his heart [or his mind/imagination]. And through that [flow of] emanation, and that cleaving of thought [to the realm above], the Words became greater and more abundant, and through joy they became revealed to him. And just like this matter was the drawing forth of prophecy. For the prophet would seclude himself [or focus himself], and would direct his heart and attach his thought [to the realm] above. And through the cleaving of prophecy, the prophet would see and know what was to happen in the future).

name of R. 'ABNeR, we can discern a spiritual ideal aimed at the elimination of physical sensibilities and concerns, as well as a radical effacement of pride and ego, insofar as these self-oriented emotions block the way to intimacy with the divine. The paradigmatic mystic is thus to be focused on the transcendence of ordinary senses and human interaction, and to be preoccupied entirely with the pursuit of an ethereal consciousness.[19]

The primary divergence between the analyses of the *hitbodedut* practice by Idel and Fenton lies in their respective interpretations of the word itself and its practical connotations. Idel argues that this term was used to connote intense intellective and meditative concentration, as opposed to the literal meaning of seclusion or isolation. He offers a wide scope of textual evidence for this claim, and he asserts that this usage by mystics was influenced by a similar use among medieval Jewish philosophers such as Abraham ibn Ezra and Moses Maimonides. Indeed, in several of the cases proffered by Idel, the word *hitbodedut* could not reasonably refer to an act of seclusion in and of itself, but rather to a more complicated and involved mystical procedure. Fenton, on the other hand, makes a sustained argument for a more literal understanding of the word *hitbodedut*, primarily predicated on the assumption that this Jewish practice was shaped by the Muslim Sufi practice of *ḥalwa*—a lengthy period of isolation undergone for the purpose of achieving a sharpened mystical consciousness. Fenton seeks to build on archeological evidence supporting the idea that

---

19. This particular formulation of the tradition—one that Isaac reports in the name of the mysterious R. 'ABNeR—can be traced to a passage found in Judah ibn Tibbon's translation of Baḥya ibn Paquda's *Ḥovot ha-Levavot*, 2: 44. It would therefore seem that this anecdote was well-circulated among Sufis and Jewish-Sufi pietists: וכבר אמרו על אחד מן החסידים שאמר לחבירו, הנשתוית? אמר לו, באיזה ענין? אמר לו, נשתוה בעיניך השבח והגנות? אמר לו, לא. אמר לו, אם כן עדיין לא הגעת, השתדל אולי תגיע אל המדרגה הזאת כי היא העליונה שבמדרגות החסידים ותכלית החמודות (They have already spoken about one of the pietists [*ha-ḥasidim*] who said to his companion: "Have you attained equanimity?" The other responded: "In what respect?" [The first one] said: "Are praise and rebuke the same in your eyes?" [The second one] said: "No." [The first one then] said: "If so, then you have not yet reached [equanimity]. Try and perhaps you will reach this rung, for it is the highest of all the rungs of the pietists, and it is the ultimate delight.") It is perfectly clear that this earlier tradition underlies the transmission preserved in Isaac of Akko's *Me'irat 'Einayim*. The ABNeR figure thus passed on a Sufi-inspired pietistic tradition that extends at least as far back as the writings of Baḥya ibn Paquda.

Muslim mystics practiced their periods of spiritual seclusion in defined caves for this purpose, one of which was discovered in recent years in the Galilee, near the town of Safed. Fenton argues that the geographical proximity of this cave (which, in light of Arabic inscriptions on the walls, was almost certainly used as a place of meditative retreat for Sufi mystics in the last decades of the thirteenth century)[20] to Jewish communities in the northern Land of Israel presents plausible evidence for the theory that Jewish mystics came into contact with their Sufi colleagues in this time and place. There is, however, a reasonable way to resolve the disparate interpretations of Idel and Fenton. It may very well be that the specific meditative practices alluded to by the word *hitbodedut* originated in seclusionary implementation (owing to the literal meaning of the word), and subsequently came to connote those meditative techniques themselves (i.e., irrespective of the physical act of isolation). This would explain the perplexing use of the word *hitbodedut* in the nonseclusionary settings that Idel so convincingly documents. The practices originally associated with seclusion (and conducted under those conditions) may therefore simply have taken on the name of their original framework, while still maintaining the mode of meditation cultivated therein.

In Isaac's *'Oẓar Ḥayyim*, the setting and practice of *hitbodedut* is linked repeatedly to the ideal of sensory detachment and nullification, and that which was articulated as a spiritual ideal in *Me'irat 'Einayim* becomes a recurrent refrain of Isaac's later work. According to Isaac, the negation of the physical מורגשות for the sake of the contemplative מושכלות is one of the hallmarks of the פרושים המתבודדים (the ascetic hermits, or the reclusive meditators), and the true kabbalist is forever in search of a transcendence of the physical:[21]

יעשה תשובה לשלול את נפשו מהמורגשות ולהשקיעה במושכלות בבית התבודדותו . . . כה אמר י"י אלהים[22] שער החצר הפנימית [הפנה קדים] יהיה סגור ששת ימי המעשה [וביום השבת יפתח] שכל אלה ירמזו לשערי תשובה והשפעת השפעים

---

20. P. Fenton, "Solitary Meditation in Jewish and Islamic Mysticism," pp. 293–296.

21. Isaac of Akko, *'Oẓar Ḥayyim*, fol. 2b.

22. The MS reads this way as the traditional pronunciation of the biblical text. The actual wording of Ezek. 46:1 is: כה אמר אדני יהו"ה.

הנפתחים לפרושים המתבודדים . . . היא הכנעת הנפש המתאוה לפני הנפש המשכלת
. . . השכל האלהי היה דואג על פרישותה מהמושכלות והשתקעותה במורגשות.

[A person] should repent by removing his soul from the physical [dimensions], and by immersing [his soul] in the intellective [dimensions] while in his house of seclusion/meditation. . . . [Ezek. 46:1] "Thus said the Lord God: The gate of the inner court which faces east shall be closed on the six working days, [and on the Sabbath day it shall be opened]." All of these [gates] allude to the gates of repentance and the flowing of efflux that open to the *perushim ha-mitbodedim*. . . .[23] [All this comes about through] the subjugation of the appetitive soul[24] before the intellective soul. . . . The Divine Intellect[25] had been anxious

23. The term *perushim* is used here to connote ascetic withdrawal from the physical life of the senses. This particular usage appears to build upon the Sufi-inspired writings of Baḥya ibn Paquda, in which the pious individual seeks to separate himself from corporeal existence and the company of others in order that he may encounter God in pure isolation and purely spiritual mind (see ibn Paquda, *Ḥovot ha-Levavot*, 2: 288–337). For other sources that understand *perishut* to be a philosophical ideal, see Klatzkin, *Thesaurus Philosophicus*, 3: 217. For Isaac of Akko (who also clearly reflects the direct or indirect influence of Sufi piety), the mystical experience of Divinity is *enabled* through a separation from, and ultimately transcendence of, physical sensation and existence. In this respect, the two words *perushim ha-mitbodedim* join to form a technical characterization of a specific social configuration. Within Jewish society in Isaac's time, there were clearly groups of individuals who practiced these forms of seclusion, ascetic separation from physical life and sensation, and the consequent mystical meditation aimed at communion or union with the Divine Intellect. The term *parush* or *perushah* in the sense of an ascetic dates back much further, however, and a significant usage can already be found in early rabbinic literature. See *Mishnah Sotah* 3:4. An extensive analysis of *perishut* in the rabbinic society of medieval 'Ashkenaz has been published by Ephraim Kanarfogel (*Peering Through the Lattices: Mystical, Magical, and Pietistic Dimensions in the Tosafist Period*, pp. 33–92), and it is quite probable that the tosafist tendencies toward asceticism exercised a major influence on Isaac of Akko in his journeys from the Land of Israel through Aragonese and Castilian Jewish communities. For consideration of this trope in early rabbinic literature, see Diamond, *Holy Men and Hunger Artists*, pp. 75–92.

24. Literally, "the desiring soul." This division of the soul into its appetitive and intellective components follows the standard medieval philosophical division as it was modeled on the thought of Aristotle. Klatzkin has noted the use of this term in a wide range of medieval Jewish philosophical sources, including the widely disseminated biblical exegesis of the Neoplatonist Abraham ibn 'Ezra' (see the latter's commentary on Exod. 23:25). See Klatzkin, *Thesaurus Philosophicus*, 2: 309; 3: 58.

25. As can be discerned from Klatzkin, *Thesaurus Philosophicus*, 1: 46–47, medieval Hebrew translators of Judaeo-Arabic philosophy generally preferred the term ענין אלהי to שכל אלהי. In this respect, Jewish philosophers sought to distinguish between the "intellective" dimensions of reality (which stand above the physical world) and the "divine element" of the universe. Nevertheless, the idea of the flow of divine intellect washing over the philosopher-prophet at the height of his ascent (one leading to union with the deity) is to be found in Maimonides,

over Its separation from the intellective [dimensions] and Its immersion in the physical [dimensions].

We may first note the significant correlation that is made between the process of repentance (*teshuvah*) and the ascetic condition of withdrawal from physical desire. The pietist's detachment from the realm of the מורגשות (the elements of physical-sensate experience), and complete immersion in the contemplative dimensions of the מושכלות, is the primary frame in which penitential transformation takes place. Isaac utterly transforms the original text of Ezekiel 46 from an ancient statement about the inner Temple courtyard (the times of its closure and its opening) into a formulation of an ascetic mystical imperative. In the text of Ezekiel, the gate to that deeper, more sanctified zone of the Temple remains closed during profane time (the six days of the week), and is opened and accessible only during the sacred time of the weekly cycle—on the Sabbath day. In the passage I have excerpted and translated above, the opening of the inner Temple gates on Shabbat is employed as a metaphor for the opening of the gates of repentance and the influx of divine energies that pour onto the receiving mystic. And just as the ancient Temple gates were only accessible at particularly sacred times, so, too, the divine flow of energy is opened with unique accessibility to the *perushim ha-mitbodedim*—the ascetic hermits who have cultivated a special refinement of body and spirit in the demarcated house of *hitbodedut* [בית התבודדותו]. Whether this last phrase here implies sustained seclusion and withdrawal from society, or if the author means only to refer to those contemplators who meditate in a defined space, is not entirely certain. It does appear, however, that Isaac is alluding to individuals who engaged in some degree of ascetic denial of physical desire, devoting themselves fully to contemplation of Divinity in a separated and so-defined meditative space. It might also be observed that the "subjugation of the appetitive soul" (הכנעת הנפש המתאוה) leads toward a kind of quietistic practice. The desires and appetites of the physical life must be quieted and subjugated so that the mystic can receive the efflux of divine energy into his soul. Only once the passions

---

Moreh Nevukhim 3:51 (in the medieval Hebrew translation of Judah ibn Tibbon): הוא השפע ההוא השכלי.

and sensations of corporeal existence have been conquered or transformed can the human being reach the spiritual height of meriting the Divine Intellect, the opening of the gates of his soul to receive the flow of divine vitality.[26] A person who fully detaches himself from physicality prepares his soul for a supernatural experience. Consider a parallel case of this trope a bit later in the manuscript:[27]

וענין ותנבאו הוא שהיו עושים תנאי המתבודדים אשר יעשו לבטל החושים המורגשים ולשלול ממחשב הנפש כל מורגש ולהלבישה רוחניות השכל. והכל תלוי במחשבה. אם דיבוק המחשבה בכל נברא . . . הרי הוא כעובד ע"ז . . . אמנם מחשבת הנפש הזכה של אליהו ז"ל דביקה עם י"ה יהו"ה אלהי ישראל לבדו.

> The meaning of "you shall prophesy" is that the *mitbodedim* made the following condition:[28] They would try to nullify the physical senses, to negate from the thought of the soul every physical sensation, and to garb it in the spirituality of the intellect.[29] And all is dependent upon the thought. If the thought is attached to any created being . . . then the individual is considered to be like an idolater. . . . Indeed, the pure thought of the soul of Elijah, of blessed memory, was attached to *YH YHVH*, the God of Israel, alone.

The stark boldness of this statement is striking, and reveals a great deal about the intersection of mind and proper devotion for the kabbalist. In order to worship God properly, the devotee must purify and empty the mind of all corporeal thoughts;[30] consciousness must ever be trained upon the ultimate subject of contemplation—the di-

---

26. The causal relation between the subjugation of physical desire and the elevated engagement with the *muskalot* of contemplation is clearly represented in Maimonides' philosophical writing. As we find in *Guide* 3:51 (trans. Pines, 2: 627): "The philosophers have already explained that the bodily faculties impede in youth the attainment of most of the moral virtues, and all the more that of pure thought, which is achieved through the perfection of the intelligibles that lead to passionate love of Him, may He be exalted. . . . Yet in the measure in which the faculties of the body are weakened and the fire of the desires is quenched, the intellect is strengthened, its lights receive a wider extension, its apprehension is purified, and it rejoices in what it apprehends."

27. Isaac of Akko, *'Oẓar Ḥayyim*, fol. 7a.

28. For the attainment of *devequt*.

29. For an analysis of the use of this term in the thought of Judah Halevi, as well as consideration of its earlier roots in Islamic thought, see Pines, "On the Term *Ruḥaniyut* and Its Sources," pp. 511–540.

30. Cf. Wolfson, *Language, Eros, Being*, pp. 209, 521 n. 131.

vine Being. For if the worshipping mind is attached to any entity of the created world, the supplicant is deemed to be nothing less than an idolater! To allow thought to be occupied with matters of physical sensation, with the objects of this-worldly existence, to desist for even a moment from the sacred contemplation of God, is tantamount to the ultimate heresy and violation of faith. Considered as such, the paradigmatic mode of mental attention and awareness is one that is directed exclusively and always toward the supernal realm of God; the true mystic is envisioned as one engaged in a perennial flight from corporeality to pure spirituality and transcendence. It is further significant to note that this practice is associated directly with the ideal path to prophecy (ענין ותנבאו). As we saw in preceding cases, the practice of *hitbodedut* reaches its apex in the moment of prophetic consciousness. To clear the mind of all sensory thoughts, to negate the structures of external perception—this was believed to stimulate the opening of a higher, more rarefied, state of consciousness. The prophecy that is associated with the *muskalot* only becomes possible once all *murgashot* consciousness has been effaced. Let us recall, however, that this ultimate effacement is preceded by a close engagement with the sensations of the physical world. Isaac of Akko was certainly attentive to the details of natural reality, and he repeatedly sought to extrapolate cosmic divine meaning from the varieties and phenomena of corporeal existence. We must assume, however, that he understood such interpretive perception to be a lower order of mystical consciousness, and that the kabbalist ultimately sought to transform all this-worldly sensation into a spiritualized encounter with the divine realm of the *muskalot*. Such would characterize an upward trajectory in spiritual consciousness—a progression in which the aspiring kabbalist seeks to attain the purity of prophetic mind. As the closing line of this passage indicates, the prophetic ideal is represented by Elijah of old—a holy man who was believed to have achieved this rung of contemplative purity through complete attachment of his mind to God alone.

In light of the seeming extremism of this attitude—an ideal that appears to advocate the nullification of sensory consciousness and the redirection of all perception to the divine *muskalot*—we should take note of a significant passage in which Isaac of Akko mitigates the absolutism of such a view and affirms the slightly more moderate position articulated more than a century earlier by Moses Maimonides. In a self-conscious paraphrase of the Maimonidean attitude, Isaac states:

> דע כי תכלית המבוקש מהאדם הוא להשכיל את בוראו ולדעת אותו כפי כח השגתו . . . ושלא יעסוק במורגשות רק להחיות גופו . . . ויקנה מדת ההסתפקות לברוח מהיתרונות ויתבודד להשכיל את המושכלות האלהיות למען תתלבש נפשו באור השכל.

> Know that the goal that is asked of a person is to contemplate his Creator, and to know Him according to the strength of his comprehension. . . . And [this person] should not engage himself in the elements of sensation [*murgashot*], except to sustain the life of his body. . . . He should attain the attribute of sufficiency [*histapqut*], such that he will flee from excess [*yitronot*]. And he should seclude himself [or concentrate] to contemplate the divine *muskalot* [intelligibles; spiritual dimensions], so that his soul will be garbed in the light of the Intellect.[31]

Here we see an acknowledgment of the need and inevitability of *some* engagement with the physical world—at least to the extent necessary for the basic sustenance of the body. In the lines that precede this passage in *'Ozar Ḥayyim*, Isaac explicitly states that he is clarifying the words of the RaMBaM, and the ideas discussed are most certainly evident in the Maimonidean corpus. For as Maimonides argues in his introductory comments to the mishnaic tractate *'Avot* (*Shemoneh Peraqim*, 5), care for the needs of the physical body is a necessity, owing to the fact that contemplation and knowledge of God (the ultimate purpose of human life, according to this philosopher) require the health and proper functioning of the body. In good Aristotelian fashion, however, Maimonides does warn his reader against excessive indulgence of the physical senses beyond what is necessary to maintain health. And it is just this point that is underscored by Isaac of Akko. Avoidance of luxury and excess, a restriction of physicality to the threshold of "sufficiency"—this is the foundation for a proper contemplation of God.

Indeed, mundane sensate experience is understood by Isaac to function as a barrier to the ultimate encounter with Divinity. The process of transcending the *murgashot* is frequently characterized as an event

---

31. Isaac of Akko, *'Ozar Ḥayyim*, fol. 32a.

of purification, and, as seen in the final line of the above-cited text, the clothing of the human self in divine light. In yet another passage, Isaac explicitly states that the ultimate spiritual goal is the theurgical attraction of divine energy into the human soul—a reception that must then be sent forth to the world from that soul. Such is the actualization of received potential energy (להוציא אותו מנפשנו מן הכח אל הפועל), while this personal reception of the divine flow first requires the opening of an unobstructed path from the lowest of the *sefirot* into the human soul. For this reason, the great majority of people—mired as they are in the filth and veils of corporeality—are left shrouded in the darkness of the mundane until, through a process of penitence, they are able to lift the veil and become illuminated by the divine Presence. The righteous ones, those who are more advanced in the spiritual life, are able to receive this divine *shefa*ʿ (energy/emanation/flow) readily and without difficulty. Others of a lower spiritual stature must undergo a rigorous purification from their engagement with the mundane—a transformation that is framed overtly as a process of *teshuvah*, of repentance:

> ההמונים הנטבעים בים המורגשות אשר היו מתהלכים בחשכת אפלת הנפש הבהמית המתאוה אשר עשו תשובה לזכך את נפשם ולטהרה מלכלוכי העבים החוצצים ומפסיקים בינה ובין האור האלהי שגם היא מוכנת לקבל שפע טהרה וקדושה כי אין לך דבר העומד בפני התשובה.
>
> [These are] the masses who are drowning in the sea of the *murgashot*, who were walking in the dark fog of the animal appetitive soul. They repented and purified their souls, purifying [that soul] from the filth of the clouds that buffer and obstruct [the way] between her and the divine light. She too is [now] ready to receive the pure and holy flow, for there is nothing that stands in the way of repentance.[32]

To be concerned with the realm of physical experience and sensation is to be covered by the dark fog of appetites and desires. The process of purification, which involves a transcendence of mundane consciousness, is characterized here as an unveiling of darkness before the light of Divinity, as the removal of obstructing clouds before the radiant sun of spiritual truth. And while there is most certainly

32. Ibid., fol. 44b.

an acknowledgment of hierarchy in mystical attainment, the floodgates of enlightenment are opened wide before the one who crosses the threshold in penitence. It is a transformation of consciousness and perception that lifts the drowning man from the perilous ocean of corporeal obsessions. On the verge of being subsumed within the ever-present waters of physical existence, the repentance of spiritual consciousness offers a new lease on life, and fresh illumination of the long coarse shadows cast by physical sensation and concerns.

The persistent challenge and imperative for the spiritual adept is to see beyond those physical layers of existence. The contemplative gaze is a cultivated skill, and the true sage will seek to develop the open eye of spiritual sight at the very same time that he seeks to nullify the gaze of corporeal perception. Indeed, the latter leads directly to the former. From a condition of mundane consciousness (מורגשות), the wise kabbalist will be led to the higher perception of the divine *muskalot*—a transformation that comes about by way of physical nullification. This is the implication, Isaac argues on another occasion, of Job 19:26, "from my flesh I will see God" (מבשרי אחזה אלוה). Once flesh-consciousness has been negated and transcended, the interiority and hidden truth of the *muskalot* will be revealed:

> מהמורגשות אתבונן במושכלות שהרוצה להיות משכיל ירגיל עצמו לשלול מהמורגש מורגשו ונגלתו ויחזה בהתבוננות לבו מושכלו ונסתרו ופנימיותו והמשכיל יבין כי עיקר גדול הוא זה להבין ולהשכיל.

> From the physical-sensory realities I shall contemplate the intellective-spiritual realities.[33] For one who wishes to be a sage [*maskil*] will train himself to negate his physical and revealed being, and he will gaze with the contemplation of his heart on his spiritual-intellective being, his hiddenness and his inwardness. And the sage will understand that this is a great and essential principle to understand and to contemplate.[34]

In this passage we may take special note of the call to a contemplation of the inward and hidden dimensions of the human self (ויחזה

33. This is formulated in the first person in direct relation to the language of Job 19:26.

34. Isaac of Akko, *'Oẓar Ḥayyim*, fol. 197a. Let us recall a parallel usage of this idea and proof text in Isaac's *Me'irat 'Einayim*, noted and discussed at the close of Chapter 4.

(בהתבוננות לבו מושכלו ונסתרו ופנימיותו)—an exhortation that implicitly likens physical-sensate being to the veil that conceals the spiritual substratum of reality. The wise kabbalist is instructed to look beyond the fleshly state of bodily existence, always seeking to behold the incorporeal divine reality that lies hidden within. Such perception is the mark of the cultivated mystic.

Physical pleasure is therefore construed to be antithetical to the path of contemplative attainment. Isaac of Akko even goes so far as to affirm the value of corporeal mortification and suffering as a means to higher mystical consciousness:[35]

[A] תענוגי הגוף הפך תענוגי הנפש שתענוגי הגוף תכלית הגופניות המורכב ותענוגי הנפש המשכלת היא הנשמה החכמה תכלית הרוחניות הפשוטה. שאין ברעה למטה מנגע ואין בטובה למעלה מעונג הן הן האותיות נגע ענג ועונג הגוף הוא [נגע] לנפש.[36]

The pleasures of the body are the opposite of the pleasures of the soul, for the pleasures of the body are the ultimate goal of composite corporeality, and the pleasures of the intellective soul, the wise soul, are the ultimate goal of the simple spiritual substance.[37] For there is nothing worse than harm [*nega*ʿ], and there is nothing better than pleasure [ʿ*oneg*]. This [is reflected] in the letters ענג/נגע, and the pleasure of the body is harm to the soul.

[B] ועל זה שבחו רז"ל שפלות ישראל ועניות[ם] וגליותם ופזורם כי הוא הוא בנין הנפש המשכלת ועלייתה ודבקותה עם האמת העליון. כן הוא האור המורגש חשך ואפלה לנפש המשכלת והאור המושכל האלהי חשך ואפלה לגוף.

Speaking about this matter, our Rabbis of blessed memory praised the humility and suffering of Israel, their exile and their dispersion, for this is the nature of the intellective soul, its ascent and adherence to the

35. Isaac of Akko, *'Oẓar Ḥayyim*, fol. 53b.

36. This is the most plausible reading of an unclear script. For while the handwriting most closely resembles the formulation ועונג הגוף הוא עונג לנפש, such a reading would run contrary to the recurrent theme of the passage.

37. In contrasting *ha-gufaniyut ha-murkav* (composite corporeality) with *ha-ruḥaniyut ha-peshuṭah* (the simple spiritual substance), Isaac is making clear use of classic Neoplatonic terminology. In that philosophical tradition, the most simple, spiritual substance is defined as the oneness of matter, while the more composite layers of physical Being are defined as the forms that cloak the basic oneness of matter. It is in this sense that the phrase *ha-ruḥaniyut ha-peshuṭah* should be understood. On this issue, see Hyman, "From What Is One and Simple Only What Is One and Simple Can Come to Be," pp. 111–135.

supernal truth. So too, the corporeal-sensate light is darkness and fog to the intellective soul, and the intellective divine light is darkness and fog to the body.[38]

[C] ושלום הגוף ושלותו הוא רעת הנפש מפני היותם גופניים אנושיים. אמנם שלום הנפש ושלותה הוא רעת הגוף מפני היותם הפכים. כי הם רוחניים שמימיים אלהיים והם ב' הפכים. שכן הנפש הבורחת מהמורגשות להדבק במושכלות שהם האור והשלום העליונים הרוחניים תבא מזה רעה גדולה לגוף סיגופין ועינויים בהתבודדות ובתנאים הידועים להמשיך הרוח האלהי שהם קשים לגוף.

The peace and tranquility of the body is the torment of the soul,[39] for these are physical human [states]. Indeed, the peace and tranquility of the soul is the torment of the body, for they are opposites. They [the peace and tranquility of the soul] are spiritual, heavenly, and divine,

---

38. Consider the following parallel use of the binaric tension between light and darkness—a passage that further elucidates Isaac's conception of the oppositional nature of physical desire and attachment to God (*'Oẓar Ḥayyim*, fols. 18b-19a): זו היא הנפש המתאוה החשוכה האוהבת חמס ובצע, שאם תברח מהמושכלות בורחת מאור החיים הולכת לחשך וצלמות. ואם תדבק במושכלות תדבק באור החיים ונמלטה מחשך וצלמות. וכאשר תגבר הנפש המשכלת על שתיהן וישמעו שתיהן בקולה, שהנפש המתאוה לא תתאוה לדבר אסור בלתי לקיים מצות האל לעסוק בתורה וחכמה ובינה וקדושה, ומעשים לעשות אשר משפט וצדקה, והנפש החיה תענה את עצמה . . . מהגאוה והשררה ואהבת הכבוד, יהיה מציאותם קיים עם מציאות הנפש המשכלת (This is the appetitive [desiring] soul, the one who is darkened, who loves violence and unjust gain. For if she flees from the *muskalot* [intellective, spiritual dimensions], she flees from the light of life, she walks into darkness and the shadow of death. But if she attaches [אם תדבק] herself to the *muskalot*, she will be attached to the light of life, and she will be saved from darkness and the shadow of death. And when the intellective soul overpowers these two [lower souls (the appetitive and the animal souls)], and the two of them hearken to her voice, such that the appetitive soul will not desire anything forbidden, but only desire to fulfill the commandment of God to engage in Torah, wisdom, understanding, and holiness—[to engage in] behavior that is just and righteous; when the animal soul deprives herself . . . of pride, power, and love of honor, then the existence [of the appetitive and animal souls] will stand with the existence of the intellective soul). The nature of reality and existence is divided along the fault line of this soul dichotomy, a chasm that separates desire, prohibition, transgression, darkness, and death from contemplative mind, wisdom, right action, holiness, and light. Only when the ideal character of the intellective soul is able to subdue and overpower the base nature of animalistic desires and impulses will the person be redeemed from the darkness of the body into the illumination of the mind. Only then will he be delivered from the shadows of death and physical mortality to the bright light of life and the eternity of the soul.

39. While not a literal rendering of the phrase *ra'at ha-nefesh*, I believe "torment of the soul" best captures the meaning of this line. Other possible translations, such as "evil of the soul," do not evoke the meaning of the phrase in context. Especially when compared with the subsequent lines about the suffering and torment of the body as the necessary correlate to the elevation and tranquility of the soul, *ra'at ha-nefesh* certainly seems to evoke torment, suffering, and disquiet. Another possible (and somewhat paraphrastic) translation might be "the peace and tranquility of the body is bad for the soul."

> and [the soul and the body] are two opposites. For the soul that flees from the corporeal-sensate elements to attach itself to the intellective-spiritual dimensions—they that are the supernal, spiritual light and peace—will bring about great torment and detriment to the body, mortification and suffering. [All this takes place] through meditative seclusion [*hitbodedut*], and by way of the known conditions that are hard on the body, and that draw down the divine spirit.

The pleasure of the body and the pleasure of the soul would therefore seem to be thoroughly irreconcilable, and the one represents the inverse reality of the other.[40] Not only is the indulgence of physical pleasure construed to have a negative impact upon the spiritual life of the soul, but the elevation and cultivation of the soul is directly linked to the suffering of the physical body. In this assertion, the tension between the *murgashot* and *muskalot* experience is taken to an entirely more extreme level of incompatibility—the corporeal self must actually suffer for the spiritual self to be liberated. If the body allows itself a state of peace and calm (without active and vigorous battle against the sensual nature of the body), the soul will result in a condition of unrest and disruption. The body must be harshly (and even violently) mortified for the sake of a higher spiritual transformation of the soul. This surprisingly bold position is underscored by the creative exegetical correlation of the words נגע (harm) and ענג (pleasure), an interpretive move that is clearly based on *Sefer Yeẓirah* and its exegesis in later kabbalistic literature.[41] Each word contains the same three Hebrew letters, though with the *'ayin* located in opposite places. Thus harm in one domain has the inverted result of pleasure in the polar realm, and vice versa. It is certainly clear from this passage that Isaac of Akko adhered to (or at least affirmed) some form

40. The language of inversion and polar opposites is also utilized in a parallel passage (Isaac of Akko, *'Oẓar Ḥayyim*, fol. 132a): אהיד"ע יושב ומשתכל בענין המורגש והאלהי המושכל שהם שני הפכים כשני אויבים (I, the young one, Isaac of Akko, was sitting and contemplating the matter of the physical-sensate and the divine-intelligible, that they are two opposites, like two enemies). Evoking a similar tenor to the passage excerpted from fol. 53b, these lines depict body and soul not only as radically polarized entities, but as states of being forever at war with each other. Read in light of the elaboration found on fol. 53b, the adversarial posture of body to soul, and vice versa, ultimately inflicts harm on the opposing side. When these enemies clash in their perpetual combat, the one emerges victorious in pleasure, while the other necessarily emerges defeated in torment and suffering.

41. See *Sefer Yeẓirah*, 2:7, and R. Isaac the Blind, *Perush le-Sefer Yeẓirah*, p. 10, lines 210–212.

of radical ascetic mortification of the body for the sake of the "peace and tranquility" of the soul. Not only a negation of the senses is necessary; the soul's spiritual purpose requires a posture of disquiet and violence toward the physical self. Such is the reason (Isaac argues) that the sages of old praised Israel for the great suffering and humility it experienced in exile. For only through a condition that undermines physical sensuality, and that even results in the degradation of corporeal torment, will the Jew be able to attain the heights of spiritual connection to the Divine and the transformation of the soul. What is more, we should take special note of the terminology employed by Isaac of Akko at the crescendo of this section. The devotee who is familiar with the techniques for elevation of the spirit will engage in the active mortification of the body—a process encapsulated in the evocative terms *sigufin* and *'inuyim* (mortifications and suffering). These practices will, Isaac acknowledges, be harsh and difficult on the body (*hem qashim la-guf*), but they are necessary for the advancement of the "intellective soul" and the drawing forth of the Divine spirit (*lehamshikh ha-ruah ha-'elohi*).

This explicit and bold prescription for the mortification and torment of the physical body in quest of a higher spiritual connection is further reflected in another passage from *'Oẓar Ḥayyim*.[42] After referring to the animal soul and the appetitive soul—those forces that stimulate strong desire for the physical pleasures of the lower world (תהיה התאוה חזקה בתענוגי העולם השפל)—Isaac states:

> ולא יקנה אדם שלימות עד אשר ישבר ויכניע שתי נפשות אלה ויגביר עליהם הנפש המשכלת . . . ובמה ישבר אדם את שתי נפשותיו? אלא בהרקה שיריק את גופו מהם. ובמה יריקם? בתעניות וסיגופים ומלקות שחשבון הכאותיו ט"ל י"י אח"ד. ואחר שיעשה זה תדבק נפשו בט"ל העליון, ואחר כל זה יבא אליו זיו אור השכינה.

> A person will not acquire completeness (or perfection) until he breaks and subjugates these two souls, and the intellective soul overpowers them. . . . And how should a person break his two souls? By emptying his body of them. And how shall he empty [his body] of them? Through fasts, mortifications, and lashes. The number of his lashes [shall be] *TaL YY EḤaD* [= 72], the dew of the one God.[43] And after

42. Isaac of Akko, *'Oẓar Ḥayyim*, fols. 87b–88a.

43. Though not stated explicitly as such, the numerical value of this phrase appears to cor-

> he does this, his soul will attach itself to the supernal dew. After all this, the light of the *Shekhinah* will shine onto him.

This is certainly one of the most overtly ascetic and bold formulations of the impulse to mortify the flesh that I have seen in Isaac of Akko's writings. In order to achieve completeness, or perfection (*sheleimut*), the devotee must harshly subjugate and break the desires of the physical life. Here we see, not only an exhortation to nullify and reject sensate experience, but also a prescription for an overtly violent approach to the body in an effort to quash the appetitive impediments to the spiritual life.[44] The exalted state of *devequt*—and the receipt of the divine light—are the direct causal results of physical mortification. The number of lashes that an individual is to inflict upon himself is even endowed with spiritual significance. Following the logic of our earlier text, the corporeal pain of the beatings has the inverse outcome of spiritual pleasure for the soul; the number of lashes corresponds directly to the nature of the spiritual result. In this way, the desires of the physical self must be beaten into submission for the intellective soul to be fully liberated and bound to the divine light. Having considered this evidence for the insight it lends into constructions of religious experience and the harsh dichotomization of body and soul, we can also glean a historical kernel of biographical information: the lived spiritual practice of Isaac ben Samuel of Akko most assuredly involved intense forms of asceticism, action that clearly included violent self-flagellation and mortification for the sake of spiritual aspiration.

---

relate to the seventy-two–letter name of God. In striking the body seventy-two times, the person receives the spiritual light of this divine name. It should be noted, however, that Y'Y may imply the tetragrammaton (YHVH), in which case the numeric value would be seventy-eight.

44. The violent tenor of this approach to physical desire is reflected in another brief comment elsewhere in the text (fol. 175b): "She is the desiring [appetitive] soul, and the man who does proper penitence must slaughter her and subjugate her before the intellective soul (היא הנפש המתאוה שצריך האיש העושה תשובה נכונה לשחוט אותה ולהכניעה לפני הנפש המשכלת). As we observed in earlier examples, the conquest of the desiring-appetitive soul is directly linked to a process of repentance (*teshuvah*). To remain bound to the precarious road of the senses and the desires that arise therefrom is to remain in a state of sin and in need of penitent transformation. Most notable in this instance, however, is the use of the language of slaughter (*lishḥoṭ*)—a term that evokes the harsh violence of ascetic practice evinced above in fols. 87b–88a, and to a lesser extent in fol. 53b. On the other hand, it should be noted that the term *lishḥoṭ* might also be rendered as "to hammer or beat" something (for the sake of improving its usefulness). See 1 Kings 10:16.

And They Become One: Union with God as a Devotional Ideal

On the basis of the foregoing discussion, it may be concluded that Isaac of Akko conceived of *devequt* as a state to be reached once the inhibiting forces of passion and desire have been conquered. The aspiring mystic seeks to reach beyond the borders of corporeality and the appetites of sensation; attachment to the *muskalot* can only be attained as the *murgashot* are subdued and transformed. This culmination of the spiritual path is represented frequently as unitive in nature—as a dissolution of the distance between deity and devotee. Within that image matrix, the rhetoric of *devequt* converges with the discourse of mystical union, and the boundaries between personal identity and the flux of divine Being are erased. To be sure, the phenomenon of mystical union in kabbalistic and hasidic sources has now received substantial attention from contemporary scholars (a trend that has served as a kind of programmatic corrective to the conclusions of Scholem and his school).[45] Nevertheless, it is critical to our larger hermeneutical task that we consider Isaac of Akko's nuanced approach to this problem in *Me'irat 'Einayim* and *'Ozar Ḥayyim*, insofar as it underlies the basic assumptions of his contemplative system and situates him within the broader landscape of experiential discourse in medieval Judaism.

As we see in the following text, the act of *devequt* takes place first and foremost in a devotional context—a devotion that is expressed through the interchangeable paradigms of sacrifice and verbal prayer. In typical

45. Consider reflections on this shift in Idel, *Kabbalah: New Perspectives*, pp. 59–61, as well as Idel's extensive analysis of the topoi of *devequt* and *unio mystica* in Jewish mysticism in *New Perspectives*, pp. 35–73, and id., *Studies in Ecstatic Kabbalah*, pp. 1–31. It should be noted, however, that important observations regarding the unitive dimension in Kabbalah were already put forth prior to Idel's work in Gottlieb, "Illumination, Attachment, and Prophecy" (particularly valuable here given its focus on Isaac of Akko's *'Ozar Ḥayyim*). Several further studies on this topic have appeared more recently. See Brody, "Human Hands Dwell in Heavenly Heights: Worship and Mystical Experience in Thirteenth-Century Kabbalah," pp. 264–395; Krassen, *Uniter of Heaven and Earth*, pp. 43–79; Wolfson, *Through a Speculum That Shines*, pp. 357–368; id., *Language, Eros, Being*, p. 209; Goldberg, "Mystical Union, Individuality, and Individuation in Provençal and Catalonian Kabbalah"; Lachter, "Paradox and Mystical Union in the Zohar."

fashion, the paradigmatic figures of olden times serve as the implicit (and explicit) models for the latter-day kabbalist.[46]

וכאשר מקריב הכהן הקרבן הוא מדביק נפשו למזבח ומתעלה הנשמה למעלה למעלה דרך עלוי והוא נקרא מלאך שנ' כי שפתי כהן ישמרו דעת ותורה יבקשו מפיהו כי מלאך י"י צבאות הוא . . . ונקרא מלאך בתחתונים. וכאשר מדביק נפשו ומעלה אותה דרך עלוי מעלה עליהם הב"ה כאלו הם בעצמם הקריבו ומתדבקים ביוצרם כי נפשות האדם באות למזבח העליון שיורדות מלמעלה לכסא שהוא כסא הב"ה ומן הראש יורדות דרך חוט השדרה לברית ומן הברית נכללות במזבח ומשם יוצאות ובאות ומתלבשות צורה בגוף השפל . . . על כן בהדביק הנפש למעלה בתחלה מתעלה רוחו של אדם כלו' שהיא יוצאת מארץ החיים ושבה לשרשה מאשר לוקחה ביציאתה לגוף ואחרי כן מתעלה למעלה עד מקום שרשה מעלוי עלוי כמו המים שעולים עד המדרגה שממנה יוצאים וזהו ברכת כהנים כאשר פורשים כפיהם לרום השמים ומברכים ישראל ומדביקים נפשם למעלה ומברכים את העם . . . כי הקרבן מתחלה מתעלה בחכמת שלמה ועולה דרך גבולו לחכמת אלהים וכן הוא ענין הנביאים כי כלם מהם דבקים מתוך התבודדותם וחכמתם לחכמת שלמה ומשם ולהלן כפי השגתם וגם כן כאשר נפרדת הנשמה מגוף השפל והיא שבה ליסודה מתחלה היא נאחזת בקרני המזבח ומשם מתעלה כפי פעולתם. וזהו תפלת החסידים שמתפללים שיצילם מדין של שמים שלא ישרף בלהב המזבח העליון.

When the priest [enacts] the sacrifice, he attaches his soul [*nafsho*] to the altar, and the soul [*neshamah*][47] ascends high above on the path of ascent. He [the priest] is called an angel [*mal'akh*][48] as it is written [Mal. 2:7]: "For the lips of a priest guard knowledge, and men seek rulings from his mouth; for he is an angel/messenger [*mal'akh*] of the Lord of Hosts.". . . He is called an angel in the lower realm. And when he attaches his soul and raises it on the path of ascent, the Holy One blessed be He raises [the people] as if[49] they themselves had [performed] the sacrifice. And they attach themselves to their Maker [*yoẓram*], for the souls of human beings come to the Supernal Altar. They descend from

46. Isaac of Akko, *Me'irat 'Einayim*, p. 140.

47. Because the English language does not reflect the same diversity on the word for *soul* as we find in Hebrew, I have had to translate both the words *nafsho* and *neshamah* as "soul." For despite the fact that *nefesh* and *neshamah* are commonly distinguished in the kabbalistic literature of this period and beyond, in this passage they appear to connote the same entity. For this reason, I have noted in the translation where each word is operative.

48. This association is also developed in the well-known "*'Ein-Dorshin*" section of BT *Ḥagigah* (fol. 15b). In that context the rabbinic figure who conducts himself with ideal character is likened to an angel of God (*mal'akh YHVH Ẓeva'ot*).

49. On the term כאלו in the context of sacrifice and ritual substitution in Judaism, see M. Fishbane, *Kiss of God*, pp. 87–124.

above to the Throne, which is the Throne of the Holy One blessed be He. And from the head[50] they descend by way of the Spinal Column to the [mark of] the covenant [*berit*],[51] and from the *berit* they are included within the Altar, and from there they go out, come forth, and become clothed in the form of an earthly [lit., lower] body. . . . Thus, when the soul [*nefesh*] attaches above, the spirit [*ruḥo*] of the human being ascends first, which is to say that she leaves[52] the land of the living and returns to the root from which she was taken when she went out to [become clothed] in a body. And after this she ascends above, all the way to the place of her root, from ascension to ascension, like the waters that rise up to the level from which they come forth. This is [the meaning of] the priestly benediction, [that which takes place] when [the priests] extend their hands to the height of the heavens, bless Israel, attach their souls above, and bless the people.[53] . . . For the sacrifice ascends first through the Wisdom of Solomon,[54] and [then] ascends through its path up to the Wisdom of *'Elohim*.[55] This is also the case with the prophets, for they all attach themselves through their concentration[56] and their wisdom to the Wisdom of Solomon, and from there onward according

---

50. Of the divine anthropos. See the next note.

51. This account of the genesis of the human soul is rooted in a medieval biology derived from Galen and was widespread in kabbalistic literature. It posited that the sperm of the male originates in the brain, travels through the spinal column, and culminates in the penis, upon which is the mark of circumcision (on Jewish males). In the logic of kabbalistic thought, this human biological process reflects a divine paradigm (given the fundamentally anthropic conception of divinity that views the human as a theomorphically structured being). As such, the seed of life that proceeds from the phallus of the male God is identical to the souls of human beings, destined to be garbed in the physical form of a body in the lower world. In the symbol structure of the *sefirot*, the male seed (which is the root of the human soul) passes from *Ḥokhmah* (which represents the brain of the divine male body) down through *Tif'eret* (which here correlates to the spinal column), down to *Yesod* (here likely represented by the phallus and mark of circumcision) into the Altar (*mizbeaḥ*) that corresponds to the womb of *'Atarah*. From the womb and opening of the tenth *sefirah*, the souls fly forth to their destinations in the corporeal realm. For a recent discussion of the kabbalistic use of the galenic biological conception in the construction of a gendered mythology and symbolic universe, see Wolfson, *Language, Eros, Being*, pp. 269–271.

52. In translating this word I have preferred the manuscript variant noted by Goldreich in *Me'irat 'Einayim* (section on manuscript variances), p. 314.

53. The phrases "bless Israel" and "bless the people" would seem redundant.

54. A cognomen for *Shekhinah*, the "lower wisdom."

55. A cognomen for *Binah*, the "upper wisdom," and the supernal correlate to *Shekhinah*.

56. *Hitbodedutam*. This word could also be translated as "their solitude," but in light of Idel's work, the former translation seems more plausible.

to their comprehension.[57] Likewise, when the soul [*neshamah*] separates from the physical body, and she returns to her foundation [*yesodah*], at first she grasps on to the horns of the altar, and from there she ascends in accordance with their actions.[58] This is the prayer of the pious ones [*ha-ḥasidim*][59] who pray that [God] save them from the judgment of Heaven, that they not be burned in the flame of the Supernal Altar.

In this text, the priest functions as the conduit for the soul-ascent of ordinary individuals ("when he attaches his soul and raises it on the path of ascent, the Holy One blessed be He raises [the people] as if they themselves had [performed] the sacrifice. And they attach to their Maker"). It is through his act of *devequt* that the nonelite are able to achieve a *devequt* of their own, a journey of return to their place of cosmic origin, a process that ultimately results in the rebirth of that soul into the physical world by way of the divine body (from brain to spinal column to phallus). Indeed, *devequt* is construed to be the climax of the sacrificial act by the priest—an experience that serves as the ultimate ritual paradigm for the kabbalist's own act of devotional contemplation and ascent into the sefirotic domain. Moreover, the mystical experience parallels and prefigures that which will take place after death—the moment of *devequt* is characterized as a departure from the realm of mortal life, a restoration to the original state of the soul before it was cast into the prison of the corporeal world. In moving through this contemplative process, the kabbalist in prayer (envisioning himself in the model of the ancient priest) concentrates on *Shekhinah* ("the Wisdom of Solomon"), and rises therefrom to *Binah* ("the Wisdom of *'Elohim*," i.e., Upper Wisdom). In this respect, the kabbalist's experience of *devequt* in prayer seeks to reenact the paradigmatic model of ancient sacrifice. Indeed, the passage appears to correlate kabbalistic devotion and action to the priestly paradigm in every way, and, as such, the kabbalist also aims to function as the cosmic channel between the world of the *sefirot*

57. Perhaps a better, but less literal translation of the word *hasagatam* would be "their ability to contemplate."

58. This appears to refer to the powerful actions of the priests and prophets mentioned above.

59. Generally a term used by kabbalists to refer to other kabbalists.

and the community of Israel below.[60] What is more, like the *kohen* of old (and the Rabbi of talmudic times),[61] the kabbalist is construed to be an angel in the lower world (or, at the very least, is compared to such an angel)—a being who bridges the celestial realm of Divinity and the earthly domain. The unitive overtones of this sacrificial service *qua devequt*, which lie at the heart of the devotional enterprise for the mystic, are further stressed in a separate passage:[62]

ודע כי ענין הקרבן לעלות רצון השפל כדי לקרבו וליחדו ברצון העליון, ולקרב רצון העליון כדי ליחדו ברצון השפל כדי שיהיה רצון העליון ורצון השפל אחד. לפיכך השפל צריך לקרב לו רצונו ועל ידי קרבן שהוא שפל שבשפלים . . . וקושר רצונו בנפש קרבנו ומעלה עליו הכתוב כאלו הקריב נפשו כדכתי' ונפש כי תקריב ורצון השפל מתקרב לרצון העליון.

Know that the point of sacrifice is to elevate the lower [human] will so as to draw it closer to, and to unite it with, the Supernal [divine] Will, as well as to draw the Supernal Will closer so as to unite it with the lower will.[63] [All this is done] *so that the Supernal Will and the lower will shall be one*.[64] Thus, the lower [being][65] must draw his will closer [to the Supernal Will], and this is accomplished through sacrifice, which is the lowest of the low [*ha-shafel she-ba-shefalim*].[66] . . . He

---

60. On this phenomenon in Jewish mystical literature, see Idel, *Hasidism: Between Ecstasy and Magic*, pp. 198–207.

61. See note 48, above.

62. Isaac of Akko, *Me'irat 'Einayim*, p. 142.

63. On the early rabbinic background to this conception, see Eilberg-Schwartz, *Human Will in Judaism*, pp. 24–31.

64. The relationship between the human and divine wills is framed in a related fashion in *Me'irat 'Einayim*, p. 48: משוים רצונם לרצון העליון והינו תוספת רוח הקדש (They equate their wills with the Supernal Will, and this is the surplus of the Holy Spirit). It remains unclear what precisely is meant by the term משוים רצונם here. While the root שוה had a rather wide usage in medieval Jewish philosophy (see Klatzkin, *Thesaurus Philosophicus*, 4: 78–81), I have not encountered any examples of the sort cited in this passage from *Me'irat 'Einayim*. It does seem that medieval Jewish philosophers used the word to connote identity between two objects, whether in the physical or the metaphysical realms. In the cited passage from *Me'irat 'Einayim*, the act of equation between the human and divine wills has the extraordinary result of prophetic experience. When the human mind is linked to its supernal model, that human being becomes infused with the Holy Spirit.

65. A reference to the human being in devotion.

66. Alternatively, "The most physical of all physical things." This is an allusion to the paradigmatically physical character of the animal sacrifice, which is composed of flesh and blood,

binds his will to the soul [or life force] of his sacrifice [*nefesh qorbano*],[67] and Scripture considers it to be as though he had sacrificed his [own] soul. As it is written [Lev. 2:1]: "when a person makes an offering" [*ve-nefesh ki taqriv*],[68] and the lower will is drawn closer to the Supernal Will.

Whereas several early kabbalists play on the word *qorban*, understanding that devotional act as a ritual method for the drawing closer (*leqarev*) of disparate cosmic elements, the stimulus of attraction here takes place not between two inner divine *sefirot*, but rather between the human and divine wills, and is a dynamic ultimately aimed at the *unification* of those two entities.[69] This assertion is precisely indicated by the verb ליחדו (to unify it) and the word אחד (one). Indeed, the ideal of kabbalistic prayer (represented by the sacrificial paradigm) is this very event of unification—a state of Being that may properly be characterized as *unio mystica*.

Another text from this corpus treats the issue with even greater elaboration and specificity.[70] In this passage, Isaac of Akko transmits a teaching heard orally from the oft-mentioned sage Rabbi Natan.[71] This

---

and whose slaughter for the act of sacrifice is an embodiment of that lower physicality in which the human being dwells.

67. This presumably refers to the soul [or life force] of the slaughtered animal, which has become the means for contemplative ascent and *devequt*.

68. The actual meaning of this biblical verse ("when a person makes an offering") does not reflect the play on the word *nefesh*, which Isaac of Akko lifts from the aforementioned midrashic text for his own kabbalistic purposes. In its interpretive use, the biblical proof text is manipulated to establish a correlation between the living essence (or soul) of the sacrificed animal and the soul of the priest (or kabbalist) whose soul must bind itself to that of the animal in order to ascend into the divine realm and unite with the Supernal Will. By binding his *nefesh* to the *nefesh* of the sacrificed animal, the devotee receives the presence of God as if he himself (the human being) had offered his own soul as a sacrifice to God. On the use of such modes of ritual substitution with respect to sacrifice, as well as the correlation between the paradigmatic sacrifice of the animal and the martyrological impulse to sacrifice the self to God, see M. Fishbane, *Kiss of God*, pp. 87–124.

69. In his seminal essay on the concept of *kavvanah* in early Kabbalah, Gershom Scholem argued that such mystical "intention" in prayer was oriented toward the *alignment* of the upper divine will and the lower human devotional will. See Scholem, "Concept of Kavvanah in the Early Kabbalah," p. 164.

70. Isaac of Akko, *Me'irat 'Einayim*, pp. 222–223.

71. As discussed earlier, Moshe Idel has identified this figure as Natan ben Sa'adyah Harar,

tradition is rooted in medieval Jewish philosophical conceptions of the cosmic hierarchy and its relationship to the human soul:

> יש לך לדעת כי השכל האלהי כשיורד ומגיע אל השכל הפועל נקרא שכל הפועל, וכאשר יורד השכל הפועל אל השכל הנקנה נקרא שכל נקנה, וכשיורד שכל נקנה אל השכל המתפעל נקרא שכל מתפעל. וכשהשכל המתפעל מגיע אל הנפש שבאדם נקרא נפש. נמצא שהשכל האלהי שבנפש האדם נקרא נפש זהו ממעלה למטה. וכאשר תשתכל בענין זה ממטה למעלה תראה כי כשהאדם פורש מהבלי העולם הזה ומדביק מחשבתו ונפשו אל העליונים בהתמדה תדירית תיקרא נפשו על שם המעלה מהמעלות העליונות אשר השיגה ונדבקה שם. כיצד אם זכתה נפש המתבודד להשיג ולהדבק בשכל המתפעל תיקרא שכל מתפעל, כאלו היא עצמה שכל מתפעל. וכן כאשר נתעלית עוד והשיגה ונדבקה בשכל הפועל הרי היא עצמה שכל פועל. ואם תזכה ותדבק בשכל האלהי אשריה כי שבהאל יסודה ושרשה ונקראת ממש שכל אלהי. והאיש ההוא יקרא איש אלהים.

> You should know that when the Divine Intellect [*ha-sekhel ha-'elohi*] descends and arrives at the Active Intellect [*ha-sekhel ha-po'el*], it is then called the Active Intellect, and when the Active Intellect descends to the Acquired Intellect [*ha-sekhel ha-niqneh*], it is then called the Acquired Intellect. And when the Acquired Intellect descends to the Agent Intellect [*ha-sekhel ha-mitpa'el*], it is then called the Agent Intellect.[72] And when the Agent Intellect reaches the soul within the human being, it is then called "soul" [*nefesh*].[73] It follows that the Divine Intellect which is within the human soul is called "soul." This is from above to below. And when you contemplate this issue from below to above you will see that when the human being separates himself from the vanities of this world, and attaches his mind and his soul to the Supernal realms with an ongoing constancy, *his soul will be called by the name of the rung from among the Supernal rungs which it has reached and*

---

disciple of Abraham Abulafia. See Idel, *Studies in Ecstatic Kabbalah*, pp. 82–83;Natan ben Sa'adyah Har'ar, *Le porte della giustizia,* ed. Idel, pp. 52–62.

72. Thus Isaac has followed the metaphysical model of medieval Jewish philosophy, in which the cosmos is structured as a hierarchical arrangement of successive "intellects." The metaphysical intellects flow forth on the paradigm of emanation from the most Supernal intellect of all—the Divine Intellect. On the details and textual manifestations of this hierarchy, as well for an analysis of the term *sekhel* (intellect) in Jewish philosophical literature, see Klatzkin, *Thesaurus Philosophicus*, 4: 93–104.

73. See ibid., 3: 57–60.

> *become attached to.*[74] How so? If the soul of the meditator [*ha-mitboded*] has merited to reach and attach to the Agent Intellect, then it is called the Agent Intellect as though it itself [the soul] was the Agent Intellect. And similarly, when it ascends further, and reaches and attaches to the Acquired Intellect, it becomes [*na'aseit*] the Acquired Intellect. And if [the soul (*nefesh*)] merits to reach and to attach to the Active Intellect, it itself becomes in fact the Active Intellect. And if it merits to reach and to attach to the Divine Intellect [*ha-sekhel ha-'elohi*], how fortunate it is! For it returns to its foundation and its root, and it is actually [*mamash*] called the Divine Intellect—and that person is called "a divine man" [*'ish 'elohim*].[75]

We have here one of the strongest and boldest formulations of *unio mystica* available in kabbalistic literature. All divisions in the cosmic order are erased, as each element of the hierarchy is progressively subsumed into the next. The soul that dwells in the human body is *identical* to the Divine Intellect, the highest and most transcendent dimension of all. For given the fact that metaphysical dimensions become identical at the moment of their emanational interaction—כי השכל האלהי כשיורד ומגיע אל השכל הפועל נקרא שכל הפועל (when the Divine Intellect descends and arrives at the Active Intellect, it is then called the Active Intellect)—whether that emanational movement be downward (toward the human soul) or upward (toward the Divine Intellect), the logical result is an

---

74. See an antecedent for this idea in the writings of 'Asher ben David as cited and observed in Amos Goldreich's notes to Isaac of Akko's *Me'irat 'Einayim*, p. 396.

75. While the phrase איש אלהים literally means "man of God," the contextual implication is clearly "divine man"—a far more radical statement. Indeed, Isaac of Akko goes on to assert that the human being whose soul has reached such heights is able to "create worlds" in a manner that parallels the divine, correlating the phrase איש אלהים with the phrase איש אלהי. The term איש האלהים is used in many places in the Hebrew Bible to describe a prophet or a holy man (the phrase appears sixty-four times in the Bible), and is used with this connotation in rabbinic sources. For an early such usage, see Finkelstein, ed., *Sifrei 'al Sefer Devarim*, p. 393, lines 5–17, and see the consideration of this motif in M. Fishbane, *Biblical Myth and Rabbinic Mythmaking*, pp. 221, 347. The idea of the human ascent through the metaphysical intellects as a process of *devequt* (one that appears to affirm the ideal of *unio mystica*) is found most prominently in Moses Maimonides, *Sefer Moreh Nevukhim* 3:51. It is most likely that it was the conflation of the rabbinic usage of the term איש אלהים with the metaphysical schema of medieval Jewish philosophy that resulted in the conception expressed in Isaac of Akko's *Me'irat 'Einayim*.

all-encompassing Oneness, a complete identity of all the component elements of cosmic Being. It is in this respect that the human soul "is actually called the Divine Intellect" (ונקראת ממש שכל אלהי), and that the human being is called "a divine man" (איש אלהים). All is One, human and Divine, and all this occurs through the human act of *devequt* (כשהאדם . . . מדביק מחשבתו ונפשו אל העליונים . . .). As the Divine Intellect descends, or as the human soul ascends, one ontic category assumes the properties and name of the next. At root this is a comprehensive monism, a veritable great chain of Being: the Divine become human, and the human Divine. The naming of entities here becomes an indicator of ontological status; the identity of the lower is subsumed within the identity of the supernal.

It is also important to note the prescriptive emphasis on *constancy* in the act of mental merging with Divinity—an instruction that underscores the nature of focus involved in kabbalistic meditation, a mode of devotional concentration that requires unwavering stability and steadfast attachment. What is more, this practice underscores the strongly anticorporeal approach surveyed above. When the mystic separates himself from the superficialities and vanities of the earthly world, he attains a complete state of *unio mystica* only if he is able to maintain an unbroken and constant connection to the supernal realm, one that directly implies a *constant* separation and detachment from the physical realm. The term *be-hatmadah tadirit* (with ongoing constancy) thus functions as a cognitive ideal for the mystic in the process of contemplation. The mind must be completely and exclusively connected to Divinity and divorced from the world of the senses. In accord with the texts studied above, there is a prescribed progression from the rigorous detachment of *perishut* to the complete merger of human mind/soul with the deity. It is also significant to note that this practice is subsumed under the discipline of *hitbodedut*—it is the skilled *mitboded* who is able to achieve the desired obliteration of individual identity, the renaming of the human with the larger force of Divinity.

Compare the bold nature of this passage with a similarly striking text from *'Oẓar Ḥayyim*,[76] one that has already achieved some attention in

76. Isaac of Akko's *'Oẓar Ḥayyim*, fol. 111a.

contemporary scholarship,[77] but that nevertheless requires review and integration in the present context:

> אהיד"ע הלכתי לשמוע ברכת מילה וראיתי סוד אש אוכלת אש . . . וסוד אכילה זו הוא הדבקות הנכונה . . . אם תרדוף אחר המושכלות ותשיגם ויהיו נעצרים ונחקקים בה שזהו ודאי סוד אכילה . . . ולדבקות זה נאמ' טעמו וראו כי טוב ה'. תדבק בשכל האלהות והוא ידבק בה, שיותר משהעגל רוצה לינק פרה רוצה להניק. ונעשית היא והשכל דבר א' כשופך כד מים במעין נובע שנעשה הכל אחד. וזהו סוד כוונת רז"ל באומרם, חנוך הוא מטט', הרי זה סוד אש אוכלת אש.

> I, the young one, Isaac from Akko, went to hear the blessing of circumcision, and I saw the secret of the fire that consumes fire. . . . And the secret of this consumption is true *devequt*. . . . If you pursue the *muskalot* and grasp them; if they are held and engraved in [your soul]—this is certainly the secret of consumption . . . and of this *devequt* it is said [Ps. 34:9], "taste and see that God is good." Attach yourself to the Divine Intellect, and He will attach Himself to [your soul], for more than the calf wants to suckle, the cow wants to nurse.[78] She [the soul] and the [Divine] Intellect become one entity, like one who pours a pitcher of water into a flowing spring, such that everything becomes one. This is the secret of the intention of our Rabbis of blessed memory, when they said: Enoch is Meṭaṭron.[79] This is the secret of a fire that consumes fire.[80]

As in the cases considered earlier, the climax of the devotee's connection to Divinity is reached through the contemplative act of training the mind on the divine *muskalot*. It is this very mental process that results in *devequt*—indeed, an attachment that is nothing less than a complete and utter unification with the divine realm. The mystic is devoured into the divine self as the larger fire consumes the smaller fire, as the larger

---

77. See Gottlieb, "Illumination, *Devequt*, and Prophecy in R. Isaac of Akko's *Sefer 'Oẓar Ḥayyim*," p. 237; Idel, *Kabbalah: New Perspectives*, p. 67; Brody, "Human Hands Dwell in Heavenly Heights: Worship and Mystical Experience in Thirteenth-Century Kabbalah," p. 279; Hecker, *Mystical Bodies, Mystical Meals*, pp. 207–208 n. 13.

78. See BT *Pesaḥim*, fol. 112a.

79. This was the standard mythic transformation central to the mystical drama of the Heikhalot literature. See Idel, "Enoch Is Metatron."

80. The phrase *'esh 'okhelet 'esh* is a rabbinic adaptation of the phrase *'esh 'okhlah*, which is of biblical origin, and is found in Isa. 29:6, 30:30, and 33:14. The rabbinic formulation is found in BT *Yoma'*, fol. 21b.

body of water consumes the water emptied into its stream. Isaac's use of the rabbinic identification of Enoch and Meṭaṭron is also instructive here. For in the ultimate ascent of the mystic to the divine realm, the separate identity of the human being is erased, morphing into the larger supernal dimension. The former identity of the man Enoch is replaced with his new status as the great angel Meṭaṭron. This metamorposis into Meṭaṭron indicates an absorption into the divine self precisely because of the identification of the Meṭaṭron and *Shekhinah* that we observed earlier. Similarly, and perhaps even more boldly, the kabbalistic devotee who grasps the *muskalot* in all their fullness becomes subsumed and united with those divine dimensions to the point where his former individual identity is erased. In so doing—in tasting and "eating" of the divine reality—he himself has been tasted and consumed by the deity.

Conclusion

In this study, I have sought to present a historical and typological analysis of Isaac ben Samuel of Akko's writings, focusing on the conception and practice of contemplative prayer and seeking to isolate and deconstruct distinct types of religious consciousness and mystical ritual. The kabbalist is simultaneously concerned with external, physical ritual on the one hand, and with internal mental conduct on the other. Moreover, this dual character is reflected in an overtly prescriptive mode of rhetoric—one in which the master seeks to communicate the proper forms of devotion to the potential disciple reading his text. In *Me'irat 'Einayim* and *'Oẓar Ḥayyim*, Isaac instructs his readers in the use of the sacred texts (in particular, the liturgical texts) as symbolic maps for the ascent of consciousness through the divine world. The devotee is exhorted to maintain simultaneous modes of focus on both root and branch elements of the divine sefirotic tree, to visualize configurations of the divine name as a mandalic focal point for contemplation of Divinity itself, and to cultivate an ascetic abnegation of the physical world in favor of an ascent to celestial heights. These specific models and techniques for mystical contemplation were predicated on a broad theurgical foundation. Both the external actions of the body in ritual (including acts of vocal utterance) and the internal conduct and behavior of the mind were conceived to be immensely powerful in their effect upon the very Being of the divine structure. As other kabbalists had claimed before Isaac of Akko, proper action results in the unifying flow of divine emanation, and improper action results in rupture and cosmic separation.

The other underlying theme of this study has been the role of transmission and creative process in the construction of kabbalistic culture.

I have sought to demonstrate the manner in which Isaac of Akko focuses upon the source of reception for a given teaching as the method for establishing the legitimacy and authority of the interpretation. Isaac's practice of reception, which arose directly out of his mobile, itinerant intellectual life, was fundamentally eclectic. In the process of wandering from the eastern Mediterranean to centers of learning in Sefarad, to his eventual migration to the Sufi-inspired environment of North Africa, Isaac endeavored to collect disparate traditions on a variety of kabbalistic and exegetical subjects. In communicating these teachings through the texts of *Me'irat 'Einayim* and *'Oẓar Ḥayyim*, Isaac was concerned with issues such as the intention of the transmitter of oral traditions or author of revered texts, the self-perception of authorship, the hermeneutical process of insight, and the act of writing as a mode of pedagogical and instructive communication with the reader.

The intellectual persona of Isaac of Akko, as well as the content and style of his literary creativity, have long been in need of systematic exposition. Isaac was a crucial figure in the spiritual landscape of fourteenth-century Jewish culture, bridging diverse religious and intellectual trends. By turns multivocal and anthological in character, his writing reflects a broad fusion of contemplative themes and practices (including deep integration of ascetic tensions) with an expansion of Naḥmanidean esotericism and exegesis. What is more, the diversity of Isaac's kabbalistic creativity is embodied in his combination of testimonial, autobiographical discourse with a pervasive posture of prescription. It is precisely in these respects that he emerges for us, not only as a figure at the crossroads of medieval intellectual trends, but also as a remarkable case study in the geographical migration of ideas, locating medieval Kabbalah within the wider discourses of the sociology of knowledge, the dynamics of contemplative intention, and the phenomenology of religion.

Bibliography

Primary Sources

Classics of Rabbinic Literature and Other Anonymous Works (by title)

Babylonian Talmud (BT). 20 vols. Jerusalem, 1975.

The Book Bahir: An Edition Based on the Earliest Manuscripts. Edited by Daniel Abrams. Los Angeles: Cherub Press, 1994.

Ma'arekhet ha-'Elohut. Mantua, 1558. Reprint, Jerusalem, 1963.

Mekhilta' de-Rabbi Yishm'a'el. Edited by H. S. Horovitz and I. A. Rabin. 2nd ed. Jerusalem: Wahrmann Books, 1970.

Midrash Bereishit Rabbah. Edited by J. Theodor and Ch. Albeck. 2nd printing with additional corrections by Ch. Albeck. Jerusalem: Shalem Books, 1996.

Midrash Tanḥuma' ha-Qadum ve-ha-Yashan. Vilna, 1885. Edited by S. Buber. Jerusalem, 1963.

Midrash Tanḥuma' Yelamedeinu. New York: Horev, 1927.

Midrash Vayiqra' Rabbah. Edited by M. Margaliot. New York: Jewish Theological Seminary of America Press, 1993.

'Oẓar ha-Ge'onim. Edited by B. Lewin. Haifa, 1928.

Pesiqta' de-Rav Kahana'. Edited and annotated by Bernard Mandelbaum. 2nd rev. ed. 2 vols. New York: Jewish Theological Seminary of America Press, 1987.

Pesiqta' Rabbati: A Synoptic Edition of Pesiqta' Rabbati Based Upon All Extant Manuscripts and the Editio Princeps. Edited by Rivka Ulmer. Atlanta, Ga.: Scholars Press, 1997.

Siddur ha-Ge'onim ve-ha-Mequbalim. Edited by M. Y. Weinstock. 17 vols. Jerusalem, 1970.

Sifrei 'al Sefer Devarim. Edited by Louis Finkelstein. New York: Jewish Theological Seminary of America Press, 1969.

Synopse zur Hekhalot Literatur. Edited by Peter Schäfer. Tübingen, Ger.: Mohr Siebeck, 1981.

Zohar. Edited by Reuven Margoliot. 3 vols. Jerusalem: Mossad Harav Kook, 1964.

All Other Primary Sources (by author's first name)

Abraham Abulafia. *Sefer ha-Ḥesheq*. Edited by M. Safrin. Jerusalem, 1998.

Abraham ben Ḥananiah Yagel. *A Valley of Vision: The Heavenly Journey of Abraham ben Ḥananiah Yagel*. Translated by David B. Ruderman. Philadelphia: University of Pennsylvania Press, 1990.

Abraham ben Natan ha-Yarḥi. *Sefer ha-Manhig*. Edited by Y. Rafa'el. 2 vols. Jerusalem: Mossad Harav Kook, 1978.

'Asher ben David. *R. Asher ben David: His Complete Works and Studies in His Kabbalistic Thought*. Edited by Daniel Abrams. Los Angeles: Cherub Press, 1996.

'Azri'el ben Menaḥem of Gerona. *Derekh ha-'Emunah u-Derekh ha-Kefirah*. In Gershom Scholem, "New Fragments," 207–213.

———. *Perush ha-'Aggadot le-Rabbi 'Azrie'el*. Edited by Isaiah Tishby. Jerusalem: The Magnes Press, 1982.

———. "R. 'Azri'el mi-Gerona—Perush ha-Tefillah: Mahadurah Biqortit." Edited by Martel Gavarin. MA thesis, Hebrew University of Jerusalem, 1984.

Baḥya ibn Paquda. *Ḥovot ha-Levavot*. Translated into Hebrew by Judah ibn Tibbon. Jerusalem, 1965.

Eliyahu de Vidas. *Rei'shit Ḥokhmah*. 2 vols. Jerusalem: Vashgal Publishing, 1997.

Ezra ben Solomon of Gerona. *Perush le-Shir ha-Shirim*. In C. D. Chavel, ed., *Kitvei RaMBaN*, 2: 476–518. 12th printing. Jerusalem: Mossad Harav Kook, 1994.

———. *Sod 'Eẓ ha-Da'at*. In Gershom Scholem, *The Kabbalah in Gerona*, 374–380.

Isaac ben Samuel of Akko. *'Oẓar Ḥayyim*. MS Moscow-Ginzburg 775.

———. "Perusho shel R. Yiẓḥaq de-min-'Akko le-Pereq Ri'shon shel Sefer Yeẓirah." Edited by Gershom Scholem. *Qiryat Sefer* 31 (1956): 379–396.

———. "Sefer Me'irat 'Einayim le-R. Yiẓḥaq de-min-'Akko." Edited by Amos Goldreich. PhD diss., Hebrew University of Jerusalem, 1981.

Isaac the Blind. *Perush le-Sefer Yeẓirah*. In appendix to Gershom Scholem, *The Kabbalah in Provence*, ed. R. Schatz. Jerusalem: Hebrew University Press, 1979.

Jacob ben Sheshet. *Sefer ha-'Emunah ve-ha-Biṭaḥon*. In C. D. Chavel, ed., *Kitvei RaMBaN*, 2: 353–448. Jerusalem: Mossad Harav Kook, 1964.

Joseph ben Shalom 'Ashkenazi (Pseudo-RABaD). *Perush Sefer Yeẓirah*. Jerusalem, 1990.

Joseph Gikatilla. *Sha'arei 'Orah*. Edited by Joseph Ben-Shlomo. Jerusalem: Bialik Institute, 1996.

Judah ben Yaqar. *Perush ha-Tefillot ve-ha-Berakhot*. 2nd ed. Jerusalem: Me'orei Yisra'el Press, 1979.

Menaḥem Recanati. *Perush ha-Tefillot*. In Menaḥem Recanati, *Sefer Ta'amei ha-Miẓvot*, 27b–43b. Basel, Switz., 1581.

Moses ben Maimon (Maimonides). *The Guide of the Perplexed*. Translated with an Introduction and Notes by Shlomo Pines. Introductory Essay by Leo Strauss. 2 vols. Chicago: University of Chicago Press, 1963.

——. *Mishneh Torah*. 6 vols. Jerusalem, 1968.
——. *Sefer Moreh Nevukhim*. Translated into Hebrew by Samuel ibn Tibbon. Reprint, Jerusalem, 1960.
Moses ben Naḥman (Naḥmanides). *Perush ha-RaMBaN ʿal ha-Torah*. Edited by C. D. Chavel. 2 vols. Jerusalem: Mossad Harav Kook, 1996.
——. *Kitvei RaMBaN*. Edited by C. D. Chavel. 2 vols. Jerusalem: Mossad Harav Kook, 1963.
Moses ben Shem Tov de Leon. *Sefer ha-Rimmon*. Edited by Elliot R. Wolfson. Atlanta, Ga.: Scholars Press, 1988.
——. "Sefer Maskiyot Kesef." Edited by Jochanan Wijnhoven. MA thesis, Brandeis University, 1961.
——. *Sefer Sheqel ha-Qodesh le-R. Moshe de Leon*. Edited by Charles Mopsik. Los Angeles: Cherub Press, 1996.
Natan ben Sa'adyah Har'ar. *Le porte della giustizia*. Edited by Moshe Idel. Milan: Adelphi, 2001. In Italian.
Plotinus. *The Enneads*. Translated by Stephen MacKenna. Boston: The Medici Society, 1926. Reprinted in Burdett, New York: Larson Publications, 1992.
Shem Ṭov Ibn Ga'on. *Baddei ha-'Aron*. Edited and introduced by David Samuel Levinger. Facsimile ed. Jerusalem: East and West Publishing, 1977.
——. *Keter Shem Ṭov*. In *Ma'or va-Shemesh*, fols. 25a–54a. Jerusalem, 1997. Reprint of Livorno, 1839.
Todros Abulafia. *Shaʿar ha-Razim*. Edited by Michal Kushnir-Oron. Jerusalem: Bialik Institute, 1989.

Secondary Sources

Abrams, Daniel. "The Boundaries of Divine Ontology: The Inclusion and Exclusion of Metatron in the Godhead." *Harvard Theological Review* 87, 3 (1994): 291–321.
——. "Critical and Post-Critical Textual Scholarship of Jewish Mystical Literature: Notes on the History and Development of Modern Editing Techniques." *Kabbalah: Journal for the Study of Jewish Mystical Texts* 1 (1996): 17–71.
——. "The Evolution of the Intention of Prayer to the Special Cherub: From the Earliest Works to a Late Unknown Treatise." *Frankfurter Judaistische Beiträge* 22 (1995): 1–26.
——. *The Female Body of God in the Kabbalah: A Study of the Forms of Divine Physical Love and Feminine Sexuality*. Jerusalem: Magnes Press of the Hebrew University, 2004. In Hebrew.
——. "From Divine Shape to Angelic Being: The Career of Akatriel in Jewish Literature." *Journal of Religion* 76, 1 (1996): 43–63.
——. "Orality in the Kabbalistic School of Nahmanides: Preserving and Interpreting Esoteric Traditions and Texts." *Jewish Studies Quarterly* 3 (1996): 85–102.
——. "Secret of All Secrets: The Idea of the Glory and Intention for Prayer in the

Writings of R. Eleazar of Worms." *Da'at: A Journal of Jewish Philosophy and Kabbalah* 34 (Winter 1995): 61–81. In Hebrew.

———. "*Sefer Shaqod* of R. Shemuel ben R. Kalonimus and the Doctrine of the *Kavod* According to a Disciple of R. Eleazar of Worms." *'Asufot* 14 (2002): 217–241. In Hebrew.

———. "The *Shekhinah* Prays Before the Holy One Blessed Be He: A New Source for a Theosophical Conception Among the German Pietists and Their Conception of the Transmission of Secrets." *Tarbiẓ* 63, 4 (1994): 509–532. In Hebrew.

———. "*Zohar, Sefer, Sefer ha-Zohar*: A History of the Assumptions and Expectations of Kabbalists and Modern Scholars." *Kabbalah: Journal for the Study of Jewish Mystical Texts* 12 (2004): 201–232. In Hebrew.

Altmann, Alexander. "Saadya's Theory of Revelation: Its Origin and Background." In A. Altmann, *Studies in Religious Philosophy and Mysticism*, 140–160. Ithaca, N.Y.: Cornell University Press, 1969.

Assis, Yom Ṭov. *The Golden Age of Aragonese Jewry: Community and Society in the Crown of Aragon, 1213–1327*. London: Littman Library of Jewish Civilization, 1997.

———. *The Jews of Spain: From Settlement to Expulsion*. Jerusalem: Rothberg School for Overseas Students, Hebrew University; Dor Hemshech Dept., World Zionist Organization, 1988.

Baer, Yitzhak. *A History of the Jews in Christian Spain: From the Age of Reconquest to the Fourteenth Century*. Vol. 1. Translated from the Hebrew by Louis Schoffman, with an Introduction by Benjamin R. Gampel. Philadelphia: Jewish Publication Society, 1992.

Beit-Arie, Malachi. "Publication and Reproduction of Literary Texts in Medieval Jewish Civilization: Jewish Scribality and Its Impact on the Texts Transmitted." In Y. Elman and I. Gershoni, eds., *Transmitting Jewish Traditions*, 225–247.

Bell, Catherine. *Ritual Theory, Ritual Practice*. Oxford: Oxford University Press, 1992.

Ben Yehuda, Eliezer. *Dictionary and Thesaurus of the Hebrew Language*. 8 vols. New York: Thomas Yoseloff, 1959.

Bielefeldt, Carl. *Dōgen's Manuals of Zen Meditation*. Berkeley: University of California Press, 1988.

Booth, Wayne C. *The Rhetoric of Fiction*. 2nd ed. Chicago: University of Chicago Press, 1983.

Brody, Seth. "Human Hands Dwell in Heavenly Heights: Contemplative Ascent and Theurgic Power in Thirteenth-Century Kabbalah." In R. Herrera, ed., *Mystics of the Book: Themes, Topics, and Typologies*, 123–158. New York: Peter Lang, 1993.

———. "Human Hands Dwell in Heavenly Heights: Worship and Mystical Experience in Thirteenth-Century Kabbalah." PhD diss., University of Pennsylvania, 1991.

Bynum, Caroline Walker. "Did the Twelfth Century Discover the Individual?" In C. W. Bynum, *Jesus as Mother: Studies in the Spirituality of the High Middle Ages*, 82–109. Berkeley: University of California Press, 1982.

Capps, Walter H. *Religious Studies: The Making of a Discipline*. Minneapolis, Minn.: Fortress Press, 1995.

Chajes, J. H. "Accounting for the Self: Preliminary Generic-Historical Reflections on Early Modern Jewish Egodocuments." *Jewish Quarterly Review* 95, 1 (2005): 1–15.

Chazan, Robert. *Barcelona and Beyond: The Disputation of 1263 and Its Aftermath*. Berkeley: University of California Press, 1992.

———. *Medieval Jewry in Northern France: A Political and Social History*. Baltimore: Johns Hopkins University Press, 1973.

Cohen, Gerson. "Esau as Symbol in Early Medieval Thought." In Alexander Altmann, ed., *Jewish Medieval and Renaissance Studies*, 19–48. Cambridge, Mass.: Harvard University Press, 1967.

———. "The Soteriology of Abraham Maimuni." *Proceedings of the American Academy for Jewish Research* 25 (1967): 75–98.

Cohen, Mark R. *Under Crescent and Cross: The Jews in the Middle Ages*. Princeton, N.J.: Princeton University Press, 1994.

Corbin, Henry. *Temple and Contemplation*. London: Islamic Publications, 1986.

Crouter, Richard E. "Schleiermacher's *On Religion*: Hermeneutical Musings After Two Hundred Years." *Zeitschrift für Neuere Theologiegeschichte / Journal for the History of Modern Theology* 6 (1999): 1–22.

Dan, Joseph. *The Esoteric Theology of Ashkenazi Ḥasidism*. Jerusalem: Bialik Institute, 1968. In Hebrew.

———. "The Hidden *Kavod*." In Moshe Hallamish and Assa Kasher, eds., *Religion and Language: Essays in General and Jewish Philosophy*, 71–78. Tel Aviv: University Enterprises, 1981. In Hebrew.

———. *Jewish Mysticism*. Vol. 2: *The Middle Ages*. Northvale, N.J.: Jason Aronson, 1998.

———. *The "Unique Cherub" Circle: A School of Mystics and Esoterics in Medieval Germany*. Tübingen, Ger.: Mohr Siebeck, 1999.

Diamond, Eliezer. *Holy Men and Hunger Artists: Fasting and Asceticism in Rabbinic Culture*. New York: Oxford University Press, 2004.

Dillon, John M. "Rejecting the Body, Refining the Body: Some Remarks on the Development of Platonist Asceticism." In Vincent L. Wimbush and Richard Valantasis, eds., *Asceticism*, 80–87.

Donini, Pierluigi. "The History of the Concept of Eclecticism." In J. M. Dillon and A. A. Long, eds., *The Question of Eclecticism: Studies in Later Greek Philosophy*, 15–33. Berkeley: University of California Press, 1988.

D'Souza, Andreas. "The Conquest of ʿAkkā (690 [1291]): A Comparative Analysis of Christian and Muslim Sources." *Muslim World* 80, 3–4 (1990): 234–250.

Durkheim, Emile. *The Elementary Forms of Religious Life*. Translated by Karen E. Fields. New York: Free Press, 1995.

Eilberg-Schwartz, Howard. *The Human Will in Judaism: The Mishnah's Philosophy of Intention*. Atlanta, Ga.: Scholars Press, 1986.

Eisen, Arnold M. *Rethinking Modern Judaism: Ritual, Commandment, Community*. Chicago: University of Chicago Press, 1998.

Eliade, Mircea. *Yoga: Immortality and Freedom*. Princeton, N.J.: Princeton University Press, 1969.

Elior, Rachel. *The Three Temples: On the Emergence of Jewish Mysticism*. Translated by David Louvish. Portland, Ore.: Littman Library of Jewish Civilization, 2004.

Elman, Y., and I. Gershoni, eds. *Transmitting Jewish Traditions: Orality, Textuality, and Cultural Diffusion*. New Haven, Conn.: Yale University Press, 2000.

Faivre, Antoine. *Access to Western Esotericism*. Albany: State University of New York Press, 1994.

Fenton, Paul B. "La 'Hitbodedut' chez les premiers Qabbalistes en Orient et chez les Soufis." In Roland Goetschel, ed., *Prière, mystique et judaïsme*, 133–157. Paris: Presses universitaires de France, 1987.

——. "Judaeo-Arabic Mystical Writings of the XIIIth–XIVth Centuries." In Norman Golb, ed., *Judaeo-Arabic Studies: Proceedings of the Founding Conference of the Society for Judaeo-Arabic Studies*, Amsterdam, 87–101. The Netherlands: Harwood Academic Publishers, 1997.

——. "Solitary Meditation in Jewish and Islamic Mysticism in the Light of a Recent Archeological Discovery." *Medieval Encounters* 1, 2 (October 1995): 271–296.

——. *The Treatise of the Pool by 'Obadyah Maimonides*. London: Octagon Press, 1981.

Fine, Lawrence. "The Contemplative Practice of Yihudim in Lurianic Kabbalah." In Arthur Green, ed., *Jewish Spirituality: From the Sixteenth-Century Revival to the Present*, 64–98.

——. *Physician of the Soul, Healer of the Cosmos: Isaac Luria and His Kabbalistic Fellowship*. Stanford, Calif.: Stanford University Press, 2003.

——. "Techniques of Mystical Meditation for Achieving Prophecy and the Holy Spirit in the Teachings of Isaac Luria and Hayyim Vital." PhD diss., Brandeis University, 1976.

Fish, Stanley. *Is There a Text in This Class? The Authority of Interpretive Communities*. Cambridge, Mass.: Harvard University Press, 1980.

Fishbane, Eitan P. "Jewish Mystical Hermeneutics: On the Work of Moshe Idel." *Journal of Religion* 85, 1 (January 2005): 94–103.

——. "Mystical Contemplation and the Limits of the Mind: The Case of *Sheqel ha-Qodesh*." *Jewish Quarterly Review* 93, 1–2 (2002): 1–27.

——. "The Speech of Being, the Voice of God: Phonetic Mysticism in the Kabbalah of Asher ben David and His Contemporaries." *Jewish Quarterly Review* 98, 4 (2008): 485–521.

———. "Tears of Disclosure: The Role of Weeping in Zoharic Narrative." *Journal of Jewish Thought and Philosophy* 11, 1 (2002): 25–47.

Fishbane, Michael. *Biblical Interpretation in Ancient Israel*. Oxford: Clarendon Press, 1988.

———. *Biblical Myth and Rabbinic Mythmaking*. New York: Oxford University Press, 2003.

———. *The Exegetical Imagination: On Jewish Thought and Theology*. Cambridge, Mass.: Harvard University Press, 1998.

The Kiss of God: Spiritual and Mystical Death in Judaism. Seattle: University of Washington Press, 1994.

Foucault, Michel. "What Is an Author?" In C. Mukerji and M. Schudson, eds., *Rethinking Popular Culture: Contemporary Perspectives in Cultural Studies*, 446–464. Berkeley: University of California Press, 1991.

Gadamer, Hans-Georg. *Truth and Method*. Translated by Joel Weinsheimer and Donald G. Marshall. 2nd rev. ed. New York: Continuum Publishing, 1995.

Garb, Jonathan. *Manifestations of Power in Jewish Mysticism: From Rabbinic Literature to Safedian Kabbalah*. Jerusalem: Magnes Press, 2004. In Hebrew.

———. "Power and Kavvanah in Kabbalah." PhD diss., Hebrew University of Jerusalem, 2000. In Hebrew.

Giller, Pinchas. *Reading the Zohar: The Sacred Text of the Kabbalah*. Oxford: Oxford University Press, 2001.

Ginsburg, Elliot K. *The Sabbath in the Classical Kabbalah*. Albany: State University of New York Press, 1989.

Gohlman, William E. *The Life of Ibn Sina: A Critical Edition and Annotated Translation*. Albany: State University of New York Press, 1974.

Goitein, S. D. "Abraham Maimonides and His Pietist Circle." In A. Altmann, ed., *Jewish Medieval and Renaissance Studies*, 145–164. Cambridge, Mass.: Harvard University Press, 1967.

Goitein, S. D., and Mordechai A. Friedman. *India Traders of the Middle Ages: Documents from the Cairo Geniza*. Leiden, Bel.: E. J. Brill, 2008.

Goldberg, Joel (Yechiel Shalom). "Mystical Union, Individuality, and Individuation in Provençal and Catalonian Kabbalah." PhD diss., New York University, 2001.

Goldin, Simha. "'Companies of Disciples' and 'Companies of Colleagues': Communication in Jewish Intellectual Circles." In Sophia Menache, ed., *Communication in the Jewish Diaspora*, 127–139.

Goodman, Lenn E. *Avicenna*. New York: Routledge, 1992.

Goshen-Gottstein, Alon. *The Sinner and the Amnesiac: The Rabbinic Invention of Elisha ben Abuya and Eleazar Ben Arach*. Stanford, Calif.: Stanford University Press, 2000.

Gottlieb, Ephraim. "Illumination, *Devequt*, and Prophecy in R. Isaac of Akko's *Sefer 'Oẓar Ḥayyim*." In *Studies in Kabbalistic Literature*, J. Hacker, ed., 231–247. Tel

Aviv: Tel Aviv University Press, 1976. Originally published in *World Congress of Jewish Studies* 2 (1969): 327–334. In Hebrew.

Graboïs, Aryeh. "Akko as a Gate for Immigration to the Land of Israel in the Crusader Period." In B. Oded et al., eds., *Studies in the History of the Jewish People and the Land of Israel*, 2: 93–106. Haifa, 1972. In Hebrew.

——. "Une conséquence du brûlement du Talmud à Paris: Le développement de l'école talmudique d'Acre." In Gilbert Dahan and Élie Nicolas, eds., *Le brûlement du Talmud à Paris, 1242–1244*, 47–56. Paris: Éditions du Cerf, 1999.

Graetz, Heinrich. *History of the Jews*. 6 vols. Philadelphia: Jewish Publication Society of America, 1894.

Green, Arthur. *Devotion and Commandment: The Faith of Abraham in the Hasidic Imagination*. Cincinnati: Hebrew Union College Press, 1989.

——, ed. *Jewish Spirituality: From the Bible Through the Middle Ages*. New York: Crossroad Publishing, 1986.

——, ed. *Jewish Spirituality: From the Sixteenth-Century Revival to the Present*. New York: Crossroad Publishing, 1987.

——. "Judaism and the Good." In Leonard Swidler, ed., *Theoria → Praxis: How Jews, Christians, and Muslims Can Together Move from Theory to Practice*, 119–138. Leuven, Bel.: Peeters, 1998.

——. *Keter: The Crown of God in Early Jewish Mysticism*. Princeton, N.J.: Princeton University Press, 1997.

Grimes, Ronald L., ed. *Readings in Ritual Studies*. Upper Saddle River, N.J.: Prentice Hall, 1996.

Guttmann, Julius. *Philosophies of Judaism: A History of Jewish Philosophy from Biblical Times to Franz Rosenzweig*. Translated by D. W. Silverman. New York: Schocken Books, 1973.

Hadot, Pierre. *Plotinus or the Simplicity of Vision*. Translated by Michael Chase. Chicago: University of Chicago Press, 1993. Originally published as *Plotin ou la simplicité du regard* (Paris: Plon, 1963; 3rd ed., Paris: Études augustiennes, 1989).

Halbertal, Moshe. *By Way of Truth: Nahmanides and the Creation of Tradition*. Jerusalem: Shalom Hartman Institute, 2006. In Hebrew.

——. *People of the Book: Canon, Meaning, and Authority*. Cambridge, Mass.: Harvard University Press, 1997.

Halbertal, Moshe, and Avishai Margalit. *Idolatry*. Cambridge, Mass.: Harvard University Press, 1994.

Hartman, Geoffrey H. *Criticism in the Wilderness: The Study of Literature Today*. New Haven, Conn.: Yale University Press, 1980.

Harvey, Peter. *An Introduction to Buddhism: Teachings, History, and Practices*. Cambridge, U.K.: Cambridge University Press, 1990.

Hatcher, Brian A. *Eclecticism and Modern Hindu Discourse*. New York: Oxford University Press, 1999.

Hecker, Joel. "Each Man Ate an Angel's Meal: Eating and Embodiment in the Zohar." PhD diss., New York University, 1996.

——. "Eating Gestures and the Ritualized Body in Medieval Jewish Mysticism." *History of Religions* 40, 2 (November 2000): 125–152.

——. *Mystical Bodies, Mystical Meals: Eating and Embodiment in Medieval Kabbalah*. Detroit, Mich.: Wayne State University Press, 2005.

Hellner-Eshed, Melila. "The Language of Mystical Experience in the *Zohar*: The *Zohar* Through Its Own Eyes." PhD diss., Hebrew University of Jerusalem, 2001. In Hebrew.

——. *A River Issues Forth from Eden: The Language of Mystical Experience in the Zohar*. Tel Aviv: Am Oved Publishers, 2005. In Hebrew.

Heschel, Abraham Joshua. *Torah from Heaven Through the Lens of the Generations*. Vol. 1. New York: Soncino Press, 1962. In Hebrew.

Hirsch, E. D. *Validity in Interpretation*. New Haven, Conn.: Yale University Press, 1967.

Hollenback, Jess Byron. *Mysticism: Experience, Response, and Empowerment*. University Park: Pennsylvania State University Press, 1996.

Huss, Boaz. "NiSAN—The Wife of the Infinite: The Mystical Hermeneutics of Rabbi Isaac of Acre." *Kabbalah: Journal for the Study of Jewish Mystical Texts* 5 (2000): 155–181.

——. "A Sage Is Preferable to a Prophet: Rabbi Shim'on Bar Yohai and Moses in the Zohar." *Kabbalah: Journal for the Study of Jewish Mystical Texts* 4 (1999): 103–139. In Hebrew.

——. "*Sefer ha-Zohar* as a Canonical, Sacred and Holy Text: Changing Perspectives on the Book of Splendor Between the Thirteenth and Eighteenth Centuries," *Journal of Jewish Thought and Philosophy* 7, 2 (1997): 257–307.

Hyman, Arthur. "From What Is One and Simple Only What Is One and Simple Can Come to Be." In Lenn E. Goodman, ed., *Neoplatonism and Jewish Thought*, 111–135. Albany: State University of New York Press, 1992.

Idel, Moshe. *Absorbing Perfections: Kabbalah and Interpretation*. New Haven, Conn.: Yale University Press, 2002.

——. "Between Authority and Indeterminacy—PaRDeS: Some Reflections on Kabbalistic Hermeneutics." In John J. Collins and Michael Fishbane, eds., *Death, Ecstasy, and Other Worldly Journeys*, 249–268. Albany: State University of New York Press, 1995.

——. "Ecstatic Kabbalah and the Land of Israel." In id., *Studies in Ecstatic Kabbalah*, 91–101.

——. *Enchanted Chains: Techniques and Rituals in Jewish Mysticism*. Los Angeles: Cherub Press, 2005.

——. "Enoch Is Metatron." *Jerusalem Studies in Jewish Thought* 6 (1987): 151–170. In Hebrew.

——. "From Platonic to Hasidic Eros: Transformations of an Idle Man's Story." In

David Shulman and Guy G. Stroumsa, eds., *Self and Self-Transformation in the History of Religions*, 216–235. New York: Oxford University Press, 2002.
——. *Hasidism: Between Ecstasy and Magic*. Albany: State University of New York Press, 1995.
——. "*Hitbodedut* as Concentration in Ecstatic Kabbalah." In id., *Studies in Ecstatic Kabbalah*, 103–169.
——. "The Image of Adam Above the *Sefirot*." *Da'at: A Journal of Jewish Philosophy and Kabbalah* 4 (1980): 41–55. In Hebrew.
——. "Intention and Colors: A Forgotten Kabbalistic Responsum." In id., Devora Dimant, and Shalom Rosenberg, eds., *Tribute to Sara: Studies in Jewish Philosophy and Kabbala*, 1–14. Jerusalem: Magnes Press, 1994. In Hebrew.
——. "Intention in Prayer in Early Kabbalah." In B. Safran and E. Safran, eds., *Porat Yosef: Studies Presented to Rabbi Dr. Joseph Safran*, 5–14. Hoboken, N.J.: Ktav Publishing, 1992. In Hebrew.
——. "Kabbalah and Elites in Thirteenth-Century Spain." *Mediterranean Historical Review* 9 (1994): 5–19.
——. *Kabbalah: New Perspectives*. New Haven, Conn.: Yale University Press, 1988.
——. *Language, Torah, and Hermeneutics in Abraham Abulafia*. Albany: State University of New York Press, 1989.
——. "*Mundis Imaginalis* and *Likkutei HaRan*." In id., *Studies in Ecstatic Kabbalah*, 73–89.
——. *The Mystical Experience in Abraham Abulafia*. Albany: State University of New York Press, 1988.
——. "Nahmanides: Kabbalah, Halakhah, and Spiritual Leadership." In id. and Mortimer Ostow, eds., *Jewish Mystical Leaders and Leadership in the 13th Century*, 15–96. Northvale, N.J.: Jason Aronson, 1998.
——. "On Isaac the Blind's Intentions for the Eighteen Benedictions." In Amos Goldreich and Michal Oron, eds., *Massu'ot: Studies in Kabbalistic Literature and Jewish Philosophy in Memory of Prof. Ephraim Gottlieb*, 25–52. Jerusalem: Bialik Institute, 1994. In Hebrew.
——. "On Mobility, Individuals and Groups: Prolegomenon for a Sociological Approach to Sixteenth-Century Kabbalah." *Kabbalah: Journal for the Study of Jewish Mystical Texts* 3 (1998): 145–173.
——, ed. *Le porte della giustizia*, by Natan ben Sa'adyah Har'ar. Milan: Adelphi, 2001. In Italian.
——. "Prayer in Provençal Kabbalah." *Tarbiẓ* 62, 2 (1993): 265–286. In Hebrew.
——. "Prometheus in Hebrew Garb." *'Eshkolot* 5–6 (1981): 119–127. In Hebrew.
——. *R. Menaḥem Recanati the Kabbalist*. Tel Aviv: Schocken Publishing, 1998. In Hebrew.
——. "The *Sefirot* Above the *Sefirot*." *Tarbiẓ* 51, 2 (1982): 239–280. In Hebrew.
——. *Studies in Ecstatic Kabbalah*. Albany: State University of New York Press, 1988.

——. "Transmission in Thirteenth-Century Kabbalah." In Y. Elman and I. Gershoni, eds., *Transmitting Jewish Traditions*, 138–165.

——. "We Have No Kabbalistic Tradition on This." In Isadore Twersky, ed., *Rabbi Moses Naḥmanides (Ramban): Explorations in His Religious and Literary Virtuosity*, 51–73. Cambridge, Mass.: Harvard University Press, 1983.

Idel, Moshe, and Bernard McGinn, eds. *Mystical Union in Judaism, Christianity, and Islam: An Ecumenical Dialogue*. New York: Continuum Publishing, 1996.

Ilan, Nahem. "The Jewish Community in Toledo at the Turn of the Thirteenth Century and the Beginning of the Fourteenth." *Hispania Judaica Bulletin* 3 (2000): 65–95.

Iser, Wolfgang. "Indeterminacy and the Reader's Response in Prose Fiction." In id., *Prospecting: From Reader Response to Literary Anthropology*, 3–30. Baltimore: Johns Hopkins University Press, 1989.

Jacoby, David. "Crusader Acre in the Thirteenth Century: Urban Layout and Topography." In id., *Studies on the Crusader States and on Venetian Expansion*, Study V, 1–45. Northhampton, U.K.: Variorum Reprints, 1989. Originally published in *Studi Medievali*, ser. 3a, 20 (Spoleto, 1979).

——. "Montmusard, Suburb of Crusader Acre: The First Stage of Its Development." In id., *Studies on the Crusader States and on Venetian Expansion*, Study VI, 205–217. Originally published in B. Z. Kedar, H. E. Mayer, R. C. Smail, eds., *Outremer—Studies in the History of the Crusading Kingdom of Jerusalem Presented to Joshua Prawer* (Jerusalem: Yad Izhak Ben Zvi, 1982).

Jaffee, Martin S. "The Oral-Cultural Context of the Talmud Yerushalmi." In Elman and Gershoni, eds., *Transmitting Jewish Traditions: Orality, Textuality, and Cultural Diffusion*, 27–73.

Jastrow, Marcus. *A Dictionary of the Targumim, the Talmud Babli and Yerushalmi, and the Midrashic Literature*. New York: Pardes Publishing House, 1950.

Jay, Martin. "Name Dropping or Dropping Names?: Modes of Legitimation in the Humanities." In M. Kreiswirth and M. A. Cheetham, eds., *Theory Between the Disciplines: Authority/Vision/Politics*, 19–34. Ann Arbor: University of Michigan Press, 1990.

Jewish Mystical Autobiographies: Book of Visions and Book of Secrets. Translated and introduced by Morris M. Faierstein; preface by Moshe Idel. New York: Paulist Press, 1999.

Jewish Mystical Testimonies. Edited by Louis Jacobs. New York: Schocken Books, 1977, 1997.

Jones, Lindsay. *The Hermeneutics of Sacred Architecture: Experience, Interpretation, Comparison*. 2 vols. Cambridge, Mass.: Harvard University Press, 2000.

Jung, Carl G. *Dreams*. Princeton, N.J.: Princeton University Press, 1974.

Kalmin, Richard. "Dreams and Dream Interpreters." In id., *Sages, Stories, Authors, and Editors in Rabbinic Babylonia*, 61–80. Atlanta, Ga.: Scholars Press, 1994.

Kanarfogel, Ephraim. "The '*Aliyah* of 'Three Hundred Rabbis' in 1211: Tosafist Attitudes Toward Settling in the Land of Israel." *Jewish Quarterly Review* 76, 3 (January 1986): 191–215.

——. *Peering Through the Lattices: Mystical, Magical, and Pietistic Dimensions in the Tosafist Period*. Detroit: Wayne State University Press, 2000.

Kedar, B. Z. "Judeans and Samarians in Crusader Kingdom of Jerusalem." *Tarbiẓ* 53, 3 (April–June 1984): 387–408.

Klatzkin, J. *Thesaurus Philosophicus*. 3 vols. New York: Philipp Feldheim, 1968.

Krassen, Miles. *Uniter of Heaven and Earth: Rabbi Meshullam Feibush Heller of Zbarazh and the Rise of Hasidism in Eastern Galicia*. Albany: State University of New York Press, 1998.

Laura, Heidi. "Collected Traditions and Scattered Secrets: Eclecticism and Esotericism in the Works of the 14th Century Ashkenazi Kabbalist Menahem Ziyyoni of Cologne." *Nordisk Judaistik* 20, 1–2 (1999): 19–44.

Lewis, Bernard. *The Jews of Islam*. Princeton, N.J.: Princeton University Press, 1984.

Liebes, Yehuda. *Ars Poetica in Sefer Yeẓirah*. Tel Aviv: Schocken Publishing House, 2000. In Hebrew.

——. "How the Zohar Was Written." In id., *Studies in the Zohar*, 85–138, 194–227. Albany: State University of New York Press, 1993.

——. *The Sin of Elisha: The Four Who Entered the Pardes and the Nature of Talmudic Mysticism*. Jerusalem: Academon Press of the Hebrew University, 1990. In Hebrew.

Lincoln, Bruce. *Authority: Construction and Corrosion*. Chicago: University of Chicago Press, 1994.

Lobel, Diana. *A Sufi-Jewish Dialogue: Philosophy and Mysticism in Bahya ibn Paquda's Duties of the Heart*. Philadelphia: University of Pennsylvania Press, 2006.

Margolin, Ron. *The Human Temple: Religious Interiorization and the Structuring of Inner Life in Early Hasidism*. Jerusalem: Hebrew University Magnes Press, 2005. In Hebrew.

Matt, Daniel. "The Mystic and the *Mizwot*." In A. Green, ed., *Jewish Spirituality: From the Bible Through the Middle Ages*, 367–404.

McGinn, Bernard. *The Growth of Mysticism: Gregory the Great Through the 12th Century*. New York: Crossroad Publishing, 1994.

Menache, Sophia, ed. *Communication in the Jewish Diaspora: The Pre-Modern World*. Leiden, Bel.: E. J. Brill, 1996.

Minnis, A. J. *Medieval Theory of Authorship: Scholastic Literary Attitudes in the Later Middle Ages*. London: Scolar Press, 1984.

Mopsik, Charles. *Les grands textes de la Cabale: Les rites qui font Dieu*. Paris: Verdier, 1993.

Moseley, Marcus. *Being for Myself Alone: Origins of Jewish Autobiography*. Stanford, Calif.: Stanford University Press, 2006.

Niehoff, Maren Ruth. "A Dream Which Is Not Interpreted Is Like a Letter Which Is Not Read." *Journal of Jewish Studies* 43, 1 (1992): 58–84.

Oppenheim, A. Leo. "The Interpretation of Dreams in the Ancient Near East—With a Translation of an Assyrian Dream-Book." *Transactions of the American Philosophical Society* 46, 3 (1956): 179–255.

Pedayah, Havivah. "Flaw and Repair of the Divinity in the Kabbalah of Rabbi Isaac the Blind." *Jerusalem Studies in Jewish Thought* 6 (1987): 157–285. In Hebrew.

———. *Nahmanides: Cyclical Time and Holy Text*. Tel Aviv: Am Oved Publishers, 2003. In Hebrew.

———. *Name and Sanctuary in the Thought of R. Isaac the Blind*. Jerusalem: Magnes Press, 2001. In Hebrew.

———. "The Spiritual vs. the Concrete Land of Israel in the Geronese School of Kabbalah." In Moshe Hallamish and Aviezer Ravitzky, eds., *The Land of Israel in Medieval Jewish Thought*, 233–289. Jerusalem: Yad Izhak Ben-Zvi, 1991. In Hebrew.

Pines, Shlomo "On the Term *Ruḥaniyut* and Its Sources and On the Thought of Yehudah ha-Levi." *Tarbiẓ* 57 (1988): 511–540. In Hebrew.

Prawer, Joshua. *The History of the Jews in the Latin Kingdom of Jerusalem*. Oxford: Clarendon Press, 1988.

Ruderman, David B. See Abraham ben Ḥananiah Yagel, in "Other Primary Sources" above.

Sartre, Jean-Paul. *"What Is Literature?" and Other Essays*. Cambridge, Mass.: Harvard University Press, 1988.

Schäfer, Peter, ed. *Konkordanz zur Hekhalot Literatur*. 2 vols. Tübingen, Ger.: Mohr Siebeck, 1986–1988.

Schein, Sylvia. "Between East and West: The Latin Kingdom of Jerusalem and Its Jewish Communities as a Communication Center (1099–1291)." In Sophia Menache, ed., *Communication in the Jewish Diaspora: The Pre-Modern World*, 141–169.

Scholem, Gershom. "The Concept of Kavvanah in the Early Kabbalah." In A. Jospe, ed., *Studies in Jewish Thought: An Anthology of German Jewish Scholarship*, 162–180. Detroit, Mich.: Wayne State University Press, 1981.

———. "*Devekut*, or Communion with God." In id., *The Messianic Idea in Judaism and Other Essays on Jewish Spirituality*, 203–227. New York: Schocken Books, 1971.

———. "The Garment of Souls." *Tarbiẓ* 24, 2 (1955): 290–306. In Hebrew.

———. *Kabbalah*. New York: Penguin Books, 1978.

———. "Kabbalah and Myth." In id., *On the Kabbalah and Its Symbolism*, 87–117. New York: Schocken Books, 1965.

———. *The Kabbalah in Gerona*. Edited by Y. Ben-Shelomo. Jerusalem: Academon Press, 1978. Based on the lectures of Gershom Scholem at the Hebrew University of Jerusalem during the 1963–1964 academic year. In Hebrew.

———. *Major Trends in Jewish Mysticism*. New York: Schocken Books, 1974.

——. "A New Documentary Witness to the Origins of Kabbalah." In id., *Studies in Kabbalah I*, edited by J. Ben-Shlomo, 7–38. Tel Aviv: Am Oved Publishers, 1998. Originally published in *Sefer Bialik*, 141–162. Tel Aviv, 1934. In Hebrew.

——. "New Fragments from the Writings of Rabbi 'Azri'el of Gerona." In *Memorial Volume for Asher Gulak and Shmuel Klein*, 201–222. Jerusalem: Hebrew University Press, 1942. In Hebrew.

——. *Origins of the Kabbalah*. Philadelphia: Jewish Publication Society; Princeton, N.J.: Princeton University Press, 1990.

——. *Rei'shit ha-Kabbalah*. Tel Aviv: Schocken Publishing House, 1948. In Hebrew.

——. "*Shekhinah*: The Feminine Element in Divinity." In id., *On the Mystical Shape of the Godhead: Basic Concepts in the Kabbalah*, 140–196. New York: Schocken Books, 1991.

——. "*Sitra Aḥra*: Good and Evil in the Kabbalah." In id., *On the Mystical Shape of the Godhead: Basic Concepts in the Kabbalah*, 56–87. New York: Schocken Books, 1991.

Schwartz, Dov. "Between Conservatism and Intellectualism: The Analytical Thought of the Circle of the Rashba." *Da'at* 32–33 (1994): 143–181. In Hebrew.

——. "From Theurgy to Magic: The Evolution of the Magical-Talismanic Justification of Sacrifice in the Circle of Nahmanides and His Interpreters." *Aleph: Historical Studies in Science and Judaism* 1 (2001): 165–213.

Segal, Alan F. *Two Powers in Heaven: Early Rabbinic Reports about Christianity and Gnosticism*. 1977. Reprint. Boston: Brill Academic Publishers, 2002.

Sendor, Mark B. "The Emergence of Provençal Kabbalah: Rabbi Isaac the Blind's Commentary on *Sefer Yeẓirah*." 2 vols. PhD diss., Harvard University, 1994.

Shulman, David, and Guy G. Stroumsa, eds. *Dream Cultures: Explorations in the Comparative History of Dreaming*. New York: Oxford University Press, 1999.

Smith, Jonathan Z. *Relating Religion: Essays in the Study of Religion*. Chicago: University of Chicago Press, 2004.

Stern, David. *Parables in Midrash: Narrative and Exegesis in Rabbinic Literature*. Cambridge, Mass.: Harvard University Press, 1991.

Strawson, Galen. *Mental Reality*. Cambridge, Mass.: MIT Press, 1994.

Ta-Shma, Israel. "Between East and West: Rabbi Asher b. Yehi'el and his son Rabbi Ya'akov." In I. Twersky and J. Harris, eds., *Studies in Medieval Jewish History and Literature*, 3: 179–196. Cambridge, Mass.: Harvard University Press, 2000.

Taylor, Charles. *Sources of the Self: The Making of the Modern Identity*. Cambridge, Mass.: Harvard University Press, 1989.

Tishby, Isaiah. *Mishnat ha-Zohar*. 2 vols. 1949, 1961. 3rd ed. Jerusalem: Bialik Institute, 1971.

———. "Symbol and Religion in the Kabbalah." In id., *Paths of Faith and Heresy*, 11–22. Jerusalem: Magnes Press, 1964. In Hebrew.

———. *The Wisdom of the Zohar*. 3 vols. Oxford: Oxford University Press, 1991.

Turner, Victor, and Edith Turner. *Image and Pilgrimage in Christian Culture: Anthropological Perspectives*. New York: Columbia University Press, 1978.

Twersky, Isadore. *Introduction to the Code of Maimonides*. New Haven, Conn.: Yale University Press, 1980.

Urbach, Ephraim E. *The Sages: Their Concepts and Beliefs*. Translated from the Hebrew by Israel Abrahams. Cambridge, Mass.: Harvard University Press, 1979.

———. *The Tosafists*. 2 vols. 5th rev. ed. Jerusalem: Bialik Institute, 1986. In Hebrew.

Vajda, Georges. "Les observations critiques d'Isaac d'Acco sur les ouvrages de Juda ben Nissim ibn Malka." *Revue des études juives,* December 1956, pp. 25–71.

———. *Recherches sur la philosophie et la Kabbale dans la pensée juive du Moyen-Age*. Paris: Mouton, 1962.

Weber, Max. "Politics as a Vocation." In Hans H. Gerth and C. Wright Mills, trans. and eds., *From Max Weber: Essays in Sociology*. New York: Oxford University Press, 1969.

———. *The Protestant Ethic and the Spirit of Capitalism*. Translated by Talcott Parsons. New York: Charles Scribner's Sons, 1958.

Werblowsky, R. J. Zwi. *Joseph Karo: Lawyer and Mystic*. Philadelphia: Jewish Publication Society of America, 1980. Originally published by Oxford University Press, 1962.

Werblowsky, R. J. Zwi, and G. Wigoder, eds. *The Oxford Dictionary of the Jewish Religion*. New York: Oxford University Press, 1997.

Wilensky, Sara Heller. "The *Guide* and the *Gate*: The Dialectical Influence of Maimonides on Isaac ibn Latif and Early Spanish Kabbalah." In R. Link-Salinger et al., eds., *A Straight Path: Studies in Medieval Philosophy and Culture—Essays in Honor of Arthur Hyman*, 266–278. Washington, D.C.: Catholic University of America Press, 1988.

Williams, Bernard. *Ethics and the Limits of Philosophy*. Cambridge, Mass.: Harvard University Press, 1985.

Wimbush, Vincent L., and Richard Valantasis, eds. *Asceticism*. New York: Oxford University Press, 1998.

Wolfson, Elliot R. *Abraham Abulafia—Kabbalist and Prophet: Hermeneutics, Theosophy, and Theurgy*. Los Angeles: Cherub Press, 2000.

———. *Along the Path: Studies in Kabbalistic Myth, Symbolism, and Hermeneutics*. Albany: State University of New York Press, 1995.

———. "Beautiful Maiden Without Eyes: *Peshat* and *Sod* in Zoharic Hermeneutics." In Michael Fishbane, ed., *The Midrashic Imagination: Jewish Exegesis, Thought, and History*, 155–203. Albany: State University of New York Press, 1993.

———. "Beyond the Spoken Word: Oral Tradition and Written Transmission in Medieval Jewish Mysticism." In Y. Elman and I. Gershoni, eds., *Transmitting Jewish Traditions*, 166–224.

———. "By Way of Truth: Aspects of Nahmanides' Kabbalistic Hermeneutic." *Association for Jewish Studies Review* 14, 2 (1989): 103–178.

———. *Circle in the Square: Studies in the Use of Gender in Kabbalistic Symbolism*. Albany: State University of New York Press, 1995.

———. "Circumcision, Vision of God, and Textual Interpretation." In id., *Circle in the Square*, 29–48, 140–155.

———. "Forms of Visionary Ascent as Ecstatic Experience in the Zoharic Literature." In Peter Schäfer and Joseph Dan, eds., *Gershom Scholem's Major Trends in Jewish Mysticism: 50 Years After*, 209–235. Tübingen, Ger.: Mohr Siebeck, 1993.

———. "Iconicity of the Text: Reification of the Idolatrous Impulse of Zoharic Kabbalah." *Jewish Studies Quarterly* 11 (2004): 215–242.

———. *Language, Eros, Being: Kabbalistic Hermeneutics and Poetic and Imagination*. New York: Fordham University Press, 2004.

———. "Left Contained in the Right: A Study in Zoharic Hermeneutics." *Association for Jewish Studies Review*, 1986, pp. 27–52.

———. "Merkavah Traditions in Philosophical Garb: Judah Halevi Reconsidered." *Proceedings of the American Academy for Jewish Research* 57 (1991): 215–235.

———. "Mirror of Nature Reflected in the Symbolism of Medieval Kabbalah." In Hava Tirosh-Samuelson, ed., *Judaism and Ecology: Created World and Revealed Word*, 305–331. Cambridge, Mass.: Harvard University Press, 2002.

———. "Mystical Rationalization of the Commandments in *Sefer ha-Rimmon*." *Hebrew Union College Annual* 59 (1988): 217–251.

———. "Mystical-Theurgical Dimensions of Prayer in *Sefer ha-Rimmon*." In David R. Blumenthal, ed., *Approaches to Judaism in Medieval Times III*, 41–79. Atlanta, Ga.: Scholars Press, 1988.

———. "Negative Theology and Positive Assertion in the Early Kabbalah." *Daʿat: A Journal of Jewish Philosophy and Kabbalah* 32–33 (1994): v–xxii.

———. "Occultation of the Feminine and the Body of Secrecy in Medieval Kabbalah." In id., ed., *Rending the Veil: Concealment and Secrecy in the History of Religions*, 113–154. New York: Seven Bridges Press, 1999.

———. "On Becoming Female: Crossing Gender Boundaries in Kabbalistic Ritual and Myth." In T. M. Rudavsky, ed., *Gender and Judaism: The Transformation of Tradition*, 209–228. New York: New York University Press, 1995.

———. "Ontology, Alterity, and Ethics in Kabbalistic Anthropology." *Exemplaria* 12, 1 (2000): 129–155.

———. "Sacred Space and Mental Iconography: *Imago Templi* and Contemplation in Rhineland Jewish Pietism." In R. Chazan, W. Hallo, and L. Schiffman, eds., *Ki Baruch Hu: Ancient Near Eastern, Biblical, and Judaic Studies in Honor of Baruch A. Levine*, 593–634. Winona Lake, Ind.: Eisenbrauns, 1999.

———. "The Secret of the Garment in Nahmanides." *Da'at: A Journal of Jewish Philosophy and Kabbalah* 24 (Winter 1990): xxv–xlix.

———. *Through a Speculum That Shines: Vision and Imagination in Medieval Jewish Mysticism*. Princeton, N.J.: Princeton University Press, 1994.

———. *Venturing Beyond: Law and Morality in Kabbalistic Mysticism*. New York: Oxford University Press, 2006.

Index of Names and Book Titles

The following entries are discussed in the text (not merely cited or mentioned in passing).

Index of Subjects and Terms

Index of Works Quoted

OTHER